Lay by Your Needles Ladies, Take the Pen

Lay by Your Needles Ladies, Take the Pen

Writing Women in England, 1500–1700

Edited by

SUZANNE TRILL
Lecturer in English, Queen's University, Belfast

KATE CHEDGZOY
Lecturer in English and Comparative Literary Studies, University of Warwick

MELANIE OSBORNE
Lecturer in English, University of Durham

ARNOLD
A member of the Hodder Headline Group
LONDON • NEW YORK • SYDNEY • AUCKLAND

First published in Great Britain 1997 by
Arnold, a member of the Hodder Headline Group
338 Euston Road, London NW1 3BH
175 Fifth Avenue, New York, NY 10010

Distributed exclusively in the USA by
St Martin's Press, Inc.,
175 Fifth Avenue, New York, NY 10010

British Library Cataloguing in Publication Data
A catalogue record for this book is available from the British Library

Library of Congress Cataloging-in-Publication Data
Lay by your needles, ladies, take the pen : writing women in England, 1500–1700 / edited by Suzanne Trill, Kate Chedgzoy and Melanie Osborne.
p. cm.
Includes bibliographical references (p.).
ISBN 0-340-69148-4 (cloth). — ISBN 0-340-61450-1 (pbk.)
1. Woman—Literary collections. 2. Women—England—History—Renaissance, 1450–1600—Sources. 3. Women—England—History—17th century—Sources. 4. English literature—Early modern, 1500–1700. 5. English literature—Women authors. I. Trill, Suzanne. II. Chedgzoy, Kate. III. Osborne, Melanie.
PR1110.W6L39 1997
820.8′09287—dc21 97–16333
CIP

ISBN 0 340 69148 4 (hb)
ISBN 0 340 61450 1 (pb)

Typeset in 9½ on 11½ pt Berling by
Phoenix Photosetting, Chatham, Kent
Printed and bound in Great Britain by JW Arrowsmith, Bristol

Contents

About the editors

The editors of this anthology met as postgraduate students at the University of Liverpool and have also co-edited a collection of essays, *Voicing Women: Gender and Sexuality in Early Modern Writing* (Keele: Keele University Press, 1996). Suzanne Trill is a lecturer in the School of English at the Queen's University of Belfast: she has also co-edited another collection of essays: *Writing and the English Renaissance* (Harlow: Longman, 1996) with William Zunder, and has written a number of essays on women and religion in the early modern period. Kate Chedgzoy is a lecturer in the Department of English and Comparative Literary Studies at the University of Warwick; she is the author of *Shakespeare's Queer Children: Sexual Politics and Contemporary Culture* (Manchester: Manchester University Press, 1996). Melanie Osborne is a lecturer in the Department of English at the University of Durham, and has published essays on Renaissance antiquarianism.

Acknowledgements

It is impossible to complete a book such as this without assistance from a variety of quarters. We would like to thank our institutions for the grants which made this project possible; in particular, the Development of Research in Northern Ireland (Young Researchers) Fund at Queen's University, the University of Warwick Research and Teaching Innovations Fund, and the Department of English at the University of Durham. We are also grateful for the help of the staff at the following libraries: the British Library, London (especially those who helped to extract vital texts from exhibitions when necessary); the Bodleian, Oxford; and Cambridge University. The extracts from the Thynne *Letters*, Halkett's *Memoirs*, Hoby's *Diary*, and DeLaval's *Meditations* are reproduced with the kind permission of, respectively, the Marquis of Bath, the British Library and the Bodleian Library.

For their assistance and advice we would like to thank Peter Davidson, Jennifer FitzGerald, Dominic Montserrat, Jane Stevenson, Peter Stoneley and Ramona Wray. We are also grateful to Nic Fulcher and Julie Sanders, for their inspiring and supportive research assistance, and Lynn Meskell and Noel McDermott for generously giving of their time to help us with the final checking process. We would also like to acknowledge the input of our students, especially those who have taken the 'Seventeenth-Century Women's Writing' module at Queen's, Belfast: their responses to early versions of the texts were invaluable in making final decisions about editorial procedure, and their enthusiasm for the material made the project even more worthwhile.

There are, of course, many others who have influenced our work, both directly and indirectly. While we cannot mention them all, we wish specifically to acknowledge Elspeth Graham, Hilary Hinds, Elaine Hobby and Helen Wilcox, editors of *Her Own Life: An Anthology of Autobiographical Writings by Seventeenth-Century Englishwomen* (London: Routledge, 1989): their book was enormously influential in the course of our own postgraduate studies and its existence enabled us to begin to develop courses specifically devoted to early modern women's writing. That anthology was a significant role model for us, as were (and are) the editors themselves. We would, therefore, like to express our respect for them, and other women working in this field.

Introduction

In the late sixteenth century, Sir Philip Sidney ended his prose romance, *The Countess of Pembroke's Arcadia*, with an invitation to others to continue his work, hoping that it 'may awake some other spirit to exercise his pen in that wherewith mine is already dulled'.[1] This request produced responses that Sidney himself apparently could not conceptualise; for he assumed that the writer(s) that would follow in his footsteps would be male, when in fact two of the four writers to take up his challenge were women, Lady Mary Wroth and Anna Weamys.[2] Sidney's assumption is understandable, insofar as the prevailing socio-cultural expectations of this period actively discouraged women from writing, usually instructing them, in Thomas Salter's words, to keep to the 'Distaffe, and Spindle, Nedle and Thimble' rather than develop 'the skill of well using a penne or wrighting a loftie vearce'.[3] However, while Sidney expects writers of romances to be male, his own romance is very specifically designed for a female readership: it was written for, and apparently in consultation with, his sister, Lady Mary Sidney, by then the Countess of Pembroke. This contradiction has other implications than the mere distinction between production as masculine and consumption as feminine. For the *Arcadia* was not simply written *for* the Countess of Pembroke, it was also edited, revised and published *by* her, leading Hugh Sanford to point out in his preface that the *Arcadia* 'is now by more than one interest The Countess of Pembroke's Arcadia – done, as it was, for her; as it is, by her'.[4] Thus, what appears to be a straightforward opposition is indicative of more complex issues surrounding the question of women's writing in early modern England.

Throughout the literature of this period, there is an ongoing debate about women's relationship to both the 'needle' and the 'pen', and the title of this anthology self-consciously reflects its more positive side. The title quotation is derived from a poem praising the literary achievements of Anna Weamys. F. Vaughan commences his dedicatory poem, prefacing her *Continuation of Sir Philip Sidney's Arcadia* (1651), thus: 'Lay by your Needles Ladies, Take the Pen'.[5] In opposition to prevailing socio-cultural expectations, Vaughan encourages women to write. Nor was he the only person to do so during this period; indeed, as more research is undertaken in this area the plethora of texts produced by early modern women is slowly being revealed. However, it is still the case that 'outside the circle of Renaissance specialists, the response to the announcement that one works on early women writers is still likely to be surprise that there were any . . . on which to work'.[6] This perception is unwittingly perpetuated by the fact that the 'female literary tradition' continues to emphasise specific periods and genres; namely, the nineteenth and the twentieth centuries, and the novel in particular.

In *Writing Women's Literary History*, Margaret J. M. Ezell points out that the 'female literary tradition' has been based upon two main assumptions: first, 'that there is a "tradition" of women's writing to be recovered'; and second, 'that this tradition reveals an evolutionary model of feminism'.[7] The rationale for these (usually unacknowledged) 'principles' is to 'provide literary ancestors' whose activities legitimate 'current women's literary activities'.[8] Following in Virginia Woolf's footsteps, feminist critics have sought the individual, professional woman writer of published 'literary' (fictional) texts, and have replicated her vision of the early modern woman writer, encapsulated in Woolf's fictional biography of 'Judith Shakespeare'. As Ezell argues, Woolf's tragic tale has served as a paradigm for interpreting early modern women's relationship to (or, more precisely, absence from) literary history. Although the suicidal culmination of Woolf's tale is not borne out by the actual lives of women writers during this period, the constraints she outlines (education, restriction to the home, parental authority, 'arranged' marriages) certainly did affect their access to literary activities. Paradoxically, the emphasis upon the cultural constraints upon women's expression in the early modern period has distorted our understanding of women's literary history: '[b]ecause of the way [feminist critics] have defined *authorship, audience, and literature*, we have effectively silenced a large number of early women's voices in our very attempts to preserve and celebrate women's writings'.[9]

While the editors of this anthology have no wish to underestimate the effect of social restrictions upon early modern women writers, it is our belief, with Ezell, that the current 'canon' of women's literature, even if inadvertently, replicates the problematics of the exclusion of women from the traditional, male canon. It is our hope that this anthology will help to break down some of the implicit assumptions that have so far formed the 'female literary tradition' by promoting the exploration of the similarities and the differences between women's lives and women's texts, both within the period 1500–1700, and between that period and the twentieth century. We hope, therefore, that it will facilitate an exploration of the dynamic interaction between continuity and discontinuity in the history of women's writing.

For perhaps the most crucial problem with the current construction of the 'female literary tradition' is the latent anxiety about whether or not 'our literary forebears were "good" feminists', which has led to many early women writers being dismissed as either 'ideologically unsound or being too acceptable to the male establishment'.[10] Correspondingly, this has simultaneously promoted a celebration of early women's texts that are perceived to be 'oppositional' or 'feminist'.[11] However, as the historian Linda Gordon puts it:

> [i]n the history of women's history, the greatest of our contradictions has been that between domination and resistance. Sometimes we feel compelled to document oppression, diagram the structures of domination, and mourn the damages. Sometimes we feel impelled to defend our honor and

> raise our spirits by documenting our struggles and identifying successes in mitigating the tyranny.[12]

The difficulty is that, more often than not, both domination and resistance occur simultaneously (as Janis Butler Holm acknowledges, in any given period of time there is usually 'a messy mixture of both'), affecting different women variously, depending on a number of factors, not just their sex.[13] The texts that we have selected provide an indication of the 'messy mixture' of both women's writing itself and the contradictory attitudes to it that co-existed, *c.* 1500–1700.

I

These contradictions are certainly evident in the conflict surrounding women's education. Thomas Salter's advice that women should focus their talents on needlework rather than writing could be said to typify conservative early modern attitudes to what constituted an appropriate realm for women's activities. This theme is reiterated in conduct books within the period covered by this anthology; J. L. Vives, for example, argues that women's education should be limited to '[t]he study of wysedome: the whiche doth enstruct their maners, and enfurme their lyvyng, and teacheth them the waye of good and holye lyfe'.[14] According to Vives, a woman has no need 'for eloquence', as she has no public role to play; moreover, when a woman learns to write, Vives suggests 'let nat her example be voyde verses, nor wanton or tryflynge songes, but some sad sentence, prudent and chaste, taken out of holy scripture'.[15] Any learning that a woman did acquire was a private activity, to be shared only with children or other women: women were not permitted to teach men. Following St Paul's injunctions in 1 Corinthians 14 and 1 Timothy 2, Vives argues that women's greatest eloquence is silence: a point that is repeatedly reaffirmed by the same biblical citations in texts by both male and female authors during this period.

These attitudes were underlined by contemporary laws: as T. E. explains in *The Lawes Resolution of Women's Rights* (1632): '[a]ll [women] are understood either married, or to be married, and their desires are subject to their husbands; I know no remedy, yet some can shift it well enough. The common law here shaketh hand with divinity'.[16] The 'inferiority' of woman was enshrined in earthly or 'common' law on the basis of God's authority, which in turn legitimated a view of women which suggested that they were 'naturally' inferior to man. Or, as the 1652 *Homily on Marriage* puts it:

> [t]he woman is a weak creature not endued with like strength and constancy of mind; therefore, they be the sooner disquieted, and they be prone

> to all weak affectations and dispositions of mind, more than men be; and lighter they be, and more vain in their fantasies and opinions.

The fact that women were characterised in this manner was used to justify male control. This was also authorised by biblical precedent, most crucially through the figure of Eve: her supposed culpability for the Fall led to the belief that women automatically inherited the wayward and capricious characteristics associated with her; consequently, it was assumed that they were susceptible to heretical or misguided ideas. As a result, women were perceived to be inherently unruly and intemperate and were aligned metaphorically with the 'body', which required the guidance of the 'head' (that is, father, husband or brother) to be kept in check.[17] In contrast to the undesirable characteristics ascribed to Eve, early modern women were ideally encouraged to be 'Chaste, Silent and Obedient'.[18] These three features were viewed as synonymous; thus, a silent woman was also assumed to be chaste and obedient and a loquacious woman was perceived to be disobedient and sexually licentious.[19] In this socio-cultural context, therefore, for a woman to express herself was simultaneously to bring her reputation into doubt: thus, the difficulties facing the women whose texts we have reproduced in this anthology should not be underestimated. But these texts also demonstrate various strategies by which early modern women writers managed to circumvent their material constraints and did indeed 'Take the Pen'.

That a large number of women did so points to the fact they did not simply internalise the negative prescriptions described above, and it suggests that attitudes to women's education and writing were not singular but rather plural and contradictory. While writers such as Vives and Salter wanted to restrict women's writing, others, such as Vaughan, obviously disagreed. Less than five years after Salter's text was published, Thomas Bentley produced what appears to be the earliest anthology of women's writing, *The Monument of Matrones* (1582). This book included texts by Katherine Parr, Elizabeth I, Lady Jane Grey, Frances Abergavenny and Elizabeth Tyrwhitt among others. In his preface, Bentley displays rather different attitudes to women's literary activities than Vives or Salter: he claims that the women whose writing he has selected 'for the common benefit of their countrie, have not ceased . . . to spend their time, their wits, their substance, and also their bodies, in the studies of noble and approoved sciences, and in compiling and translating of sundrie most christian and godlie bookes'.[20] According to Bentley, then, women's activities in the world of writing were not restricted to private interest, but were produced for the 'common benefit of their countrie'. Moreover, if one looks closely at the context surrounding Salter's advice in *The Mirrhor of Modestie*, it is not actually so diametrically opposed to Vaughan's and Bentley's position as might at first appear. Salter argues that:

> [S]uche as compare the small profit of learnyng with the greate hurt and domage that commeth to [women] by the same shall sone perceive . . . how far more convenient the Distaffe, and Spindle, Nedle and Thimble were for them with a good and honest reputation, then the skill of well

> using a penne or wrighting a loftie vearce with diffame and dishonour, if in the same there be more erudition then vertue.

While Salter stresses the needle and thimble, he does not state that women should not write *per se*, but rather insists that the content should be virtuous; like Bentley, he means 'christian and godlie bookes'. These two writers indicate that there was something acceptable about women writing on 'virtuous' or 'godlie' subjects. This apparent acceptance is, however, double-edged: although it permits some freedom it also sets limits. Moreover, such comments have led modern critics to assume that religious texts by early modern women manifest their subservience to, and internalisation of, patriarchal prescriptions. This, in turn, has led to their marginalisation within the current construction of the 'female literary tradition'.

Religious texts, especially when they are also translations, have been viewed by modern critics as the 'least oppositional' form of early modern women's writing.[21] Yet the degree to which this is accurate is questionable, not least because of the early modern equation of articulation with sexual availability. As the corollary of women's expression was to call her virtue into question, even when women produced religious translations during this period they, or their male editors, were still impelled to justify their action and protect their reputation. In his preface to Anne Cooke-Bacon's translations of Ochine's sermons, for example, B. B. defends his decision to publish them despite the fact that critics will deem it 'meeter for Docters of divinitye to meddle wyth such matters then Meydens', and finds it necessary to stress that Cooke-Bacon 'never gaddid farder then hir fathers house to learne the language'. Thus even the 'safe' realm of religious translation could still bring ignominy to a woman writer.

While many of the texts produced by women in the late sixteenth century were religious translations, this did not necessarily mean it was an acceptable mode of expression for women. Although the Bible was one of the few texts that was commonly recommended for women to read, the continual alterations and reversals in the dominant or legitimate forms of religious practice throughout the early modern period meant that adherence to a particular doctrinal position correspondingly entailed situating oneself in a precise political position. As a result, a woman's translation of a 'religious' text could be extremely controversial, as Margaret Tyler suggests:

> amongst al my il willers, some I hope are not so straight that they would enforce me necessarily either not to write or to write of divinitie. Whereas neither durst I trust mine own judgement sufficiently, if matter of controversy were handled, nor yet could I finde any booke in the tongue which would not breed offence to some.[22]

One method by which Tyler justifies her translation of a Spanish romance is to play on contemporary assumptions about women's lack of 'judgement'; she refuses to produce a religious translation because it would necessarily 'breed offence to some'. In so doing, Tyler pinpoints a crucial paradox that was to be more overtly exploited by later women writers: while the intersection of religion and politics in the early modern period was undeniably a factor which placed women in a subservient position, it also meant that for a woman to translate, or explicate, scripturally based texts inevitably involved her in the contemporary religious and political controversies from which, in theory, she was debarred.

Writing upon religious subjects did not in itself provide any guarantee of avoiding censure; even women who explicitly express their desire to remain with the culturally defined limits of femininity found themselves inadvertently transgressing them and, consequently, having to find a way to legitimate their activities. In *The Mothers Legacie, To her Unborne Childe* (1624), for example, Elizabeth Jocelin struggles to reconcile her perception of herself as an exemplary woman with her desire to write advice 'To her Unborne Childe', even though she had no intention of publishing her work. In her preface, she acknowledges that:

> I may perhaps be wondred at for writing in this kinde, considering there are so many excellent bookes, whose least note is worth all my meditations. I confesse it, and thus excuse my selfe. I write not to the world, but to mine own childe, who it may be, will more profit by a few weake instructions comming from a dead mother . . . then by farre better from much more learned.[23]

Despite her apparent humility and her attempt at self-effacement, Jocelin establishes the legitimacy of her writing on the basis of her role as a mother, which situates her as her child's earliest religious instructor, and she clearly values her own experience more than others' learning. Her own attitude to women's education is also contradictory; if her child is female, Jocelin desires:

> her bringing up may be learning the Bible, as my sisters doe, good houswifery, writing, and good workes: other learning a woman needs not: though I admire it in those whom God hath blest with discretion, yet I desired not much in my owne, having seene that sometimes women have greater portions of learning, than wisdome, which is of no better use to them than a main saile to a flye-boat, which runs it under water. But where learning and wisdome meet in a vertuous disposed woman, she is the fittest closet for all goodnesse. Shee is like a well-ballanced ship that may beare all her saile. She is – Indeed, I should but shame my selfe, if I should goe about to praise her more.[24]

Jocelin attempts to maintain the conservative line of Salter and Vives (indeed, she seems to be quoting Vives when she states 'other learning a woman needs not'), but cannot quite confine herself to this position. Ultimately she has to censor herself as she finds herself instead arguing, similarly to Richard Hyrde, that a virtuous education is a positive thing for women.[25] Jocelin's text illustrates that even she, who overtly accepted contemporary expectations of women, found herself manoeuvring between conflicting demands. The negotiations and conflicts are perhaps even more visible when the woman writer held beliefs that were not socially or politically acceptable: what for one person or group was an articulation of virtuous belief was treason for another.

II

The historical period that this anthology covers was riven with strife over the nature and form of religious beliefs, their mode of expression, and their relationship to the social and political ordering of England. Consequently, women's articulation of their own religious beliefs necessarily situated them within a political debate, whether they consciously acknowledged it or not. Initially focused on the struggle between emergent Protestantism and the recently disestablished Roman Catholic Church, in the English Civil Wars the conflict gradually became more complex as a result of the fissures within Protestantism. While Henry VIII's break away from the Roman Catholic Church is commonly believed to represent the beginning of a Reformation in England, the extent to which it produced changes in the ecclesiastical and theological organisation of the English Church is debatable: at the end of Henry VIII's reign official doctrine endorsed the communion of one kind for the laity; the celibacy of the priesthood; the permanence of vows of chastity; the benefit of private masses; auricular confession; and transubstantiation. This has led recent historians to suggest that the major changes effected by the Henrician Schism were the break away from Papal supremacy in political and economic areas, as opposed to major doctrinal alterations.[26] Over the next century, debates about doctrine, the practice of different forms of Christianity, and the relationship between religion and political rule were to have substantial effects upon English peoples' lives.

While Edward VI continued to 'reform' the English Church, the accession of Mary Tudor led to a partial re-establishment of Catholicism. These shifts led to a large degree of uncertainty in both religious and political matters, and have traditionally been seen as being assuaged by the Elizabethan Settlement. However, although the Settlement seems to have kept mainstream Protestants content, more extreme Puritans and Roman Catholics were less than satisfied and endured legal curtailment of their activities. This is most noticeable with regard to the practice of Catholicism which was outlawed during Elizabeth's reign: the Acts of Supremacy and Uniformity (1559) identified Elizabeth as 'Supreme Governor' of the Church and authorised only one form of public worship; the Act against Reconciliation to Rome (1581) made it an offence to say or sing Mass, to aid or to maintain priests, and reinforced the fine for those who did not attend public (Protestant) worship; and the treasonable nature of the aiding and maintaining of priests was further confirmed by the Act against

Jesuits and Seminary Priests (1585).[27] It is in this context that events described in Smith's *Life . . . of La. Magdalen, Viscountesse Montague* need to be situated.

While the Elizabethan Settlement sought to establish a single, national Protestant Church, many Puritans – from moderate reformers, through Presbyterian radicals to Separatists – desired more 'substantial changes to the ecclesiastical organisation of the Church, and frequently challenged the royal supremacy'.[28] While the tension between Roman Catholicism and Protestantism continued, the differences within the Protestant and Puritan groups increased: their disagreements centred not only on doctrinal issues such as transubstantiation and the decoration of a church, but also upon ecclesiastical hierarchy, which, in turn, influenced the believers' conception of political order. Those advocating a national Church, be it Catholic or Protestant, tended also to advocate a hierarchical structuring of both the Church and society. Those with more Puritan leanings wished to dispense with such hierarchies, and promoted the idea of the separation of the Church and state and a more recognisably democratic form of government. In this context it is easy to understand why Puritans objected to Archbishop Laud's 'reforms', which they saw as a return to Catholicism. Add to this the fact that Charles I had married the Roman Catholic princess, Henrietta Maria, and there seems to be some basis for their fears. It is, therefore, also interesting to note that the 1630s saw the publication of a number of texts by Catholic women dedicated to Queen Henrietta Maria, of which Susan du Verger's translation of Camus's *Admirable Events* (1639) is but one example.[29]

Although the established Church did not simply disappear during the period of the Civil Wars, 'the single most important aspect of the religious history of the period is the emergence of hundreds of independent and semi-independent congregations, the disintegration of Puritanism as well as the Church of England'.[30] Perhaps most famously characterised by Christopher Hill's use of the biblical quotation, 'the world turned upside-down', the Civil Wars witnessed an increased debate about the controversies that had been raging since the Elizabethan Settlement.[31] The groups or sects which emerged during this period – including the Levellers, Ranters, Seekers, Muggletonians, Presbyterians, Independents, Baptists, Quakers, and Fifth Monarchists – are too numerous to explain in detail. However, because some of the women whose writing is included in this anthology belonged to the Fifth Monarchists and the Quakers, it seems appropriate to provide some more information about these groups. But it is equally important to acknowledge that women were actively involved in many other sects during this period; indeed, researchers have suggested that women were particularly drawn to these sects, as many of them espoused the theory of male and female equality.[32] While in practice this was not always the case, the sects provided women with greater opportunities for speech and action than was available in the 'established' churches. Although the degree to which the Civil Wars affected women's social position in the long term is debatable, as Patricia Crawford suggests, its main effect was 'in providing greater opportunities for [women] to express their ideas individually and collectively'.[33]

The Fifth Monarchists was a millenarian group that believed in the imminent coming of Christ who would reign on earth with his 'Saints' for 1000 years.[34] This belief was based upon prophecies contained within the Books of Daniel and Revelation, which seemed to be fulfilled in the 1650s.[35] The New Model Army's success in 'purging' Parliament in 1648 had led to the establishment of the Rump Parliament in 1649. While this Parliament had authorised the dissolution of the monarchy, the execution of the King, and the disestablishment of the episcopacy, it was still perceived by some radicals, including the Fifth Monarchists, to be too moderate. These groups sought to replace it with a Church Parliament drawn from the congregations; their protests seem to have had some effect as in 1653 Cromwell dissolved the Rump Parliament and established the Barebones Parliament, which was comprised of a nominated assembly of men ostensibly chosen for their moral and religious virtues.[36] In his inaugural speech, Cromwell drew heavily upon Daniel and Revelation and was hailed as the second Moses. But his inability to deliver his promises led to severe criticism and also to the alienation of significant Fifth Monarchist leaders in Cromwell's government. One of the voices raised against him as a result was Anna Trapnel's, one of whose prophetic texts, *Strange Newes from White-Hall* (1654), is included in this anthology.[37]

One of the most radical groups during this period were the Quakers, whose name (like that of the Shakers) was derived from their behaviour, 'that is, trembling and shaking'.[38] Quakerism began in the north of England in the 1650s but soon spread to the south and became highly successful and influential. Although they did not codify their theology until the 1670s, the basis of Quakerism was a belief in the possibility of salvation for all (in contrast to the strictures of Calvinist predestination); a strong sense of unity with God and awareness of the 'Light' (or Spirit, or Christ) within; and an emphasis upon the spirit rather than the scriptures. They called for the disestablishment of the Church and the abolition of tithes, believing instead that Church members should either pay for their own ministers or that ministers should support themselves. Their anti-hierarchical beliefs aligned them with Cromwell, not so much because they approved of him but rather because they were fervently anti-monarchical. Their ensuing actions threatened the traditional symbols of social order (for example, plain dress, 'thee-ing' and 'thou-ing', and the refusal to doff hats), which led to them being perceived as representing potential anarchy.[39] The Quakers' promotion of women's preaching was also perceived as threatening, and the Quaker habit of interrupting church services led Cromwell to issue *A Proclamation Prohibiting the Disturbing of Ministers* in 1654. It would seem, therefore, that the Quakers posed a threat to nearly everyone. Their activities provoked a large degree of hostility, which Barry Reay argues '*contributed* to the Restoration of the Stuarts': while its inception was radical, one effect of Quakerism was paradoxically 'to stimulate political conservatism'.[40]

Despite the fact that the Bible was undeniably utilised as a means of restricting women's activities in all areas of life, it is important that we do not erase all sense of female agency in relation to it; as Patricia Crawford has recently argued, it is vital that we appreciate 'how women could both accept beliefs about their inferiority and transcend them'.[41] The Bible was recommended reading, on the basis that reading such a virtuous text would make the women readers virtuous themselves, but the contents of the Bible are not that clear cut. After all, it was from the Bible that two of the most striking images of women's capacity for destruction were derived: Eve and Delilah.[42] These 'disobedient' and 'destructive' women could just as easily provide challenging role models for their women readers. Moreover, women also publicly engaged in questioning the meanings ascribed to female biblical characters; perhaps most obviously in the controversy texts (i.e. those texts which debate the nature and role of women) by Rachel Speght and Ester Sowernam, but also in Anne Wheathill's prayers which question Eve's responsibility for the Fall (reproduced below). These, and many other texts produced during this period, indicate that women did find alternative ways of reading the Bible and did not necessarily read it in the same way as their male contemporaries.

Indeed, in the latter part of the period, there is an increase in texts that publicly debate the biblical precedents for and against women's speech. Most famous perhaps is Margaret Fell's *Womens Speaking Justified* (1666), but Fell's text is far from the feminist manifesto that its title would appear to suggest (a rather less well-known text, also included in this anthology, has a far more ingenious argument; that is, Mary More's *The Woman's Right* (1674–80)). *Womens Speaking Justified* paradoxically relies upon male-defined stereotypes of women to distinguish between which women could and could not speak. Although Fell's definition of 'women' actually includes men (because anyone who is out of the spirit is metaphorically represented as female), the 'women' that are explicitly excluded from speaking are depicted as sexually licentious (Jezebels): Fell's 'defence' of women's speech, like many of her male contemporaries, therefore relies upon a sense of 'virtue' as a legitimisation of expression. Furthermore, Fell's motivation for writing was arguably less to defend women's right to speak in general than an attempt to silence those women who followed the Quaker radical James Naylor, rather than Fell and her husband George Fox.[43]

Other texts which might seem at first glance to indicate a recognisably 'feminist' agenda also contain rather less radical suggestions than their titles suggest: Bathsua Pell Makin's, *An Essay to Revive the Antient Education of Gentlewomen* (1673), is a case in point. Although Makin rails against the 'custom' of keeping women ignorant, and clearly identifies the gender issues at stake in this 'custom', this has to be balanced against her following argument: 'Let not your Ladiships be offended, that I do not (as some have wittily done) plead for Female Preeminence. To ask too much is the way to be denied all. God hath made the Man the Head, if you be educated and instructed, as I propose, I am sure you will acknowledge it, and be satisfied that you are helps.'[44]

Thus, the end of education for Makin is not so far removed from that of Salter and Vives as readers may assume from its title. These points highlight the fact that the history of women's writing does not follow a simple trajectory of linear development, but is rather a complex web of contradictory strands.

III

> An anthology by nature is primarily a popular or teaching text: It is designed for readers who lack familiarity with the subject matter. It is the introduction, however, to more than the texts themselves. Anthologies as a form also help to create and to confirm canons: Their selections signal to the reader what the critical community considers to be worthy of study and also the dominant critical framework in which the texts are to be read. By their selections, anthologies thus invite readers to consider particular critical issues or questions concerning social context and literary history in addition to questions about specific authors.[45]

As the above quotation indicates, any anthology inevitably makes a contribution to the contemporary debate upon this contentious aspect of literary studies.[46] It is, therefore, vital for editors to be self-conscious about their aims and intentions in their choice of texts, and the process of compilation and organisation. While, of course, the editors do not have complete control of the reception of their text, or the meaning(s) that readers will ascribe to it, we have made our selection and organised this anthology on the basis of two main principles; first and foremost, our commitment to making the teaching of early modern women's writing a viable possibility; second, the desire to redress some of the problematic assumptions upon which the 'feminist' canon has recently been constructed.

With regard to their viability as teaching texts, the two main difficulties with most existing anthologies in this field is their expense and the brevity of the extracts. Many existing anthologies in the field of early modern women's writing provide so wide a selection that the extracts contained within them provide very little indication of the complexity of the texts from which they are derived. The tendency to organise material generically or thematically can also be misleading; the thematic organisation of women's texts tends to perpetuate the idea that they only address issues that are related to the domestic realm, which is to overlay nineteenth-century concerns onto earlier texts. Perhaps the most striking characteristic of the texts we read in the course of our research was the way in which the majority of them challenged received generic categorisation: for example, Hannah Woolley's *The Gentlewomans Companion* contains recipes, medical advice, general advice about women's conduct and the organisation of the household, and examples of how to write letters; and although Dorothy Leigh's *The Mothers Blessing* has been defined as a 'mother's advice book', it could also be read as a book of meditations and prayers.

While the primary aim of this anthology is to make more early modern women's writing accessible to students, we felt that it was important to include texts by male writers as well. We believe that in order to understand the historical context in which these women were writing, it is vital to be aware of what was expected of them; moreover, it is only by reading texts by male and female writers side by side that one gains an understanding of what points are made specifically by women and which appear to be shared ideas, or areas of contention. This does not, however, mean that the connections are simply one-sided; rather we hope that this choice will help to promote a 'commitment to the practice of gendered poetics that also re-reads men's texts in the weave of women's'.[47] This is perhaps most obvious in Rachel Speght's *A Mouzell for Melastomus*, and Ester Sowernam's, *Ester Hath Hang'd Haman*, insofar as both these texts actively promote a re-reading of the male-authored text to which they are responses. Less obvious is the way in which texts like Leigh's *The Mothers Blessing* or Anne Wheathill's *A Handfull of Holesome (though Homelie) Hearbs* react to contemporary expectations of women's sphere of activities: both of them provide prayers and spiritual guidance, the former on the basis that it is a mother's duty, the latter on the basis that 'maidens' should use their time to virtuous ends. In this, they are both following the advice contained within conduct books produced by male writers, but they prompt a reconsideration of the effects of the prescriptions contained in such books.

This kind of re-reading will, we hope, be further facilitated by the fact that we have decided to organise our selections on the basis of the date of publication or composition (in the case of manuscripts) of the excerpted text. This should also mean that the differences between texts written at around the same time will become apparent. In this way, we hope to break down the notion of an 'evolutionary' model of 'feminism', and the accompanying linear reading of history. Texts which may seem progressive to a modern feminist consciousness (for example, Margaret Fell's *Womens Speaking Justified* and Rachel Speght's *A Mouzell for Melastomus*) are side by side with those which may seem conservative (for example, Lady Elizabeth DeLaval's *Meditations*, and Elizabeth Clinton's *The Countesse of Lincolnes Nurserie*). The women whose texts are reproduced in this anthology had very different ideas about what they were writing and why, and they also had very divergent views of themselves as 'women'. It is our hope that this method of organisation will encourage readers to explore these differences: or, as Teresa de Lauretis puts it, we seek to address the fact that 'the female subject is the site of differences; differences that are not only sexual or only racial, economic, or (sub)cultural, but all of these together, and often enough at odds with one another'.[48]

These differences manifest themselves in a variety of ways throughout this collection; the women writers included represent a range of different social, religious and political positions; the kinds of texts that they produced provide an indication of the array of genres that their texts cover; and, while all the writers included here are English, they also provide some insight into questions of cultural difference, primarily in relation to Ireland and 'New England'.[49] Within the 50 texts included in this anthology, we have attempted to provide a indication of the variety of texts women writers produced throughout the period our collection covers. This challenges the straightforward notion of a 'linear development' in women's writing from religious translation to more recognisably 'literary' genres, such as prose romances: Margaret Tyler's translation of *The Mirrour of Princely Deedes and Knighthood* was produced in 1578 and Aphra Behn's translation of *Agnes de Castro* in 1688; Anne Wheathill's prayers and meditations were published in 1584 and Frances Cooke's in 1649, and the latter was published in the same year as Elizabeth Poole's second pamphlet, *An Alarum of War*. These examples perhaps suggest that the form women's writing took had less to do with the particular moment at which they were writing and rather more to do with their religious beliefs and social position. It is interesting to note, particularly in contrast with collections of women's poetry from this period, that only a quarter of the prose texts included in this anthology were produced by women of aristocratic status; a point which simultaneously challenges received notions of lower-class women's illiteracy and reinforces the notion of poetry as an elite form of literary production.[50]

While the texts included here do offer an indication of the variety of women's writing, we have purposefully decided to focus this anthology on women's *prose* writings. There were many reasons for this; first, limitations of space; second, there are a number of readily available and affordable editions of women's poetry and drama from this period; and third, although there are some anthologies of prose, they tend to focus either on one genre or one writer.[51] In contrast, our collection includes witchcraft pamphlets, letters and other manuscript material, prophetic texts, practical books and petitions, as well as the more widely recognised genres of prose fiction and autobiography. While it is important to realise that women did write prose fiction, it is equally significant to recognise that such texts account for only a small proportion of women's literary activity during this period.[52] Not only do the genres in which women wrote differ from what modern readers might expect, but it is necessary to be aware that the modern tendency to separate 'public' and 'private' modes of production can distort our understanding of early modern texts; for example, while we tend to view letters as a 'private' form of communication, in the early modern period this was not the case. Rather, they were governed by complex rhetorical rules and were highly stylised (for example, Hannah Woolley instructs women in the right style in which to write letters on a variety of occasions). Furthermore, the possibility that letters might be read by people other than the intended recipient is apparent in Lady Brilliana Harley's need to write in an encoded form.[53]

Many of the texts included in this anthology invite us to question modern concepts of authorship. While recent critical approaches have questioned the status of the author as the guarantor of a text's meaning, the response from feminist critics has been mixed: Carol Thomas Neely, for example, distrusts post-structuralism because, for her, it precludes the possibility of practising feminist criticism: '[i]f feminist criticism abandons the notion of the subject, replacing it with the much more slippery concept of subject positions, and by doing so calls into question the notion of gendered subjects, gendered authors, gendered texts, the ground of its critique is eliminated'.[54] But for other feminist critics the 'slippery concept of subject positions' is the very factor which facilitates a feminist critique.[55] Modern approaches to literary criticism are an invaluable method for investigating some of the problems posed by texts produced in the early modern period. For example, as I have argued elsewhere, a post-structuralist approach to the debate about the relative value of 'translation' and 'writing' brings their perceived opposition into doubt, because '*all* writing is a form of translation as no piece of writing is purely the property of a single, originary author'.[56] This recognition questions what is at stake in the continued marginalisation of early modern women's translations, and opens up the broader issue of what constitutes 'authorship'.

Indeed, the texts in this anthology indicate a number of disjunctions between modern concepts of 'authorship' and early modern practice. For example, whereas in the nineteenth century pseudonyms were used to obscure the writer's sex, this was not necessarily the case in the early modern period. When pseudonyms were used they tended to be gender-specific: Katherine Philips wrote poetry under the name of 'Orinda', and the writers of the controversy texts – Joseph Swetnam and Ester Sowernam (included in this volume) – did not seek to disguise the sex of the writer. The last two examples complicate this question further: although the pseudonyms are gender-specific, it is not certain that they were produced by different people as the identity of the writers is unknown. This has prompted Diane Purkiss to point out that feminist critics often set up 'a logocentric cycle . . . whereby a female signature prompts a reading strategy designed to uncover a female consciousness in texts, and this consciousness in turn is held to manifest the presence of a female author'.[57] In other words, Purkiss questions the legitimacy of assuming that because a text is ascribed to a female writer it reveals its gendered origins; rather, she suggests that *readers* project their assumptions onto the text in ways that may not be appropriate. Purkiss examines this issue specifically in relation to the controversy texts, but the points she raises are relevant to other texts included in this anthology; for example, because Anne Wheathill's *A Handfull of Holesome (though Homelie) Hearbs* (1584) is ascribed to a female writer, her representation of Adam and Eve as mutually responsible for the Fall is taken as a sign of a specifically 'female consciousness'. Yet the majority of her book is a re-working of prayers and phrases from both the Bible and *The Book of Common Prayer*, neither of which have an identifiable 'female consciousness'.

There is also another significant aspect of Purkiss's question, which can perhaps be most clearly illustrated with reference to the work of Anna Trapnel. While there is no doubt about Trapnel's existence, nor is there any record of her objecting to the publication of texts in her name, her 'authorial' role is problematised on a number of levels. First, her texts were not published by Trapnel herself but by members of her congregation, which raises the question of how much control Trapnel herself had over the content of her texts.[58] Second, while some parts of her works are identified as her own, her prophetic utterances occur while she is in an unconscious trance-like state; thus, like other female prophets, Trapnel represents her speech as given to her by God and over which she has no control. And third, her utterances are recorded by a male 'Relator' who intermittently tells us that he could not take down everything that she said because he could not hear it; thus, the extent to which the text is actually 'Trapnel's' is debatable. However, this example foregrounds one area of distinction between modern assumptions and early modern practice, that is, whereas modern readers often wish to ascribe authorship to an individual writer, this does not necessarily make sense in the early modern period.

While modern feminist critics might seek for the professional women writer, the material early modern women produced rarely falls into such a category: with the possible exception of Aphra Behn, the women whose texts are included in this anthology did not make a living from their writing. This is not solely the result of the contemporary prescriptions against women's writing; it is also affected by other factors, such as social status. Aristocratic women, for example, tended to follow the practice of their male contemporaries by producing their works in manuscript, as there was an inbuilt class suspicion of the overt self-display promoted by publication. In contrast to modern expectations, however, the fact that a text exists only in manuscript does not necessarily mean that it only had a small audience, or was intended only for private use: manuscripts were circulated (often within coterie circles) and a number of copies were frequently made, which indicates that manuscripts were read by a wider audience than the modern reader might assume. The practice of circulating manuscripts further undermines modern assumptions about individual literary creativity, as writers sometimes revised their texts on the basis of readers' comments: for example, Sir Philip Sidney, in his preface to the Countess of Pembroke, states that the *Arcadia* was 'done in loose sheets of paper, most of it in your presence, the rest by sheets sent unto you as fast as they were done'.[59]

IV

The above quotation reiterates the fact that the apparent distinction between women as consumers and men as producers was not so clear cut in the early modern period as our current understanding of the literary canon might lead us to assume. Ironically, given that women were repeatedly instructed to avoid reading romances, it is frequently within this genre that the contradictions about women's relationship to 'the Pen' were foregrounded. Contemporary responses to Pembroke's involvement in the production of the *Arcadia* reinforce this point. Hugh Sanford, for example, highlights the way in which Pembroke's editorial role culminated in a corrective role: '[a]s often in repairing a ruinous house the mending of some old part occasioneth the making of some new, so here her honourable labour, begun in the correcting of faults, ended in supplying the defects'.[60] Furthermore, Sanford continues by arguing that the changes to the *Arcadia* were all overseen by Pembroke ('most by her doing, all by her directing'); thus, Pembroke the reader and dedicatee of the *Arcadia*, became its writer. A later commentator makes this point more explicitly: the *Arcadia* 'henceforth disputed is, / Whether *Sir Philip's* or the *Countesses*'.[61] While Pembroke's part in completing her brother's works and writing her own has led her to be depicted as an exceptional sixteenth-century woman writer, it was an awareness of precisely such contradictions that enabled another sixteenth-century woman writer, Margaret Tyler, both to legitimise her translation of the Spanish romance *The Mirrour of Princely Deedes and Knighthood* in 1578 and criticise male double standards in their attitudes to women's education in general:

> [b]ut to retourn in whatsomever the truth is, whether that women may not at al discourse in learning, for men lay in their claim to be sole possessioners of knowledge, or whether they may in some maner that is by limitation or appointment in some kinde of learning, my perswasion hath bene thus, that it is all one for a woman to pen a story, as for a man to addresse his story to a woman.[62]

By the time that Anna Weamys wrote her *Continuation of Sir Philip Sidney's Arcadia* in 1651, F. Vaughan went so far as to suggest that her text represented a transferral of literary creativity from men to women: 'So when in *Sydney's* death Wit ebb'd in Men,/ It hath its Spring-tide in a Female Pen'.[63]

Traditionally, the metaphor of the pen has been so integrally associated with male writers that some modern critics identify it with the phallus; an identification which emphasises the concept of man-made language from which women were, and arguably are, excluded. Such criticism emphasises that women's association with the use of a pen is fraught with difficulty and torn by conflict, and this is the case for many of the women writers included in this anthology. Even Tyler, who undermined contemporary attitudes by justifying her use of 'the Pen', simultaneously recognises their existence; for example, she asks for acceptance of her work because the story is 'prophane' and its 'matter more manlike then becommeth my sexe'.[64] Thus, although she questions the 'naturalisation' of men's association with 'the Pen', Tyler is acutely conscious of the condemnation that her use of it might provoke. While Tyler's argument cuts a swathe through male expectations, a later woman writer's experience illustrates that the problems did not simply disappear. In 'The Introduction', which significantly was not published in her lifetime, Anne Finch, Countess of Winchilsea, argues:

Alas, a woman that attempts the pen,
Such an intruder on the rights of men,
Such a presumptuous creature is esteemed,
The fault can by no virtue be redeemed.[65]

Thus even at the very end of the period that this anthology covers, the synonymity between female expression and sexual availability remained. The texts in this anthology demonstrate that women's exclusion from the field of literary production is not as complete as has been supposed, but they also indicate the conflicts they faced as a result, both within themselves and with other people. These conflicts are indicated in the full title of this anthology; not only does the quotation stress the opposition between the 'needle' and the 'pen', but the subtitle 'Writing Women in England, 1500–1700' is double-edged. It is meant to signify that women both *wrote* literary texts during this period, but were doing so within a context which simultaneously sought to *write* them into a more restricted role. Despite the cultural prejudices and material constraints that sought to restrict women's lives and their literary activities, the texts in this anthology bear witness that many did 'Take the Pen'. However, these texts also demonstrate that women's literary history did not progress in a simple, linear trajectory, but was instead a 'messy mixture' of simultaneous domination and resistance.

Notes

1. *Sir Philip Sidney, Arcadia* ed. Maurice Evans (Harmondsworth: Penguin, 1977), p. 848. Evans's edition is of the composite *Arcadia*; however, this final sentence is the same in all three versions of Sidney's romance (*The Old Arcadia*, *The New Arcadia* and the *Arcadia*).
2. Lady Mary Wroth, *The Countesse of Mongomeries Urania* (1621), and Anna Weamys, *A Continuation of Sir Philip Sidney's Arcadia* (1651), see pp. 101–7, 175–82 in this anthology. Wroth's text is not, strictly speaking, a 'continuation' of the *Arcadia*, but it is included here as she bases her romance on the character Urania, who is marginalised in Sidney's text. The other two continuations were Gervase Markham's *The English Arcadia* (1607/1613) and Richard Belling's *A Sixth Booke of the Countesse of Pembrokes Arcadia* (1624).
3. Thomas Salter, *The Mirrhor of Modestie* (1579), see p. 47 of this anthology.
4. *Sir Philip Sidney, Arcadia*, p. 60. For further details about Pembroke's involvement in the production of the *Arcadia*, see Margaret P. Hannay, *Philip's Phoenix: Mary Sidney, Countess of Pembroke* (New York and Oxford: Oxford University Press, 1990).
5. F. Vaughan in Weamys, *Continuation*, sig. *7v.
6. Margaret J. M. Ezell, *Writing Women's Literary History* (Baltimore and London: Johns Hopkins University Press, 1993), p. 12.

7. Ezell, *Writing Women's Literary History*, p. 18.
8. Ezell, *Writing Women's Literary History*, p. 20.
9. Ezell, *Writing Women's Literary History*, p. 38, my emphasis.
10. Ezell, *Writing Women's Literary History*, p. 27. Gary F. Waller, for example, describes Tudor women writers as being 'on the margins of discourse' and as lacking 'an authentic female voice' in 'Struggling into Discourse: The Emergence of Renaissance Women's Writing', in Margaret P. Hannay, ed., *Silent But For the Word: Tudor Women as Patrons, Translators, and Writers of Religious Works* (Kent, OH: Kent State University Press, 1985), pp. 238–56.
11. See, for example, Barbara K. Lewalski, *Writing Women in Jacobean England* (Cambridge, MA and London: Harvard University Press, 1993) and Tina Krontiris, *Oppositional Voices: Women as Writers and Translators of Literature in the English Renaissance* (New York and London: Routledge, 1992).
12. Linda Gordon, 'What's New in Women's History?' in Teresa de Lauretis, ed., *Feminist Studies/Critical Studies* (Bloomington, IN: Indiana University Press, 1986), p. 23.
13. Janis Butler Holm, 'The Myth of a Feminist Humanism: Thomas Salter's *The Mirrhor of Modestie*', in Carole Levin and Jeanie Watson, eds., *Ambiguous Realities: Women in the Middle Ages and Renaissance* (Detroit: Wayne State University Press, 1987), p. 204.
14. See anthology, p. 24.
15. See anthology, p. 25.
16. T. E., *The Lawes Resolution of Women's Rights* (1632), cited in Elspeth Graham, Hilary Hinds, Elaine Hobby and Helen Wilcox, eds., *Her Own Life: Autobiographical Writings by Seventeenth-Century Englishwomen* (London: Routledge, 1989), p. 7.
17. The rationale for the connection between the (male) head and the (female) body is not solely attributable to Christian doctrine; see Ian Maclean, *The Renaissance Notion of Woman: A Study in the Fortunes of Scholasticism and Medical Science in European Intellectual Life* (Cambridge: Cambridge University Press, 1980).
18. See Suzanne Hull, *Chaste, Silent and Obedient: English Books for Women, 1475–1640* (San Marino: Huntingdon Library, 1985).
19. Peter Stallybras, 'Patriarchal Territories: The Body Enclosed', in Margaret Ferguson, Maureen Quilligan and Nancy J. Vickers, eds., *Rewriting the Renaissance: The Discourses of Sexual Difference in Early Modern Europe* (Chicago and London: University of Chicago Press, 1986), pp. 123–42.
20. Thomas Bentley, *The Monument of Matrones* (1582), vol. I, British Library (henceforth BL), sig. B1r.
21. For example, Ann Rosalind Jones argues that a woman writer's 'most submissive response' to contemporary expectations 'was to deal only with the domestic and religious concerns considered appropriate for women and to write without any ambition for publication' in *The Currency of Eros: Women's Love Lyric in Europe 1540–1620* (Bloomington and Indianapolis: Indiana University Press, 1990), p. 29.
22. Margaret Tyler, *The Mirrour of Princely Deedes and Knighthood* (1578), sig. A4v.
23. Elizabeth Jocelin, *The Mothers Legacie, To her Unborne Childe* (1624), pp. 10–11.
24. Jocelin, *The Mothers Legacie*, sig. B5v–B6v.
25. See Richard Hyrde's preface to Margaret More-Roper's *Devout Treatise upon the Pater Noster* (1526? and 1531?).

26. See Leo F. Solt, *Church and State in Early Modern England, 1509–1640* (New York and Oxford: Oxford University Press, 1990), pp. 37–8.
27. For further details of the provisions of these Acts, see J. R. Tanner, ed., *Tudor Constitutional Documents, 1485–1603* (Cambridge: Cambridge University Press, 1948), pp. 130–63.
28. Solt, *Church and State*, p. 82.
29. *John Peter Camus, Bishop of Belley, Admirable Events*, translated by Susan du Verger (1639), pp. 131–5 below.
30. J. F. McGregor and B. Reay, eds., *Radical Religion in the English Revolution* (Oxford: Oxford University Press, 1984), p. 10; for a discussion of the 'established' Church during the Civil Wars, see John Morrill, 'The Church in England, 1642–1649', in John Morrill, ed., *The Nature of the English Revolution: Essays by John Morrill* (London and New York: Longman, 1993), pp. 148–75.
31. Christopher Hill, *The World Turned Upside Down: Radical Ideas during the English Revolution* (Harmondsworth: Penguin, 1988). The central doctrinal controversies were the clothing of the clergy and their role in political rule; the decoration of the church; the number and kinds of sacraments; the paying of tithes; the relationship between the believer, the clergy and God; and the extent of 'free will' or 'predestination' to salvation.
32. On the basis of Galatians 3: 28.
33. Patricia Crawford, 'The Challenges to Patriarchalism: How did the Revolution Affect Women?' in John Morrill, ed., *Revolution and Restoration: England in the 1650s* (London: Collins and Brown, 1992), p. 119.
34. Toby Barnard, *The English Republic, 1649–1660* (Harlow: Longman, 1986), p. 97.
35. Bernard Capp, 'The Fifth Monarchists and Popular Millenarianism', in McGregor and Reay, eds. *Radical Religion*, p. 165.
36. Capp, 'The Fifth Monarchists', p. 170.
37. See pp. 193–7, below.
38. B. Reay, 'Quakerism and Society', in McGregor and Reay, eds. *Radical Religion*, p. 147.
39. Reay, 'Quakerism', p. 162.
40. Reay, 'Quakerism', pp. 163, 164.
41 Patricia Crawford, *Women and Religion in England, 1500–1720* (London and New York: Routledge, 1993), p. 1.
42. Genesis, 1–3; Judges 16.
43. For further details, see Phyllis Mack, *Visionary Women: Ecstatic Prophecy in Seventeenth-century England* (Berkeley: University of California Press, 1992) and Maureen Bell, George Parfitt and Simon Shepherd, eds., *A Biographical Dictionary of English Women Writers, 1580–1720* (New York and London: Harvester Wheatsheaf, 1990), pp. 257–63.
44. Bathsua Pell Makin, *An Essay to Revive the Antient Education of Gentlewomen* (1673), p. 240 below.
45. Ezell, *Writing Women's Literary History*, p. 40.
46. See, for example, Margaret J. M. Ezell, 'The Myth of Judith Shakespeare: Creating the Canon of Women's Literature', *New Literary History*, 21(3) (1990), pp. 579–92; John Guillory, 'Canonical and Non-Canonical: A Critique of the Current Debate', *English Literary History*, 54(3) (1987), pp. 483–527.

47. Nancy K. Miller, 'Men's Reading, Women's Writing: Gender and the Rise of the Novel', *Yale French Studies*, 75 (1988), pp. 40–55.
48. Teresa de Lauretis, 'Feminist Studies/Critical Studies: Issues, Terms, and Contexts', in de Lauretis, ed., *Feminist Studies*, p. 14.
49. Except for Anna Maria van Schurman, and her text has been translated into English.
50. We did not intentionally set out to choose texts produced by women of different social status; it did, however, strike us as significant that this was the result of our final selection.
51. See the 'Editions' section of the bibliography for further details.
52. Elaine Hobby suggests that texts produced by women represented less than 1 per cent of the total literary output for this period, *Virtue of Necessity: English Women's Writing, 1646–1688* (London: Virago, 1988), p. 6.
53. See p. 144, below.
54. Carol Thomas Neely, 'Constructing the Subject: Feminist Practice and the New Renaissance Discourses', *English Literary Renaissance*, 18 (1988), p. 13.
55. For a discussion of the advantages and disadvantages of post-structuralism for feminist criticism, see Chris Weedon, *Feminist Practice and Post-structuralist Theory* (Oxford: Blackwell, 1993) and Janet Ransom, 'Feminism, Difference and Discourse: The Limits of Discursive Analysis for Feminism', in Caroline Ramazanoglu, ed., *Up Against Foucault: Explorations of some Tensions between Foucault and Feminism* (London and New York: Routledge, 1993), pp. 123–46.
56. Suzanne Trill, 'Sixteenth-Century Women's Writing: Mary Sidney's *Psalmes* and the "Femininity" of Translation', in William Zunder and Suzanne Trill, eds., *Writing and the English Renaissance* (Harlow: Longman, 1996), p. 142.
57. Diane Purkiss, 'Material Girls: The Seventeenth-Century Woman Debate', in Clare Brant and Diane Purkiss, eds., *Women, Texts and Histories, 1575–1760* (London and New York: Routledge, 1992), p. 71.
58. Four of Trapnel's texts were published in 1654: *Strange Newes from White-Hall, The Cry of a Stone, A Report and Plea*, and *A Legacy for Saints*.
59. *Sir Philip Sidney, Arcadia*, p. 57.
60. *Sir Philip Sidney, Arcadia*, p. 59.
61. F. W. in Weamys, *Continuation*, sig. *6v.
62. Tyler, *Mirrour*, sig. A4v.
63. Vaughan in Weamys, *Continuation*, sig. *7v.
64. Tyler, *Mirrour*, sig. A4r.
65. Anne Finch, 'The Introduction' in Denys Thompson, ed., *Anne Finch, Countess of Winchilsea: Selected Poems* (Manchester: Carcanet, 1987), pp. 26–8, ll. 9–12.

Textual editing

The decision about the degree to which a text should be modernised in order to facilitate accessibility to a wider modern audience has to be balanced against the possibility of thereby erasing an awareness of the text's historical difference. To modernise texts fully alters them in ways which can make them almost unrecognisable; moreover, as Sara Jayne Steen points out, the emphasis upon modernisation can distort our understanding of manuscripts in particular: 'original punctuation and spelling are important signifiers . . . [and m]odernization, especially of punctuation, strikingly distorts the woman's voice by inserting pauses, for example, that are not indicated in the ms'.[1] Fully modernising early modern texts can also conceal an (un)conscious anxiety that women's texts in particular will appear, in modern terms, 'illiterate'. The texts in this anthology were all produced before the introduction of 'Standard English'; consequently, the fact that the spellings used by each writer vary enormously – both between different writers and within a single text – should not be taken as a sign of 'illiteracy', but rather as an indication of how the English language has altered through time. We have, therefore, opted to make minimal editorial changes, having also consulted the opinions of our students who overwhelmingly supported a less intrusive editorial style.

The editing of early modern texts, whether they were produced by male or female writers, is an area of contention in literary studies. We have edited the texts on the following principles: as is common practice, we have consistently revised the letters 'u', 'v', 's', 'j' in accordance with modern usage, and have silently expanded abbreviations ('y^{t}', '&'), contractions ('com̄end': 'commend'), and any obvious errors. Editorial omissions are signified thus: brief omissions by ellipses (. . .); larger omissions by a line break and an explanatory footnote. We have, however, opted to retain as much of the original typography as possible without making the texts unbearably difficult to read; while we have not reproduced the gothic script used in many of the very early texts and have made some alterations to paragraphing, we have retained original capitalisation and italicisation. This choice was based on the fact that although gothic script is in its own way an important indicator of historical difference, it signifies little in authorial terms and is now widely regarded as difficult to read. We have altered paragraphing for similar reasons: modern readers are unaccustomed to texts that continue for pages and pages without a paragraph break. But, during the early modern period, when paper was in short supply and was relatively expensive, it did not make sense to leave large spaces in the text: this applies to both printed texts and manuscripts.

Capitalisation and italicisation are, however, a different matter: while the names of towns were commonly italicised (or set in roman script if the text was predominantly in gothic script), the use of italics can serve other functions; for example, it was often used as a means of distinguishing between a quotation from another text (most often the Bible), or another person's speech and the narrator's expression. While this is not always the case, choosing to eradicate this form of signification can be problematic: it means that the modern editor is placing yet another layer of interpretation upon the text and is preventing modern readers from making their own decisions about its significance (or lack of it).

In order to ensure that as much of this volume as possible was devoted to the texts themselves, we have also kept annotation to a minimum. Introductions to each extract deal primarily with textual information about the mode of production, the number of editions, the overall form and content of the text, and details of the copy text from which the extracts are derived. As many early modern texts have extraordinarily long titles we have provided only the short titles of the texts unless there is a specific reason to do otherwise. We have not included detailed biographical information about the writers, as this would necessarily appear to privilege those women writers about whom information is more readily available. Furthermore (as discussed above), the problematic nature of the transmission of many of the texts means that biographical information could be misleading. Instead, we have provided a bibliography of critical texts which supply this, and other, information in far more detail than we could do here.

We have used footnotes in order to supply a gloss for words that are now obsolete and to provide contextual information where it is necessary in order to understand the extract. We have, however, used a more complex system in relation to biblical references so that they can be easily identified: those that were originally set in the main body of the text have been retained in their original form; those that were originally marginal notes have been inserted into the main text within brackets; and those references that have been supplied by the editors have been inserted into the main text in square brackets. For simplicity's sake, all references are to the Authorised Version, although, of course, some of the writers included in this anthology would actually have used the Coverdale Bible, the Bishops Bible, the Geneva Bible or the Vulgate.

Note

1. Sara Jane Steen, 'Behind the Arras: Editing Renaissance Women's Letters', in W. Speed Hill, ed., *New Ways of Looking at Old Texts* (Binghampton, NY: Medieval and Renaissance Texts and Studies, 1993), pp. 232–3.

RICHARD HYRDE (trans.)

J. L. Vives, *The Instruction of a Christen Woman* (1530)

Vives's text, translated here from Latin by Richard Hyrde, is commonly referred to as a conduct book, that is a text which sought to offer a model of ideal female behaviour. The ideas contained within it, although written for Princess Mary (the future Queen Mary), are presented as being requisite for *all* women. The text is divided into three books, which indicate how a woman's life was defined during this period; the first outlined a maid's behaviour, the second a wife's, and the third a widow's. Within each section chapters address such issues as what a woman should wear, what she should read, and how she should interact with other people. This text went through nine editions from 1529 to 1592. The copy text for the extracts included here is BL, 697. g. 9 (printed in London by Thomas Berthelet in 1530). The extracts included here are from the first book (sigs. D2r–D2v, D3r, E1r–E3r; G2r–G4v).

Of the lernyng of maydes

Of maydes some be but lyttell mete for lernynge: Lyke wyse as some men be unapte, agayne some be even borne unto hit, or at lest nat unfete for hit. Therfore they that be dulle are nat to be discoraged, and those that be apte, shuld be harted and encoraged. I perceive that lerned women be suspected of many: as who sayth, the subtyltie of lernyng shulde be a norisshement for the malitiousnes of theyr nature. Verely I do nat alowe in a subtile and a crafty woman suche lernyng, as shulde teche her disceite, and teche her no good maners and vertues: Nat withstandynge the preceptes of lyvyng, and thexamples of those that have lived well, and had knowlege to gether of holines, be the kepers of chastite and purenes, and the copies of vertues, and prickes to pricke and to move folkes to contynue in them.[1]

But you shall nat lyghtly fynde an yll woman, excepte it be suche one, as either knoweth nat, or at leste way consydereth nat what chastite and honestie is worth: nor seeth what mischiefe she doth, whan she forgoth it: nor regardethe howe great a treasure, for how fowle, for howe lyght, and transitorie an image of pleasure she changeth: what a sort of ungratiousness she letteth in, what tyme she shutteth forthe chastite: nor pondreth what bodily pleasure is, howe vayne and folyshe a thynge, whiche is nat worth the turnynge of an hande, nat only unworthy, wherfore she shulde cast away that whiche is moste goodly

1 At this point, Vives cites Aristotle in order to illustrate that whereas bad examples encourage bad behaviour, good examples promote good behaviour.

treasure, that a woman can have. And she that hath lerned in bokes to caste this and such other thynges, and hath furnyshed and sensed her mynde with holy counsailes, shal never fynde to do any vilany. For if she can fynde in her harte to do naughtyly, havyng so many preceptes of vertue to kepe her, what shulde we suppose she shulde do, havyng no knowlege of goodnes at al? And truly if we wolde call tholde worlde to remembraunce, and reherce theyr tyme, we shall fynde no lerned woman that ever was yll: where I coude brynge forth an hundred good: as Cornelia the mother of Gracchus, whiche was an example of al goodnes and chastite, and taught her children her owne selfe.[2]

Nowe if a man may be suffered amonge quenes to speke of more meane folkes, I wold reken amonge this sorte the daughters of S. T. M. Kn. M. E. and C, and with them theyr kyns woman. M. G.[3] whom their father nat content only to have them good and very chast, wold also they shulde be well lerned, supposyng that by that meane they shulde be more truely and surely chast. Wherin neyther that great wyse man is disceyved, nor none other that are of the same opinion. For the study of lernyng is suche a thyng, that it occupieth ones mynde holly, and lyfteth it up unto the knowlege of most goodly matters: and plucketh it from the remembraunce of suche thynges as be foule. And if any suche thought come in to theyr mynde, eyther the mynde, well fortyfyed with the preceptes of good lyvynge, avoydeth them awaye, or els hit gyveth none hede unto those thynges, that be vyle and foule: whan it hath other moost goodly and pure plea-sure, where with hit is delyted. And therfore I suppose that Pallas the goddes of wysedome and counnynge,[4] and all the Muses, were feyned in olde tyme to be virgins. And the mynde, set upon lernynge and wysedome shall nat only abhorre from foule luste, that is to say, the moste white thynge from soute, and the most pure from spottes: But also they shall leave all suche lyght and tryfly-nge pleasures, wherin the lyght fantasies of maydes have delyte, as songes, daunces, and suche other wanton and pevyshe playes.[5] A woman saythe Plutarche, gyven unto lernyng, wyll never delyte in daunsynge.

But here paraventure a man wolde aske, what lernynge a woman shulde be set unto, and what shall she study: I have tolde you, The study of wysedome: the whiche doth enstruct their maners, and enfurme their lyvyng, and tea-cheth them the waye of good and holye lyfe. As for eloquence I have no great care, nor a woman nedeth it nat: but she nedeth goodnes and wysedome. Nor it is no shame for a woman to holde her peace: but it is a shame for her and abominable to lacke discretion, and to lyve yll. Nor I wyll nat here condempne eloquence, which bothe Quintilian, and saint Hieronime[6] folowyng hym, say was preysed in Cornelia the mother of Gracchus, and in Hortentia the daugh-ter of Hortentius. If there may be founde any holy and well lerned woman, I

---

2 Continues list of good, learned women of high social position. **3** That is, Sir Thomas More's daughters, Margaret, Elizabeth and Cecilia. Margaret More-Roper translated Erasmus's *Devout Treatise upon the Pater Noster* (1526? and 1531?) from Latin, to which Richard Hyrde wrote an introduction where he used More-Roper's exam-ple to praise women's learning. **4** 'counnynge': knowledge. **5** 'pevyshe': silly, senseless, foolish. **6** That is, St Jerome.

had leaver[7] have her to teache them: if there be none, let us chose some man either well aged, orels very good and vertuous, whiche hath a wyfe, and that ryghte fayre ynough, whom he loveth well, and so shall he nat desyre other. For these thynges oughte to be seen unto, for as moche as chastite in bryngynge up a woman requireth the most diligence, and in a maner all to gether. Whan she shalbe taught to rede, let those bokes be taken in hande, that may teche good maners.[8] And whan she shall lerne to wryte, let nat her example be voyde verses, nor wanton or tryflynge songes, but some sad sentence, prudent and chaste, taken out of holy scripture, or the sayenges of philosophers, whiche by often wryting she maye fasten better in her memory. And in lernynge, as I poynt none ende to the man, no more I do to the woman: savyng it is mete that the man have knowlege of many and dyvers thynges, that may both profit hym selfe and the common welthe, both with the use and increasynge of lernynge. But I wolde the woman shulde be al together in that parte of philosophy, that taketh upon hit to enfourme, and teche and amende the conditions.

Finally let her lerne for her selfe alone and her yonge children, or her sisters in our lorde. For it neither becometh a woman to rule a schole, nor to lyve amonge men, or speke abrode, and shake of her demurenes and honestie, eyther all to gether or els a great parte: whiche if she be good, it were better to be at home within and unknowen to other folkes. And in company to holde her tonge demurely. And let fewe se her, and none at al here her. The apostle Paule the vessell of election, enfurmyng and teachynge the churche of the Corinthis with holy preceptes, saithe: Let your women holde theyr tonges in congregations: nor they be nat allowed to speake but to be subjecte as the lawe biddeth. If they wolde lerne any thinge, lette them aske theyr husbandes at home (I Corinthians 14). And unto his disciple Timothe he wryteth on this wyse: Let a woman lerne in silence with al subjection (I Timothy 2). But I gyve no licence to a woman to be a teacher, nor to have authorite of the man, but to be in silence. For Adam was the fyrst mayde, and after Eve, and Adam was nat betrayed, the woman was betrayed in to the breche of the commandement (Genesis 3). Thefore bicause a woman is a fraile thynge, and of weake discretion, and that maye lightly be disceyved: whiche thynge our fyrst mother Eve sheweth, whom the devyll caught with a lyght argument. Therfore a woman shulde nat teache, leste whan she hath taken a false opinion and beleve of any thyng, she spred hit in to the herars, by the auctorite of maistership, and lyghtly bringe other in to the same errour, for the lerners commenly do after the teacher with good wyll.

Of the kepyng of virginite and Chastite

Howe moche than ought that to be set by, that hath oft tymes defended women agaynst great captaynes, tyrantes, and great [h]ostes of men? We have redde of women that have ben taken and let go agayne of the moste unruly soudyours,

7 'leaver': I had rather, or I would prefer. 8 In the next chapter, Vives details both the books which a woman should be allowed to read (including the Bible) and those which she should be discouraged from reading (including Ovid).

only for the reverence of the name of virginite, bicause they sayde that they were virgins. For they ju[d]ged hit a great wickednes for a short and small ymage of pleasure, to minishe so great a treasure: And every of them had leaver that an other shuld be the causer of so wycked a dede than hym selfe. O cursed mayde, and nat worthy to live,[9] the whiche wyllyngly spoyleth her selfe of so precious a thyng, whiche men of warre, that are accustomed to all myschiefe, yet drede to take awaye. Also lovers, whiche be blinde in the heat of love, yet they stay and take avisement. For there is none so outragious a lover, if he thynke she be a virgine, but he wyll alwaye open his eyes, and take discretion to hym and deliberation, and take counsayle to change his mynde. Every man is so sore adrad to take awaye that, whiche is of so great price, that afterward neither can they their selfe kepe nor restore agayne: though they shal have no losse by the meanes: And the ungratious mayde douteth nat to lose that, whiche ones gone, she shall by no meanes recover agayne: whan she hath ones lost the greattest treasure that ever she had. And if motions of the mynde may do ought, whiche if they be reasonable and honest, ought to beare great rule. Let her, that hath loste her virginite, turne her whiche way she wyl, she shal fynde al thynges sorowful and hevy, wailyng, and mournyng, and angry, and displeaserfull. What sorowe wyll her kynnes folkes make, whan every one shall thynke them selfe dysshonested by one shame of that mayde? What mournyng, what teares, what wepynge of the father and mother and bryngers up? Dost thou quite them with this pleasure for so moche care and labour? Is this the rewarde of thy bryngyng up? What cursyng wyl ther be of her aquaintance? What talke of neighbours, frendes, and companyons, cursynge that ungratious yonge woman? What mockynge and bablynge of those maydens, that envied her before? What a lothyng and abhorryng of those that loved her? What fleyng of her company and desertnes, whan every mother will kepe nat only their doughters, but also theyr sonnes from the infection of suche an unthriftie maide? And woars also, if she had any, all fle away from her. And those that before sembled love with her, they openly hate her: Yea and nowe and than with open wordes, wyll caste the abominable dede in her tethe: that I wounder howe a yonge woman, seing this, can eyther have joye of her lyfe, or live at all, and nat pine away for sorowe. Nowe wherto shulde I reherce the hate and anger of folkes? For I knowe that many fathers have cut the throtes of their doughters, bretherne of their systers, and kynnesmen of their kynneswomen.[10]

Histories be full of examples, and dayly ye se: neither hit is marvaile that these be done of fathers and frendes, and that the affection of love and charite is tourned so sodaynly in to hate: whan the women taken with the abominable and cruell love, all love caste quite out of theyr harte, hate theyr fathers and mothers, bretherne and children: nat only theyr frendes and aquayntance. And this I wolde nat that onely maidens shulde thynke spoken unto them, but also maryed women and wydowes, and fynally all women.

9 In the 1529 text, this reads 'love', but other editions substitute 'live'. 10 Vives continues by giving examples of such events.

Nowe let the woman turne to her selfe and consydre her owne ungratiousnes, she shal feare and abhorre her selfe: nor take reste day nor nyght: but ever vexed with the scourge of her owne conscience, and bourned as hotte fyre brondes: shall never loke stedfastlye upon any bodye, but she shal be in feare, leste they knowe some what of her lewdenes: that than no body shall speake softely, but she shall thynke they speake of her unthryftynes. She shall never here talkynge of noughty women, but she shall thynke hit spoken bycause of her. Nor she shall never here name of corruption spoken by an other, but she shall thynke hit ment by her, or of her selfe. Nor no body shall stoure prively in the house, but she shal feare, lest her ungratiousnes be opened, and that she shall be punyshed streyght. What realme woldest thou bye[11] with suche perpetuall vexation. Whiche many a man supposeth to be none other paine in hell. The same payne have wycked men, and women farre sorer, bycause theyr offences be rekened fouler, and they be more timorous[12] of nature. And doutles, if hit be well consydred, women be worthy these punyshementes, and moche worse, that kepe nat theyr honestie diligently. For as for a man nedeth manye thynges, as wysedome, eloquence, knowlege of thynges, with remembraunce, some crafte to lyve bye, Justice, Liberalite, lustye stomake, and other thynges moo[re], that were to longe to reherce: And though some of these do lacke, hit is nat to be disliked, so that many of them be had, but in a woman, no man wyll loke for eloquence, great witte, or prudence, or crafte to lyve by, or ordrynge of the commen weale, or justice, or liberalite: Finally no man wyl loke for any other thing of a woman, but her honesty: the whiche onely, if hit be lacked, is lyke as in a man, if he lacke al that he shulde have. For in a woman the honestie is in stede of all.

It is an evill keper, that can nat kepe one thyng wel, committed to her kepyng, and put in truste to her with moche commendation of wordes: and specially whiche no man wil take from her agaynst her wyll, nor touche hit, excepte she be wyllynge her selfe. The whiche thynge onely, if a woman remembre, hit shall cause her to take better hede, and to be a more ware keper of her goodnes: whiche alone, thoughe all other thynges be never so well in safetie, so loste, all other thynges perysshe to gether there with. What can be safe to a womb saieth Lucrecia, whan her honesty is gone? And yet had she a chast mynde in a corrupt body. Therfore as Quintillian sayth, she thrust a sworde into her body, and avenged the compulsion, that the pure mynde myght be seperated from the defyled body, as shortly as coude be. But I saye nat this because other shuld folowe the dede, but the mynde: Bycause she that hath ones lost her honestie, shulde thynke there is nothynge lefte. Take from a woman her beautie, take from her kynrede, riches, comelynes, eloquence, sharpenes of wytte, counnynge in her crafte, gyve her chastite, and thou hast gyven her al thynges. And on that other syde, gyve her all these thynges, and calle her a noughty packe,[13] with that one worde thou haste taken all from her, and hast left her bare and foule.

---

11 'bye': buy. **12** 'timorous': fearful, timid. **13** 'noughty packe': as the OED puts it, 'a woman of bad character' or 'a wicked or dissolute man'.

LADY ANN COOKE-BACON (trans.)

Fouretene Sermons of Barnardine Ochyne (1550)

Ochine was an Italian Calvinist and his sermons focus on the thorny theological issue of predestination and election: they cover such topics as 'If we maie knowe in this present lyfe, whether we be in the grace of God, and one of his electe or not, and in what manner', 'Howe it ought to be answered to them that lament that God hath created them forseying theyr dampnacion', and 'Wherfore God hathe elected us'. While other, later translations of Ochine's sermons were popular, there was only one separate edition of Bacon's text. However, her translations were reproduced in two other editions, together with more of Ochine's sermons (1551 and 1570). Ann Cooke-Bacon had three sisters, Mildred, Elizabeth and Katherine, each of whom also produced translations, although Mildred's translation of St Chrysostom from Greek has not yet been traced. The copy text is BL, C 12. c. 22 (printed in London by John Day, 1550). The following extracts include the prefatory material (sigs. A2r–A4v) and the twelfth sermon (sigs. G2r–G4v).

To the Christen Reader

When these translated sermons of the famous Barnadine were come to myne hand, Jentyll Reader, I thought it mete to publysh them to the ende so Godly Aposotlyke doctryne should not be private to those onely whych understande the Italian toung, synce thorow the honest travel of a wel occupied Jentelwoman, and verteouse meyden they speake in Englyshe: whose shamfastnes would rather have supprest theym, had not I to whose handes they were commytted halfe agaynst hyr wyll put them fourth, biddyng them blush that deserve blame: for thys of her parte I dare safely affyrme craveth perpetual praise and if any prety pryckemydantes[1] shal happen to spy amote in thys godly laboure (as I doughte not but the nisytes[2] wyl) seynge it is meeter for Docters of divinitye to meddle wyth such matters then Meydens, let them remember howe womanly they wast their tyme the one part in pryckeynge and trymmynge to vayne hethennyshe ostentacion, and in devisyng newe fashyons of apparel, to whome if in their glasse appered the fowle fautes of their fylthy condicions as playnely as the defautes of theyr forsayde faces, I doubt much whether thei wold delight to toote[3] therin so often as thei do: the other part speakyng in prynt lyke parates wyth solemne countenaunces, debate matters of importaunce, and grave weight, as though the ordre of realmes appartained to them, or els warbling wordes of scripture in all their

1 'pryckemydantes': person or people excessively concerned with trifles. 2 'nisytes': people who are fastidious or over-particular. 3 'toote': peer or gaze.

doynges, deface the thyng they most bable of. But I require the (Christian Reader) wyth judgement to reade, and in the equal balaunce of Scripture to way these learned and godly sermons, whych thou shalt fynde (I dout not) of just weyght with the sacred word of God: I forbare to prayse them, lest I should say to lytle, defend them I nede not the authour lyvinge and here amongest us: a man whose lyfe wythout wordes were a suffyciente protection to hys worcke. If oughte be erred in the translacion, remember it is a womans, yea, a Jentylwomans, who commenly are wonted to lyve Idelly, a maidens that never gaddid farder then hir fathers house to learne the language. Fare wel and use hyr labor to the amendement of thy life.

B.B.

To the right worshypful and worthyly beloved Mother, the Lady. F. hyr humble Daughter wysheth encrease of spirituall knowledge, with ful fruicion of the fruites thereof

Since the Orygynal of what so ever is, or may be converted to ani good use in me, hath frelye proceded (thoughe as the minister of GOD) of youre Ladyshyppes mere carefull, and Motherly goodnes, as well in procurynge all thynges thereunto belongeynge, as in youre many, and most Godly exhortacyons, wherein amonge the rest it hath pleased you, often, to reprove my vaine studye in the Italyan tonge, accompting the sede thereof, to have bene sowen in barayne, unfruitful grounde (syns God thereby is no whytte magnifyed) I have at the last, perceived it my duty to prove howe muche the understandyng of youre wyll, could worcke in me towardes the accomplyshynge of the same. And for that I have wel knowen your chyfe delight, to rest in the destroynge of man hys glorye, and exaltynge wholy the glory of God: whych may not be unles we acknowledge that he, doth fore se and determyne from wythout begynnynge, al thynges, and cannot alter or rewarde after our deserved worckes, but remayne stedefaste, accordynge to hys immutable wyll, I have taken in hande to dedicate unto your Ladyship this smale number of Sermons, for the excelent fruit sake in them conteined, proceding from the happy spirit of the santified Barnadyne, which treat of the election and predestinacion of God, wyth the rest (although not of the selfe title) aperteyni[n]g to the same effect to the end it might appere, that your so many worthy sentences touching the same, have not utterly ben without some note in my weake memory, and al be it, they be not done in such perfection, as the dignitie of the matter doth requyre: yet I trust and know, ye wil accept the humble wil of the presenter, not weghing so much the excelnecy of the translacion, al thoughe of ryghte it oughte to be such as should not by the grosnes therof deprive the aucthor of his worthynes. But not meanynge to take upon me the reache, to his hygh style of thealogie, and fearyng also, least in enterprisynge to sette forth the bryghtnes of hys eloquence, I shuld manyfest my selfe unapte, to attaine unto the lowest degre therof. I descend therefore, to the understanding of myne own debilitye. Only requiring, that it may please youre Ladyshippe to vouchsafe that thys my smal labor may be alowed at your handes under whose proteccion only it is commited wyth humble reverence, as yeldyng some parte of the fruite of your Motherly admonicions, in this my wyllinge servyce.

Your Ladyshyppes Daughter
most boundenly obedient.
A.C.

Howe God dothe dispose his grace: the twelfe Sermon

Ther are many whiche thinke that god to every one continually doth offer his grace, and that it is in the power of man to accepte it or not, as thoughe they had it in a boudget, and were in their arbitrement to open and take at their owne wil. And that of this their dead, false, and erronious opinion, groweth that they live most wickedly, thinking and saiyng, god never fayleth with his grace, and it is at our choyse to receyve it at our wyll.

Therfore we may take leisure and lyve a vicious life after our owne way, for we shal be saved alwaies, a moment of time is enough for us to repent and be saved, sence it is in our power. Therfore for to flye such an evell, I have judged it good to shewe that it is not so. It is no doute that god hath created the world for his electe, so that if god had forsene that none should have bene saved, he would not have created it. Ffor them also he dyd preserve it, to them he hath geven the Aungels for kepers, and of them as a father he hath moste singular care and providence (Heb. 1; I Cor. 1; Rom. 8). God wyl not suffer that they be tempted above their power, yea everi thyng worketh and serveth well to their salvacion. Seven times in a day the just shal fal, and ryse againe, because God is with them, and helpeth them in such sorte, that the more thei are in great perils and necessitie, so muche the more is god beneficial to them (Prov. 24). Ffor them god gave the lawe to the world, sent Moses and the Prophetes, them he calleth inwardly in suche maner, that they heare his voice, and answere him of them he molifieth the herte, and draweth them to Christ, as the adamant doth Iron:[4] If they erre, he dothe correcte and chasten them as chyldren, as it is read of David, (Ps. 31; Jhon. 10; Jhon. 9) to them he doth not impute their sinne, he doth quicken and glorify them, and finally al that god hath wrought, and shall worke for hym selfe, is for the electe, for them he sent Christ, and when he came, for them he toke upon hym theyr sinnes, only for them he prayed, for them he wepte, preached, and dyd miracles, for them he shed his bloude, dyed, rose, ascended in to heaven, sent the holye goste, and shal come to judge the quicke and the dead: yea all that he hath suffered, wrought and shall worke, is for the electe, whom he loveth in so excessive maner, that he

4 This was the name of a rock or mineral which was alleged to have remarkable properties. The most relevant in this context is the fact that it was thought to be magnetic.

doth attribute to him selfe al that is done to them. God then beyng gratified with the electe in Christ, doth geve unto them his spirite (Jhon. [3][5]), the lyvely lyghte of hym, faythe, hope, with all the reste of vertues and graces essencial and necessary to salvacion. And moreover he geveth them grace to use in the honor of god, and be served in his glorye, of all the gyftes and graces which maye be comune both to the good, and to the evel, to be used wel and evel, as riches, honour, dignitie, healthe, long lyfe, chyldren, frindes, science, the giftes of the tongue, to do miracles and such lyke. Of them in parte, Paule made mencion, wryting to the Corinthes (I Cor. 12). And also geveth them grace to use in his glorie, povertie, ignomine, infamie, infirmitie, with all adverstitie, and the privacion of lyke gyftes, even to the death, god geveth them such grace that with every wind, they saile to the porte, and they knowe that they are no lesse bounde to thanke god when they are without such giftes, and in all adversitie, then when they have suche thinges wyth the prosperitie of the world, sence that bi the grace which god geveth them, all thinges worke to good [Rom. 8: 28].

Therfore they are ever contented to bee in the state which pleaseth the Lorde, neither wolde they chaunge it, if they myght (without the wyll of god) and onlye for that they fele the divine goodnes, no lesse in adversitie then in the worldly prosperitie. In thend when they are fallen to any sinne, god openeth theyr eies, and maketh them se, not only the evell that they have done, but also that he hath so permitted it for their benefite, to thend they maye the better know theyr owne miseries and the bountie of god. But speaking of the reprobate,[6] I saye, that it is enough for us to knowe that god is not bonde, nor necessited to geve them his grace for theyr good worckes: because that the grace findeth not good worckes, but doth make them to be done.

God neither hath, nor may have any bonde wyth his creatures. The bondes are all oures wyth god, and so muche the more, as that we beyng all loste in Adam, he myghte justly, not only abandon us, but damne and punyshe us. He is not also compelled of hys perfecte goodnes, mercie and charitie, to not have created the worlde, he myghte nowe brynge it to nothinge, and dispose all creatures after his owne waye, being styl moste perfectlye juste, as he is nowe, and was from without beginning, before he did create the worlde. God maye geve of his grace as much as it pleaseth him, when and to whome he thinketh good (Matth. [10][7]), yea, and not to geve it without beyng unjust, or doinge any injurie. God also hath ben of power, without doyng any unrighteousnes, to create the reprobate, foreseynge theyr damnacion, to serve his owne turne, and to use them for instrumentes, or exercise the elect in vertue, to the ende that their victories and triumphes, and likewise Christes, myght be the more glorious, and finally all for his owne greater glorye.

And moreover I saye, that Christe hydeth hym selfe and his grace manye times frome persons (John. 7; Prov.[1][8]), so that althoughe they seeke hym, crie after hym, and recommend them selves to hym, they fynde him not, nor

5 The chapter reference here is illegible. 6 'reprobate': one rejected by God; one who has fallen away from grace or religion and is lost in sin. 7 The chapter reference here is illegible. 8 Again, the chapter reference is illegible.

he heareth them not, notwythstandynge those such as are not moved to seke him, or commit them selves to him, by the spirite, nor from the zeale of the honoure of God, but for their proper interest, yea and mani times he doth blinde and indurate[9] the people, and all is most justlie done. And although it be written that God hath cure of all, calleth all, wolde save al, died for al, doth illuminate al, dothe raine and power[10] his grace upon all; and lyke sentences: I saye, it is to be understand, that he hath cure of al ingeneral, but of the elect in special, and so he calleth al, with a vocacion universall, but the elect with an inward and singuler. When Paule saide also, that he wold save all, he understoode that, to be of everie sorte of persones. His death also was sufficient to save all, but it is not effectuous but to the elect, and so where it is written, that he doth illuminate and geve grace to al, it is understand of the elect, of those that are illuminate. Therfore saide Christe to the Apostels, to you it is geven to knowe the misteries of the Kingdome of heaven (Matth. 13), Paule said likewise, that the faith which is the gifte of God, is not al mens (Eph. 2; II Thess. 2). It is well true also, that God doth illuminate al, in asmuch as there is no person that hath not had some lighte and knowledge of God. Let us then geve him thanckes, sence that of his mere goodnes, he hath connumerat[11] us among the elect, and praye we him that he geve us so much light of his goodnes, that in every place and time we mai render him perfecte laude, honoure and glorye, by Jhesu Christe oure Lorde.

Amen.

JOHN KNOX

The First Blast of the Trumpet against the Monstrous Regiment of Women (1558)

This famous tract was written in Dieppe whilst Knox was, like many Protestant reformers, in exile from Mary Tudor's Catholic reign. Published in Geneva, the tract aimed to call into question the legality of Mary's government by drawing upon patriarchal commonplaces (classical, Christian and patristic) that denounced women's right to hold any position of authority, including that of monarch. However, Knox's purpose was undermined, owing to the unfortunate timing of its publication: it appeared just months before Mary's death and it was not welcomed by the succeeding Protestant Queen, Elizabeth I. The

9 'indurate': to harden morally, to be stubborn or obstinate. 10 'power': pour. 11 'connumerat[e]': literally, to reckon or count together; in this context, then, it means to include.

following extract has been taken from the first part of the tract (copy text: BL, C. 12. b. 18: sigs. 9v–15v; 16v–18v), the complete text being 57pp. The italicised texts within square brackets indicate original marginal comments.

The First Blast to Awake Women degenerate

To promote a woman to beare rule, superioritie, dominion or empire above any realme, nation, or citie, is repugnant to nature, contumelie[1] to God, a thing most contrarious to his reveled will and approved ordinance, and finallie it is the subversion of good order, of all equitie and justice.

In the probation of this proposition, I will not be so curious, as to gather what soever may amplifie, set furth, or decore the same, but I am purposed, even as I have spoken my conscience in most plaine and fewe wordes, so to stand content with a simple proofe of everie membre, bringing in for my witnesse Goddes ordinance in nature, his plaine will reveled in his worde, and the mindes of such as be most auncient amongest godlie writers.

And first, where that I affirme the empire of a woman to be a thing repugnant to nature, I meane not onlie that God by the order of his creation hath spoiled[2] woman of authoritie and dominion, but also that man hath seen, proved and pronounced just causes why that it so shuld be. Man, I say, in many other cases blind, doth in this behalfe see verie clearlie. For the causes be so manifest, that they can not be hid. For who can denie but it repugneth to nature, that the blind shall be appointed to leade and conduct such as do see? That the weake, the sicke, and impotent persones shall norishe and kepe the hole and strong, and finallie, that the foolishe, madde and phrenetike[3] shal governe the discrete, and give counsel to such as be sober of mind? And such be al women, compared unto man in bearing of authoritie. For their sight in civile regiment, is but blindnes: their strength, weaknes: their counsel, foolishenes: and judgement, phrenesie, if it be rightlie considered.

I except such as God by singular priviledge, and for certein causes knowen onlie to him selfe, hath exempted from the common ranke of women, and do speake of women as nature and experience do this day declare them. Nature I say, doth paynt them furthe to be weake, fraile, impacient, feble and foolishe: and experience hath declared them to be unconstant, variable, cruell and lacking the spirit of counsel and regiment.[4] And these notable faultes have men in all ages espied in that kinde, for the whiche not onlie they have removed women from rule and authoritie, but also some have thoght that men subject to the counsel or empire of their wyves were unworthie of all publicke office. For this writeth Aristotle in the seconde of his Politikes: what difference shal we put, saith he, whether that women beare authoritie, or the husbandes that obey the empire of their wyves be appointed to be magistrates? For what insueth the one, must nedes folowe the other, to witte, injustice, confusion and

---

1 'contumlie': insolent reproach or abuse; contemptuous language or treatment. **2** 'spoiled': damaged, impaired, defective; deprived of good or effective qualities. **3** 'phrenetike': insane; mentally deranged. **4** 'regiment': rule, government.

disorder. The same author further reasoneth, that the policie or regiment of the Lacedemonians (who other wayes amongest the Grecians were moste excellent) was not worthie to be reputed nor accompted amongest the nombre of common welthese, that were well governed, because the magistrates, and rulers of the same were to muche geven to please and obey their wyves.

What wolde this writer (I pray you) have said to that realme or nation, where a woman sitteth crowned in parliament amongest the middest of men. Oh fearefull and terrible are thy judgementes (o Lord) whiche thus hast abased man for his iniquitie! [*Reade Isaie the thirde chaptre.*] I am assuredlie persuaded that if any of those men, which illuminated onelie by the light of nature, did see and pronounce causes sufficient, why women oght not to beare rule nor authoritie, shuld this day live and see a woman sitting in judgment, or riding frome parliament in the middest of men, having the royall crowne upon her head, the sworde and sceptre borne before her, in signe that the administration of justice was in her power: I am assuredlie persuaded, I say, that such a sight shulde so astonishe them, that they shuld judge the hole worlde to be transformed into Amazones, and that suche a metamorphosis and change was made of all the men of that countrie, as poetes do feyn was made of the companyons of Ulysses, or at least, that albeit the owtwarde form of men remained, yet shuld they judge that their hartes were changed frome the wisdome, understanding, and courage of men, to the foolishe fondnes and cowardise of women. [*Amazones were monstruouse women, that coulde not abide the regiment of men, and therfore killed their husbandes. Reade Justine.*] Yea they further shuld pronounce, that where women reigne or be in authoritie, that there must nedes vanitie be preferred to vertue, ambition and pride to temperancie and modestie, and finallie, that avarice the mother of all mischefe must nedes devour equitie and justice. [*Arist. 2. Politic.*]

But lest that we shall seme to be of this opinion alone, let us heare what others have seen and decreed in this mater. In the rules of the lawe thus it is written: Women are removed from all civile and publike office, so that they nether may be judges, nether may they occupie the place of the magistrate, nether yet may they be speakers for others. [*Lib. 50. de regulis juris.*][5] The same is repeated in the third and in the sextenth bokes of the digestes: Where certein persones are forbidden, *Ne pro aliis postulent*, that is, that they be no speakers nor advocates for others. And among the rest are women forbidden, and this cause is added, that they do not against shamefastnes intermedle themselves with the causes of others, nether yet that women presume to use the offices due to men. The law in the same place doth further declare, that a naturall shamfastnes oght to be in womankind, whiche most certeinlie she loseth, when soever she taken upon her the office and estate of man. As in Calphurnia was evidentlie declared, who having licence to speake before the senate, at length became so impudent and importune, that by her babling she troubled the hole assemblie. And so gave occasion that this lawe was established.

5 Knox's frequent citing of legal references has been omitted due to pressure on space.

In the first boke of the digestes, it is pronounced that the condition of the woman in many cases is worse then of the man. As in jurisdiction (saith the lawe) in receiving of cure and tuition, in adoption, in publicke accusation, in delation,[6] in all popular action, and in motherlie power, which she hath not upon her owne sonnes. The lawe further will not permit, that the woman geve anything to her husband, because it is against the nature of her kinde, being the inferiour membre to presume to geve anything to her head. The lawe doth more over pronounce womankinde to be the most avaricious (which is a vice intolerable in those that shulde rule or minister justice). And Aristotle, as before is touched, doth plainly affirme, that wher soever women beare dominion, there must nedes the people be discorded, livinge and abounding in all intemperancie, geven to pride, excesse, and vanitie. And finallie in the end, that they must nedes come to confusion and ruine. [*England and Scotland beware.*]

Wold to god the examples were not so manifest, to the further declaration of the imperfections of women, of their naturall weaknes, and inordinat appetites. I might adduce histories, proving some women to have died for sodein joy, some for unpaciencie to have murthered them selves, some to have burned with such inordinat lust, that for the quenching of the same, they have betrayed to strangiers their countrie and citie: and some to have bene so desirous of dominion, that for the obteining of the same, they have murthered the children of their owne sonnes. Yea and some have killed with crueltie their owne husbandes and children. [*Romilda the wife of Gisulphus betrayed to Cacanus the dukedome of friaul in Italie. Jane quene of Naples hanged her husband. Athalia, 4. Reg. II. Hirene, Anton, Sabell.*] But to me it is sufficient (because this parte of nature is not my most sure foundation) to have proved, that men illuminated onlie by the light of nature, have seen and have determined, that it is a thing most repugnant to nature, that women rule and governe over men. For those that will not permit a woman to have power over her owne sonnes, will not permit her (I am assured) to have rule over a realme: and those that will not suffer her to speake in defense of those that be accused, nether that will admit her accusation intended against man, will not approve her, that she shal sit in judgement crowned with the royall crowne, usurping authoritie in the middest of men.

But now to the second part of nature: In the whiche I include the reveled will and perfect ordinance of God, and against this parte of nature, I say, that it doth manifestlie repugne that any woman shal reigne or beare dominion over man. For God first by the order of his creation, and after by the curse and malediction[7] pronounced against the woman, by the reason of her rebellion, hath pronounced the contrarie. First, I say, that woman in her greatest perfection, was made to serve and obey man, not to rule and command him: As saint Paule doth reason in these wordes. Man is not of the woman but the woman of the man. [*Woman in her greatest perfection was made to serve man. I Cor. 11.*] And man was not created for the cause of the woman, but the woman for the

6 'delation': denunciation; to bring a charge against or to inform. 7 'malediction': utterance of a curse; the condition of being subject to a ban or curse.

cause of man, and therfore oght the woman to have a power upon her head (that is a coverture in signe of subjection). Of which words it is plaine that the Apostle meaneth, that woman in her greatest perfection shuld have knowen, that man was Lord above her: and therfore that she shulde never have pretended any kind of superioritie above him, no more then do the angels above God the creator, or above Christ Jesus their head. [*A good comparison.*] So, I say, that in her greatest perfection woman was created to be subject to man. But after her fall and rebellion committed against God, their was put upon her a newe necessitie, and she was made subject to man by the irrevocable sentence of God, pronounced in these wordes: I will greatlie multiplie thy sorowe and thy conception. [*A newe necessity of womans subjection.*] With sorowe shalt thou beare thy children, and thy will shall be subject to thy man: and he shal beare dominion over the. [*Woman by the sentence of God subject to man. Gene. 3.*] Herebie may such as altogither be not blinded plainlie see, that God, by his sentence, hath dejected all woman frome empire and dominion above man. For two punishmentes are laid upon her, to witte, a dolour,[8] anguishe and payn, as oft as ever she shal be mother; and a subjection of her selfe, her appetites and will, to her husband, and to his will. Frome the former parte of this malediction can nether arte, nobilitie, policie, nor lawe made by man, deliver womankinde, but who so ever atteineth to that honour to be mother, proveth in experience the effect and strength of goodes word.

But (alas) ignorance of God, ambition, and tyrannie have studied to abolishe and destroy the second parte of Goddes punishment. For women are lifted up to be heades over realmes, and to rule above men at their pleasure and appetites. But horrible is the vengeance, which is prepared for the one and for the other, for the promoters, and for the persones promoted, except they spedelie repent. For they shall be dejected from the glorie of the sonnes of God, to the sclaverie of the devill, and to the torment that is prepared for all suche, as do exalte them selves against God. Against God can nothing be more manifest, then that a woman shall be exalted to reigne above man. For the contrarie sentence hath he pronounced in these wordes: Thy will shall be subject to thy husband, and he shall beare dominion over the. [*Gen. 3.*] As God shuld say: forasmuch as thou hast abused thy former condition, and because thy free will hath broght thy selfe and mankind in to the bondage of Satan, I therfore will bring the in bondage to man. For where before, thy obedience shuld have bene voluntarie, nowe it shall be by constreint and by necessitie: and that because thou hast deceived thy man, thou shalt therefore be no longar maistresse over thine own appetities, over thine owne will nor desires. For in the there is nether reason nor discretion, whiche be able to moderate thy affections, and therfore they shall be subject to the desire of thy man. He shall be Lord and governour, not onlie over thy bodie, but even over thy appetites and will. This sentence, I say, did God pronounce against *Heva*,[9] and her daughters, as the rest of the Scriptures doth evidentlie witnesse. So that no

8 'dolour': physical or mental suffering and pain. 9 'Heva': Eve.

woman can ever presume to reigne above man, but the same she must nedes do in despite of God, and in contempt of his punishment and malediction.

I am not ignorant, that the most part of men do understand this malediction of the subjection of the wife to her husband, and of the dominion, which he beareth above her: but the holie ghost geveth to us an other interpretation of this place, taking from all women all kinde of superioritie, authoritie and power over man, speaking as foloweth, by the mouth of saint Paule: I suffer not a woman to teache, nether yet to usurpe authoritie above man. [*I Tim. 2*] Here he nameth women in generall, excepting none, affirming that she may usurpe authoritie above no man. And that he speaketh more plainlie, in an other place in these wordes: Let women kepe silence in the congregation, for it is not permitted to them to speake, but to be subject as the lawe sayeth. [*I Cor. 14*]. These two testimonies of the holy ghost, be sufficient to prove what so ever we have affirmed before, and to represse the inordinate pride of women, as also to correct the foolishnes of those that have studied to exalt women in authoritie above man, against God, and against his sentence pronounced.

The apostle taketh power frome all woman to speake in the assemblie. *Ergo* he permitteth no woman to rule above man. The former parte is evident, whereupon doth the conclusion of necessitie folowe. For he that taketh from woman the least parte of authoritie, dominion or rule, will not permit unto her that which is greatest: But greater it is to reigne above realmes and nations, to publish and to make lawes, and to commande men of all estates, and finallie to appoint judges and ministers, then to speake in the congregation. For her judgement, sentence, or opinion proposed in the congregation, may be judged by all, may be corrected by the learned, and reformed by the godlie. But woman being promoted in sovereine authoritie, her lawes must be obeyed, her opinion folowed, and her tyrannie mainteined: supposing that it be expreslie against God, and the prophet of the common welth, as to manifest experience doth this day witnesse. And therfore yet againe I repete that, whiche before I have affirmed: to witt, that a woman promoted to sit in the seate of God, that is, to teache, to judge or to reigne above man, is a monstre in nature, contumelie to God, and a thing most repugnant to his will and ordinance. For he hath deprived them as before is proved, of speakinge in the congregation, and hath expreslie forbidden them to usurpe any kinde of authoritie above man. Howe then will he suffer them to reigne and have empire above realmes and nations? He will never, I say, approve it, because it is a thing most repugnant to his perfect ordinance, as after shalbe declared, and as the former scriptures have plainlie geven testimonie.

To the whiche, to adde any thing were superfluous, were it not that the worlde is almost nowe comen to that blindnes, that what soever pleaseth not the princes and the multitude, the same is rejected as doctrine newelie forged, and is condemned for heresie. I have therfore thought good to recite the mindes of some auncient writers in the same mater, to the end that suche as altogither be not blinded by the devil, may consider and understand this my judgement to be no newe interpretation of Goddes scriptures, but to be the uniforme consent of the most parte of godlie writers, since the time of the apostles. Tertullian in his boke of womens apparell, after that he hath shewed many causes why gorgious apparell is abominable and odiouse in a woman, addeth these wordes, speaking as it were to every woman by name: Dost thou not knowe (saith he) that thou art Heva? the sentence of God liveth and is effectuall against this kind, and in this worlde of necessity it is, that the punishment also live. [*Tertulian. de habitue mulierum.*] Thou art the porte and gate of the devil. Thou art the first transgressor of godes law, thou didest persuade and easly deceive him whome the devil durst not assault. For thy merit (that is for thy death) it behoved the son of god to suffre the death, and doth it yet abide in thy mind to decke the above thy skin coates? By these and many other grave sentences, and quicke interrogations, did this godlie writer labour to bring everie woman in contemplation of her selfe, to the end that everie one depelie weying, what sentence God had pronounced against the hole race and doughters of Heva, might not onely learne daily to humble and subject them selves in the presence of God, but also that they shulde avoide and abhorre what soever thing might exalte them or puffe them up in pride, or that might be occasion, that they shuld forget the curse and malediction of God. And what, I pray you, is more able to cause woman to forget her own condition, then if she be lifed up in authoritie above man? It is a thing verie difficile to a man, (be he never so constant) promoted to honors, not to be tickled some what with pride (for the winde of vaine glorie doth easelie carie up the drie dust of the earth). But as for woman, it is no more possible, that she being set aloft in authorite above man, shall resist the motions of pride, then it is able to the weake reed, or to the turning wethercocke, not to bowe or turne at the vehemencie of the unconstant wind.

MARGARET TYLER (trans.)

D. Ortunez de Calaharra, *The Mirrour of Princely Deedes and Knighthood* (1578)

Tyler translated a Spanish romance, which tells the tale of the 'worthinesse of the Knight of the Sunne, and his brother Rosicleer, sonnes to the great Emperour Trebatio: with the strange love of the beautifull and excellent Princesse Briana, and the valiant actes of other noble Princes and knightes'. Her address 'to the Reader' has been much anthologised, due to her ingenious means of justifying her actions, of which the following are but two examples: 'But my defence is . . . if men may and do bestow such of their travailes upon gentlewomen, then may we women read such of their works as they dedicate unto us, and if we may read them, why not farther wade in them to the serch of a truth. And then much more why not deale by translation in such arguments' (sig. A4r); and 'my perswasion hath bene thus, that it is all one for a woman to pen a story, as for a man to addresse his story to a woman. But amongst al my il willers, some I hope are not so straight that they would enforce me necessarily either not to write or to write of divinitie. Whereas neither durst I trust mine own judgement sufficiently, if matter of controversy were handled, nor yet could I finde any booke in the tongue which would not breed offence to some' (sig. A4v). The text itself, however, is less widely available; for this reason we have included a brief extract from the beginning of the tale (pp. 1-8). The copy text (BL, C. 56. d. 15) was printed in London by Thomas East in 1578.

The Mirrour of Knighthood. Cap. I

After that the greate Emperour *Constantine* had peopled the Citie of *Constantinople*, with the race of the noble Citizens of *Rome*, and had reedified the auncient buildings founded by *Pansanias* king of the *Parthes*. Among all the Emperours which succeeded in that Empire of *Greece*, none seemed to have raysed his owne name, or to have made it so famous, as the great and mightie Emperour *Trebatio*. Whose worthy deedes with the valiant actes of the Knights of his time, I will report here, according as *Artimidoro* the *Grecian* hath left them written in the great volumes of his Cronicle.

The story sayth thus: That if at any time Fortune, being alwaies uncerteine and variable, shewed hir selfe more freindly to the *Greekes*, then to all men besides: and if ever the *Grecians* were feared in all the worlde, it was in the time of *Trebatio* the sonne of *Alicante*, which man by right line discended from the noble and auncient blood of *Molosso*, the second sonne of strong *Pyrrhus*, and in the third discent from the great *Achilles*, which was slayne in the warres of *Troye*.

This *Trebatio*, in the xxv. yeare of his age, reigned in *Epirus*, wher the sayd *Pyrrhus* and his auncestours had bene kings. He was strong and valiant in armes, and endowed with so many graces, that his fame in that time was spred over all the world, and that there was neither king nor Emperour, but[1] he was glad to hold him for his friend.

Now it happened in his time by the death of the Emperour *Theodoro*, the state of the Empire to be voyde, for that *Theodoro* had no sonne, and the Empire was to be given by election: So that the Electors not fynding any whom with so good reason they might chuse for Emperour as the great *Trebatio*, as well for his great valure, as for his discent from so noble a race. They with the willing and joint assent of all the Emperials named him unto the Empire, and brought him with great honour to Constantinople. Where, (if before, for his great fame they had praised and honored him) now much more they held him deere, having in some part seene and knowen him. Bicause he

1 'but': in sixteenth-century usage, this often meant 'except', as it does in the above example.

was of conditions very noble, pleasant, loving to all, liberall, courteous, sufferable,[2] pitifull, and above all very desirous to entertein in his court, valiant and worthy knights, whom he honoured above all the Princes of the earth. So that his court florished with princes and knights, as wel subjects as straungers, which much magnified his great estate, and him selfe held continuall exercise in armes with them, as being like enclined to nothing. His vertue by the report of such as knew him, was so rare that it was generally thought none of his predecessors to have had advauntage over him, but rather he was of greater force then any one of them all. For many men were witnesses of his mightie strokes. He was called the great *Trebatio*, bicause he was viii. foote in height, and very strong timbred,[3] so that without proofe of his manhood, they might therby make conjecture of his force.

In his life, customes, and conditions he was alway so affable, and courteous, that never might be noted in him one little fault. Wherfore his historians say, that he was the crown of the *Greeks*, and the cleere mirrour of all the Princes and knights of the world. Whence also this his chronicle boroweth this title, especially having therein to remember the mervailous deedes of the knight of the Sunne with *Rosicleer* both sons unto *Trebatio*. Since whose time, all the adventures of the auncient and famous knights were cleane forgotten, and since whose time, neither *Ulisses*, of whom *Homere* speaketh, neither any other songs or sonets, ballads or enterludes, wer heard in *Greece*, onely with these two knightes they were familiarly acquainted. Of these they made great volumes, and with a thousand devises in verse they sang of their love. They made no building nor painture[4] without some storie of them and their memorie therin declared. In such sort that you might passe by no part of all *Greece* where was not recited, song or painted the histories and noble deeds of these knights. As if no other thing but armes or love were fitting for them.

And bicause that in the time to come so noble things should not be put in oblivion, some of the *Grecians* compiled this noble Historie, to the encouraging of all Nations, that shall either heare or reade this Historie.

The king of Hungary pretending a title to the Empire, setteth him selfe against the Emperour Trebatio. Cap. 2

It appeareth by an auncient *Greeke* Chronicle, that the Emperour *Helio*, the third predecessor in the Empire of *Trebatio* had two sons, the eldest of which two, the father being deceased, was chosen Emperour, the other was married with a Princesse inheritrix of the kingdome of *Hungary*, whereby he became Lord and ruler of that kingdome. The first son which was elected for Emperour departed without issue. For which cause the *Grecians* chose an other which was the predecessor of *Theodoro*. This seeing, the second son of *Helio* which

2 'sufferable': long-suffering, patient. 3 'timbred': physical build. 4 'painture': painting.

then reigned in *Hungary*, and judging that with most reason the Empire was his, as greeved with the election he assembled his power against the *Grecians*, thinking to be Lord over them by force. In the end as he was not so mightie as they, so he was vanquished and slaine before he might atteine his purpose. Yet from that time foorth al the kings which succeded in *Hungary*, pretended alway that the right of the Empire rested in them by way of inheritaunce, and there never failed warres and dissentions betweene the *Hungarians* and the *Greeks* upon this occasion.

In like manner when the great *Trebatio* was chosen for Emperour, then reigning in *Hungary* the king *Tiberio*, a very strong man and of great courage, besids of more might then all his auncestours. For he held in his subjection beside the kingdome of *Hungary* many other provinces, as *Holland*, *Zeland*, *Flaunders*, *Zweueland*, *Bavare*, *Austrich*, *Almaine*, *Alba*, *Denmarke*, *Marcomandia*, *Persia*, and other regions, with the which he deemed himselfe one of the mightiest kings in the world. This *Tiberio* knowing the election of the Emperour *Trebatio*, and beeinge more attached with the desire of the Empire then any of his predecessors were, (as it was to bee gotten by war) so he assembled by summons the greatest of estate throughout his lande, and declaring unto them his will, hee commaunded to gather all the people they might for to invade *Greece*.

Besides this, to the ende his power might yet bee greater, he determined to marry his daughter unto such a one, as would and could mainteine his quarrel. This maiden was called *Briana*, the most bewtifull Princesse that was to be found in all those partes, beeinge by the onely reporte of hir eccellencie, sued unto by many worthy Princes, especially by Prince *Edward*, sonne of *Olyverio* king of the great *Britaine*. This young knight strong and valiant, and greatly enamored on the Princesse *Briana*, through the great fame of hir bewtie, had before dispatched his ambassadors towards the king hir father, to request hir for wife. To the which hir Father bicause hee had already undertooke the battaile against the Emperour *Trebatio*, easely condesended, upon condition that the Prince should come into *Hungary* with *20,000* chosen men of warre for to aide him in the presuite of his claime, against the Emperour.

This, when Prince Edward understoode, hee had so great desire to have the Princesse *Briana*, that by and by he graunted his request, and so as speadely as he might, he gathered the people that the king *Tiberio* required of him, and with the consent of his Father hee departed from great *Britaine* towarde *Hungary*, giving intelligence before unto the King *Tiberio*, of his comming. The king knowing the succours which came unto him, appointed a day when all his hoast should meet together, and finding him selfe of so great power, in the meane while untill the Prince came, hee resolved to make a rode into *Greece*, sacking all the little townes he might, before that the Emperour *Trebatio* should perceive it. Afterwardes if the Emperour *Trebatio* should come to succour his subjectes, then to joyne battaile with him, at such time as the Prince should approch, which thing he put in practise diligently. For with that power which he had, he entered into *Greece* forraging the countrey, taking little townes of great force, burning and wasting so much as he might, to the intent that the people of other fenced cities stroken with feare, might abandon themselves to flight, and enfeeble their forces. Howbeit king *Tiberio* had not passed into *Greece* xxx. myles, when the Emperour *Trebatio* having knowledge of it, came against him with an hoast of knights so valiant, that at the first alarme, the *Hungarian* reculed,[5] and by the chase of his enimies was forced to retire home into the citie of *Belgrado*, which is in *Hungary*. Ther he fortified himselfe, and manned the towne, unwilling as yet to goe unto the feelde, untill the Prince of greate *Britaine* should arrive: by whose comming their powers beeing joyned, he thought he might give the battaile unto the Emperour *Trebatio*. Albeit he caryed about him a mayme incurable in his body, not by any stroke lent him by his enimie, but by the onely conceit of the Emperours vertue. For he had seene the Emperour demeane[6] him selfe more worthely, then any of those which came with him, and namely in a kinsman of his, a very strong knight, whom the Emperour at one blow, as it were, devided in two peeces. This, as it might be, made him keepe his chamber, bicause he himselfe confessed the valour of the Emperour to be above the report of men, not withstanding he had heard sufficiently of the Emperours prowesse. But bicause these things are not mentioned, but to give beginning to this history, we run them briefly over, not rehearsing the great deeds of armes that the Emperour and his people did in besieging the citie, bicause we have other matters more noble in hand, in comparison whereoff, these thinges were needlesse. The story hereoff, begins in the chapter following.

The Emperour Trebatio by the hearesay of hir beautie, was surprised with the love of the princesse Briana, ca. 3

Certeine daies the Emperour *Trebatio* lay at the sidge of *Belgrado*, hoping that the king *Tiberio* would come out to give them battaile, for that he had greate desire to be avenged of the great harmes which he had received in *Greece*, but the king would in no wise leave the towne, still abiding the comming of Prince *Edward* and his army out of England. The Emperour mervailing much at it, commaunded a prisoner to be brought before him, whom he had taken in the former battaile, of him he demaunded the cause why the king *Tiberio* held himself so close with so many good knights mewed up in the citie, and why hee came not out to give the battaile, with promise of life and liberty if he told trouth, otherwise the certeintie of most cruel death. The prisoner thus placed before the Emperour, what with feare of death, and hope of libertie, durst not declare other then the truth, and therfore thus made answere unto him.

"Know you mightie Emperour, that when the king of *Hungary* my master, first tooke upon him the entry into *Greece*, he would not have done it,

5 'reculed': recoiled, retreated. 6 'demeane': behave.

(although he hath so mightie an hoast as is seene) but in hope that before he should be espied and met withall, there should come to his helpe Prince *Edward*, sonne to the king of great *Britaine* with *20,000* knights. This number was promised upon condition that the prince should have the kings daughter, the princesse *Briana* to wife, which princesse I beleeve is the fayrest maide in all the world, and by such fame the prince is become enamoured of hir, so as we heere that he is already departed from greate *Britaine* with the number appointed, and shal take landing very soone in this countrey, the king *Tiberio* abideth his comming, and is determined to give the onset, as soone as their forces shalbe united."

This sayd the prysoner, but the Emperour minding to knowe more of the matter, demaunded of him where the Princesse *Briana* remayned, and of what age shee myght be. The prisoner aunswered him, "My Lord, she is with the Queene *Augusta* hir Mother in the monastry of the ryver which is neere to *Buda*, a pleasant and delectable house, wherin none are lodged but Nonnes, and the Queenes gentlewomen. The Princesse is of the age of xiiii. years, and be you assured that so many as shal see hir, wil judge hir rather a goddesse then a woman, so much hir beautie doth excell all the gentlewomen of the world. Now so soone as the prince shall land, he will straight waies take his journey towards the monastery of the river, bicause it is so appointed by the king hir father. The king him selfe will not be there, bicause he will not be absent in such a busy time from the citie." When the prisoner had thus sayde, the Emperour *Trebatio* demaunded him to be set free without speaking other thing to his people, but with a sorowfull and troubled countenaunce, he withdrew himselfe into a secret chamber of his Imperiall tent. Where tossing in his conceit divers and sundry fancies, he endured a wilful imprisonment, without any baile or maynprise.[7] Thus that force, which neither by tilt, turney,[8] nor barriers, neither by speare nor swoord, neither by mallice of the enimy, nor pride of the mightie, might at any times be subdued, was nowe vanquished by the onely hearesay of a gentlewomans commendation. Nay the valiant heart which he held forcible inough against all the world, failed in his own defence against a delicate damzel whom he had never seene. What force is it that may repulse this evil, sith that with such flattering closes, it overthroweth so many noble hearts and strong bodies.

But to retourne, the Emperour *Trebatio* so much burned in love with the Princesse *Briana*, that already he hath forgotten the damage received in his countrey, his travaile out of his countrey with a huge army, the consuming of his treasure for to wreake his anger on the king *Tiberio*, onely he devised upon this, howe to give remedie unto his amorous passion. For as the fire was great which enflamed him, so was the remedy by all semblaunce farre from him. Bicause that on the one part he was hindred by the enmitie betweene him and hir father, so that he durst not require hir for wife, and on the other side she was already promised to the Prince of greate *Britaine*, who had put himselfe on his journey for the atteining of hir person, so that likewise the king could not

7 'maynprise': surety; legal responsibility. 8 'turney': tournament.

take hir from him to give unto his enimy. These things bred such griefe unto the Emperour as that he hoped for nothing, but to dye. And so tourning and overtourning in his thought a thousand sort of remedies, without finding any which might satisifie him, he convaied him selfe into his most secret tent, and ther remained .iii daies, not suffering any of his people to have accesse unto him or speach with him, except some squiers servitors, from whom likewise he would willingly have exempted himself, but that he would not die so deperately. Those of the camp which sawe the sodeine chaunge and alteration in the Emperour, as they knew not the cause of it, so were they much abashed and carefull to know what it might bee. Some immagined that the delay of the warre, and the comming of prince *Edward* were the occasions of his trouble, and so hoping that he should well overcome that griefe shortly, they left him to his rest, untill he had resolved upon the pursuite of this which followeth in the next Chapter.

THOMAS SALTER

A Mirrhor mete for all Mothers, Matrones and Maidens, intituled the Mirrhor of Modestie (1579)

Although this text was initially believed to be Salter's own, original work, Janis Butler-Holm points out that the *Mirrhor of Modestie* is 'for the most part a close translation of Giovanni Michele Bruto's *La Institutione di vna faniculla nata nobilmente*'.[1] Butler-Holm also notes the connection between Salter's text and W. P.'s later translation entitled *The Necessarie, Fit, and Convenient Education of a yong Gentlewoman* (1592). In addition to the *Mirrhor*, the book contains 'A . . . Dialogue betweene Mercurie, and Vertue' (sigs. D7r–E3r). The text exists in only one edition, a copy of which is held in the British Library (printed in London for Edward White, 1579, C. 40. a. 20), and it 'is primarily a gathering of common-places about female training' (p. 7). The following extracts provide an outline of contemporary expectations about women's education and behaviour (sigs. A6r–A6v; B2v–B3r; B7r–C4r; C6r–C7r; D2r–D5r).

For as muche as the weakenesse of our nature is suche, as wee are more inclined and prone to imitate and followe those thynges that bee hurtfull unto

1 Janis Butler-Holm, ed., *A Critical Edition of Thomas Salter's The Mirrhor of Modestie*, The Renaissance Imagination, vol. 32 (New York and London: Garland, 1987), p. 1.

us, then those that bee good and profitable. In my judgemente there is nothyng more meete, especially for yong Maidens then a *Mirrhor*, there in to see and beholde how to order their dooyng, I meane not a Christall *Mirrhor*, made by handie Arte, by whiche Maidens now adaies, dooe onely take delight daiely to tricke and trim their tresses, standyng tootyng[2] twoo howers by the Clocke, lookyng now on this side, now on that, least anythyng should bee lackyng needefull to further Pride, not sufferyng so muche as a hare to hang out of order, no I meane no suche *Mirrhor*, but the *Mirrhor* I meane is made of an other maner of matter, and is of muche more worthe then any Christall *Mirrhor*; for as the one teacheth how to attire the outwarde bodie, so the other guideth to garnishe the inwarde mynde, and maketh it meete for vertue, and therefore is intituled a *Mirrhor*, meete for Matrones and Maidens, for Matrones to knowe how to traine up suche young Maidens as are committed to their charge and tuission, and for maidens how to behave them selves to attaine to the seate of good fame.[3]

[B]efore I passe any farther, I will staye too shewe the use of many unwise Fathers, who beyng more daintye, and effeminate in followyng their pleasures, then wise and diligent in seekyng the profite of their Daughters, doe give them, so sone, as they have any understandyng in readyng, or spellyng, to cone and learne by hart bookes, ballades, Songes, sonettes, and Ditties of daliance excityng their memories thereby, beyng then moste apt to retayne for ever, that whiche is taughte theim, to the same maner of order, for the hartes of youth, are therein to bee compared to newe vesselles, whiche for ever will keepe the savour and tast, of that licore where with it is first filled and seasoned, therefore I would wish our good Matrone to eschew suche use, as apestilent infection, for no doubt the weake age of youth, and evell conversation of manye, geves copious, and aboundant matter enough to evill, and muche more then wise Parentes would wish, I am sure without neede to bee taught it so longe tyme before, but in steede of suche bookes and lascivious ballades, our wise Matrone, shall reade or cause her Maidens to reade, the examples and lives of godly and vertuous Ladies, whose worthy fame, and bright renowme, yet liveth and still will live for ever, whiche shee shall make choise of, out of the holy Scripture, and other histories both auncient and of late dayes whiche, bookes will not onely delight them, but as a spurre it will pricke and incite their hartes, to follow vertue, and have vice in horror and disdaine.[4]

[B]ut my intent is not, neither was it ever, to attribute suche evill as springeth from the mallice of wicked men, and their corrupte nature, to the sacred studie of learnyng, to whiche I have given my mynde so muche as in me laye all my life tyme. But my purpose is to prove that in a vertuous Virgine, and

2 'tootyng': peering, gazing. 3 Salter continues by outlining the qualities that a 'Matrone' should have. 4 Here, Salter discusses what learning is, or is not, appropriate for women, and produces examples which he claims prove that women's education can be detrimental to a nation.

modest Maiden, suche use is more daungerous and hurtfull, then necessarie or praise woorthie. Some perhaps will alledge that a Maiden beyng well learned, and able to searche and reade sonderie aucthors, maie become chaste and godlie, by readyng the godlie and chaste lives of diverse: but I aunswere who can deny, that, seyng of her self she is able to reade and understande the Christian Poetes, . . . that shee will not also reade the Lascivious bookes, of *Ovide, Catallas, Propercius, Tibullus*, and in Virgill of *Eneas*, and Dido, and amonge the Greeke Poettes of the filthie love (if I maie terme it love) of the Goddes themselves, and of their wicked addulteries and abhominable Fornications, as in Homer and suche like, and to the same also (seyng that Parentes will be so Ambicious, as they will take delight to see their daughters dispute in Philosophers Schooles) who can warrant that when it seemes good unto her, that she will not as well defende the perverst oppinion of the *Epicure*. . . . [A]nd sure I suppose there is no Manne of reason and understandyng, but had rather love a Mayden unlearned and chast, then one suspected of dishonest life, though never so famous and well learned in Philosophie. Wherefore I wish all Parentes too beware and take heede, how they suffer their young Daughters beyng fraile of Nature, to be bolde disputers, and to the ende I maie not be thought naked of examples to prove the contrarie, I maintaine (seyng it behoveth mee more to contende with aucthoritie then reason) that where these obstinate defendoures of learning to be meete and necessarie in women, can bryng in one example, I will alledge a nomber to the contrarie.

For the Histories as well ancient as of those of late daies are full of the Noble factes and renowmed deedes done by rare and Excellent Ladies, whiche as well for their noble courage and magnanimous harts as for their chast and vertuous lives have beene and for ever wilbee moste Famous and renowmed in the worlde, and yet had no learning, as it hath beene seene, bothe in *Sparta, Rome, Persia, Phocia, Chios, Argiva*, and dyvers other places, whose names have beene celebrated in tyme past, and to our tyme present have leaft behinde them more matter to wright on touchyng their vertue, then ever either *Erinna, Sappho*, or *Corinna*, did write them selves of excellent and famous men. And who is it that will denie that it is not more praies and honnour too doe noble deedes, then to write of them, sure I thinke none, I am therefore of this advise, that it is not mete nor convenient for a Maiden to be taught or trayned up in learnyng of humaine artes, in whome a vertuous demeanour and honest behaviour, would be a more sightlier ornament, then the light or vaine glorie of learnyng, for in learnyng and studiyng of the artes there are twooe thynges finallie proposed unto us, that is recreation and profitte, touchyng profitte, that is not to bee looked for, at the handes of her that is geven us for a companion in our labours, but rather every woman ought wholelie to be active and diligent about the governement of her housholde and familie, and touchyng recreation by learnyng that cannot bee graunted her, without greate daunger and offence to the beautie and brightnesse of her mynde; seyng then that the governement of estates and publike weales are not committed into the handes of women, neyther that it is lawfull or convenient for them to wright lawes, by whiche men should bee ruled and governed, . . . neither as professours of

Science and facultie, to teache in Schooles the wisedome of Lawes and Philosophie, and seing also that in suche studies, as yeldeth recreation and pleasure, there is no lesse daunger, that they will as well learne to be subtile and shamelesse Lovers, as connyng and skilfull writers, of Ditties, Sonnetes, Epigrames, and Ballades, let them be restrained to the care and governement of a familie, and teache them to bee envious in followyng those, that by true vertue have made little accoumpte of those, that to the prejudice of their good names, have beene desirous to bee reputed *Diotimes, Aspaties, Sapphoes,* and *Corinnes*.

For suche as compare the small profit of learnyng with the greate hurt and domage that commeth to them by the same shall sone perceive (although that they remaine obstainate therein) how far more convenient the Distaffe, and Spindle, Nedle and Thimble were for them with a good and honest reputation, then the skill of well using a penne or wrighting a loftie vearce with diffame and dishonour, if in the same there be more erudition then vertue; moreover who is hee that will doubte that the Maide, will not become perfitte and well accomplished (how be it that it be harde to be beleved, seyng that now adaies they bee wedded and committed to the government of a housholde so young) whiche in companie, and by the instruction of manie bothe wise and vertuous and by longe experience have beene taught the manner, how to governe a housholde wisely, sure I will never condiscende that any Maiden surmounting in her selfe the estate of an active wife, or for too name her by one woorde *Economicall*, should by climyng up the Ladder of naturall Philosophie, beyng so difficile, adventure to get to the contemplation of suche thynges, as rather of idle menne, whiche have bin many yeres exercised in readyng, is to bee desired then hoped for . . .

[A]nd yet notwithstandyng al this, I would not have a Maiden altogether forbidden, or restrained from reading, for so muche as the same is not onely profitable to wise and vertuous women, but also a riche and precious Jewell, but I would have her if she reade, to reade no other bookes but suche as bee written by godlie Fathers, to our instruction and soules healthe, and not suche lascivious Songes, filthie Ballades, and undecent bookes as be moste commonly now a daies sette to sale, to the greate infection of youth, the names of whiche to recite would require a long tyme, and to write a greate volume beyng more pleasaunte[5] then profitable, long then learned, gallant then godlie. Wherefore leavyng theim as unworthie to bee mentioned, I would have our Maiden, I meane her that will attire her minde by this *Mirrhor* to read, (if she delight to bee a reader) the holie scripture, or other good bookes, as the bookes of *Plutarche*, made of suche renowmed and vertuous women as lived in tyme paste, and those of *Boccas* tendyng to the same sence or some other, nerer to our tyme, and lette her in readyng, consider what she reade, for in theim she shall not onely reade woordes, whiche if thei bee not garnished with good examples, be naught worth. But also godly deedes and holie enterprises of vertuous Virgines and worthie Women, by whiche she maie increase and

5 'pleasaunte': amusing or ridiculous.

augmente her vertue by immytatyng their lives. Lette her reade I saie and with the same print in her minde the lives of suche noble Ladies as lived in *Troie, Sabina, Phocia, Argiva*, and *Rome*, for no doubte she shall learne greate example of pitie to her Countrie, by *Megestona, Aretaphila, Polioreta*, and by *Judith* and *Hester*. And true love and loialtie to their housbandes by *Lucres, Portia*, and *Camma*, in somme to make an ende of strangers, she shall finde example of vertue, Religion, and holinesse in a number of Virgines, as in *Cicile, Agathe, Theodore, Barbara*, and infinite other who with the prise of their bloudes, did suffer incredible tormentes, for the profession of a godly faithe. And above all for delight, if she love to bee delighted in vertue, let her reade that worthie booke of Martyres, compiled by that famous Father and worthie man of God maister Foxe. . . .

[B]ut now adaies it semeth to some, and that to the moste parte, that it is a godly ornament, and a brave settyng out to a yong Maiden, if she emong the rest can shewe her self, to be an excellent fine singer, or a cunnyng[6] player uppon Instrumentes, whiche thynge, although it bee confirmed by some gallant glosyng[7] reasons: I for my part doe not onely discommende, but judge that a thing of no little daunger, which ought in all women to be eschewed. For as Musicke if it be used to a laudable and good intention, hath no evill in it, but deserverth a place emong the other Artes, the whiche appertainyng properly to menne, be called Liberall: Yet notwithstandyng, under the shadowe of vertue (as for the moste parte all other Artes and faculties, bee foolishely acknowledged for vertues) it beareth a swete baite, to a sowre and sharpe euill.

Therefore I wishe our Maiden, wholie to refrain from the use of Musicke, and seeyng that under the coverture of Vertue, it openeth the dore to many vices, she ought so muche the more to be regarded, by how muche the more the daunger is greate, and lesse apparent. I must confesse that the use of singing and delicate plaiyng uppon Instrumentes and sweete harmonie is necessarie, but for whom? For those that bee overworne with greef, sorowe, trouble, cares, or other vexasion, have neede of recreation, as *Agamemnon* had in *Homer*, and *Saule* in the holie Scripture, by the Harpe and sweete syngyng of *David*, who therewith pacified his fierce and furious passions, and revoked them to a milde and quiete Spirite [1 Sam. 16: 14–23], but in steade of usyng it to so good an intention, it is converted to a poison, for it is onely at bankettes and feastes, to whiche as if the delicious and sweete meates, did not sufficiently effeminate the myndes of men and women: the excellentest Musitians are called, where to the sweete accordes of sondrie Instrumentes, often tymes artificiall lascivious songes are adjoyned therby, no other wise, then as dried wood beyng laied on the fire with little blowyng, will kindle and burne, to kindle in their hartes the flames of leude affections, that are not yet strongly staied up by vertue, and by suche newe devises to burne theim. It is saied, that from the false sweetenesse of the *Sirens* songes, *Ulisses* a Prince famous emong the Grekes, and saied to be nourished with heavenly foode, in the verie bosome of *Sapience, Jupiters* doughter, could hardly escape, and shall wee then without

6 'cunnyng': skilful. 7 'glosyng': flattering interpretation.

feare, give so muche trust to a young Maiden, daintely and tenderly trained up, that she not onely by hearyng, but by learnyng so wanton an Arte, will not become wanton and effeminate?[8]

I would not have her that will attire her minde by this *Mirrhor*, to be a babbler or greate talker, but to consider that alwaies muche babbling and speaking is occasion of many faultes, not onely in youth, in whiche more then in other it behoveth to learne but also in those of ripe yeeres and gravitie, whiche ought to be instructors and teachers of good demeanors. I therefore wishe her diligentlie to harken to all. But especially being in the companie of grave and wise women, I wishe her to be attentive to heare that whiche they saie, and she not to speake to often, for as she that speaketh often is in danger to faile. So shee that hereth much is in possibilitie to become more wise and learned, whiche thing to the ende it maie happen to our Maiden, I would wishe her to take heede and note that whiche is uttered to the praies or dispraies of any, and thereafter to frame her life. Whiche thing shee maie easely discerne by the jestures and behaviours of the hearers, who alwaies with cherefull countenances are accustomed to rejoyce at that whiche is good, contrarie with a sower and sharpe looke and as it were with grief thei accorde to that whiche is evill and tolde without respecte of place, tyme, persone, or of suche thinges as they talke of, or of them selves. In this wise shee shall make election and choise of that whiche she ought to keepe silent setting a lawe to her self, to doe the one and eschue the other, for she ought to know that the use of the toung is to be used soberly and discretly, for to that ende nature, that wise woorke woman ordained the toung to bee inclosed as with a hedge within twoo rowes of teeth, where contrarie shee hath leaft our eares open, the one to be readie to heare, and the other slowe to speake. . . .

For truely as too muche boldnesse (beeyng a thyng more conveniente for those that to reprove vice, use the partes of divers personages in Comedies and Tragedies, then for a modeste or milde Maiden) is to bee shonned and eschewed, as a fault infamous: So to the contrary, too muche fearfulnesse or shamefastnesse where it is needelesse, is a pointe of greate follie, fitter for babes to use, then suche a one as I wishe our Maiden to bee, that delighteth to decke her minde by this *Mirrhor*, therefore restrainyng these twoo extremities, if any commit offence proper to yong age, let them be shamefast, onely in acknowledging their fault and not otherwise, and so not beeyng obstinate in deniyng, they shall shewe greate signe of amendemente. And sure there can not bee a greater chasticemente, then the fame that suche a one shall conceive.[9]

8 Salter continues to discuss the detrimental effects of music. He then moves on to the issue of honesty and the need to confess errors and sins, and how a maiden should behave in company. 9 'conceive': beget, i.e., what will ensue.

Likewise where it behoveth her to shewe her vertue, she shall bee readie but not to bolde, and by a sodaine blushyng, whiche immediatly will overspread her lillie cheekes with roseat red, she shall shewe that she beareth in her breaste a reverente harte, farre separated from infamous and reprochfull shame. In suche wise I saie, she shall with a cherefull countenaunce, and a well tempered gravitie, castyng her eyes to the yearth, shewe of her self that whiche neverthelesse, although she knowes it will redounde[10] to her praise and commendation, she would willingly dissemble and faine[11] not to care for. With this commendable confidence, when it behoves her through request to recite any Psalme, or other Spirituall song, or godlie sentence, she shall set her self forthe to doe it with a milde refusall, yet altogether voide of undecent affectyng, which thyng the moste parte of people can hardly eschewe, and yet her prudente Matrone, to the ende that our Maiden maie bee still in doubte of this affectyng, shall holde her in suspecte of her refuse.

ANNE WHEATHILL

A Handfull of Holesome (though Homelie) Hearbs (1584)

Anne Wheathill's collection of prayers was dedicated 'to all religious ladies, Gentlewomen, and others'. While the book itself is a small, tightly bound duo-decimo volume, it spans to 144 pages and contains 49 prayers on different subjects. In addition to those reproduced below, Wheathill addresses such subjects as faith, repentance, confession and God's fatherly love, and concludes with 'A praier shewing that God is alwaies our protection'. Her writing is informed by Reformist doctrine and, as Elaine Beilin notes, '[s]he writes plainly, in the style long established as appropriate for godly instruction'.[1] The copy text is BL, C. 145. f. 13, printed in London by H. Denham, 1584, sigs. a. iir–a. iiir; b1r–b2r; b7v–b9v; f2r–f5v; h8v–h10r; k7r–k10v.

10 'redounde': reflect. 11 'faine': feign, pretend. 1 Elaine V. Beilin, *Redeeming Eve: Women Writers of the English Renaissance* (Princeton: Princeton University Press, 1987), p. 53.

To all Ladies, Gentlewomen, and others, which love true religion and vertue, and be devoutlie disposed; Grace mercie, and peace, in Christ Jesus

For a testimonall to the world, how I have and doo (I praise God) bestowe the pretious treasure of time, even now in the state of my virginitie or maidenhood; lo heare I dedicate to all good Ladies, Gentlewomen, and others, who have a desire to invocate and call upon the name of the Lord, a small handfull of grose hearbs; which I have presumed to gather out of the garden of Gods most holie word. Not that there is anie unpurenes therein, but that (peradventure) my rudenes[2] may be found to have plucked them up unreverentlie, and without zeale.

Whereupon of the learned I may be judged grose[3] and unwise; in presuming, without the counsell or helpe of anie, to take such an enterprise in hand: nevertheles, as GOD dooth know, I have doone it with a good zeale, according to the weakenes of my knowledge and capacitie. And although they be not so pleasant in taste, as they can find out, to whom God hath given the spirit of learning: yet doo I trust, this small handfull of grose hearbs, holesome in operation and workeing, shall be no lesse acceptable before the majestie of almightie God than the fragrant floures of others, gathered with more understanding.

But without presumption I may boldly saie, they have not sought them with a more willing hart and fervent mind; nor more to the advancement of Gods glorie, and the desire of acceptation, than I have doon. Which if I may obtaine, with the good judgement and liking of all my brethren and sisters in the Lord, I shall thinke my time most happilie bestowed: for that thereby I did avoid idlenes, to the pleasing of almightie God; and have gained those, whom I know not, as well strangers to me, as my acquaintance, to be my freends, that shall taste these grose hearbs with me.

The Lord Jesus Christ, who moisteneth all his elect[4] with his most pretious blood, give us all a sweete taste in him: whome I humblie beseech, from the bottome of my hart, to give unto those that are vertuouslie bent, a desire to increase therein; and those, which have not yet reached thereunto, I praie the holie Ghost to inspire their hearts from above, that they and we may be worthie to meete together, in the blessed kingdome of our heavenlie father, which his deare sonne our saviour Jesus Christ did purchase for us; whose blessed name, with the living father, and the holie Ghost, be praised and magnified now and for ever, Amen, Amen.

Yours in Christ,
Anne Wheathill,
Gent

---

2 'rudenes': ignorance; lack of knowledge or education. 3 'grose': uninstructed, lacking in refinement.
4 'elect': those chosen by God for salvation or eternal life, in contrast to those who are damned (the reprobate).

1. A Praier for the *Morning*

O Mightie maker and preserver of all things, God omnipotent, which like a diligent watchman, alwaies attendest upon thy faithfull people, so that whether they sleepe or wake, live or die, thy providence never forsaketh them: looke favourablie upon me, O Lord, thy poore and sinfull servant, which am not woorthie, but through thy great mercies offered to me in Christ, once to lift up mine eies unto thy mercie seat.

Wherefore in the name of thy deere sonne my Lord and Saviour, I offer unto thee, through him, the sacrifice of praise and thanks giving; that thou hast preserved me both this night, and all the time and daies of my life hitherto, untill this present houre. I beseech thee of thy great mercie to illuminate my understanding, that I may lead and frame my life as thou hast taught me in thy holie word, that my light may so shine here on earth, that my heavenlie father may be glorified in me, through Jesus Christ our Lord and redeemer; for whose sake heare me deare father, and send thy holie Ghost to direct me in all my dooings. To thee O glorious and blessed Trinitie, the Father, the Sonne, and the holie Ghost, be given all honor and praise, now and for ever more, Amen.

4. An Evening praier

O Everlasting light, whose brightnesse is never darkned; looke favourablie upon me thy poore and sinfull servant, who hath not onelie this daie, but all the daies and time of my life hitherto, untill this present houre, offended thy divine Majestie, in thought, word, and deed; wherby I have most justlie provoked thy wrath and indignation against me. And now I bow the knees of my hart unto thee most mercifull and heavenlie father, beseeching thee for Jesus Christ his sake, to forgive me all my sinnes, negligences and ignorances. For I confesse how wickedlie I have mispent the talent that thou gavest me, abusing thy gifts of grace manie waies, burieng the same in obscure darknesse, woorse than the servant that hid his maisters treasure, not putting it to anie increase; for he delivered the principall againe [Matt. 25: 14–30].

But I most miserable creature, can shew unto thy majestie no part of that which thou gavest me, to use to thine honor and glorie: for the which I am most hartilie sorie, and doo unfeinedlie repent, having no meane to helpe myselfe, but onelie to lift up the eies of my faith unto thy deare sonne Jesus Christ, beseeching him most instantlie to make perfect my wants, and to renue whatsoever is lacking in me. For I commit my bodie and soule, this night and evermore, into his most holie hands; hoping, O Christ, thou wilt make me an acceptable sacrifice unto thy father.

I have no place to flie unto, but to shrowd me under the wings of thine almightie power, who wast so loving unto us, that thou wast contented to shed thy most pretious bloud, for the sinnes of the whole world; for the which I most humblie and hartilie yeeld unto thee thanks, honor, praise and glorie.

O lambe of God, sonne of the father, heare thou me, thou that saiedst; I am thy health and salvation, I am thy peace and life; cleave fast unto me, and thou shalt live. O Lord I am the woonded man, and thou art the good Samaritane: powre oile into my wounds, and bind them up [Luke 10: 25–37]. Lord heale thou me, and I shall be whole: for thou art my God and Saviour.

Heare thou therefore my supplications from heaven, and have mercie. Take from me all my sinnes and wickednesse, and give me thy grace and holie spirit. Lighten mine eies, that I sleepe not in death: so shall I joiefullie, after this sluggish sleepe of sinne, rise againe, living in thy feare all the daies of my life. Which grant me to doo, O Father, Sonne, and holie Ghost, three persons and one true GOD, world without end, Amen.

21. A praier of the *creation of mankind, of the true* Samaritane, and for strength against temptation

O Father of heaven, of power almightie, which with thine onlie word diddest create and make all the whole world, and all for the profit and service of man, whom thou diddest create of all other a most noble and perfect creature, giving him power upon earth, the waters, and all the fowles and birds of the aire; thou madest him also after thine own similitude and likenes, induing him with a reasonable soule, and all the powers thereof, thou also diddest put him in the pleasant garden of paradise, excepting nothing from him, but the eating of the onelie tree of knowledge of good and evill: and further, for his helpe, comfort, and companie, of a ribbe of his side thou madest for him a woman, and gavest hir to him to be his wife [Gen. 1–3].

There had they instructions given them, and the lawe of life for an heritage. Before them was laid both life and death, good and evill, with a freewill given them to take which liked them best. But their frailtie was such, that they, through a small intisement, chose the evill, and left the good: they left life, and chose death. Thus Lord, through sin and breaking of thy commandements, man lost the freewill that was given him in his creation, and purchased death to all his posteritie.

In the waie as he went to Jerusalem and Jericho, he fell in the hands of theeves, who hurting and wounding him sore, departed, leaving him halfe dead; so that he could have helpe of none, but only the good Samaritan, who, as he passed by the same waie, powred wine and oile into his wounds, and tooke the cure of him.

This onelie Samaritan was thy deare Sonne Christ, which tooke upon him all the iniquities of mankind, and laid them on his backe by his death, purging and clensing him, not onelie from the originall sin of our father *Adam*, but also from all our sins which we commit from time to time, by the vertue of his passion, and the sacrament of baptisme upon our repentance. For as by *Adam*, death came to mankind, so by Jesus Christ was mankind restored to life.[5]

For this great and high benefit of thy sonnes blessed passion for our redemption, we thy poore creatures praise and thanke thee, most humblie acknowledging his inestimable love towards us, in that thou vouchsafedst to die for us, being then sinners, and thy mortall enimies. Neverthelesse, most mercifull father, we are of our selves not able to do any thing that good is, no not so much as to thinke a good thought, without thine aid and assistance. We wander here miserablie, in the lowe parts of the vile earth; our strength will not serve us to clime to the high of the hilles, where thou dwellest in thy mount Sion, a place prepared for thine elect, a chosen inheritance of thy faithfull servant *Abraham*, and his seed.

Wherefore since we, being burthened with the affects of worldlie pleasures, and also with other cares and troubles, can by no meanes ascend to thee, that art on the top of so high a mountaine, (so manie legions of angels attending on thy Majestie) we have no remedie, but with the prophet *David* now to lift the eies of our harts and minds towards thee, and to crie for helpe to come down from thee to us thy poore and wretched servants.[6]

We wander here below as lost sheepe, having no shepheard; we are assailed on every side with manifold enimies; the divell ravening and hungering, seeketh whom he may devoure; the world allureth us also to hir deceitfull vanities; our flesh also, which we carrie about us, is our enimie readie and prone to drawe us unto all vices and pleasures. From this can we by no meanes be defended, but by thee Lord.

Send us therfore thy helpe and holie angell, to assist and strengthen us: for of thee most mercifull Father floweth all bountie and goodnes. Thou O Lord God madest heaven and earth for thine honour, and mans commoditie; establish therefore good Lord the chosen works of thy hand with thy eternall helpe: from heaven send us downe the welspring of thy grace, and thy strong angell to aide us by his helpe, that no assault of our spirituall enimies doo prevaile against us: but from all evils by thy word defend us, Lord, both touching the bodie, and also the soule, that no temptation prevaile against us.

Thou hast beene our protectour, even from our mothers wombe [Ps. 22: 9]; and our trust is that thou wilt so continue all the daies of our life, and speciallie at the houre of our death, that we may ascend to the heavenlie Jerusalem, where we shall reast in the bosome of our father *Abraham*, the father of all faithfull beleevers, there to praise thee, and thy loving Sonne, and the holie Ghost, world without end, Amen.

31. A praier that we may *heare the word of* God and keepe it

I am thy servant, Lord, give me understanding, that I may learne thy lawe and decrees: incline my soule to the words of thy mouth, bicause thy talke floweth

5 Note Wheathill's reinterpretation of the Fall; Beilin suggests that 'Wheathill avoids both the misogynistic attribution of guilt to Eve and the ingenious acquittals of her defenders' (p. 53) by representing Adam and Eve as sharing the responsibility for the Fall. 6 Allusion to Psalm 123.

like unto dew. The Israelites said unto *Moses*; Speake thou unto us, and we will heare thee, but let not the Lord speake, least we die [Exod. 20: 19]. Howbeit, I praie not so, O Lord, but rather with the prophet *Samuel* I doo humblie and earnestlie beseech thee thus; Speake on Lord, for thy servant dooth hearken [1 Sam. 3: 9, 10], for thou art the giver and inspirer of life, who art able without anie to instruct me.

Thy Ministers speake for thee thy secreats, but thou unlockest the understanding of the things pronounced; they rehearse to us thy commandements, but it is thy aid and helpe that giveth strength to walke over the same, and givest light unto the minds. Wherefore, bicause thou art the everlasting truth, speake thou Lord my God unto me, least I die, and be made unfruitfull: for thou hast the words of everlasting life. Speake therefore that thing, which may bring both comfort unto my soule, and amendment unto my life, and also may cause glorie and immortall honor unto thee. For man dooth perish, but thy truth indureth, O God, for ever.

Blessed are they therefore, whom thou instructest and givest knowledge unto O Lord, and doost teach thy lawe, that thou maist helpe them in time of trouble, that they perish not. Looke favourablie upon me, O GOD, and graunt (I praie thee) that thy truth may teach me, keepe me, and bring me unto a happie end. Let the same deliver me from all wicked lusts, and from inordinate love. Thou hast infinit means, and all creatures are at thy commandement; therefore good Lord shewe some signe, whereby I shall be delivered, and send thine holie angell before me, to keepe me in thy waie, and to bring me to the place which thou hast provided for me, that I may live with thee everlastinglie, world without end, Amen.

39. A praier of *lamentation, wherein the sinner lamenteth* his miserable estate, and crieth for mercie

My God, when I do earnestlie behold mine owne state, whereunto I am brought through sinne, not onelie being naked and bare of all goodnes, but also to be overwhelmed in the depth of all iniquitie; I cannot but lament, moorne, and crie for helpe, as dooth a woman, whose time draweth neere to be delivered of hir child; for she can take no rest, till she be discharged of hir burthen.

No more can I, Lord, as long as I feele my selfe loden with my heavie burthen of sinne, the weight wherof draweth me downe to the deepe bottome of all miserie; from whence I can by none be delivered, but onelie by thee, that art the guide and the eie to those that are blind through ignorance, the succor of the oppressed, the comfort of the weake, the life of those that are dead; so that they repent and turne unto thee.

It is not the long distance of us from thy highnesse, which keepeth our praiers from thee; thine eares are readie in the hearts of all that are willing to crie for the help of thy grace. Who so is made farre from thee, through sinne, by repentance is made neere unto thee. He that is in the bottom of the sea of miserie, if he beginne to call for thy helpe, he shall not be suffered to sinke. From all deepe dangers most mercifull God deliver me.

I crie and call pitiouslie unto thee, which art onelie able to helpe me. Heare therefore, I most hartilie praie thee, my sorowfull praier, and let my poore petition pearse the eares of thy Godhed. And since thy sonne Christ died for to release us of sinne, let not my sinnes be a staie, whereby my praiers should not be heard, but wipe them cleane awaie, that they never more appeere. For I miserable sinner doo flie to the gentlenes, of thy favourable mercie, whose nature and propertie is to have pitie and compassion.

From thee floweth all mercie and grace, which was so great unto us, that it mooved thee to send thine onlie Sonne to die for our redemption; whereby thy justice was satisfied, and thy mercie found that it sought. O how fervent was this thy noble charitie to us vile wretches! It tooke root and beginning in thy mightie deitie, and from thence it was derived to mankind; being an example that we thy christian people should, like loving brethren, beare one anothers burthen.

Wherefore I am most willinglie contented, to remit all injuries doon to me; as it hath pleased thy goodnes to forgive me much greater offenses comitted against thee. And whensoever it shall please thee to scourge and punish me, I will gladlie receive thy chastisement, for that I knowe it proceedeth of love for my wealth and suretie; trusting that after my long abiding and suffering in this life, I shall surelie obteine thy reward, by thy promise, that is; If we suffer with Christ, we shall also reigne with him [Rom. 8: 17].

Such sure hope have I ever had in thee Lord, and by the same hope I trust to have thy favour, and live for ever. For blessed are they that trust in thee, most mercifull Father; and cursed are they that trust in man. Of thy grace and mercie onelie commeth all goodnes; thy mercie forgiveth onelie our sinnes dailie and hourelie, and the painfull death of thy sonne Christ delivereth us from all the paines due for our sinnes. Thou boughtest us not with gold and silver, but with the pretious bloud of that lambe without spot, thy blessed Sonne, whose death had beene sufficient for thousands of worlds.

The greatnes of thy love caused the plentifull paiment of the price of our redemption. The charitie of our Lord Jesus Christ hath burnt up, and consumed, by his death, all our iniquities. Wherefore the faithfull, being thus delivered from all dangers, by thine onlie goodnesse, may now give thanks unto thy mightie Majestie, resting in hope to have, after this life, everlasting joie and felicitie; through Jesus Christ our mercifull Lord and redeemer; to whom with thee O deare Father, and the holie Ghost, be given all honor, glorie, and praise, now and for ever, Amen.

PHILIP STUBBES

A Christal Glasse, for Christian Women (1591)

A *Christal Glasse* is Philip Stubbes's exemplary biography of his wife Katherine; it also contains her confession of faith on her deathbed, and ends with 'A most wonderfull Conflict between Satan and her soule, and of her valiant Conquest in the same, by the power of Christ', in which Stubbes articulates her assurance of salvation and refutes Satan's temptations: '[Y]ea Satan, I was chosen and elected in Christ to everlasting salvation, before the foundations of the world were laid: and therefore thou maist get the packing, thou damned dog, and go shake thine eares, for in me thou hast nought' (sig. C2v). This text was enormously popular, arguably the most popular text of its kind, going through 24 editions between 1591 and 1637. The copy text (BL, 4902. b. 63) was printed in London by Richard Jhones, 1591: the extract is from the beginning of the text, sigs. A2r–B1r.

Calling to remembrance (most Christian Reader) the finall ende of mans creation, which is to glorifie God, and to edifie one another in the way of true godlinesse, I thought it my dutie as well in respect of the one, as in regarde of the other, to publish this rare and wonderfull example, of the vertuous life, and Christian death of mistresse *Katherine Stubbes*, who whilest she lived, was a myrrour of woman-hoode, and now being dead, is a patterne of true Christianitie. She was of honest and wealthie parentage, and her father had borne office of worship in his companie: he was zealous in the truth, and of a sound Religion. Her mother was a Dutch woman, both discreete and wise, of singular good grace and modestie: and which did most of all adorne her, she was both religious, and verie zealous. This couple living together in the Citie of London certain yeares, it pleased God to blesse them with children, of whom this *Katherine* was youngest save one. But as she was youngest save one by course of nature: so was she not inferiour to any of the rest, or rather farre excelled them all without comparison by manie degrees, in the induments[1] and qualities of the mind.

At xv. yeares of age (her father being dead) her mother bestowed in marriage to one maister *Stubbes*, with whom she lived foure yeares, and almost an halfe, verie honestly and godly, with rare commendations of all that knewe her, as well for her singular wisedome, as also for her modestie, courtesie, gentlenesse, affabilitie and good government. And above all, for her fervent zeale which she bare to the truth, wherein she seemed to surpasse manie: Insomuch as if she chanced at any time to be in place where either

1 'induments': attributes.

Papists, or Atheists were, and heard them talke of religion, of what countenance or credite soever they seemed to be, she would not yeeld a jote, or give place unto them at all, but would most mightily justifie the truth of God, against their blasphemous untruthes, and convince them: yea, and confound them by the testimonies of the worde of God. Which thing how could it be otherwise? for her whole heart was bent to seeke the Lorde, her whole delight was to bee conversant in the Scriptures, and to meditate upon them day and night [Ps. 1: 2]: insomuch that you could seldome or never have found her without a Bible, or some other good booke in her hands. And when she was not reading, she would spend the time in conferring, talking and reasoning with her husband of the worde of God, and of Religion: asking him: what is the sence of this place, and what is the sence of that? Howe expounde you this place, and howe expounde you that? What observe you of this place, and what observe you of that? So that shee seemed to bee, as it were ravished with the same spirit that *David* was, when hee saide, The zeale of thy house hath eaten me up [Ps. 69: 9].

Shee followed the commaundement of our Saviour Christ, who biddeth us to search the Scriptures, for in them you hope to have eternal life. She obeied the commandement of the Apostle, who biddeth women to be silent, and to learne of their husbands at home [1 Cor. 14: 35]. She would suffer no disorder or abuse in her house, to be either unreproved, or unreformed. And so gentle was shee and curteous of nature, that she was never heard to give to any the lie, nor so much as to (thou) any in anger. Shee was never knowen to fall out with any of her neighbours, nor with the least childe that lived: much lesse to scolde or brawle, as many will now adayes for everie trifle, or rather for no cause at all. And so solitarie was shee given, that shee woulde verie seldome, or never, and that not without great compulsion go abroade with any, either to banquet or feast, to gossip or make merie (as they tearme it) inso much, that shee hath beene accused to doo it in contempt and disdaine of others.

When her husbande was abroade in London, or elsewhere, there was not the dearest friend she had in the world that coulde get her abroad to dinner or supper, or to any other exercise whatsoever: neither was she given to pamper her bodie with delicate meates, wine or strong drinke, but refrained them altogether. And as she excelled in the gift of sobrietie: so she surpassed in the vertue of humilitie. For it is well knowne to diverse yet living, that she utterly abhored all kind of pride, both in apparell, and otherwise. She coulde never abide to heare any filthie or uncleane talke of scurrilitie, neither swearing nor blaspheming, cursing nor banning,[2] but would reprove them sharply, shewing them the vengeance of God due for such deserts. And which is more, there was never one filthy, uncleane, undecent, or unseemly word heard to come forth of her mouth, nor never once to curse or ban, to sweare or blaspheme God any maner of way: but alwayes her speach were such, as both glorified God, and ministred grace to the hearers, as the Apostle speaketh [Eph. 4: 29]. And for her conversation, there was never any man or woman that ever opened their

2 'banning': cursing.

mouthes against her, or that ever either did or could accuse her of the least shadow of dishonestie, so continently she lived,[3] and so circumspectly she walked, eschewing ever the outward appearance or shewe of evill.

Againe, for true love and loyaltie to her husband, and his friends, she was (let me speake it without offence) I thinke, the rarest in the worlde: for shee was so farre from perswading her husbande to bee lesse beneficiall to his friends, that shee woulde perswade him to bee more beneficiall to them. If she sawe her husband merrie, then shee was merrie: if hee were sadde, she was sadde, if he were heavie, or passionate, shee would endevour to make him glad: if he were angrie, she would quickely please him, so wisely shee demeaned[4] her selfe towardes him. Shee woulde never contrarie him in any thing, but by wise counsail, and politike advice, with all humilitie and submission, seeke to perswade him. And so little given was she to this worlde, that some of her neighbours marvayled why shee was no more carefull of it, and would aske her sometimes, saying: Mistresse *Stubbes* why are you no more carefull for the things of this life, but sit alwayes poaring uppon a booke, and studying? To whome she woulde answere: If I shoulde be a friend to this worlde, I shoulde be an enemie to GOD: for God and the worlde are two contraries. *John* biddeth mee, love not the world, nor any things in the world: affirming, that if I love the world, the love of the Father is not in me [I John 2: 15]. Againe, Christ biddeth mee, first seeke the kingdome of heaven, and the righteousnesse thereof, and then all these worldy things shall be given to me [Matth. 6: 33]. Godliness is great riches if a man be content with what he hath. I have chosen with good *Martha* the better part, which shall never be taken from me.[5] Gods treasure (shee would say) is never drawne drie, I have enough in this life, God make me thankeful, and I know I have but a short time to live here, and it standeth me upon to have regard to my salvation in the life to come.

Thus this godly yong woman helde on her course three or foure yeares after shee was married: at which time it pleased God, that she conceyved with a man childe: after which conception she would say to her husband, and many other her good neighbours and friends, not once, nor twice, but manie times, that she should never beare more children, that, that child woulde bee her death, and that shee shoulde live but to bring that childe into the worlde. Which thing (no doubt) was revealed unto her by the Spirite of God, for according to her prophecie, so it came to passe.

The time of her account being come, shee was delivered of a goodly man childe, with as much speede, and as safely in all womens judgements, as any could be. And after her deliverie, she grewe so strong, and lustie,[6] that she was able within foure or five dayes to sit up in her bed, and to walke up and downe her chamber, and within a fortnight, to goe abroade in the house, being throughly well, and past all daungers, as everie one thought.

But presently upon this so sudden recoverie, it pleased God to visite her

---

3 'continently': self-restrainedly. **4** 'demeaned': only became derogatory in the eighteenth century. At this time it referred to how one conducted oneself or behaved towards other people. **5** For the story of Martha and Mary, see John 12: 1–8. **6** 'lustie': joyful, merry, cheerful, lively.

againe, with an extreame hot and burning quotidian Ague,[7] in which sicknes she languished for the space of six weekes, or there aboutes. During all which time, shee was never seene, nor perceived to sleep one houre together, neither night nor day, and yet the Lord kept her (which was miraculous) in her perfect understanding, sence, and memorie, to the last breath, praysed bee the Lorde therefore. In all her sickenesse, which was both long and grievous, she never shewed any signe of discontenment, or impatiencie: neither was there ever heard one worde come forth of her mouth, sounding either of desperation, or infidelitie: of mistrust, or distrust, or of any doubting or wavering, but alwayes remayned faithfull, and resolute in her God. And so desirous was she to be with the Lorde, that these golden sentenses were never forth of her mouth,[8] I desire to be dissolved, and to be with Christ. And, Oh miserable wretch that I am, who shall deliver me from this bodie subject to sinne. Come quickly Lord Jesus, come quickly [Rev. 22: 20]. Like as the heart desireth the water springs, so dooth my soule thirst after thee O God [Ps. 42: 1–2]. I had rather bee a doore keeper in the house of my God, then to dwell in the tentes of the wicked [Ps. 84: 10]: with manie other heavenly sentences, which (least I should seeme tedious) I willingly omit. She would alwaies pray in her sicknesse absolutely, that God would take her out of this miserable worlde: and when her husband and others would desire her to pray for health, if it were the will of God: Shee would answere, I pray you, pray not that I shoulde live, for I thinke it long to be with my God. Christ is to me life, and death is to me advantage. I cannot enter into life, but by death, and therefore is death the doore or enterance into everlasting life to me. I knowe and am certainly perswaded by the Spirite of God, that the sentence of my death is given alreadie, by the great Judge, in the Court or Parliament of heaven, that I shall nowe depart out of this life: and therefore pray not for me, that I might live here, but pray to God to give me strength, and patience, to persevere to the ende, and to close up mine eyes in a justifying faith in the blood of my Christ.

Sometimes she would speake very softly to herselfe, and sometimes very audibly, these words doubling them a thousande times together, Oh my good God, why not nowe? Why not nowe, o my good God? I am readie for thee, I am prepared, oh receyve me nowe for thy Christ his sake. Oh send thy messenger death to fetch me, send thy sergeant to arest me, send thy pursevant[9] to apprehend me, thy herauld to summon me: oh send my Jailour to deliver my soule out of prison, for my bodie is nothing else but a filthie stinking prison to my soule. Oh sende thy holie Angels to conduct my soule into the everlasting kingdome of heaven. Other some times she would lie as it were in a slumber, her eyes closed, and her lips uttering these words very softly to her selfe: Oh my sweete Jesus, oh my love Jesus: why not nowe sweete Jesus, why not nowe: as you heard before. Oh sweete Jesus, pray for mee, pray for me sweete Jesus, repeating them many times together. These and infinite the like were her dayly

7 'quotidian Ague': recurrent fever, marked by successive fits or paroxysms, consisting of a cold, hot and sweating stage. 8 'forth': i.e. out of her mouth. 9 'pursevant': summoner, formerly a junior heraldic officer.

speaches, and continuall meditations: and never worser worde was there heard to come forth of her mouth, during all the time of her sicknesse.

She was accustomed many times as she lay, verie suddenly to fall into a sweete smiling, and sometimes into a most heartie laughter, her face appearing right faire, redde, amiable, and lovely: and her countenaunce seemed as though she greatly rejoyced at some glorious sight. And when her husband would aske her why she smiled and laughed so: she woulde say, if you sawe such glorious visions and heavenly sights as I see, you would rejoyce and laugh with me: for I see a vision of the joyes of heaven, and of the glorie that I shall go to: and I see infinite millions of Angels attendant upon me, and watching over me, readie to carrie my soule into the kingdome of heaven. In regard whereof, she was willing to forsake herselfe, her Husband, her childe, and all the world besides. And so calling for her childe, which the Nurse brought unto her, shee tooke it in her armes, and kissing it, said: God blesse thee my sweete babe, and make thee an heire of the kingdome of heaven: and kissing it againe, delivered it to the Nurse, with these words, to her husband standing by. Beloved husband, I bequeath this my child unto you, he is now no longe mine, he is the Lords and yours, I forsake him, you, and all the worlde, yea, and mine owne selfe, and esteeme all things dungue, that I may winne Jesus Christ. And I pray you, bring up this child in good letters, in discipline, and above all things, see that he be brought up in the exercise of true Religion.

The childe being taken away, she spyed a little Puppie or Bitch, (which in her life time she loved well) lying upon her bed: she had no sooner spied her, but she beate her away, and calling her husband to her, said: Good husband, you and I have offended God grievously in receyving this Bitch many a time into our bed: the Lord give us grace to repent for it and al other vanities. And afterward could shee never abide to looke upon the Bitch any more.

Having thus godly disposed of all things, she fell into an extasie, or into a traunce, or sownde,[10] for the space almost of a quarter of an houre, so as every one thought she had beene dead. But afterward she comming to her selfe, spake to them that were present, (as there were many both worshipfull and others) saying. Right worshipfull and my good neighbours and friends, I thanke you all, for the great paines you have taken with me: and whereas I am not able to requite you, I beseech the Lord to reward you in the kingdome of heaven. And for that I knowe that my hower-glasse is runne out, and my time of departure hence is at hande, I am perswaded, for three causes to make a confession of my faith before you all. The first cause that moveth me is, for that those (if there be any such here) that are not thorowly resolved in the trueth of God, may heare and learne what the spirite of God hath taught me out of his blessed and alsaving worde. The second cause that moveth me hereto, is, for that none of you shoulde judge that I died not a perfect Christian, and a lively member of the mysticall bodie of Jesus Christ, and so by your rash judgement might incurre the displeasure of God. The thirde and last

---

10 'sownde': swoon or faint.

cause, is for that, as you have beene witnesses of part of my life: so you might bee witnesses of my Faith and beliefe also.

And in this is my confession, I woulde not have you to thinke, that it is I that speake unto you, but the spirite of God which dwelleth in me, and in all the elect of God, unlesse they be reprobates: For Paul sayeth *Rom.* 8. If any one have not the spirite of Christ dwelling in him, he is none of his. This blessed spirite, hath knocked at the doore of my heart, and God hath given mee grace to open the doore unto him, and hee dwelleth in me plentifully. And therefore I pray you give me pacience a little, and imprint my wordes in your hearts, for they are not the wordes of flesh and blood, but of the spirite of God, by whom I am sealed to the day of redemption.

LADY MARY SIDNEY, COUNTESS OF PEMBROKE (trans.)

Philippe de Mornay, *A Discourse of Life and Death* (1592)

Philippe de Mornay was a controversial French Huguenot leader, writer and soldier who was admired by Protestants in Elizabeth I's court. Sir Philip Sidney, the Countess of Pembroke's brother, met him in Paris in 1572 at the time of the St Bartholomew's Day massacre, and they formed a close friendship. It seems that de Mornay sent Sidney a copy of the first French edition of his text, and that Pembroke referred to it in her translation. There had been an earlier translation of de Mornay's text by Edward Aggas, to which Diane Bornstein suggests Pembroke also referred.[1] However, Bornstein claims that Pembroke's work is 'an independent – and superior – translation' (p. 128). Pembroke's *Discourse* appeared in two versions. The first, and earliest edition, was accompanied by Pembroke's translation of Robert Garnier's *Antonius*; a significant combination as the latter text involves a representation of suicide. The second version, an edition of the *Discourse* alone, appeared in four editions (1600–8). The copy text is the first edition (BL, C. 57. d. 16), printed by W. Ponsonby, 1592. Extracts are from sigs. A2r–A3r; B1v–B4v; D2r–D3r; E2r–E3r.

It seemes to mee strange, and a thing much to be marveiled, that the laborer to repose himselfe hasteneth as it were the course of the Sunne: that the

1 Diane Bornstein, 'The Style of the Countess of Pembroke's Translation of Philippe de Mornay's *Discour de la vie et de la mort*', in Margaret P. Hannay, ed., *Silent But for the Word*, pp. 126–34.

Mariner rowes with all force to attayne the porte, and with a joyfull crye salutes the descryed land: that the traveiler is never quiet nor content till he be at the ende of his voyage: and that wee in the meane while tied in this world to a perpetuall taske, tossed with continuall tempest, tyred with a rough and combersome way, cannot yet see the ende of our labour but with griefe, nor behold our porte but with teares, nor approch our home and quiet abode but with horrour and trembling. This life is but a *Penelopes* web, wherein we are alwayes doing and undoing: a sea open to all windes, which sometime within, sometime without never cease to torment us: a weary jorney through extreame heates, and coldes, over high mountaynes, steepe rockes, and theevish deserts. And so we tearme it in weaving at this web, in rowing at this oare, in passing this miserable way. Yet loe when death comes to ende our worke, when she stretcheth out her armes to pull us into the porte, when after so many dangerous passages, and lothsome lodgings she would conduct us to our true home and resting place: in steede of rejoycing at the ende of our labour, of taking comfort at the sight of our land, of singing at the approch of our happie mansion, we would faine (who would beleeve it?) retake our worke in hand, we would againe hoise saile to the winde, and willinglie undertake our journey anew. No more then remember we our paines, our shipwracks and dangers are forgotten: we feare no more the travailes nor the theeves.

Contrarywise, we apprehende death as an extreame payne, we doubt it as a rocke, we flye it as a theefe. We doe as litle children, who all the day complayne, and when the medicine is brought them, are no longer sicke: as they who all the weeke long runne up and downe the streetes with payne of the teeth, and seeing the Barber comming to pull them out, feele no more payne: as those tender and delicate bodyes, who in a pricking pleurisie complaine, crie out, and cannot stay for a Surgion, and when they see him whetting his Launcet to cut the throate of the disease, pull in their armes, and hide them in the bed, as, if he were come to kill then. We feare more the cure then the disease, the surgion then the paine; the stroke then the impostume.[2] We have more sence of the medicins bitternes soone gone, then of a bitter languishing long continued: more feeling of death at the end of our miseries, then the endlesse misery of our life. And whence proceedeth this folly and simplicitie? we neyther knowe life, nor death. We feare that we ought to hope for, and wish for that we ought to feare. We call life a continuall death: and death the issue of a living death, and the entrance of a never dying life. Now what good, I pray you, is there in life, that we should so much pursue it? or what evill is there in death, that we should so much eschue it? Nay what evill is there not in life? and what good is there not in death?[3]

Come we to ambition, which by a greedines of honor fondly holdeth occupied the greatest persons. . . . Of those that geve themselves to courte ambition,

2 'impostume': an abscess, a swelling or cyst in some part of the body. 3 The argument continues by examining experiences of 'death' during different stages of 'life' (A3r). From this point, it continues by illustrating the temptations and vexations of different periods of one's life, and then focuses upon the specific dangers of covetousness and ambition.

some are great about Princes, others commanders of Armies: both sorts according to their degree, you see saluted, reverenced, and adored of those that are under them. You see them appareled in purple, in scarlet, and in cloth of gould: it seemes at first sight there is no contentment in the world but theirs. But men knowe not how heavy an ounce of that vaine honor weighes, what those reverences cost them, and how dearely they pay for an ell[4] of those rich stuffes: who knewe them well, would never buy them at the price. The one hath attained to this degree, after a long and painefull service hazarding his life upon every occasion, with losse ofttimes of a legge or an arme, and that at the pleasure of a Prince, that more regards a hundred perches of ground on his neighbours frontiers, then the lives of a hundred thousand such as he: unfortunate to serve who loves him not: and foolish to thinke himselfe in honor with him, that makes so litle reckening to loose him for a thing of no worth. Others growe up by flattering a Prince, and long submitting their toongs and hands to say and doe without difference whatsoever they will have them: whereunto a good minde can never commaund it selfe. They shall have indured a thousand injuries, received a thousand disgraces, and as neere as they seeme about the Prince, they are nevertheles alwayes as the Lions keeper, who by long patience, a thousand feedings and a thousand clawings hath made a fierce Lion familiar, yet geves him never meate, but with pulling backe his hand, alwayes in feare least he should catch him: and if once in a yere he bites him, he sets it so close, that he is paid for a long time after. Such is the ende of all princes favorites. When a Prince after long breathings hath raised a man to great height, he makes it his pastime, at what time he seemes to be at the top of his travaile, to cast him downe at an instant: when he hath filled him with all wealth, he wrings him after as a sponge: loving none but himself, and thinking every one made, but to serve, and please him.

These blinde courtiers make themselves beleeve, that they have freends, and many that honor them: never considering that as they make semblance to love, and honor everybody, so others do by them. Their superiors disdaine them, and never but with scorne do so much as salute them. Their inferiors salute them because they have need of them (I meane of their fortune, of their foode, of their apparell, not of their person) and for their equalls betweene whome commonly frendship consistes, they envy each other, accuse each other, crosse each other; continually greeved either at their owne harme, or at others good. Nowe what greater hell is there, what greater torment, then envie? which in truth is nought else but a feaver *Hectique* of the minde: so they are utterly frustrate of all frendship, ever judged by the wisest the chiefe and soveraigne good among men. Will you see it more clearely? Let but fortune turne her backe, every man turnes from them: let her frowne, every man looks aside on them: let them once be disroabed of their triumphal garment, no body will any more knowe them. Againe, let there be apparelled in it the most unworthie, and infamous whatsoever: even he without difficultie by vertue of his robe, shall

4 'ell': literally, a measurement of 45 inches; used proverbially to denote an unfair measurement or, in this case, payment.

inherit all the honours the other had done him. In the meane time they are puffed up, and growe proude, as the Asse which caried the image of *Isis* was for the honours done to the Goddesse, and regard not that it is the fortune they carry which is honored, not themselves, on whome as on Asses, many times she will be caried.

But you will say: At least so long as that fortune endured, they were at ease, and had their contentment, and who hath three or foure or more yeeres of happy time, hath not bin all his life unhappie. True, if this be to be at ease continually to feare to be cast downe from that degree, whereunto they are raised: and dayly to desire with great travaile to clime yet higher.

Those (my friend) whome thou takest so well at their ease, because thou seest them but without, are within farre otherwise. They are faire built prisons, full within of deepe ditches and dungeons: full of darkenes, serpents and torments. Thou supposest them lodged at large, and they thinke their lodgings straite. Thou thinkest them very high, and they thinke themselves very lowe. Now as sicke is he, and many times more sicke, who thinkes himselfe so, then he who in deed is. Suppose them to be Kings: if they thinke themselves slaves, they are no better: for what are we but by opinion? you see them well followed and attended: and even those whome they have chosen for their guard, they distrust. Alone or in company ever they are in feare. Alone they looke behinde them: in company they have an eye on every side of them. They drinke in gould and silver; but in those, not in earth or glasse is poison prepared and dronke. They have their beds soft and well made: when they lay them to sleepe you shall not heare a mouse stur in the chamber: not so much as a flie shall come neere their faces. Yet . . . in the middest of all this silence and delicacie, [they] do nothing but turne from side to side, it seemes still that they heare some body, there rest itselfe is without rest. Lastly, will you knowe what the diversitie is betwene the most hardly intrated prisoners and them? both are inchained, both loaden with fetters, but that the one hath them of iron, the other of gould, and that the one is tied but by the body, the other by the mind. The prisoner drawes his fetters after him, the courtier weareth his upon him. The prisoners minde sometimes comforts the paine of his body, and sings in the midst of his miseries: the courtier tormented in his minde weerieth incessantly his body, and can never give it rest.

And as for the contentment you imagine they have, you are therein yet more deceived. You judge and esteeme them great, because they are raised high: but as fondly, as who should judge a dwarfe great, for being set on a tower, or on the top of a moutaine. . . . But could you enter into their mindes, you would judge, that neither they are great, true greatnes consisting in contempt of those vaine greatnesses, whereunto they are slaves: nor seeme unto themselves so, seeing dayly they are aspiring higher, and never where they would be. Some one sets downe a bound in his minde. Coulde I attaine to such a degree, loe, I were content: I would then rest my selfe. Hath he attained it? he geves himselfe not so much as a breathing: he would yet ascend higher. That which is beneath he counts a toy: it is in his opinion but one step. He reputes himselfe lowe, because there is some one higher, in stead of reputing himselfe high, because there are a million lower. And so high he climes at last, that either his breath failes him by the way, or he slides from the top to the bottome. Or if he get up by all his travaile, it is but as to finde himselfe on the top of the Alpes: not above the cloudes, windes and stormes: but rather at the devotion of lightnings, and tempests, and whatsoever else horrible, and dangerous is engendered, and conceived in the aire: which most commonly taketh pleasure to thunderbolt and dash into pouder that proude height of theirs. It may be herein you will agree with me, by reason of the examples wherewith both histories, and mens memories are full.

But say you, such at least whome nature hath sent into the world with crownes on their heads, and scepters in their hands: such as from birth she hath set in that height, as they neede take no paine to ascend: seeme without controversie exempt from all these injuries, and by consequence may call themselves happie. It may be in deed they feele lesse such incommodities, having bene borne, bred and brought up among them. . . . Yet free doubtles they are not when the lightning often blasteth a flowre of their crownes, or breakes their scepter in their handes: when a drift of snowe overwhelmes them: when a miste of heavines, and grief continually blindeth their wit, and understanding. Crowned they are in deede, but with a crowne of thornes. They beare a scepter: but it is of a reede, more then any thing in the world pliable, and obedient to all windes: it being so far off that such a crowne can cure the maigrims[5] of the minde, and such a scepter keepe off and fray away the griefes and cares which hover about them: that it is contrariwise the crowne that brings them, and the scepter which from all partes attracts them.[6]

Conclude I say, that life is but a wishing for the future, and a bewailing of the past: a loathing of what wee have tasted, and a longing for that wee have not tasted, a vaine memorie of the state past, and a doubtfull expectation of the state to come: finally, that in all our life there is nothing certaine, nothing assured, but the certaintie and uncertaintie of death. Behold, now comes Death unto us: Behold her, whose approch we so much feare. We are now to consider whether she be such as wee are made to beleeve: and whether we ought so greatly to flie her, as commonly wee do. Wee are afraide of her: but like little children of a vizarde, or of the Images of *Hecate*. Wee have her in horror: but because wee conceive her not such as she is, but ougly, terrible, and hideous: such as it pleaseth the Painters to represent unto us on a wall. Wee flie before her: but it is because foretaken with such vaine imaginations, wee give not our selves leisure to marke her. But staie wee, stande wee stedfast, looke wee her in the face: wee shall finde her quite other then shee is painted us: and

5 'maigrims': deficiency or headache. 6 The narrator continues by providing classical and biblical examples to prove this point, and then moves on to consider the impossibility of achieving things for yourself without upsetting others. The discussion proceeds to consider whether 'man' would be better off if 'he' did not live socially; and instead retired to a country life. However, this does not help, '[f]or the life of man upon earth is but a continual warfare' (C3v). There then follows a discussion of the significance of private study, which eschews 'earthly' learning and concludes 'with *Salomon*, that the beginning and end of wisedome is the feare of God' (C4v). From this the narrator returns to the evils of the world.

altogether of other countenauce then our miserable life. Death makes an ende of this life. This life is a perpetuall misery and tempest: Death then is the issue of our miseries and entraunce of the porte where wee shall ride in safetie from all windes. And shoulde wee feare that which draweth us from misery, or which draws us into our Haven?

Yea but you will say, it is a payne to die. . . . The entraunce indeede is hard, if our selves make it harde, comming thither with a tormented spirite, a troubled minde, a wavering and irresolute thought. But bring wee quietnesse of mind, constancie, and full resolution, we shall not finde anie daunger or difficultie at all. Yet what is the paine that death brings us? Nay, what can shee soe with those paines wee feele? Wee accuse her of all the evilles wee abide in ending our life, and consider not howe manie more greevous woundes or sicknesses wee have endured without death: or howe many more vehement paines wee have suffered in this life, in the which wee called even her to our succour. All the paines our life yeeldes us at the last houre wee impute to Death: not marking that life begunne and continued in all sortes of paine, must also necessarily ende in paine. . . . We thinke we dye not, but when we yeeld up our last gaspe. But if we marke well, we dye every day, every houre, every moment. We apprehend death as a thing unusuall to us: and yet have nothing so common in us. Our living is but continuall dyeng: looke how much we live, we dye: how much we encrease, our life decreases. We enter not a step into life, but we enter a step into death. . . . Briefely, this whole life is but a death: it is as a candle lighted in our bodies: in one the winde makes it melt away, in an other blowes it cleane out, many times ere it be halfe burned: in others it endureth to the ende. Howsoever it be, looke how much it shineth, so much it burneth: her shining is her burning: her light a vanishing smoke: her last fire, hir last wike, and her last drop of moisture. So is it in the life of man, life and death in man is all one. If we call the last breath death, so must we all the rest: all proceeding from one place, and all in one manner. One onely difference there is betweene this life, and that we call death: that during the one, we have alwayes wherof to dye: and after the other, there remaineth only wherof to live. In summe, even he that thinketh death simply to be the ende of man, ought not to feare it: in asmuch as who desireth to live longer, desireth to die longer: and who feareth soone to die, feareth (to speake properlie) lest he may no longer die.[7]

By this reckoning, you will tell me death is a thing to be wished for: and to passe from so much evill, to so much good, a man shoulde as it seemeth cast away his life. . . . Yet is it not that I conclude. We must seeke to mortifie our flesh in us, and to cast the world out of us: but to cast our selves out of the worlde is in no sort permitted us. The Christian ought willingly to depart out of this life but not cowardly to runne away. The Christian is ordained by God to fight therein: and cannot leave his place without incurring reproch and

7 Indeed, the argument continues, as Christians believe in an after life, and 'true life' is to be found in the spirit, true Christians should welcome death.

infamie. But if it please the grand Captaine to recall him, let him take the retrait in good part, and with good will obey it. For hee is not borne for himselfe, but for God: of whome he holdes his life at farme, as his tenant at will, to yeeld him the profites. It is in the landlord to take it from him, not in him to surrender it, when a conceit takes him. Diest thou yong? praise God as the mariner that hath had a good winde, soone to bring him to the Porte. Diest thou olde? praise him likewise, for if thou hast had lesse winde, it may be thou hast also had lesse waves. But thinke not at thy pleasure to go faster or softer: for the winde is not in thy power, and in steede of taking the shortest way to the Haven, thou maiest happily suffer shipwracke. God calleth home from his worke, one in the morning, an other at noone, and an other at night. One he exerciseth til the first sweate, another he sunne-burneth, another he rosteth and drieth throughly. But of all his he leaves not one without, but brings them all to rest, and gives them all their hire, every one his time. Who leaves his worke before God call him, looses it: and who importunes him before the time, looses his reward. We must rest us in his will, who in the middest of our troubles sets us at rest.

To ende, we ought neither to hate this life for the toiles therein, for it is slouth and cowardise: nor love it for the delights, which is follie and vanitie: but serve us of it, to serve God in it, who after it shall place us in true quietnesse, an replenish us with pleasures whiche shall never more perish. Neyther ought we to flye death, for it is childish to feare it: and in flieng from it, wee meete it. Much lesse to seeke it, for that is temeritie: nor every one that would die, can die. As much despaire in the one, as cowardise in the other: in neither any kind of magnanimitie. It is enough that we constantly and continually waite for her comming, that shee may never finde us unprovided. For as there is nothing more certaine then death, so is there nothing more uncertaine then the houre of death, knowen onlie to God, the onlie Author of life and death, to whom wee all ought endeavour both to live and die.

Die to live,
Live to die.

LADY MARGARET HOBY

Diary (1599–1605)

Lady Hoby's *Diary* is one of the earliest known diaries produced by a woman. It provides a fascinating insight into Hoby's life, although its formulaic nature provokes varying reactions from modern readers. It is a prime example of a text that challenges received definitions of generic classification. There has been much recent debate about the gendering of the generic distinctions between a 'diary' and an 'autobiography', which challenges the traditional notion that the latter is of greater literary value. The following extract is from 1600 to 1601: it indicates the different dating system used during this period (1601 begins in March). The extracts are based on the manuscript of Hoby's *Diary* in the British Library (British Museum, Egerton 2614). The manuscript is unpaginated. There are two striking characteristics of Hoby's manuscript: firstly her total lack of punctuation; and secondly, the large gaps that she leaves in the margins. When Dorothy M. Meads edited the whole diary in 1930, she retained original spelling but modernised punctuation. While this could be said to help the modern reader it also distorts the character of Hoby's text, so we have left the text unpunctuated.

The Lordes day 25	this day I hard Mr fuller preach at my Lord Burleys wher I dined and after diner Came in Mr Ewry[1] so that we Came away rather givinge place to him then our affections whic might have binn provoked after I Came home Mr Hoby rede to me a Sarmon of Udale[2] and After I Lay downe being not well when after a litle sleepe Mr fuller Came in and he repeated to us the substance of Mr Egerton Sarmon
The 26 day	this day I beinge not well praied and reed in mine owne chamber and had Mr Bettnam to diner after I had talke with Mr Betnam touchinge my Mothers assurance and then beinge agreed that he should drawe the bookes Mrs Thornborowe Came in and after she was gonne My Aunte Cooke with hir Sons and Daughters after I went to praiers and so to Supper

from the :26: of Jaunarie unto the :8: of feb I remained weake and so ill that I Could not goe out of my chamber And unpon the Lordes day in the morninge begann the treason of the Earles of Esix Suthhamton and Rutland with their assotiates to appeare to the vewe of all that were not over partially blind from that day I remained saikly but not so ill tell the: 16: day upon which day was Captain Lea Arained [and the day following][3]

this 19 day Came our Horsses to London from Shepie	Executed] for his intention to Murther the Quens Majestie the :19: day was the Earle of Suthamton and Esixe Arained and Condemned this day I thank god I was better then before so that I Continewed my orderarie exercises in my Cchamber

The 20: day was 3[4] Arained and Condemned Sir Edward Mr John Litelton and Orill which was of the Consperisie[5]

---

1 According to Meads this was 'an awkward situation, since a law-suit between them in the star-chamber was not yet concluded'. 2 John Udall, a puritan preacher who had been arrested on suspicion of complicity in the printing of the Marprelate tracts (considered to be heretical tracts) in 1590 and condemned to death in 1591. Although he was pardoned, he died soon after his release from prison. 3 The text in square brackets has been inserted above the main text. 4 In the manuscript the word 'Knight' has been crossed out here. 5 The Essex Rebellion. Hoby was the sister-in-law of the Earl of Essex by her first marriage and had been brought up in the same household as the Devereuxs – Essex's sisters.

The 21: day — I was well recovered and kept Mr Betnam Companie who dined with us and Mr Stillington at night I praied and so went to bed

The Lordes day :22: day — this day was rainie so that I Could nor durst goe abroad but exersised in the house with prainge and reading and singing Psa and Conferinge in the after none Came Mr fuller from Mr Egertons sarmon and he delivered unto us the some of what he had delivered after I praied and supped and so went to bed

The :23: day: — After privatt praiers I went to my worke after I had reed of the bible sonne after to Dinner then we went to packinge some thinges for the Contrie after Came in Mr John Mansfeeld[6] who treated with Mr Hoby and my selfe touchinge a privatt agrement with his Cosine Ewrie Mr Robert Stillington like wise Came to visitt us after all was gone I went to privat praier and after I went to supper and after to bed

The :24: day — After prairs I went to work and havinge reed a Litle I talked with some that Came to Dine with us as Mr Betname Mr Stillington and Mr Smith after diner I talked with Mr Betname and after a whill Cam in Mr Etherington Mr Jenkins and Mr Briges after I Concluded with Mr Betnam touchinge a recognesance[7] and so I went to privat prairs after I bought a Whell[8] then Mr Yeardly Came in and after that Mr Smith who staied supper

The :25: day — After privat praiers I brake my fast and reed and sonne after Came in Mr Stillington and tould us of the Death of the Late Earle of Esixe at the Tower after we went to diner and after I wrett a letter to Mr Rhodes

The :26: day — After privatt praers I reed of the bible and then went to worke after I dined after diner I wrought[9] a whill and after I talked with those that Came with my Cosine Dakins and others Came in to se me after I went to privat readinge and medetation

The 28: day — I went to the Court to se my Lady warwick and the next day I went againe to se the Quene and the Day followinge I trussed upe our stuffe to be sent into the Cuntrie the next day beinge the 2 day of March I tooke my Journie towardes Yorkshire and the Lordes even

---

6 '[T]hen' has been crossed out in the manuscript. 7 'recognesance': a bond or obligation, entered into and recorded before a court or magistrate, by which a person engages him or herself to perform some act or observe some condition; also a sum of money pledged as a surety for such performance and rendered forfeit by neglect of it. 8 'whell': wheel. 9 'wrought': worked, i.e. at sewing or embroidery, etc.

followinge I Came to Mrs Terlingtons house wher I staied the Lordes day the day after I Came the water side and the next morninge I havinge a faire tide to Hull I Came that night to Linton wher I beinge sicke staied there from the 10 to the :18: of March[10] and then I Came home to Hacknes wher I remained very well untell the 25 which night I was Verie sicke of a fitt as I think of the stone and Collike for one hower and an halfe after which time I praise god I havinge ease, tooke good rest all the night after

March 1601: The 26: day: this day I kept my chamber and as I was able I wrought and reede and had Mr Ardington to read to me and Mr Rhodes some time we sung psa: and att my accustomed times I went to privatt praier and medetation

The 27: day After my accustomed prairs I did eate and read after I was busie tell diner tim[11] then after diner I paied /10^{li}/ to Mr Lacie of Seamer and Continewed to exercis my selfe in some beusenes tell praier, having Mr Rhodes and Mr Ardington to read to me after I went to supper and so to the Lecture after I went to bed well I thank god

The Lordes euen 28: day After prairs I was busie tell diner time after I talked with Mrs Bell who Came to offer me the sarvice of one of hir Daughters after I hard Mr Ardington Read and reed my selfe a Catzisimie[12] of the Lord supper and preparinge my selfe by priaer and medetation, I sonne after went to supper

The 29: the Lordes day After privat prairs I tooke leave of Mr Ardington and Mr Netelton and then tell diner time was busie packinge stuffe to send to Yorke after I had dined I was busie in the kicthine and at my accustomed time went to privatt prairs and so to supper

The 30: After privatt praier I went downe and wrought with my maides before diner I praied and read of the bible after diner I went downe again and was busie tell 4 a clock then I wrought and hard Mr Rhodes read and after I went to privat medetation and praier

The 31: After prairs I went about the house and wrought tell all most Diner time then I praied and reed dined and was busie tell all most night in the house and then I went to privat medetation and praier

The :1: day: this day for prainge readinge and workinge I Continewed my ordenarie exercises with much Comfort and peace of

10 Marginal note: 'March 1601 :25:'. **11** 'tim[e]': There are many occasions in Hoby's manuscript when the last letter of a word is missing, not because it is indicative of the vagaries of early modern spelling, but because she reaches the edge of the manuscript. **12** 'Catzisimie': catechism, an elementary treatise for instruction in the principles of the Christian religion, in question and answer form.

	Conscience I thanke god havinge Learned some thing from Mr. Rhodes his readinge unto me as first that no Callinge is lawfull with growne[13] for itt in godes word 2° that the title of Lord Archbusshopes are UnLawfull 3° that no minister should be made without a minestrie and charge unto which he should be[14] ordained
The 2: day	Havinge my health I thanke god I Continewed my accustomed exercises
The 3: day	this day we were accompaned with Mr Crakeroffe att diner and John Dowson Mr Hoby wrett Concerninge Mr Bankes his dealinge by him unto the Counsill att Yorke and att night I went to privat praier and examenation
Aprill :4:	this day I performed my accustomed exercises I praise god and was all most all the after none in the Garden Sowinge seed whether Mr Busshill came to se us after I returned in to my Chamber and there reed and praied tell all most I went to supper
The Lordes day :5:	Havinge praied I brake my fast and then went to the church wher havinge hard the sermon and received the Lordes supper I returned home and privatly gave thankes the rest of the day after the afternone sermon I spent in readinge singing praing and hearinge repeticions
The 2 day of the week :6:	I havinge praied according to my Use I wrought in the house with my maides all the afternone tell I went to privatt medetation and praier
The 7: day	After prairs and readinge I kept Mr Gatt Companie after Diner I wrought and hard Mr Rhodes read sent away besse Stafford after walked about with Hoby and then returned to privatt reading and praier
The 8: day	After I had praied and that Mr Hoby was gone [towardes][15] Yorke I went about the howse and then reed and wrought a whill before diner after I went with my Maides in to the Garden and towardes night, [I kept] Mr Maude Compenie a whill [then] I went to privatt prairs and medetation and readinge
The :9: day	this day I Continewed my ordenarie exercises I praise god without sicknes or trouble and so like wise the 10 and :11: day
The Lordes even 11: day home	After privat praiers I was busie in the Kitchine [and garden] tell diner time and after tell Mr Hoby Came and after I had walked a litle abroad I went to privatt prairs and examenation

13 'growne': ground. 14 In the manuscript, the word 'made' has been crossed out here. 15 This and the other words in this entry in square brackets are either inserted above the main text or in the margin.

The Lordes day :12: day	This day I praise god I hard the exersices and received the sacrementes with much Comfort and in health Continewed my Custom
The 2 day of the weeke 13: day	As through corruption we use not the blessinge of peace as we ought so are we to expecte new temptations to humble us for our former necclegence and so I have benne this day boffeted for better heed
The 3 day of the weeke :14:	After I had reed and praied I went about the house made a salve for a sore beast then I Came to worke into my chamber and so went to diner after I walked a whill and spake to John Dowson for Mault and so went to worke tell praier time
The 15 day The 16 day	These 2 daies I Continewed my accustomed exercises and wrought most of a token I sent to London
The 17 day	This day blakeborn Cutt his foot with a hatchett
The :18: day	this day I finished my worke wrott Letters to London talked with Mr Stillington praied at my accustomed times and dressed Tho Blackbornes foott and after went to readinge and preparation for the next day
The Lordes day :19:	this day it pleased god to blesse my reading and medetation and in the afternone my hearinge of Mr Urpith after I Came home and Caused Mr Stillington to Read of Grenhame and after I went to privatt readinge and praier
The 2 day, of the weeke, the 20: 21: day	this day my Mother Came to Hacknes and staied the next day which was when Mr Hoby tooke his journie to London att which time I thank god I Continewed my exercises in good health and at night hard John Corrow praie
The 22	my Mother went in the morninge betimes and after she was gonne I dressed up my Closett and was buseed about that all the day tell night at which time John Corrow praied and reed publeckly and after I had performed som privat dutie I tooke order for peters going to the markett and went to bed
The 23 day	Mistress Brutnell accompaned me at diner and in the after none Mr Rhodes Cam home and his brother Edward who brought me a booke from his wiffe after I talked with Mr Coniers of Scarborow who went to London and after he was gone I praied and dressed Tho Blackbourns Legg and after went to readinge and medetation
Aprill The 24:	This day I performed my ordenarie exercises and wrett to Mr Hoby by Mr Coniers
The :25: day:	After praers and breakfast I went to church when the sarmen was done I praied and dressed blackbourns Legge

	after diner I went Diverse busenes about the howse and hard Mr Rhodes read and after went to privatt examenation and praier
The Lordes day :26:	After I was readie I went to the church and after praers and sermon I Came home and dressed Blackbourns foote after I dined and after I talked and reed to some good wiffes after I praied and reed and wrett notes in my bible of the morninge exercise after I went to the church and after sarmon I dressed a poore mans hand and after that I walked a broad and so Came to privat examenation and praier
The 27 day	After privat praier I was busie about the house and dressed my sarvants foot and another poore mans hand and talked with others that Came to aske my Counsill after I went into the garde, and gave some hearbes unto a good wiffe of Erley for his garden after I Came to diner praied and went to diner after I talked a whill with Mr Rhodes and his brother and after that went to worke and hard Mr Rhodes read of Mr perkins[16] new booke and after went to walke and about the house And then went into my Clositt and then examened my selfe and praied
The 28 day	After privat praier I went to worke and before diner time came my Cosine John Bouser with whom I kept Companie untell diner after we walked forth and when he was gone I dressed packeringes hand after I hard Mr Rhodes read of perkins and after I went to privat examenation and praier
The :29: day :	After prairs I wrett to Mr Hoby and my Cossine Bouchier after I dined and wroughte tell allmost night then I praied and after supper I hard Mr Aston praie and reade and so went to bed
The :30: day	After praers I went downe and before diner Came Mr Hunter with whom I kept Companie tell his goinge away After I went and wrought with my Maides tell allmost night and then I went to privat examenation and praier
May :1: day	After I had hard the sarmon at the church I praied and dined and after diner wrett to Mr Hoby by Mr Etherington after He was gone I went to privat examen ation and praier
The 2 day the Lordes even	After I had praied I wound yearne tell dinner time then I praied and dined in the afternone I received Letters by Mr Urpith from Mr Hoby and after he was gon I went to privat praier and examenation

16 Meads suggests that this could be *A Warning against the Idolotrie of the Last Times* published in 1601. There were two other texts published by Perkins in that year: *How to Live, and That Well* and *The True Gaine*.

The Lordes day :3:	After I had ben at the church I praied and after diner talked of good thinges to some of my neighbours and when they were at Catizisinge I wrett notes in my bible of the chapter after I dressed the sores I had in hand and when I had wretten a letter to my Mother I went to privat examenation and praier
The 4 day	After a few drowsie praiers I went about the house omittinge thorowe neccIegence some exercise before I practised after diner I walked abroad god notwithstandinge givinge me comfort in some thinges beyond hope after I praied and after supper hard the Lecture
The :5: day of May 1601:	After praers I went to the church wher I hard a sarmon after I Came home and hard Mr Rhodes read after diner I went abroad and when I was come home I dresed some sores after I hard Mr Rhodes read and wrought with in a while after I went to see a calfe at Munckmans which had :2: great heades 4 eares and had to ether head a throte pipe besides the heades had longe heares Like brissels about the mouths such as n'other Cowe hath the hinder Legges had no parting from the rumpe but grewe backward and were no longer but from the first Joynte also the backe bone was parted about the midest of the bicke and a rowne howle was in the midest into the bodie of the Calfe but one would have thought that to have comed of some strocke it might gett in the Cowes bely after this I Came in to privat medetation and praier

MARIA THYNNE

Letters (1604–1607)

Maria Thynne, née Audley, was the elder sister of Lady Eleanor Davies, and their shared fluency as writers indicates that they had received a good deal of education. In 1594, Maria married Thomas Thynne hastily and in secret: although her family were happy with the match, his were not, and Maria's letter to her mother-in-law Joan (below) clearly shows that more than a decade after the marriage relations were still difficult. Maria's letters, like Dorothy Osborne's, are undated: those reproduced here clearly date from the period after she and her husband had taken possession of Longleat, the Thynne family seat, and show Maria taking on a good deal of responsibility for the running of the estate in Thomas's absence. Maria's letters are in volume VIII of the Thynne Papers, still held at Longleat, which contain many other letters (and some poetry) by female members of the family. The copy text for this edition is BL microfilm 904, reel 4; in the absence of dates, folio numbers are given for each letter.

Maria to Thomas Thynne (f. 2)

Myne owne Sweete Thomken, I have no longer ago than the very last nighte wryghten such a large volume in prayse of thy kindness to me, thy doggs thy hawkes the hare and the foxes, and also in commendation of thy greate care of thy bussinesses in the countrye, that I think I need not amplifye anye more on that texte, for I have crowned thee for an admirable good husband with poetycall Lawrell, and admired the inexpressible singularitye of thy love in the cogitations of piamature,[1] I can saye no more but that in waye of gratuitye, the doggs shall without interdiction expell ther excremental coruption in the best roome (which ys thy bed) whensoever full feedinge makes ther bellyes Ake, and for my owne parte since you have in all your letters given me authoritye to care enoughe, I wyll promyse to be inferyor to none of my deverill[2] Neighbours in playeinge the good huswyfe, though they stryve tyll they stinke, Now yf for my better incouragement, and in requyttall thou wylte at my earneste intreatye butt for thys tyme spare diggrye, I shall be so much Bownde, that nothinge butt a stronge purgation can lose me / for yf you wyll beleeve me in sober sadnes, my cosin Stantore hath upon speech with me, made ytt appeer that hee hath disgested manye uncivell and unbecominge words from 3 of your servants, hee doth not desyre you to remite diggries faulte, butt to dispence with hys apparance for hys sake this tyme, becawse ytt conscerns hym in hys profyt, and when you come in to the countrye my cosin wyll come and throughly satysfye all matters in controversye between you / I wyll not intreate too earnestlye becawse I know thow arte chollerike[3] with me ever in these cases, but though thow doste manye tymes call me foole for yeeldinge to the intysing of fayer woords, yett yf you marke ytt, I have never yett craved anye thinge of such greate Importance as hath ever been prejudiciall to your reputation or profit, if so (As yt ys to true yt ys so) Name me anye man that hath a wyfe of that rare temper, No, in good fayth thys age wyll not helpe you to an equall, I meane for a wyfe, alas I sitt att home and lett thy doggs eatte parte with me, and wear clothes that have worne oute their prentyshipe[4] a yeare and halfe sithence, when my systers wyll be in London att ther pleasure, I am talkeinge of foxes and rudder Beasts at home / well doo but make hast home and make much of thy Mall when thow doste come home, I wyll not be Mallenchollye, butt with good courage spend my life and waste my sperits in anye course to please thee, excepte fighteing, and in thys busines satysfye my

1 'piamature': Latin 'pia mater', tender mother. In *Two Elizabethan Women* (Devizes: Wiltshire Record Office, 1983), an edition of letters by Maria and her mother-in-law Joan, Alison Wall suggests that Maria may have been pregnant at this time. 2 Brixton Deverill, Hill Deverill, Kingston Deverill, Longbridge Deverill and Monkton Deverill are a collection of small settlements a few miles from Longleat. 3 'chollerike': short-tempered. 4 'prentyshipe': apprenticeship.

request as you thinke I deserve, and do not be angrye with me for Importuning you, butt aske all the husbands in Lundon, or aske the questyon in the lower house,[5] what requests they grante their wives, and then good husband thinke upon your foole at home as ther ys cause

Thine

Maria Thynne

I wyll saye nothinge of anye busines, for I have thys last nighte wryghten you a whole sheet of paper and given you knowledge accordinge to your apoyntments of all your affayers, yf your leasure wyll not serve good sweet cause Exall to wryghte in hys owne name butt this and this ys my master's pleasure and yt shall serve the turne, for I know your trouble in matters of more waighte there ys greate and I leek[6] not hys wryghtinge in your name for ytt ys as thou were angrye god in heaven send thee well and speeddily home.

Maria Thynne to Thomas Thynne (f .4)

My fayer Tomken: I have nothinge to saye butt how dost thow, and that I hope to see thee well shortly, as thou lovest me be exceedinge careful of cominge in to any shopes, for ther ys the greatest danger,[7] I have since thy goeinge lerned an aproved medicen for the plague yf yt be used in tyme etc. take dragon water a good draughte, and mingle therewith as much treacle or mettridott in quantitye as an ordinarye wallnutte, and add to thiss so much readdinge pownded as a greate hassell nutt (such readdinge as is given piggs for the murraine), sture all this together and drinke ytt, yf you do butt never so lyttle suspect your selfe, I know thow wylte laugh to hear me preach phisike so long before hand, but consyder medicen comes to late when the deseas is past cure, good sweet be not with owt sume thinge to take in an instaint, in good fayth I assure you this hath been tryed by manye, yf you coulde indure to eate in a morninge butt 3 or fower leaves of rue putt in to sume reasons[8] of the Sunne, you would fynd ytt with gods helpe a good preservative against infection, good Tomken remember wee are bownd in conscience to maintayne lyfe as long as ys possible, and though gods power can work mericles, yet wee canot builde upon ytt that be cawse he can, he wyll, for then he wolde not saye He made herb[s] for the use of man. / I much feare Brownwints libbertye maye breed danger, I can saye no more being in exceeding hast, but that I wyll be a carefull officer in your absence, and Even so god in heaven preserve thy health, as long as I live, and contynue thy love so to me, as I maye have cawse to love thee no less then I doo, which ys yett as my own soule

Thyne

Maria Thynne

heer is not so much as halfe an [iota] of busines to acquaynt you withall.

---

5 'Lower House': of Parliament. 6 'leek': like. 7 Maria is anxious about the possibility of plague infection – there were outbreaks in London in 1604, 1607 and 1609. 8 'reasons': raisins.

Maria Thynne to Thomas Thynne (f. 6)

My best beloved Thomken, and my best little Sirra, know that I have not, nor wyll forgett how you made my modest blood flush up into my bashfull cheeke att your first letter, thou threatned sownde payement, and I sownd repayement, so as when we meet, ther wyll be paye, and repay, which wyll pass and repass, allgiges ultes fregnan tolles,[9] thow knowest my mind, though thow doste not understand me well now laying on side my high choller,[10] know in sober sadnes that I am att Longe Leate, reddye and unredy to receeve thee, and heer wyll attend thy cominge, remember that your last dayes journye wyll be the longer by 5 or 6 miles, and therfore determine accordingly, your horses are taken up, and I wyll take thee up when thou comest home for stayeing so longe from me, I know your cheefest business is now butt with your Kempsford tenants, and for them the next term wyll best serve, I wryte to you this weeke by our neighbour Sir Jeffery the clothier, then had you intelligence of all your affayers and my hope is that you wyll come down so soon thatt I wyll not trouble you with the knowledg of much busines now, though I assure you ther be more than many thinges to be determined of, Sudlow hath seen the extreats[11] but knowes not what to do tyll you come home, Hals keepes bake the tenants rent towards reperations of the house at Monkshame, but his owne half yeers rent woodlands hath latelye received, besydes £30 of me; monye walkes awaye apace heer, for woodlands hath had £60 of me since you went, I heer no tyddings of Cabble, butt I warant he wyll not be longe hence for his mony, if you wer come downe, Usher wyll not repaye the £240 tyll hee have his owne byll agayne, therefore keep ytt safe, or send ytt safe downe, for ther is all I have for to testyfie the delivery of ytt to hym; all my comfort is that Cogswell sayeth hee is an honeste man, in good fayeth Thomken the uttermost farthinge that wyll be scraped up together wyll butt make up £150 towards payeinge of Cabble, and now I assure thee ther ys no one peny to be received thatt I know of tyll Christmas, and then butt radoks £20 neyther, thus doo I tell thee all the yll newes in every letter sume that thy anger maye be past before thou comest to me, I had allmost forgotten to tell thee yt is the mare which wylliams ryd up which hath cast her foale, the horses in the parke get in to the copse for which Carr scolds, I have caused the baylye to place them somewhere else tyll your pleasure be knowne, they dare not putt them into bushes grownd for feare of steallinge

my lady[12] hath wrytten to me touching a payer of folkes which her Ladyship thinketh very fytt for our servise, and in that respect hath made the fyrst offer of them to us, when thou goest next to Clarkenwell I praye thee vew them and I wyll promise not to be jelous though one of them is a shee, if they be as my Lady wrytes I would wee had taken them in the roome of sume we have all-

9 The meaning of this phrase is unclear; Wall suggests that Maria is deliberately using inaccurate Latin to encode a sexual reference. 10 Punning on colour (referring back to her blush), choler (anger), and the fashion for high collars on women's clothes. 11 'extreats': extracts or copies of financial records. 12 Her mother, Lady Lucy Audley, then residing at Clerkenwell in London.

readye, for then boyes and groomes would be better looked to, for his part, and husewifery better for her part. Halliwell I heer is weary of his office, and then doo I not know who to place yn yt, Mr Morgan is more than halfe spoylt with the dogge boye and the other boyes so as I desyre nothinge more than to have one to cudgell them to ther work, all my desyr is thou shouldest see these cattell, and yf you like not, leave, I hear woodlands wyll staye butt tyll the audience the reason in good fayeth I knowe not, unless yt be my receiving the rents, yf that be ytt I wyll offend his worshipe no more, Even so, being as mellencolly as a red herring and as made as a pilchard and as prowde as a peece of argon ling, I salute thy best beloved selfe with the returne of thyne owne wyshe in thy last letter, and so once more fare ever well, my best and sweetest Thomken, and many thousand tymes more than these many thankes 10000000000000000000000000 for thy kind wanton letters

Thine and only all thine

Maria

Maria Thynne to Thomas Thynne (f. 8)

My best Thomken I know thow wylt say (receiving 2 letters in a daye from me) that I have tryed the vertue of Aspen leaves under my tounge, which makes me prattle so much; but consyder that all is busines, for of my owne naturall dispossission I assure thee ther ys not a more silent woman living than my selfe / butt to the purpose: you must understand that I received this daye being Sundaye my grandfather's letter to Mr Sampford, and dyd forthwith sende halliwell awaye with ytt to hym, so as what maye be dun in reason besydes shall not be neglected / Smith of deverell sent to me for mony to discharge the kinges rente, hee sayeth the rent of deverell wyll not dyscharge ytt, butt I have apoynted hym to bring in the rent and lett the other allone, for that I understand by you, your selfe would discharge yt wherby you mighte the better be allowed you father's fee and your owne, if I have not done in ytt as I should, then lerne not to place a foole in an office: / Salsbury hath been heer with his fyne and hath offered £5 to my Uncle Thomas more than is due so he wyll not take the forfyture of his bond, but whatsoever become of it he wyll not give one peny more, my uncle desyers to knowe your pleasure speedilie for he feareth lest upon ther goeing to my uncle harry he wyll receive ther monye and give a release and so lose the £5 too, because he made the bargaine, all the means hath been made that maye be to get hym leave the mills, and take his bond agayne, but Shore wyll not, the lawe shall take yt from them ere they wyll leave ytt now, I pray lett us know whether you wyll take the forfyture or no, for yf you doo not, the sooner wee have the mony the better / Curtyse of deverell was heer with his master but not a worde of Shute tyll I begane, he sayeth you have lett ytt for a yeer to one that husbands ytt very yll, so as he cannot enter upon ytt to his profyte, and to keep his mony tyll the tyme be expyerd, that he cannot neyther: hee wyll not give one peny more than £370 and for any thinge I see hee is now very careles of it, for those respects affore sayed, I never heard that you had so much bydden for it by any other: lett me knowe what you wyll doo, for on Saturdaye next I shall know whether ever hee wyll deal yn yt agayne, but yf he doo, he wyll looke the tenant now in ytt shall be his tenante.

You trunk is sent, and therwith a letter from me, also £60 which marchant (Cogswells sonne) is to paye from me, and this I thinke wyll be all woodland's[13] and I shall helpe you to tyll allhallowtyd,[14] yf Salsburys shall be received, then shall you presently have that to, with as much as maye be gathered, remember I praye thee to paye as many debts as is possible, and then wylte thou lett Idle expences allone tyll hereafter: I hard thee talke of cuttinge down sume parte of the copse in Long Leat parke, my uncle Thomas sayeth yf he mighte advise you thee should be as much as maye have utterance be sould, and this is his advice, to have the sale cryed in the markets and none to be cutt butt as ther shall come fyrst a chapman to bye yt, and then when the bargine is made (the wood standing) lett his aker that hath bought be apoynted out lettinge the rest stand tyll more chapmen come, by which means you shall be sure to have no spoyle nor waste, for what wyll not be sould shall growe, your pleasure must be knowne in this for Allhallowtyd is the best tyme, he thinketh yf you please ther wyll be lyttle lefte by midsummer / I thinke I have given thyne eyes a surfyt with a letter by this tyme, wherfore I wyll now end, wyshinge thy life hapyiness and contentment maye never end, tyll thy love to me hath end

Thyne

Maria Th[ynne]

In any wyse sweet lett sume body receive my other letter of the carryer for ytt is all business to

Maria Thynne to Joan Thynne (f. 10)

Good Lady out of my care to your health lett me intreat you to temper your choller, esspeciallye consyderinge you canot comforte your selfe with hope that Mr Thynne will greeve much at yt: for my parte (resspectinge your alliance with hym) I wyll not withowt leave tell you that yf you gave anye fee to a cowncellor to indighte your letter, ytt was bestowed to lyttle purpose, for ther should have bin consyderation that Mr Thynne lookes in to waste and spoyle on your joyntur, as to a tenant for term of life, and so your scribe can prove no nessecarye consequence for you to wryghte disgracefullye or contemptyouslye in business which concerns you not, indeed yf you or your heyers have an expectation in reversion of Longleate house or garden, ther were reason your speach should pass currante withowt offence or exception, but

13 This refers to a person called Woodlands, not the plan for woodland management outlined below. 14 All Souls' Day, 1 November.

the case beinge as yt ys, methinkes you should not unkindlye intermeddle, more than Mr Thynne doth with all your lands of inheritance

I confess (withowt shame) ytt ys true my garden ys to ruinous, and yett to make you more merry you shall be of my cowncel, that my intente ys before it be better, to make ytt worse, for, finding that greate expence can never alter ytt from being lyke a porridge pote, nor never by report was lyke other, I intend to plowe yt up and sowe all varietye of fruits at a fytt season, I beseech you laugh, and so wyll I at your captiousnes / now whereas you wryghte your grownd putt to bassest uses ys better manurde than my garden, surelye yf ytt wer a grandmother of my owne and equall to my selfe by bearth, I should answere that oddious comparison with tellinge you I beleeve so corpulent a Lady cannot butt do much your selfe towards the soyllinge of lande, and I think that hath bin, and wyll be all the good you intend to leave behinde you at Corslye / you saye Mr Thynne ys starke blinde in his owne faultes, butt trulye I take ytt ther wanted spectacles on sume bodyes nose when they could not see a more becominge civill course (that ys your phrase) to be practysed amongst freinds of equall woorth: you talke too much of mallice and revenge, your wyll to shew mallice maye be as greate as please you, butt your power to revenge is a bugg beare that one that knowes hys owne strength no better than Mr Thynne doth, wyll never be affrayde of, how far your bountyous lyberalitye hath extended towards him in former tymes I know not, butt I have called my memorye to a strict accompte, and canot finde anye obligacion of debts recorded there that hath not bine substanciallye cancelled, for your well wyshings (which are all the benefyts I am accessorye to) hath ever bin requyted with the lyke both in quantatye and quallitye, So all things consydered lett the insufficiencye of sence you speake of rest dew on your owne parte, beinge a reproch allotted by you to the unthankfull; to conclude good Lady, having vowed to fullfyll the Scripture in thys poynt of runninge from father and mother for my husband, surely I will forsake all [some words illegible: bottom of sheet torn off] if thay affoord me more love than thay are wylling he should partake of, and therfore Maddam yf your intent be to yeeld hym no dew respecte, I praye know my desyer ys in that as in other woorse fortuns, to be a partner with hym in your displeasure / If butt I doo wysh you should remember your owne children's estymacion and creadite, for yf Mr Thynne deserve but slender accompte, they must expecte rate after rate, he being the best flower in their garland / And so he that made you save you, and I wyll rest your daughter and assured friende yf you please

Maria Thynne

JOSEPH SWETNAM

The Arraignment of Lewd, Idle, Froward and Unconstant Women (1615)

This tract was published under the pseudonym Thomas Tell-Troth, but was quickly associated with Joseph Swetnam, who was possibly a fencing master. Although part of a long tradition of formal treatises on the subject of 'Woman', Swetnam's tract initiated a pamphlet war on this issue and this anthology includes two responses to the tract, those of Rachel Speght and Ester Sowernam. Unlike the latter two pamphlets, Swetnam's tract went into a number of editions (nine by 1640); in 1641 the tract was translated into Dutch, which ran into five editions. The copy text (BL, C. 142. cc. 30) is the first edition printed in London by George Purslowe for Thomas Archer, 1615. The following extracts are from pages 1–4; 14–16; 36–7; 45–7.

Chap. I

Moses describeth a Woman thus: At the first beginning (saith hee) a woman was made to be a helper unto man, and so they are indeede: for she helpeth to spend and consume that which man painefully getteth. Hee also saith that they were made of the ribbe of a man, and that their froward nature sheweth; for a ribbe is a crooked thing, good for nothing else, and women are crooked by nature: for small occasion will cause them to be angry.

Againe, in a manner, shee was no sooner made, but straightway her mind was set upon mischiefe, for by her aspiring minde and wanton will, shee quickly procured mans fall, and therefore ever since they are and have beene a woe unto man, and follow the line of their first leader.

For I pray you let us consider the times past, with the time present; first, that of *David* and *Salomon*, if they had occasion so many hundred yeares agoe to exclaime so bitterly against women, for the one of them said, that it was better to be a doore-keeper, and better dwel in a den amongst Lyons, then to be in the house with a froward and wicked woman: and the other said, that the climing up of a sandy hill to an aged man was nothing so wearisome, as to be troubled with a froward woman: and further he saith, that the malice of a beast is not like the malice of a wicked woman, nor that there is nothing more dangerous then a woman in her fury.

The Lyon being bitten with hunger, the Beare being robbed of her young ones, the Viper being trod on, all these are nothing so terrible as the fury of a woman. A Bucke may be inclosed in a Parke, a bridle rules a horse, a Woolfe may be tyed, a Tyger may be tamed: but a froward woman will never be tamed, no spur will make her goe, nor no bridle will holde her backe; for if a woman holde an opinion, no man can draw her from it: tell her of her fault, she will not beleeve that she is in any fault: give her good counsell, but she will not take it; if you doe but looke after another woman, then she will be jealous, the more thou lovest her, the more she will disdaine thee; and if thou threaten her, then she will be angry, flatter her, and then she will be proud; and if thou forbeare her, it maketh hir bold, and if thou chasten her, then she will turne to a Serpent; at a word, a woman will never forget an injury, nor give thanks for a good turne: what wise man then will exchange gould for drosse, pleasure for paine, a quiet life for wrangling brawles, from the which the married men are never free.

Salomon saith, that women are like unto wine, for that they will make men drunke with their devises.

Againe, in their love a woman is compared to a pommis-stone, for which way soever you turne a pommis stone, it is full of holes; even so are womens heartes, for if love steale in at one hole, it steppeth out at another.

They are also compared unto a painted ship, which seemeth faire outwardly, and yet nothing but ballace within her; or as the Idolls[1] in *Spaine*, which are bravely gilt outwardly, and yet nothing but lead within them; or like unto the Sea, which at somtimes is so calm, that a cockbote[2] may safely endure her might, but anon againe without outrage she is so growne, that it overwhelmeth the tallest ship that is.

A froward woman is compared to the wind, and a still woman unto the Sunne: for the Sunne and the wind met a traveller upon the way, and they laide a wager, which of them should get his cloake from him first; then first the wind began boistrously to blow, but the more the wind did blow, the more the traveller wrapped and gathered his cloake about him; now when the wind had done what he could, and was never the neerer, then began the Sun gently to shine upon him, and he threw off, not onely his cloake, but also his hat and jerkin: this morall sheweth, that a woman with high words can get nothing at the hands of her husband, never by froward meanes, but by gentle and faire means she may get his heart-bloud to doe her good.

As women are compared unto many things, even so many, and many more troubles commeth galloping after the heeles of a woman, that young men beforehand doe not thinke of; for the world is not made of ote-meale, nor all is not gold that glittereth, nor the way to Heaven is not strewed with rushes, no more is the cradle of ease in a womans lappe. If thou wert a Servant or in bondage before, yet when thou doest marry, thy toile is never the neerer ended, for even then and not before, thou doest change thy golden time for a drop of hony, which presently afterwards turneth to be as bitter as worm-wood.

Yet there are many young men which cudgell their wits, and beate their braines, and spend all their time in the love of women, and if they get a smile or but a favour at their Loves hand, they straight-way are so ravished with joy, yea so much, that they thinke they have gotten God by the hand, but within a while after they will finde that they have but the Devill by the foot. A man

1 'idolls': images of divinity. 2 'cockbote': a small boat.

may generally speake of women, that for the most part thou shalt find them dissembling in their deeds, and in all their actions subtill and dangerous for men to deale withall: for their faces are lures, their beauties are baytes,[3] their looks are netts, and their wordes charmes, and all to bring men to ruine. . . .

Chap. II

First, that of *Salomon*, unto whom God gave singular wit and wisedome, yet hee loved so many women, that he quiet forgot his God, which alwaies did guide his stepps, so long as he lived godly, and ruled justly: but after hee had glutted him selfe with women, then he could say, vanity of vanites, all is but vanity: he also in many places of his booke of Proverbs exclaimes most bitterly against lewd women, calling them all that naught is, and also displayeth their properties: and yet I cannot let men go blamelesse, although women goe shamelesse; but I will touch them both: for if there were not receivers, then there would not be so many stealers: if there were not some knaves, there would not be so many whoores; for they both hold together to bolster each others villany: for alwaies birdes of a feather will flocke together hand in hand, to bolster each others villany. Men I say may live without women, but women cannot live without men: For *Venus* whose beauty was excellent faire, yet when she needed mans helpe, she tooke *Vulcan* a clubfooted Smith. And therefore if a womans face glister, and her Jesture pearce the Marble wall, or if her tongue be so smooth as oile, or so soft as silke, and her wordes so sweet as hony: or if she were a very Ape for wit, or a bagge of gold for wealth: or if her personage have stolne away all that nature can affoord, and if she be deckt up in gorgeous apparell, then a thousand to one but she will love to walke where she may get acquaintance; and acquaintance bringeth familiarity, and familiarity setteth all folies abroach: and twenty to one that if a woman love gadding, but that shee will pawne her honesty to please her fantasie.

Many must be at all the cost, and yet live by the losse; a man must take all the paines, and women will spend all the gaines: a man must watch and ward, fight and defend, till the ground, labour in the vineyard; and looke what he getteth in seven yeares, a woman will spread it abroad with a forke in one yeare, and yet little enough to serve her turne, but a great deale too little to get her good will: nay, if thou give her never so much, and yet if thy personage please not her humour, then will I not give a halfe-penny for her honesty at the yeares end.

For then her breast will be the harbourer of an envious heart, and her heart the storehouse of poysoned hatred, her head will devise villany, and her hands are ready to practice that which their heart desireth. Then, who can but say that women sprung from the Devill, whose heads, hands, hearts, mindes and soules are evill? for women are called the hooke of all evill, because men are taken by them, as fish is taken with the hooke.

---

3 'baytes': enticements; entrapments.

For women have a thousand waies to entice thee, and ten thousand waies to deceive thee, and all such fooles as are sutors unto them: some they keepe in hand with promises, and some they feed with flattery, and some they delay with dalliances, and some they please with kisses: they lay out the foldes of their haire, to entangle men into their love; betwixt their brests is the vale of destruction, and in their beds there is hell, sorrow and repentence. Eagles eat not men till they are dead, but women devoure them alive: for a woman will pick thy pocket, and empty thy purse, laugh in thy face and cut thy throat: they are ungratefull, perjured, full of fraud, flouting and deceit, unconstant, waspish, toyish, light, sullen, proud, discurteous and cruell, and yet they were by God created, and by nature formed, and therefore by policy and wisedome to bee avoided; for good things abused, are to be refused, or else for a moneths pleasure shee may hap to make thee goe stark naked, she will give thee rost-meat, but she will beat thee with the spitte: if thou hast crownes in thy purse, shee will be thy heartes gold, untill shee leave thee not a whit of white money: they are like summer birdes, for they will abide no storme, but flocke about thee in the pride of thy glory, and flye from thee in the storms of affliction; for they aime more at thy wealth, then at thy person, and esteeme more thy money, then any mans vertuous qualities for they esteeme of a man without money, as a horse doth of a faire stable without meate, they are like Eagles, which will alwaies flie where the carrion is. . . .

Chap. III

There are sixe kinds of women which thou shouldest take heede that thou match not thy selfe to any one of them: that is to say, good nor bad, faire nor foule, rich nor poore, for if thou marriest one that is good, thou maist quickly spill her with too much making of her: for when provender pricks a woman, then shee will grow knavish: and if bad, then thou must support her in all her bad actions, and that will be so wearisome unto thee, that thou hadst as good draw water continually to fill a bottomlesse tub: if she be faire then thou must doe nothing else but watch her: and if she be foule and loathsom, who can abide her? if shee be rich then thou must forbeare her because of her wealth: and if she be poore, then thou must maintaine her.

For if a woman be never so rich in dowry, happy by her good name, beautifull of body, sober of countenance, eloquent in speech, and adorned with vertue, yet they have one ill quality or other, which overthroweth all the other: like unto that Cow which giveth great store of milke and presently striketh it downe with her foote, such a cow is as much to be blamed for the losse, as to be commended for the gift: or like as when men talke of such a man, or such a man, he is an excellent good workeman, or he is a good Chirurgian, or a good Phisition, or hee is a pretty fellow of his hands, but if they conclude with this word, But it is pitty hee hath one fault, which commonly in some men is drunkennesse, then I say, if he were endued with all the former qualities, yet they cannot gaine him so much credit to counterpoise[4] the discredit that commeth thereby. . . .

Now if thou aske me howe thou shouldst choose thy wife? I anwsere, that thou hast the whole world to make choyse, and yet thou maiest be deceyved. An ancient father being asked by a young man how hee should choose a wife, he answered him thus, When thou seest a flock of maydens together, hudwinke[5] thy selfe fast, and runne amongst them, and looke which thou chasest, let her be thy wife: the young man told him that if he went blindfolded, he might be deceyved: and so thou maiest (quoth the old man) if thy eyes were open; for in the choyse of thy wife, thou must not trust thy owne eyes, for they will deceive thee and be the cause of they woe: for she may seeme good whose waste is like a wand, or she which hath a spider fingered hand, or she which on her tiptoes still doth stand, and never read but in a golden booke, nor will not be caught but with a golden hooke; or such a one as can stroke a beard, or looke a head, and of every flea make herselfe afraide if one had a spring, such a wench would make him a begger if he were halfe a King: then this is no bargaine for thee. But harke a little further: the best time for a young man to marry, is at the age of twenty and five, and then to take a wife of the age of seventeene yeares, or thereabout, rather a maid then a widdow; for a widdow is framed to the conditions of another man, and can hardly be altered, so that thy pains will be double: for thou must unlearne a widdow, and make her forget and forgoe her former corrupt and disordered behaviour, the which is hardly to be done: but a young woman of tender yeares is flexible and bending, obedient and subject to doe anything, according to the will and pleasure of her husband.

And if thy state be good, marry neere home, and at leisure; but if thy state be weake and poore, then to better thy selfe after enquiry made of her wealth and conditions, go farre off, and dispatch it quickly, for doubt lest tattling speeches, whiche commonly in these cases runne betwixt party and party, and breaks it off, even then when it is come to the up-shot: but as I have already said, before thou put thy foote out of doores, make diligent enquiry of her behaviour; for by the market-folke thou shall heare how the market goeth: for by enquiry thou shalt heare whether she be wise, vertuous and kinde, wearing but her owne proper haire, and such garments as her friends estate will afford, or whether she love to keepe within the house, and to the servants have a watchfull eye, or if she have a care when to spend, and when to spare, and to be content with what God doth send, or if she can shed no kinde of unstained teares, but when just cause of hearty sorrow is, and that in wealth and woe, in sicknesse and in health, she will be all alike, such a wife will make thee happy in thy choise.

Although some happen on a devillish and unhappy women yet al men doe not so, and such as happen ill it is a warning to make them wise, if they make a second choise, not that all other shall have the like fortune, the sunne shineth upon the good and bad, and many a man happeneth sooner on a shrew then a ship: Some thrive by dicing, but not one in an hundreth, therefore dicing is ill husbandry, some thrive by marriage, and yet many are undone by marriage, for

4 'counterpoise': counterbalance. **5** 'hudwinke': blindfold.

marriage is either the making or marring of many a man, and yet I will not say but amongst dust there is Pearle found, and in hard rockes Dyamonds of great value, and so amongst many women there are some good, as that gracious and glorious Queene of all womankinde the Virgin *Mary*, the mother of al blisse: what won her honour, but an humble minde, and her paines and love unto our Saviour Christ.

RACHEL SPEGHT

A Mouzell for Melastomus (1617)

Speght's pamphlet was written in response to Swetnam's *Arraignment* and forms part of the gender debates of this period. The title refers to the muzzling or silencing of slanderous attacks on women. Other responses included Ester Sowernam's 'Ester hath Hang'd Haman' (1617) and Constantia Munda's 'The Worming of a mad Dogge' (1617). Prior to the following extract, Speght asserts in the Preface that Swetnam has 'plainely displayed [his] owne disposition to be Cynicall' and that although he arraigns 'lewd, idle, froward and unconstant women', he fails to make a distinction in his text between good and bad women. The copy text is BL, 8415. e. 24, printed in London by Nicholas Okes for Thomas Archer, and the following extracts are from sigs. A3r–A4v; pp. 3–9; pp. 15–19; E2v–E3r.

To all vertuous Ladies *Honourable or Worshipfull, and to all other of* Hevahs *sex fearing God, and loving their just reputation, grace and peace through Christ, to eternall glory*

It was the similie of that wise and learned *Lactantius*, that if fire, though but with a small sparke kindled, bee not at the first quenched, it may worke great mischiefe and dammage: So likewise may the scandals and defamations of the malevolent in time prove pernitious, if they bee not nipt in the head at their first appearance. The consideration of this (right Honourable and Worshipfull Ladies) hath incited me (though yong, and the unworthiest of thousands) to encounter with a furious enemy to our sexe, least if his unjust imputations should continue without answere, he might insult and account himselfe a victor; and by such a conceit deale, as Historiographers report the viper to doe, who in the Winter time doth vomit forth her poyson, and in the spring time sucketh the same up againe, which becommeth twise as deadly as the former: And this our pestiferous[1] enemy, by thinking to provide a more deadly poyson for women, then already he hath foamed forth, may evaporate, by an addition unto his former illeterate Pamphlet (intituled *The Arraignement of Women)* a more contagious obtrectation[2] then he hath already done, and indeed hath threatned to doe. Secondly, if it should have had free passage without any answere at all (seeing that *Tacere is, quasi consentire*)[3] the vulgar ignorant might have beleeved his Diabolicall infamies to bee infallible truths, not to bee infringed; whereas now they may plainely perceive them to bee but the scumme of Heathenish braines, or a building raised without a foundation (at least from sacred Scripture) which the winde of Gods truth must needs cast downe to the ground. A third reason why I have adventured to fling this stone at vaunting *Goliah* is to comfort the mindes of all *Hevahs* sex, both rich and poore, learned and unlearned, with this Antidote, that if the feare of God reside in their hearts, maugre[4] all adversaries, they are highly esteemed and accounted of in the eyes of their gracious Redeemer, so that they need not feare the darts of envy or obtrectators:[5] For shame and disgrace (saith *Aristotle)* is the end of them that shoote such poysoned shafts. Worthy therefore of imitation is that example of *Seneca*, who when he was told that a certaine man did exclaime and raile against him, made this milde answere; Some dogs barke more upon custome then curstnesse; and some speake evill of others, not that the defamed deserve it, but because through custome and corruption of their hearts they cannot speake well of any. This I alleage as a paradigmatical patterne for all women, noble and ignoble to follow, that they be not enflamed with choler against this our enraged adversarie, but patiently consider of him according to the portraiture which he hath drawne of himselfe, his Writings being the very embleme of a monster.

This my briefe Apologie (Right Honourable and Worshipfull) did I enterprise, not as thinking my selfe more fit then others to undertake such a taske, but as one, who not perceiving any of our Sex to enter the Lists of encountring with this our grand enemy among men, I being out of all feare, because armed with the truth, which though often blamed, yet can never be shamed, and the Word of Gods Spirit, together with the example of vertues Pupils for a Buckler, did no whit dread to combate with our said malevolent adversarie. And if in so doing I shall bee censured by the judicious to have the victorie, and shall have given content unto the wronged, I have both hit the marke whereat I aymed, and obtained that prize which I desired. But if *Zoilus* shall adjudge me presumptuous in Dedicating this my C*hirograph*[6] unto personages of so high ranke; both because of my insufficiency in literature and tendernesse in yeares: I thus Apologize for my selfe; that seeing the *Bayter of Women* hath opened his mouth against noble as well as ignoble, against the rich as well as

1 'pestiferous': plague-bringing. 2 'obtrectation': detraction, disparagment, slander, calumny. 3 'To keep quiet is to give consent'. 4 'maugre': in spite of, notwithstanding. 5 'obtrectators': detractors. 6 'Chirograph': written document.

the poore; therefore meete it is that they should be joynt spectators of this encounter: And withall in regard of my imperfection both in learning and age, I need so much the more to impetrate[7] patronage from some of power to sheild mee from the biting wrongs of *Momus*, who oftentimes setteth a rankling tooth into the sides of truth. Wherefore I being of *Decius* his mind, who deemed himselfe safe under the shield of *Caesar*, have presumed to shelter my selfe under the wings of you (Honourable personages) against the persecuting heate of this fierie and furious Dragon; desiring that you would be pleased, not to looke so much *ad opus*, as *ad animum*:[8] And so not doubting of the favourable acceptance and censure of all vertuously affected, I rest

Your Honours and Worships
Humbly at commandement.
Rachel Speght.

Of Womans Excellency, with the causes of her creation, and of the sympathie which ought to be in man and wife each toward other

The worke of Creation being finished, this approbation thereof was given by God himselfe, That *All was very good*; If All, then *Woman*, who, excepting man, is the most excellent creature under the Canopie of heaven (Gen. 1: 31). But if it be objected by any.

First, that woman, though created good, yet by giving eare to Sathans temptations, brought death and misery upon all her posterity.

Secondly, That *Adam was not deceived, but that the woman was deceived, and was in the transgression* (I Tim. 2: 14).

Thirdly, that Saint *Paul* saith, *It were good for a man not to touch a woman* (I. Cor. 7: 1).

Fourthly, and lastly, that of *Salomon*, who seemes to speake against all of our sex; I *have found one man of a thousand, but a woman among them all have I not found*, whereof in it due place (Eccles. 7: 30).

To the first of these objections I answere; that Sathan first assailed the woman, because where the hedge is lowest, most easie it is to get over, and she being the weaker vessel was with more facility to be seduced: Like as a Cristall glasse sooner receives a cracke then a strong stone pot. Yet we shall finde the offence of *Adam* and *Eve* almost to paralell: For as an ambitious desire of being made like unto God, was the motive which caused her to eate, so likewise was it his; as may plainely appeare by that *Ironia*, *Behold, man is become as one of us* (Gen. 3: 22): Not that hee was so indeed; but heereby his desire to attaine a greater perfection then God had given him, was reproved. Woman sinned, it is true, by her infidelitie in not beleeving the Word of God, but giving credite to

7 'impetrate': obtain by request, especially by application to an authority. 8 '*ad opus*, as *ad animum*': on the work, as on the spirit.

Sathans faire promises, that *she should not die* (Gen. 3: 4); but so did the man too: And if *Adam* had not approoved of that deed which *Eve* had done, and beene willing to treade the steps which she had gone, hee being her Head would have reproved her, and have made the commandement a bit to restraine him from breaking his Makers Injunction: For if a man burne his hand in the fire, the bellowes that blowed the fire are not to be blamed, but himselfe rather, for not being carefull to avoyde the danger: Yet if the bellowes had not blowed, the fire had not burnt; no more is woman simply to bee condemned for mans transgression: for by the free will, which before his fall hee enjoyed, hee might have avoyded, and beene free from beeing burnt, or singed with that fire which was kindled by Sathan, and blowne by *Eve*. It therefore served not his turne a whit, afterwardes to say, *The woman which thou gavest mee, gave mee of the tree, and I did eate* (Gen. 3: 12): For a penalty was inflicted upon him, as well as on the woman, the punishment of her transgression being particular to her owne sex, and to none but the female kinde: but for the sinne of man the whole earth was cursed (Gen. 3: 17). And he being better able, then the woman, to have resisted temptation, because the stronger vessell, was first called to account, to shew, that to whom much is given, of them much is required; and that he who was the soveraigne of all creatures visible, should have yeelded greatest obedience to God.

True it is (as is already confessed) that woman first sinned, yet finde wee no mention of spirituall nakednesse till man had sinned: then it is said, *Their eyes were opened*, the eyes of their mind and conscience (Gen. 3: 7); and then perceived they themselves naked, that is, not onely bereft of that integritie, which they originally had, but felt the rebellion and disobedience of their members in the disordered motions of their now corrupt nature, which made them for shame to cover their nakednesse: then (and not afore) is it said that they saw it, as if sinne were imperfect, and unable to bring a deprivation of a blessing received, or death on all mankind, till man (in whom lay the active power of generation) had transgressed. The offence therefore of *Adam* and *Eve is* by Saint *Austin* thus distinguished, *the man sinned against God and himselfe, the woman against God, her selfe, and her husband:* yet in her giving of the fruit to eate she had no malicious intent towardes him, but did therein shew a desire to make her husband partaker of that happinesse, which she thought by their eating they should both have enjoyed. This her giving *Adam* of that sawce, wherewith Sathan had served her, whose sowrenesse afore he had eaten, she did not perceive, was that, which made her sinne to exceede his (I Pet. 3: 7): wherefore, that she might not of him, who ought to honour her, be abhorred, the first promise that was made in Paradise, God makes to woman, that by her Seede should the Serpents head be broken (Gen. 3: 15): whereupon *Adam* calles her *Hevah, life*, that as the woman had beene an occasion of his sinne, so should woman bring foorth the Saviour from sinne, which was in the fullnesse of time accomplished (Gal. 4: 4); by which was manifested, that he is a Saviour of beleeving women, no lesse then of men, that so the blame of sinne may not be imputed to his creature, which is good; but to the will by which *Eve* sinned, and yet by Christs assuming the shape of man was it declared, that his mercie was equivalent to both Sexes; so that by *Herods* blessed Seed (as Saint *Paul* affirmes) it is brought to passe, that *male and female are all one in Christ Jesus* (Gal. 3: 28).

To the second objection I answer, That the Apostle doth not heereby exempt man from sinne, but onely giveth to understand, that the woman was the primarie transgressour; and not the man, but that man was not at all deceived, was farre from his meaning: for he afterward expresly saith, that as *in Adam all die, so in Christ shall all be made alive* (I Cor. 15: 22).

For the third objection, *It is good for a man not to touch a woman:* The Apostle makes it not a positive prohibition, but speakes it onelie because of the *Corinths* present necessitie, who were then persecuted by the enemies of the Church, for which cause, and no other, hee saith, *Art thou loosed from a wife? seeke not a wife*: meaning whilst the time of these perturbations should continue in their heate; *but if thou art bound, seeke not to be loosed: if thou marriest, thou sinnest not*, only increasest thy care: *for the married careth for the things of this world, And I wish that you were without care, that yee might cleave fast unto the Lord without separation: For the time remaineth, that they which have wives be as though they had none* (I. Cor. 7): for the persecuters shall deprive you of them, eyther by imprisonment, banishment, or death; so that manifest it is, that the Apostle doth not heereby forbid marriage, but onely adviseth the *Corinths* to forbeare a while, till God in mercie should curbe the fury of their adversaries. For (as *Eusebius* writeth) *Paul* was afterward married himselfe, the which is very probable, being that interrogatively he saith, *Have we not power to leade about a wife, being a sister, as well as the rest of the Apostles, and as the brethren of the Lord and Cephas* (I Cor. 9: 5)?

The fourth and last objection, is that of *Salomon, I have found one man among a thousand, but a woman among them all have I not found:* for answere of which, if we looke into the storie of his life, wee shall finde therein a Commentary upon this enigmaticall Sentence included: for it is there said, that *Salomon* had seven hundred wives, and three hundred concubines, which number connexed make one thousand (Eccle1. 7: 30). These women turning his heart away from being perfect with the Lord his God, sufficient cause had hee to say, that among the said thousand women found he not one upright (I King. 11: 3). Hee saith not, that among a thousand women never any man found one worthy of commendation, but speakes in the first person singularly, I *have not found*, meaning in his own experience: for this assertion is to be holden a part of the confession of his former follies, and no otherwise, his repentance being the intended drift of *Ecclesiastes.*

Thus having (by Gods assistance) removed those stones, whereat some have stumbled, others broken their shinnes, I will proceede toward the period of my intended taske, which is, to decipher the excellency of women: of whose Creation I will, for orders sake observe; First, the efficient cause, which was God; Secondly, the materiall cause, or that whereof shee was made; Thirdly, the formall cause, or fashion, and proportion of her feature; Fourthly and lastly, the finall cause, the end or purpose for which she was made.[9]

The Kingdome of God is compared unto the marriage of a Kings sonne: *John* calleth the conjunction of Christ and his Chosen, a Marriage (Rev. 19: 7): And not few, but many times, doth our blessed Saviour in the Canticles, set forth his unspeakable love towards his Church under the title of an Husband rejoycing with his Wife; and often vouchsafeth to call her his Sister and Spouse, by which is shewed that with *God is no respect of persons,* Nations, or Sexes (Rom. 2: 11): For whosoever, whether it be man or woman, that doth *beleeve in the Lord Jesus,* such *shall bee saved* (John. 3: 18). And if Gods love even from the beginning, had not beene as great toward woman as to man, then would hee not have preserved from the deluge of the old world as many women as men; nor would Christ after his Resurrection have appeared unto a woman first of all other, had it not beene to declare thereby, that the benefites of his death and resurrection, are as availeable, by beleefe, for women as for men; for hee indifferently died for the one sex as well as the other: Yet a truth ungainesayable is it, that the *Man is the Womans head* (I Cor. 11: 3): by which title yet of Supremacie, no authoritie hath hee given him to domineere, or basely command and imploy his wife, as a servant; but hereby is he taught the duties which hee oweth unto her: For as the head of a man is the imaginer and contriver of projects profitable for the safety of his whole body; so the Husband must protect and defend his Wife from injuries: For he is her *Head, as Christ is the Head of his Church* (Ephes. 5: 23), which hee entirely loveth, and for which hee gave his very life; the deerest thing any man hath in this world (Job 2: 4); *Greater love then this hath no man, when he bestoweth his life for his friend,* saith our Saviour (John 15: 13): This president passeth all other patternes, it requireth great benignity, and enjoyneth an extraordinary affection, for *men must love their wives, even as Christ loved his Church.* Secondly, as the Head doth not jarre or contend with the members, which *being many,* as the Apostle saith, *yet make but one bodie* (I Cor. 12: 20); no more must the husband with the wife, but expelling all bitternesse and cruelty hee must live with her lovingly, and religiously, honouring her as the weaker vessell (Col. 3: 19; I Pet. 3: 7). Thirdly, and lastly, as hee is her Head, hee must, by instruction, bring her to the knowledge of her Creator, that so she may be a fit stone for the Lords building (I Cor. 14: 35). Women for this end must have an especiall care to set their affections upon such as are able to teach them, that as they *grow in yeares, they may grow in grace, and in the knowledge* of *Christ Jesus our Lord* (I Pet. 3: 18).

---

9 At this point, Speght continues by arguing that God's creation of humanity 'can not chuse but be good'; that Eve was created not 'from [Adam's] head to be his superior, but from his side, neare his heart, to be his equal', and that God had stated 'Let them rule over the fish of the sea', thereby suggesting that He 'makes their authority equal, and all creatures to be in subjection to them both'; she affirms the version that 'in the Image of God were they both created'; and finally, that woman was made 'to glorify God, and to be a collaterall companion for man to glorify God'.

Thus if men would remember the duties they are to performe in being heads, some would not stand a tip-toe as they doe, thinking themselves Lords and Rulers, and account every omission of performing whatsoever they command, whether lawfull or not, to be matter of great disparagement, and indignity done them; whereas they should consider, that women are enjoyned to submit themselues unto their husbands no otherwaies then as to *the Lord* (Ephes. 5); so that from hence, for man, ariseth a lesson not to bee forgotten, that as the Lord commandeth nothing to be done, but that which is right and good, no more must the husband; for if a wife fulfill the evill command of her husband, shee obeies him as a tempter, as *Saphira* did *Ananias* (Actes 5: 2). But least I should seeme too partiall in praysing women so much as I have (though no more then warrant from Scripture doth allow) I adde to the premises, that I say not, all women are vertuous, for then they should be more excellent then men, sith of *Adams* sonnes there was *Cain* as well as *Abel*, and of *Noahs*, *Cham* as well as *Sem;* so that of men as of women, there are two sorts, namely, good and bad, which in *Mathew* the five and twenty chapter, are comprehended under the name of *Sheepe* and *Goats.* And if women were not sinfull, then should they not need a Saviour: but the Virgin *Mary* a patterne of piety, *rejoyced in God her Saviour: Ergo,* she was a sinner (Luke 1: 47). In the *Revelation* the Church is called the Spouse of Christ; and in *Zachariah*, wickednesse is called a woman (Zach. 5: 7), to shew that of women there are both godly and ungodly: For Christ would not *Purge his Floore* if there were not Chaffe among the Wheate; nor should gold neede to bee fined, if among it there were no drosse (Gen. 18: 25). But farre be it from any one, to condemne the righteous with the wicked, or good women with the bad (as the Bayter of women doth:) For though there are some scabbed sheepe in the Flocke, we must not therefore conclude all the rest to bee mangie: And though some men, through excesse, abuse Gods creatures, wee must not imagine that all men are Gluttons; the which wee may with as good reason do, as condemne all women in generall, for the offences of some particulars. Of the good sort is it that I have in this booke spoken, and so would I that all that reade it should so understand me: for if otherwise I had done, I should have incurred that woe, which by the Prophet *Isaiah is* pronounced against them that *speake well of evill*, and should have *justified the wicked, which thing is abhominable to the Lord* (Esay [Isaiah] 5: 20; Prov. 17: 15).

The Epilogue or upshut of the premises

Great was the unthankefulnesse of *Pharaohs* Butler unto *Joseph;* for though hee had done him a great pleasure, of which the Butler promised requitall, yet was hee quite forgotten of him (Gen. 40: 23): But farre greater is the ingratitude of those men toward God, that dare presume to speake and exclaime against *Woman*, whom God did create for mans comfort. What greater discredit can redound to a workeman, then to have the man, for whom hee hath made it, say, it is naught? or what greater discurtesie can be offered to one, that bestoweth a gift, then to have the receiver give out, that hee cares not for it: For he needes it not? And what greater ingratitude can bee shewed unto GOD then the opprobrious speeches and disgracefull invectives, which some diabolicall natures doe frame against women?

Ingratitude is, and alwayes hath beene accounted so odious a vice, that *Cicero* saith, *If one doubt what name to give a wicked man, let him call him an ungratefull person, and then hee hath said enough*. It was so detested among the *Persians*, as that by a Law they provided, that such should suffer death as felons, which prooved unthankefull for any gift received. And *Love* (saith the Apostle) *is the fulfilling of the Lawe* (Rom. 13: 10): But where Ingratitude is harbored, there Love is banished. Let men therefore beware of all unthankefulnesse, but especially of the superlative ingratitude, that which is towards God, which is no way more palpably declared, then by the contemning of, and rayling against women, which sinne, of some men (if to be termed men) no doubt but God will one day avenge, when they shall plainely perceive, that it had been better for them to have been borne dumbe and lame, then to have used their tongues and hands, the one in repugning, the other in writing against Gods handie worke, their owne flesh, women I meane, whom God hath made equall with themselves in dignity, both temporally and eternally, if they continue in the faith: which God for his mercie sake graunt they alwayes may, to the glory of their Creator, and comfort of their owne soules, through Christ Amen.

To God onely wise be glorie now and for
ever, AMEN.

ESTER SOWERNAM

Ester Hath Hang'd Haman (1617)

Ester Sowernam's (pseud.) pamphlet was the second response to Swetnam (the first was written by Speght). The majority of her pamphlet refutes Swetnam's attack by describing virtuous women from the scriptures, from the classical and pagan past, and it includes a eulogy of Elizabeth I. The full text is divided into two parts: 'The first proveth the dignity and worthinesse *of Women, out of divine Testimonies.* The second shewing the estimation of the Foeminine Sexe, in ancient and Pagan times; all which is acknowledged by men themselves in their daily actions'. The copy text (BL, C. 132. h. 29 (2)) was printed in London for Nicholas Bourne, 1617. The following extract has been taken from the end of her pamphlet, where Sowernam takes issue with Swetnam's arguments directly, deconstructing passages of his pamphlet line by line (pp. 31–7, 42–8).

Chap. VII

The answere to all objections which are materiall, made against Women

Right Honourable and Worshipfull, and you of all degrees; it hath ever beene a common custome amongst Idle and humerous Poets, Phamphleters, and Rimers, out of passionate discontents, or having little otherwise to imploy themselves about, to write some bitte Satire-Pamphlet, or Rime, against women: in which argument he who could devise any thing more bitterly, or spitefully, against our sexe, hath never wanted the liking, allowance, and applause of giddy headed people. Amongst the rable of scurill writers, this prisoner now present hath acted his part, whom albeit women could more willingly let passe, then bring him to triall, and as ever heretofore, rather contemn such authors then deigne them any answere, yet seeing his booke so commonly bought up, which argueth a generall applause; we are therfore enforced to make answere in defence of our selves, who are by such an author so extreamely wronged in publike view.

You all see hee will not put himselfe upon triall: if we should let it so passe, our silence might implead us for guiltie, so would his Pamphlet be received with a greater currant and credite then formerly it hath beene: So that as well in respect of our sexe, as for a generall satisfaction to the world, I will take this course with our prisoner, I will at this present examine all the objections which are most materiall, which our adversarie hath vomited out against woman, and not onely what he hath objected, but what other authors of more import then *Joseph Swetnam* have charged upon women: alas, seely man he objecteth nothing but what he hath stolne out of English writers, as *Euphues*, the *Palace of Pleasure*, with the like, which are as easily anwered as vaynly objected. He never read the vehement and profest enemies against our sexe, as for *Grecians, Euripeides, Menander, Simonides, Sophocles*, with the like, amongst Latine writers *Juvenall, Plautus*, etc.

But of all that ever I read, I did never observe such general sinceretie in any, as in this adversarie, which you shall finde I will make as manifest as the Sunne to shine at mid-day.

It is the maine end that our adversarie aimeth at in all his discourse, to prove and say that women are bad; if he should offer this upon particulars, no one would denie it: but to lavish generally against all women, who can endure it? You might *Mr Swetnam*, with some shew of honestie have sayd, some women are bad, both by custome and company, but you cannot avoide the brand, both of blasphemie and dishonestie, to say of women generally they are all naught, both in their creation and by nature, and to ground you inferences upon Scriptures.

I let pass your objections in your first page; because they are formerly answered, onely whereas you say, *woman was no sooner made, but her heart was set upon mischiefe*: if you had then said, she had no sooner eaten of the fruit, but her heart was set upon mischief, you had had some colour for your speaches; not in respect of the womans disposition, but in consideration both of her first Tutor and her second instructor: For whereas scripture doth say, *Woman was supplanted by a Serpent Joseph Swetnam* doth say, *she was supplanted by the devil, which appeared to her in the shape of a beautifull yong man.* Men are much beholding to this author, who will seeme to insinuate, that the devill would in so friendly and familier a manner, put on the shape of man, when he first began to practise mischiefe. The devill might make bold of them, whom he knew in time would prove his familier friends. Hereupon it may be imagined it commeth to passe that Painters, and Picture-makers, when they would represent the devill, they set him out in the deformed shape of a man; because under that shape he began first to act the part of a devill: and I doubt he never changed his suite sithence. Here it is to be observed, that which is worst is expressed by the shape of a man; but what is the most glorious creature is represented in the beautie of a woman, as Angels. Woman at the first might easily learne mischiefe, where or how should she learne goodnes? her first Schoole-master was aboundant in mischiefe, and her first husband did exceede in bad examples. First, by his example he taught her how to flye from God: next how to excuse her sinne: then how to cample[1] and contest with God, and to say as *Adam* did, thou art the cause, for, the woman whom thou gavest me, was the cause I did eate. What *Adam* did at the first, bad husbands practice with their wives ever sithence, I meane in bade examples. It was no good example in *Adam*, who having received his wife from the gift of God, and bound to her in so inseperable a bond of love, that forthwith he being taken tardie would presently accuse his wife and put her in all the danger; but the woman was more bound to an upright judge, then to a loving husband: it would not serve *Adams* turne, to charge her, therby to free himselfe: It was an hard and strange course, that he who should have beene her defender, is now become her greatest accuser. I may heare say with Saint *Paul, by one mans sinne, death*, etc so by the cantagion of originall sinne in *Adam*, all men are infected with his diseases; and looke what examples he gave his wife at the first, the like examples and practises doe all men shew to women ever sithence. Let mee speake freely, for I will speake nothing but truly, neither shall my words exceede my proofe.

In your first and second Page, you alledge *David* and *Salomon*, for exclaiming bitterly against women: And that *Salomon* saith, *Women (like as Wine) doe make men drunke with their devices*. What of all this?

Joseph Swetnam, a man which hath reason, will neither object that unto his adversary, which when it commeth to examination will disadvantage himselfe. Your meaning is, in the disgrace of women to exalt men: but is this any commendation to men, that they have been and are over-reacht by women? Can you glory of their holinesse, whom by women prove sinfull? or in their wisedome, whom women make fooles? or in their strength, whom women overcome? can you excuse that fall which is given by the weaker? or colour that soyle which is taken from women? Is holinesse, wisedome, and strength, so

1 'cample': enter into a wordy conflict; to wrangle or quarrel.

slightly seated in your Masculine gender, as to be stained, blemished, and subdued by women? But now I pray you let us examine how these vertues in men so potent, came by women to be so impotent. Doe you meane in comparative degree, that women are more holy, more wise, more strong, then men? if you should graunt this, you had small cause to write against them. But you will not admit this: What is, or are the causes then why men are so overtaken by women? You set downe the causes in your fourth Page; there you say, *They are dangerous for men to deale withall, for their faces are Lures, their beauties baytes, their lookes are nets, and their words are charmes*, and all to bring men to ruine: *Incidit in Scyllam qui vult vitare Charybdim*,[2] whilst he seeketh to avoide one mischiefe, he falleth into another. It were more credit for men to yeeld our sexe to be more holy, wise, and strong, then to excuse themselves by the reasons alleaged: for by this men are proved to have as little wit as they are charged to exceed in wickednesse. Are external and dumbe shews such potent baites, nets, lures, charmes, to bring men to ruine? Why? wilde Asses, dotterels, and woodcockes, are not so easily entangled and taken? are men so idle, vaine, and weake, as you seeme to make them? Let mee now see how you can free these men from dishonest mindes, who are overtaken thus with beautie, etc. How can beautie hurt? how can it be a cause of a mans ruine, of it selfe? what, do women forcibly draw? why, men are more strong? are they so eloquent to perswade? why, men are too wise; are they mischievous to entise? men are more holy; how then are women causes to bring men to ruine? direct causes they cannot be in any respect; if they be causes, they are but accidentall causes: A cause as Philosophers say, *Causa sine qua non*: a remote cause, which cause is seldome alleaged for cause, but where want of wit would say somewhat, and a guilty conscience wou'd excuse it selfe by something. Philosophers say, *Nemo leditur nisi a seipso*, no man is hurt but the cause is in himselfe. The prodigall person amongst the *Gracians* is called *Asotos*, as a destroyer, an undoer of himselfe: When an heart fraughted with sinne doth prodigally lavish out a lascivious looke out of a wanton eye; when it doth surfeit upon the sight, who is *Asotos*? who is guiltie of his lascivious disease but himselfe? *Volenti non fit iniuria*, hee who is wounded with his owne consent, hath small cause to complaine of anothers wrong: Might not a man as easily, and more honestly, when he seeth a faire woman, which doth make the best use that she can to set out her beautie, rather glorifie God in so beautifull a worke, then infect his soule with so lascivious a thought? And for the woman, who having a Jewell given her from so deare a friend, is she not to be commended rather that in the estimate which she sheweth, shee will as carefully and as curiously as she may set out what she hath received from Almighty God, then to be censured that she doth it to allure wanton and lascivious lookes?[3]

2 Each time she uses a Latin phrase, Speght immediately offers an English paraphrase. 3 Sowernam continues that men have no cause to complain that women seek to allure them by the way in which they dress, since such complaints only reveal the way in which men perceive women and that, furthermore, men themselves spend a great deal on their own clothing.

This is the true application of the Morrall. As for that crookedness and frowardnesse with which you charge women, looke from whence they have it; for of themselves and their owne disposition it doth not proceede, which is prooved directly by your owne testimonie: for in your 45 Page, Line 15. You Say, *A young woman of tender yeares is flexible, obedient, and subject to doe any thing, according to the will and pleasure of her Husband.* How commeth it then that this gentle and milde disposition is afterwards altered? your selfe doth give the true reason, for you give a great charge not to marrie a widdow. But why? because say you in the same Page, *A widdow is framed to the conditions of another man.* Why then, if a woman have froward conditions, they be none of her owne, she was framed to them. Is not our adversarie ashamed of himselfe, to raile against women for those faults which doe all come from men? Doth not hee most grievously charge men to learne their wives bad and corrupt behaviour? for hee saith plainely, *Thou must unlearne a widdow, and make her forget and forgoe her former corrupt and disorder behaviour.* Thou must unlearne her, *Ergo*, what fault shee hath, shee learned, her corruptnes commeth not from her own disposition, but from her Husbands destruction. Is it not a wonder, that your Pamphlets are so dispersed? Are they not wise men to cast away time and money upon a Booke which cutteth their owne throates? 'Tis pittie but that men should reward you for your writing; if it be but as the Roman *Sertorius* did the idle Poet, hee gave him a reward, but not for his writing, but because he should never write more; as for women, they laugh that men have no more able a champion. This author commeth to baite[4] women, or as hee foolishly sayth, the *Beare bayting of Women*, and he bringeth but a mungrell Curre, who doth his kinde, to braule and barke, but cannot bite. The milde and flexible disposition of a woman is in philosophy proved in the composition of her body, for it is a Maxime, *Mores animi sequntur temperaturam corporis*, The disposition of the minde is answereable to the temper of the body. A woman in the temperature of her body is tender, soft, and beautifull, so doth her disposition in minde corresponde accordingly; she is milde, yeelding, and vertuous; what disposition accidentlly happeneth unto her, is by the contagion of a froward husband, as *Joseph Swetnam* affirmeth.

And experience proveth. It is a shame for a man to complaine of a froward woman, in many respects all concerning himselfe. It is a shame he hath no more government over the weaker vessell. It is a shame he hath hardned her tender sides, and gentle heart with his boistrous and Northren blasts. It is a shame for a man to publish and proclaime houshold secrets, which is a common practise amongst men, especially Drunkards, Leachers, and prodigall spend-thrifts: These when they come home drunke, or are called in question for their riotous misdemeanours, they presently shew themselves, the right children of *Adam*. They will excuse themselves by their wives, and say that their unquitenesse and frowardnesse at home, is the cause that they runne abroad. An excuse more fitter for a beast than a man. If thou wert a man thou wouldest take away the cause which urgeth a woman to griefe and discontent,

4 'baite': to persecute or harass.

and not by thy frowardnesse encrease her distemperature: forbeare thy drinking, thy luxurious riot, thy gaming, and spending, and thou shalt have thy wife give thee as little cause at home, as thou givest her great cause of disquiet abroad. Men which are men, if they chance to be matched with froward wives, either of their own making or others marring, they would make a benefit of the discommodity, either try his skill to make her milde, or exercise his patience to endue her curstnesse: for all crosses are inflicted either for punishment of sinnes, or for exercise of vertues; but humorous[5] men will sooner marre a thousand women, then out of an hundred make one good.

And this shall appeare in the imputation which our adversarie chargeth upon our sexe, to be lascivious, wanton and lustfull: He sayth, *Women tempt, alure, and provoke men*. How rare a thing is it for women to prostitute and offer themselves? how common a practise is it for men to seeke and solicit women to lewdnesse? what charge do they spare? what travell doe they bestow? what vowes, oathes, and protestations doe they spend, to make them dishonest? They hyer Pandors,[6] they write letters, they seale them with damnations, and execrations, to assure them of love, when the end proves but lust: They know the flexible disposition of Women and the sooner to overreach them, some will pretend they are so plunged in love that except they obtaine their desire they will seeme to drown'd, hang, stab, poyson, or banish themselves from friends and countrie: What motives are these to tender dispositions? Some will pretend marriage, another offer continuall maintenance, but when they have obtained their purpose, what shall a woman finde, just that which is her everlasting shame and griefe, shee hath made her selfe the unhappie subject to a lustfull bodie, and the shamefull stall of a lascivious tongue. Men may with foule shame charge women with this sinne which they had never committed if shee had not trusted, nor had ever trusted if shee had not beene deceived with vowes, oathes, and protestations. To bring a woman to offend in one sinne, how many damnable sinnes doe they commit? I appeale to their owne consciences. The lewd disposition of sundry men doth appeare in this: If a woman or maide will yeeld unto lewdnesse, what shall they want? But if they would live in honestie, what helpe shall they have? How much will they make of the lewd? how base account of the honest? how many pounds will they spend in bawdie houses? but when will they bestowe a penny upon an honest maide or woman, except it be to corrupt them.

Our adversary bringeth many examples of men which have beene overthrowne by women. It is answered, before the fault is their owne. But I would have him, or any one living, to shew any woman that offended in this sinne of lust, but that she was first sollicited by a man.

Helen was the cause of *Troyes* burning; first, *Paris* did sollicite her; next, how many knaves and fooles of the male kind had *Troy*, which to maintaine whoredome would bring their Citie to confusion.

---

5 'humorous': concerning disposition or temperament. In ancient and medieval physiology an individual's physical and mental qualities were thought to be determined by the relative proportions of the four humours of the body (that is, blood, phlegm, choler and melancholy or black choler). 6 'pandor': a pimp or procurer.

When you bring in examples of lewd women, and of men which have been stained by women, you shew you selfe both franticke, and a prophane irreligious foole to mention *Judith* for cutting of *Holofernes* head, in that rancke.

You challenge women for untamed and unbrideled tongues; there was never woman was ever noted for so shameless, so brutish, so beastly a scold as you prove your selfe in this base and odious Pamphlet: You blaspheme God, you raile at his Creation, you abuse and slander his Creatures; and what immodest or impudent scurilitie is it, which you doe not expresse in this lewd and lying Pamphlet?

Hitherto I have so answered all your objections against Women, that as I have not defended the wickednesse of any; so I have set downe the true state of the question. As *Eve* did not offend without the temptation of a Serpent; so women doe seldome offend, but it is by provocation of men. Let not your impudencie, nor your consorts dishonestie, charge our sexe hereafter, with those sinnes of which you your selves were the first procurers. I have in my discourse, touched you, and all yours, to the quick. I have taxed you with bitter speaches; you will (perhaps) say I am a rayling scold. In this objection, *Joseph Swetnam*, I will teach you both wit and honestie: The difference betwixt a railing scold, and an honest accuser, is this, the first rageth upon passionate furie, without bringing cause or proofe; the other bringeth direct proofe for what she alleageth: you charge women with clamorous words, and bring no proofe; I charge you with blasphemie, with impudencie, scurilitie, foolery, and the like. I shew just and direct proofe for what I say; it is not my desire to speake so much, it is your desert to provoke me upon just cause so fare; it is no railing to call a Crow blacke, or a Wolfe a ravenour, or a drunkard a beast; the report of the truth is never to be blamed, the deserver of such a report, deserveth the shame.

Now, for this time, to draw to an end; let me aske according to the question of *Cassius, Cui bono?* what have you gotten by publishing your Pamphlet; good I know you can get none. You have (perhaps) pleased the humors of some giddy, idle conceited persons: But you have died your selfe in the colours of shame, lying, slandering, blasphemie, ignorance, and the like.

The shortnesse of time and the weight of business call me away, and urge me to leave off thus abruptly, but assure your selfe where I leave now, I will by Gods grace supply the next Terme, to your small content.[7] You have exceeded in your furie against Widdowes, whose defence you shall heare of at the time aforesaide, in the meane space recollect your wits, write out of deliberation, not out of furie; write out of advice, not out of idleness; forbeare to charge women with faults which come from the contagion of Masculine serpents.

7 There is no record of a further response by Sowernam.

LADY MARY WROTH

The Countesse of Montgomeries Urania (1621)

When the first part of Wroth's prose romance, *The Urania* (together with her sonnet sequence *Pamphillia to Amphilanthus*) was published in 1621, it provoked a scandal: Lord Edward Denny claimed that Wroth had written a *roman à clef* in which she had slandered him, his daughter and his son-in-law in an episode concerning Sirelius. It would seem that, whatever the truth of Denny's claims, this had an effect on Wroth: the first part of *The Urania* was withdrawn from publication and the second part remains in manuscript. Thus, although Wroth explicitly utilised her family connections – the title page declares her book was 'Written by the right honorable Lady Mary Wroath. Daughter to the Right Noble Robert Earle of Leicester. And Neece to the ever famous, and renowned Sr. Phillip Sidney knight. And to the most exelent Lady Mary Countesse of Pembroke late deceased' – this did not protect her from public censure. The first part of *The Urania* is comprised of four books: book one is currently available in *An Anthology of Seventeenth-Century Fiction*, edited by Paul Salzman (Oxford: Oxford University Press, 1991). The extract reproduced below is from the opening of the second book. As *The Urania* has a very convoluted narrative, we have selected an extract which centres on the romance's heroine, Pamphilia. In this episode, Pamphilia's virtue and self-containment is contrasted with the actions of Nereana, Queen of Stalamina. The copy text is BL, 86. h. 9, printed for John Marriot and John Grismond, pp. 147–8, 159–64.

All this journey did *Urania* passe with much griefe inwardly suffered, and so borne, desirous to know where her love was, yet bashfull, durst not aske, till one day *Perissus* sitting betweene her and *Limena*, tooke occasion to speake of his first finding her, and so of the obligation they remaind tied unto her in, for all the fortunes they enjoyd; and so from that, to speake of the rescue *Parselius* brought *Limena* at her last breathing, as shee thought. I wonder (said *Urania)* where that Prince is, since so many brave men being here, mee thinkes hee should not bee absent; nor could I have thought any but himselfe might have ended this adventure. Truly (said *Perissus)* when we parted with him, I never saw a more afflicted man then hee was (except once my selfe), and all was for the losse of you. I thought rather (said she) he had been offended with us for adventuring; which well he might, considering by that folly we lost him. Nay, said *Allimarlus* (who was then come to them), hee had no cause to blame you, having committed as great an error, and the same, himselfe, then told hee all the story to her, of what had past after the drinking the water, and so much as he knew, or heard by others of him, while he was heard of. Then came *Pamphilia* and *Amphilanthus.* who went on with the discourse, that now

Urania was resolved, and assured of his affection, which so much joyd her, as the absence of him, grew the more terrible to afflict her.

Then to *Delos* they came, whose milke-white rockes looked smooth with joy to receive within their girdle, the worlds treasure of worth, now being in their presence richer, then when most treasure was within her: then tooke they directly to the Pallace, at the entring into the vault meeting the grave *Mellissea*, who with her maides carrying torches of white waxe, conducted the Prince through that into the Gardens, all now in hope or feare to know their fortunes. *Urania* desiring to know her selfe; *Pamphilia* to be resolved, whether she should gaine by her loyalty. *Amphilanthus* when he should enjoy, and *Antissius* longing to be assured, if hee should have *Selarina*, who as much desired the same knowledge of gaining him, such affection had growne betweene them, he being (as shee did verily perswade her selfe) the selfe same little King, that beckned to her out of the enchanted Garden. *Allimarlus* must by any meanes be gaind by the Shepheardesse. . . .

The Queene of all brave beauty, and true worth, *Pamphilia*, thinking it long to heare her fate in Love, yet daring not for modesty to aske, what most she coveted to understand, faign'd a desire to returne againe unto her People, who expected her, this also was a truth, and therefore just excuse.

The Lady [Mellissea] knowing most things, also found this drift, yet did as finely strive to cover it; wherefore one day dinner newly done, she tooke her company into a roome, the fairest and best furnish'd of that place, and by a witty sleight divided them into the windowes, and some pretty places every one a sunder from their friend, each one imagining she was with 'tother, then came shee to *Pamphilia* and thus spake: Rarest of women for true loyalty, I know your longing which proceeds from love, and grieve I doe, that I cannot be blessed with power to tell that happinesse you seeke, but Destiny that governes all our lives hath thus ordain'd, you might be happy, had you power to wedd, but daintinesse and feare will hinder you: I cannot finde that you shall marry yet, nor him you most affect many afflictions you must undergoe, and all by woman kinde, beware of them, and so the better speed.

Pamphilia onely sigh'd, and turnd her blushing face unto the window, while the Lady went unto *Urania*, to whom she thus discours'd. Fayrest, and sweetest, leave off your laments for ignorance of your estate, and know that you are daughter to a mighty King, and sister to the bravest living Prince, the honour of all Knights, and glory of his Country, renowned *Amphilanthus;* the manner, and the reason for your losse, shall bee brought to you in a fitter place. Now for your love, alas that I must say, what Destinie foretels, you shall be happy, and enjoy, but first, death in apparance must possesse your daintie bodie, when you shall revive with him you now love, to another love, and yet as good, and great as hee. Bee not offended for this is your fate, nor bee displeased, since though that must change, it is but just change, bringing it from him alike disquieted.

The Lady left her, who impatient of her ill went to *Pamphilia*, whom shee found still without speech, and as (if one would say) fix'd like the heaven, while the world of her thoughts had motion in her griefe. *Urania* likewike vex'd in her soule, shewed in her face the small content shee knew; they both stood gazing in each others face, as if the shining day Starre had stood still to looke her in a glasse, their bloud had left their cheeks, and sunke into their hearts, as sent in pitty downe to comfort them; at last assured confidence did come and plead for part, and so they sate and spake; while *Mellissea* pass'd unto the King, to whom shee onely told that faire *Urania* was his sister, and that although so deare to him, yet to make her live contentedly, he, and none else must throw her from the Rocke of St. *Maura* into the Sea; feare not, but doe it (said shee) for this must make her live, and forget her unfortunate love, (which vertue that water hath.) For his Love, she did assure him hee was bless'd in that, if being certaine of her heart, could bring it him; but yet said she; Nay, say no more, cry'd he, this is enough, and let me this enjoy, Ile feare no ills that Prophesies can tell.

Then went he to the window, where hee found the sad sweet couple, whom he comforted, kissing his Sister, and with eyes of joy, telling *Pamphilia*, he was happy yet: then *Ollorandus* came, also *Perissus* with his Queen, who *Mellissea* had assuredly foretold, the constant being of their happy dayes. *Antissius* was the joyfull'st man alive, for he had such a lucky fortune given, as to love well, and to bee well belov'd, and what was most, to gaine that he most sought, and happily still to continue so; the like had *Selarina*, so as well it might be said, these of all the others had the happiest states. Good *Allimarlus*, and his loving love had promise to obtaine, so all are bless'd but those to whom best blessings did belong. All thus resolv'd, they thinke of their returne; *Pamphilia* homewards needs would take her way, but *Amphilanthus* gain'd so much at last, with helpe of faire *Urania*, and the rest, as she resolv'd to see *Morea* first, and therfore sent *Mellisander* unto *Pamphilia* to satisfie the Councell of her course, and to assure them of her speedy coming to them, after she had seene her Fathers Court; so with kind farewells they left *Delos*, soone after landing in *Messenia*, and with all this royall troope came to the aged King, whose joy was expresselesse grown, to see this company, the glory of those parts. Much did he welcome faire *Urania*, glad in his heart to see her, who he knew would bring such comfort and content unto her father, his beloved friend. Feasts were proclaim'd throughout the kingdom, Justs,[1] and all exercises were brought forth to welcome these brave Princes to the Court, *Pamphilia's* honour, honouring all the rest; yet could not that, or any other joy (though all joyes were so plentifully there, as bare accepting had injoyed them) give least delight to her, whose wounded heart did feede upon the sore, was lately given by cursed foretelling of her loosing fate. Into the garden woods (her old sad walke) she therefore went, and there as sadly did againe complaine. Alas *Pamphilia*, said shee, lucklesse soule, what cruell Planet governd at thy birth? what plague was borne with thee, or for thee, that thou must but have a vertue, and loose all thereby? Yet 'tis all one, deere love, maintaine thy force well in my heart, and rule as still thou hast: more worthy, more deserving of all love, there breaths not then the Lord of my true love. Joy then *Pamphilia*, if but in thy choice, and

---

1 'justs': jousts.

though henceforth thy love but slighted be, joy that at this time he esteemeth me. Then went shee to the Ash, where her sad sonnet was ingraved, under which she writ:

Teares some times flow from mirth, as well as sorrow,
Pardon me then, if I againe doe borrow
Of thy moist rine some smiling drops, approoving
Joy for true joy, which now proceeds from loving.

As she past on, she heard some follow her, wherefore looking backe, she discernd *Urania* and *Amphilanthus*, to whom she straight returnd, and with them walked a while Up and downe the wood, til *Amphilanthus* advised them to sit downe, so laying his Mantle on the grasse, the two incomparable Princesses laid themselves upon it, the king casting himselfe at their feete, as though the only man for truth of perfection that the world held, yet that truth made him know, that they were so to be honourd by him; then laying his head in *Uranias* lap, and holding *Pamphilia* by the hand, he began to discourse, which they so well liked, as they past a great part of the day there together, *Pamphilia* still desiring him to tell of his adventures, which hee did so passing finely, as his honour was as great in modestly using his victories in relation, as in gaining them: but when hee spake of *Steriamus*, his finding him and his passions, he did it so pretily, as neither could procure too much favor for him, nor offend her with telling it, yet still did she hasten the end of those discourses, which he no whit dislikt: but *Urania* desird stil to heare more particularly of him, as if she had then known what fortune they were to have, together; at last the king proceeded to the comming to the Iland, now cald *Stalamine*, anciently *Lemnos*, where (said he) the Lady is called *Nerena*, a woman the most ignorantly proud that ever mine eyes saw; this Ladies ill fortune was to fall in love with *Steriamus*, who poore man was in such fetters, as her affection seemd rather a new torture, then a pleasure to him: yet left she not her suite, telling him she was a Princesse descended from the kings of *Romania*, absolute Lady of that Iland, and for his honor (if he knew truly what honour it was to him) his love. He told her, 'Twere more credit he was sure for her, to be more sparingly, and silently modest, then with so much boldnesse to proclaime affection to any stranger. Why (said shee) did ever any man so fondly shew his folly till now, as to refuse the profferd love of a Princesse? and such an one, as if a man would by marriage bee happy, should bee onely chosen as that blessing? I am (said hee) truly ashamed to see such impudent pride in that sexe most to be reverenced: but to let you know, that you too farre exceede the limits of truth and understanding by vainely over-esteeming your selfe, I will assure you that I love a Princesse, whose feete you are not worthy to kisse, nor name with so fond a tongue, nor see, if not (as the Images in old time were) with adoration: nor heare, but as Oracles; and Yet this is a woman, and indeed the perfectest, while you serve for the contrarie. How call you this creature, said she? *Steriamus* was so vext that plainly she cald you so, as he in very fury flung out of the house, nor for the two daies which wee staid there, afterwards ever came more in: shee perplexing him still, leaving him in no place quiet, till she got your name. Then made shee a vow to see you, and follow him till shee could win him, letting her proud heart bow to nothing but his love, wherein the power of love is truely manifested. I would be sorry (said *Pamp[h]ilia)* to see her upon these termes, since she must (fild with so much spite against me) with all malice behold me. I wish she were here (said *Urania)*, since it is a rare thing surely to see so amorous a Lady.

Thus pleasantly they passed a while, till they thought it time to attend the King, who about that houre still came forth into the Hall, where they found him, and the adventure soone following, which he last spake of: for the kings being set, there entred a Lady of some beauty, attended on by ten knights, all in Tawny, her selfe likewise apparreld in that colour; her Pages, and the rest of her servants having that liverie. The knights being halfe way to the State, stood still, making as it were a guard for the Princesse to passe through, who went directly to the king; then making a modest, but no very low reverence, she thus spake.

Although your Majesty may well wonder, first at my comming, then at the cause, yet (I hope) that excuse I bring with it, will pleade for my justification. It is not (I am most assured) unknowne to you, although one of the greatest Christned Kings, that loves power is such, as can command over your hearts, when to all other powers, you scorn so much as yeelding. This hath made me a subject, though borne absolute; for whatsoever I seeme here to be, yet I am a Princesse, and Lady of the sweet, and rich *Stalamine:* but alas to this Iland of mine, came three knights (knights I call them, because they honor that title, with esteeming it higher then their own titles, for Princes they were, and the rarest some of them of Princes, as when you heare them namd, you wil confesse with me). One of these, my heart betraying me, and it self never before toucht unto the subjection of his love, wherof if he had bin so fortunat as to be able to see the happines was falle unto him in it he might have justly boasted of it. But hee slighting what his better judgement would have reverenc'd refused my affection, mine, which onely was worthy of gaine, being so well knowing as to dispise liberty in giving it selfe to any of meaner qualitie then *Steriamus*, whose proud refusall, yet makes me love him, and take this journey in his search, comming hither where I hop'd to find him, both because I heard he lived much in this Court, and that hee had bestowed his love upon your surpassing daughter *Pamphilia:* these brought me assurance to win him, having given my selfe leave to show so much humility as to follow him: next to see that beauty which he so admired, and as if in scorne contemned mine in comparison of it, which I thinke, Sir, if you well behold, you will judge rather to merit admiration then contempt.

Fair Lady said the King, that Prince you speake of hath been much in my Court, and not long since, but now indeed is absent, nor have we heard any thing of him, since his departure: for your love, it is so rare a thing to bee found in one of your sexe in such constant fury, as to procure, and continue such a journey, as that of it selfe (without the mixture of such perfections as you see in your selfe) were enough to conquer one, that could be overcome: but for his love to my daughter, there she is to answer you if she please, and cleare that doubt, since it is more then ever I knew that the *Albanian* Prince did love her, more then in respect unto her greatnesse.

Nereana turning to *Pamphilia*, earnestly, and one might see curiously, and like a rivall, therefore spitefully beholding her, thus spake. Well might hee (brave Princesse) bestow his affections where such unusuall beauties do abide; nor now can I blame him for prostrating his heart before the throne of your excellent perfections. *Pamphilia* blushed, both with modesty, and anger, yet she gave her this answer. *Madam* (said she) I know you are a Princesse, for before your comming hither, I heard the fame of you, which came swifter then your self, though brought by love: and in truth I am sorry, that such a Lady should take so great and painefull a voyage, to so fond an end, being the first that ever I heard of, who took so Knight-like a search in hand; men being us'd to follow scornefull Ladies, but you to wander after a passionate, or disdainefull Prince, it is great pitie for you. Yet *Madam*, so much I praise you for it, as I would incourage you to proceede, since never feare of winning him, when so many excellencies may speake for you: as great beauty, high birth, rich possessions, absolute command, and what is most, matchlesse love, and loyaltie: besides, this assurance you may have with you, that to my knowledge hee loves not me, and upon my word I affect not him, more then as a valiant Prince, and the friend to my best friends. Thus are you secure, that after some more labour you may gaine, what I will not accept, if offered me, so much do I esteeme of your affectionate search.

These words were spoken so, as, though proud *Nereana* were nettled with them, yet could she not in her judgement finde fault openly with them, but rather sufferd them with double force to bite, inwardly working upon her pride-fild heart, and that in her eyes she a little shewed, though she suffered her knees somewhat to bow in reverence to her. Answere shee gave none, scorning to thanke her, and unwilling to give distaste; having an undaunted spirit, she turned againe to the King, using these words.

For all this (said she) great King, I cannot thinke but *Steriamus* loves this Queene, for now doe I find a like excellent mind inclosed within that all excelling body, such rarenes I confesse living in her beauty, as I cannot but love his judgement for making such a choice and the rather do I believe he loves her, because he affects hardest adventures, and so impossible is it I see to win her heart, as it may proove his most dangerous attempt, yet bravely doth he, in aspiring to the best. Then brave king, and you faire Lady, pardon me, and judge of my fault or folly with mild eyes, since neither are mine wholly, but the Gods of love, to whom I am a servant. The King told her, more cause he had to commend, and admire her, then to contemne her, since for a woman it was unusuall to love much, but more strange to be constant. After this, and some other passages, *Amphilanthus* and *Ollorandus* came, and saluted her, giving her many thankes for their royall welcome: she kindly received them, desiring them to give her some light how to find *Steriamus:* they answered her, that from *Delos*, he was directed to an Iland, called *St. Maura*, but more they knew not, nor heard of him since his going thither with another good Prince, calld *Dolorindus.*

Having this little hope of finding him, she gave them thankes, and so took her leave, nor by any meanes could they perswade her stay, in her soule hating the sight of her, who though against her will had won, and then refused that, which shee for her onely blessing did most seeke after, yet would she honour her worth, which openly she protested, but never affect her person. Thus this strange Princesse departed, neither pleased nor discontented, despising any passion but love should dare think of ruling in her: but because she must not be left thus, this story shall accompany her a while, who tooke her way to the sea, thinking it better to trust her selfe with *Neptune*, then the adventures which might befall her, a longer journey by land.

DOROTHY LEIGH

The Mothers Blessing (1621)

In *Redeeming Eve*, Elaine Beilin identifies a category of texts produced by women which she calls 'Mothers' Advice Books', which includes Leigh's and Clinton's texts (both excerpted in this anthology).[1] Like other writers in this genre, Leigh wrote her text to guide her children in spiritual matters; thus most of these texts could perhaps also be classified as prayer books or books of meditations. However, unlike, for example, Elizabeth Jocelin, whose text was published posthumously by her husband, Leigh actively promotes her text for public consumption and makes the decision to publish it herself: she dedicates her book to Princess Elizabeth (the future Elizabeth of Bohemia, daughter of James I) and, in her dedication, it is apparent that she expects her book to be a guide for other parents, as well as for her own children. However, Leigh still makes reference to contemporary social mores when, in her epistle to her sons, she makes it clear that a major motivation for writing her book was to fulfil her role as a mother and her duty to her husband. Leigh's book was remarkably popular, going through over 15 editions between1616 and 1639. The copy text for the extracts reproduced below is BL, 4405. aa. 50, printed in London for John Budge in 1621, pp. 1–6; 14–17; 24–17; 46–53; 102–5.

Chap. 1. *The occasion of writing this Booke, was the consideration of the care of Parents for their Children*

My Children, when I did truely weigh, rightly consider, and likewise perfectly see the great care, labour, travaile, and continuall study, which parents take to

1 Elaine V. Beilin, *Redeeming Eve*, pp. 266–85.

inrich their children, some wearing their bodies with labour: some breaking their sleepes with care, some sparing from their owne bellies, and many hazzarding their soules, some by bribery, some by simony, others by perjury, and a multitude by usury; some stealing on the Sea: others begging by Land, portions from every poore man, not caring if the whole Common-wealth be impoverished, so their children be inriched: for them selves they can be content with meate, drinke, and cloth, so that their children, by their meanes, may be made rich, alwaies abusing this portion of scripture: *He that provideth not for his owne Family, is worse then an Infidel* (1. Tim. 5: 8.): ever seeking for the temporall things of this world, and forgetting those things which be eternall: when I considered these things, I say, I thought good (being not desirous to inrich you with transitory goods) to exhort and desire you to follow the counsell of Christ: *First seeke the Kingdome of God and his righteousnesse, and then all these things shall bee administred unto you* (Matt. 6: 33).

Chap. 2. *The first cause of writing, is a motherly affection*

But lest you should marvaile, my children, why I doe not according to the usual custome of women, exhort you by words and admonitions, rather then by writing: a thing so unusuall among us, and especially in such a time, when there bee so many Godly bookes in the World, that they mould in some mens Studies, while their Masters are mard, because they will not meditate upon them; as many mens garments moth-eate in their Chests, while their Christian Bretheren quake with cold in the streete for want of covering; knowe therefore that it was the Motherly affection that I bare unto you all, which made mee now (as it often hath done heretofore) forget my selfe in regard of you: neither care I what you or any shall thinke of mee, if among many words I may write but one sentence, which may make you labour for the spiritual food of the soule, which must bee gathered every day out of the Word, as the children of Israel gathered Manna in the Wildernesse [Exod. 16: 15, 35]. By the which you may see it is a labour: but what labour? A pleasant labour, a profitable labour: a labour, without the which the soule cannot live. For as the children of Israel must needs starve, except they gathered every day in the Wildernesse and fedde of it: so must your soules, except you gather the spirituall Manna out of the Word every day, and feede of it continually: for as they by this Manna comforted their hearts, strengthned their bodies, and preserved their lives; so by this heavenly Word of God, you shall comfort your soules, make them strong in faith, and grow in true godlinesse, and finally preserve them with great joy, to everlasting life, through faith in Christ; whereas, if you desire any foode for your soules, that is not in the written Word of God, your soules die with it even in your hearts and mouthes; even as they, that desired other food, dyed with it in their mouthes, were it never so dainty: so shall you, and there is no recovery for you.

Chap. 4. *The second cause is, to stir them up to write*

The second cause, my sonnes, why I write unto you (for you may thinke that I had but one cause, I would not have changed the usuall order of women) is needfull to bee knowne, and may doe much good. For where I saw the great mercy of God toward you, in making you men, and placing you among the wise: where you may learne the true written Word of God, which is the pathway of all happinesse, and which will bring you to the chiefe Citie new Jerusalem: and the seven liberall Sciences, whereby you shall have at least a superficiall sight in all things: I thought it fit to give you good example, and by writing to intreate you, that when it shall please GOD to give both vertue and grace with your learning, hee having made you men, that you may write and speake the Word of God, without offending any, that then you would remember to write a book unto your children of the right and true way to happinesse, which may remaine with them and theirs for ever.

Chap. 5. *The third cause is, to move women to be carefull of their children*

The third is, to encourage women (who, I feare, will blush at my boldnesse) not to bee ashamed to shew their infirmities, but to give men the first and chiefe place: yet let us labour to come in the second; and because wee must needes confesse that sinne entred by us into our posteritie; let us shew how carefull we are to seeke to Christ, to cast it out of us and our posterity, and how fearefull we are that our sinne should sinke any of them to the lowest part of the earth; wherefore, let us call upon them to follow Christ, who will carry them to the height of heaven.

Chap. 8. *The sixt cause is, to perswade them to teach their Children*

The sixt reason is, to intreat and desire you, and in some sort to command you, that all your children, be they Males or Females, may in their youth learn to reade the Bible in their own Mother tongue; for I know, it is a great helpe to true godlinesse. And let none of you pleade poverty against this; for I know, that if you be neither covetous, prodigall, nor idle, either of which sins will let no vertue growe where they come, that you need not faile in this: but if you will follow the Commandement of the Lord, and labour sixe dayes, and keepe the seventh holy to the Lord, and love him with all your heart, soule, and strength, you will not onely bee willing, but also able to see them all brought up to reade the Bible. *Salomon* that was wise by the Spirit of GOD, said, *Remember thy Creatour in the dayes of thy youth* (Eccles. 12: 1). And yee are also commanded, to *write it upon the walles of your houses, and to teach it youre children* (Deut. 11: 19, 20). *I know* (saith God) *that Abraham will teach his children, and his childrens children, to walke in my commandements* (Gen. 18: 19). Also I further desire you; because I wish all well, and would bee glad you should doe as much good as could bee in the Wildernesse of this world, that if any shall at any time desire you to bee a Witnesse to the baptizing of their Childe, that then you shall desire the person so desiring, to give you his faithfull word, that the Child shall be taught to reade, so soone as it can conveniently learne, and that it shall so continue, till it can reade the Bible. If this will not bee granted, you shall refuse to answer for the Child: otherwise doe not refuse to be a Witnesse to any: for it is a good Christian duety. Moreover, forget not, whether you answer for the Childe or no, to pray, that the Childe baptized may receive the Holy Ghost, with all other children of the faithful, especially when you are where a Child is baptized; for it is your duety to pray for the increase of the Church of God. *Pray for the peace of Jerusalem* (saith the Psalmist) *let them prosper that love thee* (Psal. 122: 6).

Chap. 11. *Children to bee taught betimes, and brought up gently*

I am further also to entreate you, that all your Children may bee taught to reade, beginning at foure yeeres old or before, and let them learne till ten, in which time they are not able to doe any good in the Commonwealth, but to learne how to serve GOD, their King and Country, by reading. And I desire, entreate, and earnestly beseech you, and every one of you, that you will have your Children brought up with much gentlenesse and patience. What disposition so ever they bee of, gentlenesse will soonest bring them to vertue; for frowardnesse and curstnesse doth harden the heart of a Child, and maketh him weary of vertue. Among the froward thou shalt learne frowardnesse: let them therefore bee gently used, and alwaies kept from idlenesse, and bring them up in the Schooles of learning, if you bee able, and they fit for it. If they will not bee Schollers, yet I hope they will bee able by Gods grace to reade the Bible, the Law of God, and be brought to some good Vocation or Calling of life. *Salomon* saith, *Teach a Child in his youth the trade of his life, and hee will not forget it, nor depart from it when he is old* (Prov. 22: 6).

Chap. 12. *Choice of Wives*

Now for your Wives the Lord direct you; for I cannot tell you, what is best to be done. Our Lord saith. *First seeke the Kingdome of God, and his righteousnesse, and all things else shall be ministred unto you* [Matt. 6: 33]. First, you must seek a godly Wife, that shee may be a helpe to you in godlinesse: For GOD said, *It is not good for man to bee alone, let him have a helper meet for him* (Gen. 2: 18): And shee cannot bee meete for him, except shee be truely godly; for God counteth that the man is alone still, if his Wife bee not godly. If I should write unto you, how many the Scripture maketh mention of, that have beene drawne to sinne, because they married ungodly wives, it would be tedious for you to reade.

The world was drowned because men married ungodly wives (Gen. 6: 2, 3). *Salomon*, who was not only the wisest man that ever was, but was also mightily indued with the Spirit of God, by marrying idolatrous women, fell for the time to idolatry (I. Reg. [Kings] 11: 4): Never thinke to stand, where *Salomon* fell. I pray God, that neither you, nor any of yours may at any time marry with any of those, which hold such superstitions, as they did, or as some doe now; as namely, to pray to Saints; to pray in Latine, to pray to go to Purgatory, etc. Let no riches or mony bring your posterity to this kind of tradition. The beloved Apostle of Christ saith: *Love not the world, nor the things that are in the world* (I John. 2: 15): for he knew well, that a little that a man loveth not, would suffice him: a little with a godly Woman, is better then great riches with the wicked. *Rebecca* saith, *I shall be weary of my life, if* Jacob *take a Wife of the daughters of* Heth [Gen. 27: 46], as if shee should say, If my sonne marry an ungodly Wife, then all my comfort of him and his is gone, and it will bee a continuall griefe to me, to see him in league and friendship amongst the wicked. If such a shame and sinne commeth upon my Sonne, as can by no meanes be helped, nor by no meanes be comforted, what availeth me then to live?

Bee not unequally yoked, (saith the Holy Ghost (2 Cor. 6: 14)). It is indeed very unequall, for the godly and ungodly to bee united together, that their hearts must be both as one, which can never bee joyned in the feare of God, and Faith of CHRIST. Love not the ungodly: marry with none, except you love her, and bee not changeable in your love: let nothing, after you have made your choyce, remove your love from her; for it is an ungodly, and very foolish thing for a man to mislike his owne choyce, especially since God hath given a man much choyce among the godly; and it was a great cause that mooved GOD to command his to marry with the godly, that there might bee a continuall agreement betweene them.

Chap. 25. *How to reade with profit*

I pray reade the story of *Job*, and not onely reade, but gather some fruit out of it, and ever when you begin to reade any part of the Scripture, lift up your hearts, soules and minds unto God, and pray privately or publikely; but of private prayer never faile: and desire God, for Christs sake, to enlighten your understandings, to sanctifie your hearts, and to make them fit to receive the good seed of his Word, and to give you grace to bring forth fruit to Gods glory: for Christ saith; *In this is my Father glorified, that you bring forth much fruit, and be made my Disciples* (Joh. 15: 8). And againe he saith, *Let your light so shine before men, that they may see your good workes, and glorifie your Father which is in heaven* [Matt. 5: 16]. Heere you may see you must glorifie God, and you must leave an example to the Church, that you serve and love God; this did *Job*: and, I pray God, for Christs sake, that you may doe the like; and that you may doe it, you must pray to God continually, yea, and in private, for his grace and assistance.

Chap. 26. *The preeminence of private Prayer*

This is the most excellent vertue and happinesse, that belongeth to private prayer, no man by any meanes can deprive a man of it. Some have had their Bibles taken away, that they could not reade: Preachers have been banished, that they could not heare: they have beene separated from company, that they could not have publike prayer, yet private prayer went with them: therby they talked with God, and made all their miseries knowne unto him, and craved his assistance in all their troubles. And this is the greatest comfort that all good Christians have, that no man can barre them from private conference with God. Then take heed you doe not barre your selves from it, since none else can doe it, and you know not what neede you shall have of it, nor what accident may happen to you in your lives, nor what need you shall have of it in the houre of death. Therefore, if you would alwaies have it, you must alwaies use it, and then you will see what profit will come by it, and then you will be humbly, faithfully, and familiarly acquainted with God.

WILLIAM GOUGE

Of Domesticall Duties (1622)

This text outlines the rules governing the orderly household, with a particular focus upon the relationship between a husband and wife. It is divided into eight treatises, moving from an examination of the relationship between a husband and wife, to the particular duties of wives, husbands, children, parents, servants and masters. Each treatise is divided into numbered subsections and includes a question and answer section, where Gouge anticipates objections to his points. Indeed, in the preface to this edition it is clear that Gouge has himself been subjected to criticism, as he writes: '*[t]his just Apologie I have been forced to make, that I might not ever be judged (as some have censured me)* an hater of women' (sig. π4r). In an attempt to placate his audience's objections to his delineation of women's subjection, Gouge inserts cross-references to the corresponding duties of husbands (footnoted in the following extract). The extracts reproduced below are from the third treatise, 'Particular Duties of Wives' (pp. 277–82; 284–6). The copy text (BL, 722. i. 22) was printed in London by John Haviland.

9. *Of wive-like sobriety*

A wives[1] outward reverence towards her husband is a manifestation of her inward due respect of him. Now then seeing the intent of the heart, and inward disposition cannot be discerned by man simply in it selfe, that the husband may know his wives good affection towards him, it is behovefull that she manifest the same by her outward reverence.

A wives outward reverence consisteth in her reverend { *Gesture.* / *Speech.* }

For the first, that a reverend gesture and carriage of her selfe to her husband, and in her husbands presence, beseemeth a wife, was of old implied by the *vaile* which the woman used to put on, when she was brought unto her husband, as is noted in the example of *Rebekah*: whereunto the Apostle alludeth in these words, *the woman ought to have power on her head* (Gen. 24. 65; I Cor. 11. 10). That cover on the womans head, as in generall it implied *subjection*, so in particular this kinde of subjection, viz. *a reverend carriage* and gesture. But most expresly this dutie set downe by Saint *Peter* who exhorteth wives to order their *conversation* before their husbands, so as it be pure, *with reverence* (I Pet. 3: 1).

This reverend conversation consisteth in a wive-like *sobrietie, mildnesse, courtesie,* and *modestie.*

By sobriety I meane such a comely, grave, and gratious carriage, as giveth evidence to the husband that his wife respecteth his place and the authority which God hath given him. Sobriety in generall is required of all women by reason of their sexe; and surely it doth well become them all: but much more doth it become wives: most of all, in their husbands presence. The Apostle in particular enjoyneth it to *Deacons wives*, yet not so proper unto them, but in a further respect appertaining to them not only as wives, but as the wives of Deacons.

Contrary to this sobriety is lightnesse and wantonnesse: which vices in a wife, especially before her husband, argueth little respect, if not a plaine contempt of him.

Object. Thus shall all delightfull familiarity betwixt husband and wife be taken away.

Answ. Though the aforenamed sobriety be opposed to lightnesse and wantonesse, yet not to matrimoniall familiarity: which is so farre permitted to man and wife, as if any other man and woman should so behave themselves one towards another as an husband and wife lawfully may, it might justly be counted lightnesse and sinne: instance the example of *Isaak* and *Rebekah*, who so sported together, as *Abimelech*, knowing them to be such as feared God,

---

1 Treatise 4. 4: 'Of Husbands Particular Duties'; 'Of an husbands wife maintaining his authority'.

gathered by that *sporting* that they were man and wife: for he thought that otherwise they would not have beene so familiar together (Gen. 26: 8, 9).

This familiarity[2] argueth both *liking* and *love*: and sheweth that the man and wife delight in one anothers person. But the lightnesse here condemned in a wife, is not so much a mutuall familiarity with her husband by his good liking, as a wanton dallying with others to his griefe and disgrace.

10. Of *wive-like mildnesse*

Mildnesse in a wife hath respect also to the ordering of her countenance, gesture, and whole cariage before her husband, whereby she manifesteth a pleasingnesse to him, and a contentednesse and willingnesse to be under him and ruled by him.[3] Excellently is this set forth in the spouse of Christ whose eies are said to be as *doves eies*, her *lips to drop as honie combs*, and she her selfe every way *pleasant* (Cant. [Song of Songs] 4, 6, 7): whereupon it is noted that she appeared to her husband as the *bright morning*, and that his heart was wounded with her. Assuredly the cleere skie is not more pleasant in time of harvest, then a milde and amiable countenance and carriage of a wife in her husbands presence. And though her husband should be of an harsh and cruell disposition, yet by this means might he be made meeke and gentle. For the keepers of Lions are said to bring them to some tamenesse by handling them gently and speaking to them fairely.

Contrary to this mildnesse is a frowning brow, a lowring eie, a sullen looke, a powting lip, a swelling face, a deriding mouth, a scornefull cast of the armes and hands, a disdainfull turning of this side and that side of the body, and a fretfull flinging out of her husbands presence: all which and other like contemptuous gestures are as thicke clouds overspreading the heavens in a Summers day, which make it very uncomfortable. They oft stirre up much passion in the man, and bring much mischiefe upon the wife her selfe.

11. Of *wive-like courtesie and obeysance*

Courtesie is that vertue whereby a wife taketh occasion to testifie her acknowledgement of her husbands superiority by some outward obeysance to him.[4] *Rebekah*, so soone as she saw *Isaak*, whom she had taken for a husband, lighted from her Camell and came to him on foot, which was a kinde of obeysance. This is not so to be taken as if no difference were to be made betwixt the carriage of a servant, or childe, and a wife: or as if a wife should bow at every word that she speaketh to her husband. Though in the kinde and extent of many duties the same things are required of wives which are required of children and servants, because God hath made them all inferiours, and exacted

2 Treatise 4. 42: 'Of an husbands familiar gesture with his wife'. **3** Treatise 4. 13: 'Of an husbands kinde acceptance of such things as his wife doth'; 4. 22: 'Of an husbands mildnesse'. **4** Treatise 4. 15: 'Of husbands courteous accepting their wives reverend carriage'.

subjection of all: yet in the manner and measure of many duties there is great difference: as in this, the obeysance of children and servants ought to be more submissive and more frequent. Yet because God hath placed authority in the husband over his wife, she is in every way to testifie her reverend respect of her husband, and therefore at some times, on some occasions (as when he is going on a journey for a time from her, or when he returneth home againe, or when she hath a solemne and great sute to make unto him, or when he offereth an especiall and extraordinary favour unto her, or (as I have observed such wives as know what beseemeth their place, and are not ashamed to manifest as much) when she sitteth downe or riseth up from the table) to declare her reverence by some obeysance. This cannot but much worke on the heart of a good and kinde husband, and make him the more to respect his wife, when he beholdeth this evidence of her respect to him. Yea it cannot but be a good patterne to children and servants, and a motive to stirre them up to yeeld all submissive obeysance both to her husband and to her selfe. For it may make them thus to reason with themselves, shall we scorne or thinke much to yeeld that to our father or master which our mother or mistresse thinketh not much to yeeld to her husband? Shall she bow to him, and shall not we much more bow to her? Thus a wives honouring of her husband by yeelding obeysance to him, maketh both him and her selfe to be more honoured of others.

Contrarily minded are they, who not only altogether omit this dutie, but also gibe and scoffe at the very hearing thereof, saying, thus wives shall be made no better then children or servants. But though scornefull dames deride these outward evidences of their subjection, yet such wives as feare the Lord ought not to be hindered thereby from doing their dutie: for by such evill examples they might be discouraged from every good dutie. It is sufficient that such holy women as trusted in God so behaved themselves. But for this particular, we know that equals scorne not upon occasions to performe this kinde of courtesie in making obeysance one to another: how much lesse ought wives, who are their husbands inferiours?

12. *Of wife-like modestie in apparell*

Modestie appertaining to a wife[5] is much manifested in her apparell. S. *Paul* requireth this modestie in generall of all sorts of women: but S. *Peter* presseth it in particular upon wives (I Tim. 2: 9; I Pet. 3: 3). For as it beseemeth all women, so wives after a peculiar manner, namely, in attiring themselves, to respect rather their husbands place and state, then their owne birth and parentage, but much rather then their owne minde and humour. A wives modestie therefore requireth that her apparell be neither for costlinesse above her husbands abilitie, nor for curiousnesse unbeseeming his calling. As a poore mans wife must not affect costly apparell, so neither Ministers, grave

5 Treatise 4. 49: 'Of an husbands providing things needfull for his wives body'; 4. 52: 'Of an husbands providing for his wife according to his own estate and ability'.

Counsellours, sage Magistrates, no nor conscionable Professours wives, hunt after new fashions, or in light and garish apparell attire themselves. It is a token of great reverance in a wife towards her husband, to have an eye to his place and state in her apparell.

On the contrarie, such proud dames as must have their owne will in their attire, and thinke it nothing appertaineth to their husbands to order them therein, who care not what their husbands abilitie, or what his place and calling be, they shew little respect and reverance to their husbands. Such are they, who are no whit moved with their husbands example: but though the mans apparell be plaine and grave, yet the wives shall be costly and garish. Yea many there be that stand in some more awe of their husbands sight, but shew little more respect unto him, who have their silken gownes, Beaver hats, and other like attire not agreeable to their place and state, lie in the countrey, if they be of the citie; or in the citie, if they be of the countrey, in a friends house where their husbands shall not know it, and when their husbands are not with them, weare them, and paint their faces, lay out their haire, and in everie thing follow the fashion. What can they which behold this thinke, but that such a wives care is more to please other light vaine persons, then her grave, discreet husband: or that her husband can nothing at all prevaile with her: which as it staineth her owne credit, so it leaveth a blot of dishonour even upon him. If the care of a wife were to give evidence of the reverence which she beareth to her husband, his desire and example would in this respect more prevaile with her, then the humour of her owne heart.

13. *Of a wives reverend speech to her husband*

As by gesture, so by speech also, must a wives reverence[6] be manifested: *this* must be answerable to *that*. For by words as well as by deeds, the affection of the heart is manifested, *Out of the abundance of the heart the mouth speaketh* (Matt. 12: 34). A wives reverence is manifested by her speech, both in her husbands presence, and also in his absence. For this end in his presence her words must be few, reverend and meeke. First few: For the Apostle enjoyneth *silence* to wives in their husbands presence, and inforceth that dutie with a strong reason in these words: *I permit not the woman to usurpe authoritie over the man, but to be in silence* (I Tim. 2: 12): the inference of the latter clause upon the former sheweth that he speaketh not only of a womans silence in the Church, but also of a wives silence before her husband: which is further cleared by another like place, where the same Apostle enjoyneth wives to *learne of their husbands at home* (I Cor. 14: 35). The reason before mentioned for silence, on the one side implieth a reverend subjection, as on the other side too much speech implieth an usurpation of authoritie.

Obiect. Then belike a wife must always be mute before her husband.

Answ. No such matter: for silence in that place is not opposed to speech, as

6 Treatise 4. 24: 'Of the titles which an husband giveth his wife'.

if she should not speake at all, but to loquacitie, to talkativenesse, to overmuch tatling: her husbands presence must somewhat restraine her tongue, and so will her verie silence testifie a reverend respect. Otherwise silence, as it is opposed to speech, would imply stoutnesse of stomacke, and stubbornesse of heart, which is an extreme contrarie to loquacitie. But the meane betwixt both, is for a wife to be sparing in speech, to expect a fit time and just occasion of speech, to be willing to hearken to the word of knowledge comming out of her husbands mouth. This argueth reverence. *Elihu* manifested the reverend respect, which as a younger he bare to his elders, by forbearing to speake while they had anything to say (Job. 32: 6). How much more ought wives in regard both of their sex and of their place?

Contrarie to this practise, who must and will have all the prate.[7] If their husbands have begun to speake, their slipperie tongues cannot expect and tarrie till he have done: if (as verie hastie and froward they are to speake) they prevent not their husbands, they will surely take the tale out of his mouth before he have done: Thus they disgrace themselves, and dishonour their husbands.

15. *Of wives meeknesse in their speeches*

Meeknesse in a wives manner of framing her speech to her husband, doth also commend her reverend respect of him.[8] This is an especiall effect of that *meeke* and *quiet spirit* which *S. Peter* requireth of wives; which dutie he doth strongly inforce by this weighty argument, *which is before God a thing much set by* (I Pet. 3: 4). Is a wives meeknesse much set by before God, and shall not wives hold it both a bounden dutie, and comely ornament, and grace unto them? As the forme of words which a wife useth in asking or answering questions, or any other kinde of discourse which shee holdeth with her husband, so her moderation in persisting, arguing and pressing matters, yea and the milde composition of her countenance in speaking, declare her meeknesse. If she be desirous to obtaine any thing of him, fairely she must intreat it, as the *Shunemite* (2 Kings. 4: 10): If she would move him to performe a bounden dutie, mildly she must perswade him. If she would restraine and keepe him from doing that which is evill, even that also she must doe with some meeknesse, as *Pilats* wife (Matt. 27: 19): If she have occasion to tell him of a fault, therein she ought to manifest humilitie and reverence, by observing a fit season, and doing it after a gentle manner as *Abigail* (2 Sam. 25: 31, 37): who as she wisely behaved her selfe in this respect with her husband in observing a fit season, so also with *David* by intimating his fault unto him, rather then plainely reproving him, when she said, *It shall be no griefe nor offence unto my Lord, that he hath not shed bloud causelesse.* This meeknesse requireth also silence and patience, even when she is reproved.

---

7 'prate': chatter, suggests speaking a lot and to little purpose. 8 Treatise 4. 24 (see footnote 6 above).

Contrary is the waspish and shrewish disposition of many wives unto their husbands, who care not how hastily and unadvisedly they speake to them, like *Rahel*; nor how angerly and chidingly, like *Jezebel*; nor how disdainfully, and spightfully, like *Zipporah*; nor how scoffingly, and frumpingly,[9] like *Michal*; nor how reproachfully and disgracefully, like *Jobs* wife (Gen. 30: 1; I King. 21: 7; Exo. 4: 25, 26; 2 Sam. 6: 20; Job. 2: 9). If they be reproved by their husbands, their husbands shall be reproached by them: and they are ready to answer again, not only word for word, but ten for one. Many wives by their shrewish speeches, shew no more respect to their husbands, then to their servants, if so much. The least occasion moveth them not only inwardly to be angry and fret against them, but also outwardly to manifest the same by chiding and brawling. The very object whereupon many wives usually spit out their venomous words, is their husband; when their stomacks are full, they must needs ease them on their husbands: wherein their fault is doubled.

Let wives therefore learne first to moderate their passion, and then to keepe in their tongues with bit and bridle, but most of all to take heed that their husbands taste not of the bitternesse thereof, no not though they should by some oversight of their husbands be provoked. It is to be noted how *Salomon* calleth the jarres which are betweene man and wife, *the contentions of a wife* (Prov. 19: 13), whereby he intimateth that she commonly is the cause thereof, either by provoking her husband, or not bearing with him.

16. *Of a wives speech of her husband in his absence*

The reverence which a wife beareth to her husband, must further be manifested by her speeches of him in his absence.[10] So did *Sarah* manifest her reverence, and so must all such as desire to be accounted the daughters of *Sarah* (Gen. 18: 12). The Church speaking of her Spouse, doth it with as great reverence, as if she had spoken to him. It was for honour and reverence sake, that the Virgin *Mary* called *Joseph* the *Father of Jesus*, when she spake of him (Cant. 5: 10; Luke 2: 48).

This sheweth that a wives reverend speeches in presence of her husband and to his face, are not in flatterie to please him and fawne upon him, but in sinceritie to please God and performe her dutie.

Contrary therefore to their dutie deale they, who in presence can afford the fairest and meekest speeches that may be to their husbands face, but behinde their backs speake most reproachfully of them.

---

9 'frumpingly': cross, ill-tempered; sneering or jeering. 10 Treatise 2: 'Of common mutuall duties betwixt man and wife'. Part 2. 36: 'Of husbands and wives like affection towards one anothers credit'.

LADY ELIZABETH CLINTON

The Countesse of Lincolnes Nurserie (1622)

Unlike other women writers in the 'Mothers' Advice Book' genre, Clinton is not writing from her deathbed and her advice is directed towards mothers in general, rather than to her children specifically. Moreover, whereas other texts in this genre were apparently very popular, Clinton's *Nurserie* exists in only one edition. Her central concern is to inform mothers of their duty to breastfeed: she dedicates her text to her daughter-in-law 'LA. Briget Countesse of Lincolne', who she claims practises this duty (sig. A2r). In addition to Clinton's dedication, there is a preface to the reader by Thomas Lodge praising both the form and the content of Clinton's text (sigs. A4r–A4v). Apart from this prefatory material, the text is reproduced below almost in entirety (pp. 1–12; 15–16; 17–21). The copy text is BL, C. 40. d. 30, which was printed in Oxford by John Lichfield and James Short 'Printers to the famous Universitie'.

Because it hath pleased God to blesse me with many children, and so caused me to observe many things falling out to mothers, and to their children; I thought good to open my minde concerning a speciall matter belonging to all childe-bearing women, seriously to consider of: and to manifest my minde the better, even to write of this matter, so farre as God shall please to direct me; in summe, the matter I meane, *Is the duty of nursing due by mothers to their owne children*.

In setting downe whereof, I wil first shew, that every woman ought to nurse her owne childe; and secondly, I will endeavour to answere such objections, as are used to be cast out against this dutie to disgrace the same.

The first point is easily performed. For it is the expresse *ordinance* of God that mothers should nurse their owne children, and being his ordinance they are bound to it in conscience. This should stop the mouthes of all replyers, for *God is most wise* (Isa. 31: 2), and therefore must needs know what is fittest and best for us to doe: and to prevent all foolish feares, or shifts, we are given to understand that he is also *All sufficient* (Gen. 17: 1), and therefore infinitely able to blesse his owne ordinance, and to afford us meanes in our selves (as continuall experience confirmeth) toward the observance thereof.

If this (as it ought) bee granted, then how venterous[1] are those women that dare venter to doe otherwise, and so to refuse, and by refusing to dispise that order, which the most wise and allmighty God hath appointed, and in steed thereof to chuse their owne pleasures? Oh what peace can there be to these

1 'venterous': taking a risk of incurring danger.

womens consciences, unlesse through the darknes of their understanding they judge it no disobedience?

And then they will drive me to prove that this nursing, and nourishing of their own children in their own bosomes is Gods ordinance; They are very willful, or very ignorant, if they make a question of it. For it is proved sufficiently to be their dutie, both by Gods word, and also by his workes.

By his word it is proved, first by *Examples*, namely the example of *Eve.* For who suckled her sonnes Cain, Abel, Seth, etc. but her selfe? Which shee did not only of meere necessitie, because yet no other woman was created; but especially because shee was their mother, and so sawe it was her duty: and because shee had a true naturall affection, which moved her to doe it gladly. Next the example of *Sarah* the wife of *Abraham*; For shee both gave her sonne *Isaac* suck (Gen. 21: 7), as doing the dutie commanded of God: And also tooke great comfort, and delight therein, as in a duty well pleasing to her selfe; whence shee spake of it, as of an action worthy to be named in her holy rejoycing. Now if *Sarah*, so great a *Princesse*, did nurse her own childe, why should any of us neglect to doe the like, except (which God forbid) we thinke scorne to follow her, whose daughters it is our glory to be, and which we be only upon this condition, that we imitate her well-doing (I Pet. 3: 6). Let us looke therefore to our worthy Pattern, noting withall, that shee put her selfe to this worke when shee was very old, and so might the better have excused her selfe, then we yonger women can: being also more able to hire, and keep a nurse, then any of us. But why is shee not followed by most in the practise of this duty? Even because they want her vertue, and piety. This want is the common hinderance to this point of the womans obedience; for this want makes them want love to Gods precepts, want love to his doctrine, and like step-mothers, want due love to their own children.

But now to another worthy example, namely that excellent woman *Hannah* (I Sam. 1: 23), who having after much affliction of minde obtained a sonne of God, whom shee vowed unto God, shee did not put him to another to nurse, but nursed him her owne selfe untill shee had weaned him, and carried him to be consecrate unto the Lord: As well knowing that this duty of giving her childe sucke, was so acceptable to God, as for the cause thereof shee did not sinne in staying with it at home from the yearely sacrifice: but now women, especially of any place, and of little grace, doe not hold this duty acceptable to God, because it is unacceptable to themselves: as if they would have the Lord to like, and dislike, according to their vaine lusts.

To proceed, take notice of one example more, that is, of the *blessed Virgin*: as her womb bare our *blessed Saviour*, so her papps gave him sucke. Now who shall deny the own mothers suckling of their owne children to bee their duty, since every godly matrone hath walked in these steps before them: *Eve* the mother of al the living; *Sarah* the mother of al the faithfull; *Hannah* so gratiously heard of God; *Mary* blessed among women, and called blessed of all ages. And who can say but that the rest of holy women mentioned in the holy scriptures did the like; since no doubt that speech of that noble Dame, saying, who would have said to *Abraham* that *Sarah* should have given children sucke? (Gen. 21: 7) was taken from the ordinary custome of mothers in those lesse corrupted times.

And so much for proofe of this office, and duty to be Gods ordinance, by his own *Word* according to the argument of *Examples*: I hope I shall likewise prove it by the same word from plaine *Precepts* (I Tim. 5: 14). First from that *Precept*, which willeth the younger women to marry, and to *Beare* children, that is, not only to *Beare* them in the wombe, and to bring them forth; but also to *Beare* them on their knee, in their armes, and at their breasts (I Tim. 5: 10): for this *Bearing* a little before is called nourishing, and bringing up: and to inforce it the better upon womens consciences, it is numbred as the first of the good workes, for which godly women should be well reported of. And well it may be the first, because if holy Ministers, or other Christians doe heare of a good woman to be brought to bed, and her child to bee living; their first question usually is, whether she her selfe give it sucke, yea, or no? if the answer be she doth, then they commend her: if the answer be she doth not, then they are sorry for her.

And thus I come to a second *Precept*: I pray you, who that judges aright, doth not hold the suckling of her owne childe the part of a true mother, of an honest mother, of a just mother, of a syncere mother, of a mother worthy of love, of a mother deserving good report, of a vertuous mother, of a mother winning praise for it? All this is assented to by any of good understanding. Therefore this is also a *Precept*, as for other duties, so for *This* of mothers to their children; which saith, whatsoever things are true, whatsoever things are honest, whatsoever things are just, whatsoever things are pure, whatsoever things be worthy of love, whatsoever things be of good report, if there be any vertue, if there bee any praise, thinke on these things, these things doe, and the God of peace shall be with you (Philip. 4: 8).

So farre for my promise, to prove by the word of God, that it is his ordinance that women should nurse their owne children: now I will endeavour to prove it by his *workes*: First by his *workes of judgement*; if it were not his ordinance for mothers to give their children sucke, it were no *judgement* to bereave them of their milke, but it is specified to be a great *judgement* to bereave them hereof, and to give them dry breasts, therefore it is to be gathered, even from hence, that it is his ordinance, since to deprive them of meanes to doe it, is a punishment of them.

I adde to this *the worke that God worketh in the very nature of mothers*, which proveth also that he hath ordained that they should nurse their owne children: for by his secret operation, the mothers affection is so knit by natures law to her tender babe, as she findes no power to deny to suckle it, no not when shee is in hazard to lose her owne life, by attending on it; for in such a case it is not said, let the mother fly, and leave her infant to the perill, as if she were dispensed with: but onely it is said *woe to her*, as if she were to be pittied, that for nature to her child, she must be unnaturall to her selfe: now if any then being even at liberty, and in peace, with all plenty, shall deny to give sucke to their owne children, they goe against nature: and shew that God hath not done so much for them as to worke any good (Lam. 7: 3), no not in their nature, but left them more savage then the Dragons, and as cruell to their little ones as the Ostriches.

Now another *worke* of God, proving this point is the *worke of his provision*, for every kinde to be apt, and able to nourish their own fruit: there is no beast that feeds their young with milke, but the Lord, even from the first ground of the order of nature; *Growe, and multiplie*; hath provided it of milke to suckle their owne young, which every beast takes so naturally unto, as if another beast come toward their young to offer the office of a Damme unto it, they shew according to their fashion, a plaine dislike of it: as if nature did speake in them, and say it is contrary to Gods order in nature, commanding each kinde to increase and multiplie in their owne bodies, and by their owne breasts, not to bring forth by one Damme, and to bring up by another: but it is his ordinance that every kinde should both bring forth, and also nurse its owne fruit.

Much more should this work of God prevaile to perswade women, made as man in the image of God, and therefore should be ashamed to bee put to schoole to learne good nature of the unreasonable creature. In us also, as we knowe by experience, God provideth milke in our breasts against the time of our childrens birth, and this hee hath done ever since it was said to us also, *Increase, and multiplie*, so that this worke of his provision sheweth that hee tieth us likewise to nourish the children of our owne wombe, with our own breasts, even by the order of nature; yea it sheweth that he so careth for, and regardeth little children even from the wombe, that he would have them nursed by those that in all reason will looke to them with the kindest affection, namely their mothers; and in giving them milke for it, hee doth plainely tell them that he requires it.

Oh consider, how comes our milke? is it not by the direct providence of God? Why provides he it, but for the child? The mothers then that refuse to nurse their owne children, doe they not despise Gods providence? Doe they not deny Gods will? Doe they not as it were say, *I see,* O *God, by the meanes thou hast put into me, that thou wouldst have me nurse the child thou hast given me, but I will not doe so much for thee*. Oh impious, and impudent[2] unthankfulnesse; yea monstrous unnaturalnesse, both to their own natural fruit borne so neare their breasts, and fed in their owne wombes, and yet may not be suffered to sucke their owne milke.

And this unthankfulnesse, and unnaturalnesse is oftner the sinne of the *Higher*, and the *richer sort*, then of the meaner, and poorer, except some nice and prowd idle dames, who will imitate their betters, till they make their poore husbands beggars. And this is one hurt which the better ranke doe by their ill example; egge, and imbolden the lower ones to follow them to their losse: were it not better for *Us greater persons* to keepe Gods ordinance, and to shew the meaner their dutie in our good example? I am sure wee have more helpes to performe it, and have fewer probable reasons to alleage against it, then women that live by hard labour, and painfull toile. If such mothers as refuse this office of love, and of nature to their children, should hereafter be refused, despised, and neglected of those their children, were they not justly requited according

2 'impudent': disrespectful, insolent.

to their owne unkind dealing? I might say more in handling this first point of my promise; but I leave the larger, and learneder discourse hereof unto men of art, and learning: only I speake of so much as I reade, and know in my owne experience, which if any of my sexe, and condition do receave good by, I am glad: if they scorne it, they shall have the reward of scorners. I write in modestie, and can reape no disgrace by their immodest folly.[3]

Now if any reading these few lines returne against me, that it may bee I my selfe have given my own children suck: and therefore am bolder, and more busie to meddle in urging this point, to the end to insult over, and to make them to bee blamed that have not done it. I answer, that whether I have, or have not performed this my bounden duty, I will not deny to tell my own practise. I knowe and acknowledge that I should have done it, and having not done it; it was not for want of will in my selfe, but *partly I was overruled by anothers authority,* and *partly deceived by somes ill counsell, and partly I had not so well considered of my duty in this motherly office,* as since I did, when it was too late for me to put it in execution. Wherefore being pricked in hart for my undutifullnesse, this way I studie to redeeme my peace, first by *repentance* towards God, humbly and often craving his pardon for this my offence: secondly by *studying how to shew double love to my children,* to make them amends for neglect of this part of love to them, when they should have hung on my breasts, and have beene nourished in mine owne bosome: thirdly *by doing my indeavour to prevent many christian mothers* from sinning in the same kinde, against our most loving, and gratious God. . . .

I doe knowe that the Lord may deny some women, either to have any milke in their breasts at all, or to have any passage for their milke, or to have any health, or to have a right minde: and so they may be letted from this duty, by *want,* by *sicknesse,* by *lunacy,* etc. But I speake not to these: I speake to you whose *consciences* witnesse against you, that you cannot justly alleage any of those impediments.

Doe you submit your selves, to the paine and trouble of this ordinance of God? trust not other women, whom *wages hyres* to doe it, better then your selves, whom *God, and nature ties* to doe it. I have found by grievous experience, such dissembling in nurses, pretending sufficiency of milke, when indeed they had too much scarcitie; pretending willingnesse, towardnesse,[4] wakefulnesse, when indeed they have beene most wilfull, most froward,[5] and most slothfull, as I feare the death of one or two of my little Babes came by the defalt of their nurses. Of all those which I had for eighteene children, I had but two which were throughly willing, and carefull: divers have had their children

---

3 In the next two pages, Clinton answers possible objections: firstly that Rebecca had a nurse and therefore did not breastfeed her child. Clinton argues that, as the nurse is later referred to as a 'maid' (i.e., virgin), she could not have been breastfeeding the child. Second, Clinton rejects the objection that breastfeeding ruins women's clothes, calling it an 'uncomely and unchristian' response. Third, in reply to the objection that it may endanger some women's health, Clinton argues that in that case they should not have got married or become pregnant. All these objections, but especially the last, according to Clinton, demonstrate women's disobedience of God. **4** 'towardnesse': readiness. **5** 'froward': disposed to go counter to what is demanded; difficult to deal with; ungovernable.

miscarry in the nurses hands, and are such mothers (if it were by the nurses carelesnesse) guiltlesse? I knowe not how they should, since they will shut them out of the *armes of nature*, and leave them to the will of a *stranger*; yea to one that will seeme to *estrange* her selfe from her *owne child*, to give sucke to the *nurse-child*: This she may faine to doe upon a *covetous composition*, but she frets at it in her minde, if she have any naturall affection.[6]

Therefore be no longer at the trouble, and at the care to hire others to doe your *owne worke*: bee not so *unnaturall* to thrust away your owne children: be not so *hardy* as to venter a *tender Babe* to a *lesse tender heart*: bee not *accessary* to that disorder of causing a *poorer woman to banish her owne infant*, for the entertaining of a *richer womans child*, as it were, bidding her *unlove her owne to love yours*. Wee have followed *Eve* in transgression, let us follow her in obedience. When God laid the sorrowes of conception, of breeding, of bringing forth, and of bringing up her children upon her, and so upon us in her loynes, did shee reply any word against? Not a word; so I pray you all mine owne *Daughters*, and others that are still child-bearing reply not against the duty of suckling them, when God hath sent you them.

Indeed I see some, if the wether be wet, or cold; if the way be fowle; if the Church be far off, I see they are so coy, so nice,[7] so luke-warme, they will not take paines for their *own soules:* alas, no marvell if these will not bee at trouble, and paine to nourish their *childrens bodies*, but feare God, bee diligent to serve him; approve all his ordinances; seeke to please him; account it no trouble, or paine to doe any thing that hath the promise of his blessing: and then you will, no doubt, doe this *good, laudable, naturall, loving duty* to your children.

If yet you be not satisfied, inquire not of such as refuse to doe this: consult not with your owne conceit: advise not with flatterers: but aske counsell of syncere, and faithfull Preachers. If you be satisfied; then take this with you, to make you doe it cheerefully. Thinke alwaies, that having the child at your breast, and having it in your armes, you have *Gods blessing* there. For children are Gods blessings. Thinke againe how your Babe crying for your breast, sucking hartily the milke out of it, and growing by it, is the *Lords owne instruction*, every houre, and every day, that you are suckling it, instructing you to shew that you are his *new borne Babes*, by your earnest desire after his word, and the syncere doctrine thereof, and by your daily growing in grace and goodnesse thereby, so shall you reape pleasure, and profit. Againe, you may consider, that when your child is at your breast, it is a fit occasion to move your heart to pray for a blessing upon that worke; and to give thanks for your child, and for ability and freedome unto that, which many a mother would have done and could not; who have tried and ventured their health, and taken much paines, and yet have not obtained their desire. But they that are fitted every way for this *commendable act*, have certainely great cause to be thankfull: and I much desire that God may have glory and praise for every good worke, and you much comfort, that doe seeke to honour God in all things. *Amen.*

---

6 'faine': pretend; 'covetous composition': excessive desire for anything, especially money. **7** 'nice': reluctant, unwilling.

C. F. (trans.)

Richard Smith, *The Life of the most Honourable and Vertuous Lady, the La. Magdalen, Viscountesse Montague* (1627)

The Life of the . . . La. Magdalen, Viscountesse Montague is an exemplary biography of a Catholic noblewoman written by her priest. While the chapter titles indicate that the qualities which defined an exemplary woman during this period did not differ according to religious affiliation, the means by which these qualities were manifested (and their political significance) were distinct. In both his preface and the text itself, Smith is acutely conscious of the connection between exemplary femininity and religious identification; in chapter III (which describes Magdalen's life at the court of Queen Mary), Smith comments: 'I desire my Countrymen to consider the notable purity of the maydes of Honour under Queene *Mary*, and the infamous reproches which some of them have incurred under Q. *Elizabeth*; and they will find what difference there is between a most chast Religion, and a most impure Heresy' (p. 7). The copy text is BL, 4903, bb. 47; the extracts are from pp. 27–31; pp. 34–8.[1]

Of her Zeale and Constancy in supporting, and professing the Catholike Fayth. Chap. XI

How gratefull i[t] is unto God to professe his fayth, it appeareth by those words of Christ our Saviour: *Every one that shall confesse me before men, I also will confesse him before my Father* (*Matth.* 10). And also on the contrary, how odious it is unto God to deny his fayth, is evident by that which followeth: *But he that shall deny me before men, I also will deny him before my Father which is in heaven.* But how constant the La. *Magdalen* was, not only in keeping, but even in professing the fayth of Christ, is evident, not by one act, but by the whole progresse of her life. For in those times, so turbulent, and so exceeding subject to mutation under the Kings *Henry* the VIII. and *Edward* the six, and Q. *Elizabeth*, she remayned most constant in her fayth. And if in the beginning of the raigne of Q. *Elizabeth* she went sometimes to hereticall Churches, that may rather be imputed to the defect of instruction, then want of zeale. For when she understood it to be unlawfull, she did most constantly abhorre it. And albeit that under Q. *Elizabeth* she endured no other persecution for matter of Religion, then that she was once accused to the pretended Bishop of *Canterbury*, her house twice searched, and her Priest once taken, and

1 The pagination is misleading here; the correct numbers should be 35–9.

imprisoned; yet was she prepared to suffer whatsoever it should please God, and did expose herselfe to the perill therof.

For wheras she had two goodly Mansion houses, the one upon the Thames side neere London-Bridge, in which, from the first beginning of persecution by Q. *Elizabeth* was a common retire for Priests comming in, and going out of England; and also a refuge for such as resided in London; wherin also one Priest had his residence, to minister the Sacraments to such Catholikes as resorted thither. In this house happened a matter worthy observation, which by the way I thought requisite to relate. When in the chappell of this house (which sometime appertayned to the Canons-Regular) some persons did dig in the place where the high Altar had formerly stood, under the same altar, or neere therunto they found a leaden coffin, and within it the body of a Religious man lapped[2] in linnen, and bound hard with cords, there buryed for many yeares before, so sound, flexible, and of so lively a colour, as it seemed alive. The La. Magdalen, as her selfe told me, putting her fingers into his mouth, did a little pull out his tongue, which was fleshly red and dry; and another with a knife cut a slash in the flesh, which within seemed very sound and fatty, no signe appearing either of Balme, or any other thing that could conserve that body from corruption. And of this matter many eye witnesses worthy of credit are yet living.

In her other house, which, being distant foure miles from *Hastings*, of that famous field which there was fought betweene *William* the Conquerour and King *Herald*, is called *Battell*, where herselfe with her family did for the most part reside, she kept there three Priests, one of whome was *M. Thomas More*, great grandchild, and direct heire of that famous *Syr Thomas More* sometime Lord Chauncellor of England, and a most worthy Martyr; who seeking to participate rather of the vertues, then of the lands of his great grandfather, having resigned unto his yonger brother a most ample patrimony,[3] and being worthily adorned with learning and vertues, and made Priest, devoted himselfe wholy to the conversion of his Country; in which industry he hath laudably employed himselfe these 20. yeares. Another was *M. Thomas Smith* Bachelor of divinity, a man no lesse venerable for his learning, worthy piety, and unwearyed endevour in helping his Country, then for his gravity of yeares. The third was my selfe. These did minister the word of God and the Sacraments, not only to the La. *Magdalen*, and her family, but to all Catholikes repayring thither. She built a chappell in her house (which in such a persecution was to be admired) and there placed a very faire Altar of stone, wherto she made an ascent with steps and enclosed it with railes: and to have every thing conformable, she built a Quire for singers, and set up a pulpit for the Priests, which perhaps is not to be seene in all England besides.

Here almost every weeke was a sermon made, and on solemne feasts the sacrifice of the Masse was celebrated with singing, and musicall instruments, and sometimes also with Deacon and subdeacon. And such was the concourse and resot of Catholikes, that sometimes there were 120 together, and 60

2 'lapped': wrapped up, disguised. 3 'patrimony': inheritance of property or estate.

communicants at a time had the benefit of the B. Sacrament. And such was the number of Catholikes resident in her house, and the multitude and note of such as repayred thither, that even the heretikes, to the eternall glory of the name of the La. *Magdalen*, gave it the title of *Litle Rome*. O happy woman, and true mayntainer of the Romaine fayth, who, where the very name of *Rome*, is to most so odious, that they use all their industry and utmost endevour to extinguish it; there, she did not only preserve the memory therof, but made it so famous, as she deserved to have the title therof given to her house. Let others nominate their houses by what titles they please, this only title of *Litle Rome*, given by Heretikes unto thy house, O Honorable *Magdalen*, by reason of the Romane fayth there professed, appeareth more famous, and more illustrious then all other titles!

Whiles she was present either at Masse or Sermon, she did not conceale herselfe for feare to be betrayed by some false brother, as it sometimes happeneth in England, but she did serve God publikely in the sight of all, that by her example she might encourage all; and when she walked abroad, by her Beads, or Crosse which she used to weare about her neck, she professed herselfe to be a Catholike, even to whatsoever Hereticall beholders; and so manifest was her religion, that scarce any in England had heard her name, who knew her not also to be a Catholike. She hindered none from hearing Masse in her house, if any Catholike had but the least knowledge of them, using these words: *Let these poore people come, they desire comfort as much as we.* And that which to others did strike a feare of trobles, was unto her occasion of great joy: to wit, when on festivall dayes, she saw a great number of Catholiks in her Chappell, in so much as she would sometimes shed teares for joy, and would thanke God, that by her meanes so many pious soules received spirituall consolation. Yea so far streched the fortitude of this blessed woman, in propagating the Catholike fayth, that she twice offered me leave to set up a Presse to print Catholike bookes in her house; which had bin done but that it was most difficult, and almost impossible in such an ample family to conceale such a matter from Heretikes.

This her couragious Constancy bred her great Envie, in her Hereticall neighbours: wherwith some of them being moved, presented her name, and the names of almost all her family [t]o the Judges in publike assises, for not observing the law of comming to Church every month. By which law it is commanded, that whatsoever person of the age of 16. yeares shall abstaine, for a month, from the Protestant Churches, shalbe confined within the compasse of five miles of his house, and shall pay, at the choyce of the King, either 20. ^{ff} every month, or two thirds of his lands and tenements, with the losse of all his goods: and if he keep any Catholike servant, he shall pay besides for each one, 10 ^{ff} every month. Upon which law the La. Magdalen was the first of the Nobility, that ever in England was accused in publike judgment. But she was so far from being terrified with this most hard proceeding, or dismissing of any of her servants, that, having intelligence therof, with a pleasing Countenance she sayd: *If the King will have two thirds of mine estate, I will joyfully live with the rest, and I thank God, who hath permitted me to enjoy it hitherto, and now permitteth that it be taken from me, for profession of his fayth.*

When there was danger of searching her house, she was more sollicitous of her Priests then of herselfe, and when in the time of that notorious powder-treason, she was terrifyed with extreme and imminent dangers, that she should not be able to keep a Priest in her house, she did not yet give way therunto, but dismissing the advertiser with a manly courage and full confidence in God, she sayd to her Confessor: *Let us say the litanies, and commit this matter to God.* And as well at other times often, as when she lay in her extreme infirmity, she strictly commaunded her children, encouraged her servants, and importunately exhorted all persons, to neglect the wealth of the world, constantly to retaine the Catholike fayth, and to repose their hopes in God. At which time Almighty God gave unto her this consolation, that by her example and admonitions she reduced[4] two of her neerest kinred into the lap of the church. And certainly it is to be much attributed to her Piety, that wheras she left living above thirty of her children, Nephewes and Neeces, she left them all constant professors of the Catholike fayth. And albeit she most tenderly affected her children; yet she so much preferred fayth before nature, that she would often say, she should exceedingly rejoyce to see any of them dye for the Catholike fayth. Neither do I doubt, but if Almighty God had tryed her, we should have seene in her the courage of the Mother of the Machabees.

Of the admirable Providence of God, towards the La. Magdalen. Chap. XIII

As this holy woman had a peculiar care to serve and please God, so it appeareth that correspondently he had a particuler providence, and care over her, wherof I will alleadge a few examples. Whiles she was a marryed woman she fell into an extreme, and continuall griefe and affliction of mind, upon the ruine of her family procured (as she sometymes sayd) by him in whome she had placed the hope of best reliefe therof; which melancholy affliction being such as exceeded the art of all Phisitians, and the counsaile and comfort of her friends, almighty God at length compassionating his servant, vouchsafed to cure her by another meanes. For in a dreame (as she particulerly related unto me) it was clearly and manifestly demonstrated unto her, what she should do to be freed of her inward griefe. Which when she had performed, (it being a very pious action) she was instantly cured of that affliction of mind, which no humane art, medicine, or counsaile could prevaile in. Of this triall, as she often confessed, she obtayned a better knowledge of her selfe, and more benefit then of any other thing; in so much that she confidently affirmed, that by her owne experience, she had learned that God worketh all things for our good [Rom. 8: 28]. And by this meanes almighty God did mervailously free her from spirituall desolations, and did convert them to her advantage and consolation; neither did he lesse protect her from her corporall enemies.

4 'reduced': brought back to a previous state or position; especially to right belief or conduct.

For wheras some few years before her death certaine Protestants, in hatred of her Religion, sought the destruction of her, and all her family, yet did they not prevaile in their malice. For the principle of them *Syr Tho. May*, being a Knight and Justice of peace, and having given commaundment for apprehending the servants of the La. *Magdalen*, was himselfe a litle after ignominiously convented[5] before publike authority, and cast into prison for debt, where he lay long, and at the setting forth of this worke, was shamefully dismissed of the Commission of the Peace. But the author and firebrand of all evils was *Nicholas Cobbe*, who a litle after he began to seeke the ruine of the La. *Magdalen*, had a knife thrust into his belly by his owne wife; and being for some hainous fact apprehended by officers, and even by heretikes pursued to punishment, did at length by letters beg pardon of the La. *Magdalen*; and what affliction yet expecteth him, almighty God knoweth. The third inveterate Heretike called *N. Benet*, who perceyving that nothing, of what himselfe and his Confederates had conspired agaynst the devout Lady, tooke effect, on a market-day held at *Battell*, falling on his knees before the gate-house of the Viscountesse, did vomit out his bitter imprecation, praying God to confound her, and all her family. But the dart which the impious fellow cast against heaven, did soone fall upon his owne head. For the third day after going early in the morning out of his house, he drowned himselfe in a pit at the townes end, towards *London*: Whereupon being taken up by Protestants, and by their judgement found guilty of his owne death, he was buryed like a dog in the high way.

At another time also when (as before is sayd) she was called in question for not going to hereticall service, she was so farre from incurring any detriment therby, as that it wrought her more security then before. For the Kings Councell by their publike letters addressed to the Attorny Generall dated the 19. of April 1607. commaunded that no sentence should proceed agaynst her. Which letters because they testify both the true allegiance of the Lady *Magdalen* to the King in temporalityes, and also that her molestation was meerly for Religion, I will here set downe part of them out of the originall which is in my custody. *For so much* (say they) *as the Lady Montague the wife of Antony Viscount Montague deceased, is lately called in question for default of conformity in Religion according to the lawes of this Kingdome; in regard that she is a Noble-woman, aged, and by reason of her fidelity, in the tyme of Q. Elizabeth, was never called in question, it pleaseth the Kings Majesty that in her old yeares she be free from molestation. These therfore, shalbe to require you, that you forthwith doe procure the accusation which is presented against her in the County of Sussex or elsewhere to be removed by writ of* Certiorari,[6] *into his Majesties Court of the Kings bench, and therby you shall have power to stay all processe against her person, grounded upon that presentment, or whatsoever other, till we shallbe further certifyed.*

---

5 'convented': summoned before a judge for trial or examination. **6** 'Certiorari': a writ issuing from a superior court, upon the complaint of a party that s/he has not received justice in an inferior court, by which the records of the cause are called up for trial in the superior court.

And in the same manner, when under pretence of search for the powder-traytors, Protestants did often search her house, she obtayned letters from the Kings Councell dated the 5. of April 1606. and subscribed by ten of the same Councell, that none besides fower by her self nominated, should search her house. By which letters she obtayned, that herselfe, whose house especially was alwayes free to all Catholikes, and who, in admitting Catholikes to the Sacraments, exposed herselfe to danger more then all others, proved thence forward to be more free from perill then any else. Whiles she lay in London in the yeare 1606. a Protestant seeing one goe into her house, whome he suspected (but falsely) to be one of those whome the King had proclaymed guilty of the powder-treason, declared the same to the Kings Councell, who instantly authorized Officers that most watchfully beset both hers, and the adjoyning houses, from Wednesday at two of the clocke in the morning, till Saturday noone following, and in that tyme very diligently searched hers, but especially her neighbours houses. The Lady *Magdalens* Priest was then absent, who was gone towards *Battell*, she intending immediatly to follow him; but understanding that two of her family were fallen grievously sick, instantly taking horse, returned to *London*, the same day that the search began. But almighty God so protected the Lady *Magdalen*, that at that very instant when the Priest, suspecting no danger, entred into the house, the Watchmen for a quarter of an hower were gone aside. And even two dayes after when it was esteemed most dangerous for him to remayne there any longer, he went againe out of the house in the middest of the watch, not one of them apprehending him, albeit amongst them there were three that knew him well, to be a Priest, and did speake of him to each other, and with their fingers pointed at him.

Not many monthes after the same Priest going from the house of the Viscountesse at *Battell*, was discovered to the aforesayd impious *Cobbe*, and the Priest being scarce out of sight, *Cobbe* having a vehement malicious desire to apprehend him, ran every way to hyre a horse to pursue him; but Almighty God did so preserve the Lady *Magdalen*, that he permitted not any Protestant, though her grievous enemyes, to lend *Cobbe* a horse, nor suffered him to follow the Priest a foote, or by out-cry (as is the manner in England) to rayse the people to pursue him; whereas the Priest, not suspecting any danger, walked on a foote pace, expecting one that was to accompany him, might easily have byn apprehended. Both which escapes the Priest himselfe ascribed to the piety of this Lady whome God protected, least her Priest being taken, her lyfe had byn brought in question for entertayning him.[7]

7 This chapter concludes with a brief 'rehearsall' of an incident in which a woman was miraculously unhurt when a slab of marble stone fell on top of her.

SUSAN DU VERGER (trans.)

John Peter Camus, Bishop of Belley, Admirable Events (1639)

In her dedication to Queen Henrietta Maria, du Verger suggests what the reader may gain from such a text: '[h]istories are the store-houses, where vertues are faithfully conserved to posterities veneration, and vices detestation . . . a glasse wherein to behold, adorne, and fashion out the life to what is worthy imitation, and to have in horrour and avoidance . . . they are the only monuments of truth, which they purely deliver, no way flattering, or concealing any thing' (A4v). In addition to prefatory material, the extract below includes one tale from the 'Singular Events' section of the book. The *STC*[1] entry for this text suggests that 'The Moral Relations' section was in fact translated by T. B. The copy text is BL, 243. k. 5 printed in London by T. Harper, 1639 (second issue); the extracts are from sigs. A6r–A7r; A8r–A8v, a7r–a7v; tale, pp. 125–31.

The Translator to the *Reader*

It is no small hazard that they runne, who oppose their writings to the view of the world, being subject to the detraction of every base tongue. I know full well considering the rudenesse of my wit, that it had beene very fit for me to have looked well, before I had leaped, and that this labour of mine might well have beene spared; but considering with my selfe, that there is not any Book, out of the which some good may not be drawn, it may be possible, that although my wit be wanting, and the refined language which many will expect (which wanting in the Author) because as hee saith; hee minded more the benefit which might arise by the matter, then the adorning it with curious termes, could not be supplyed by mee, unlesse I should both wrong the Author, and the History, by perverting the sence, yet the zeale which I had to profit others, may supply that defect. This makes mee not to use prolixe circumlocutions[2]*, but as much as possibly, to follow the Author: it is true, that many French words have divers significations, yet all tend to one sence, which if the Reader perceive any mistake thereby, I remit my selfe to his correction. I crave his upholding hand to helpe my weakenesse, and put my selfe under his faire censure. Reade so as becomes thee to reade, and do not scoffe at the Histories being good in themselves, though wronged by my want of language, doe not cast them into some corner of oblivion, but thinke with thy selfe that therein may remaine some parings*

1 *STC* is A. W. Pollard and G. R. Redgrave, *A Short Title Catalogue of Books Printed in England, Scotland and Ireland, and of English Books Printed Abroad, 1475–1640*, second edn. revised by W. A. Jackson, F. S. Ferguson and K. F. Pantzer (London: Bibliographical Society, 1986), 3 vols. 2 'prolixe circumlocutions': lengthy or protracted, circuitous expressions.

of great value, as a little gold lyes hid in a great masse of earth, keep them therefore together, and put them into thy consideration, and seriously examine them, and I assure thee thou shalt extract some pretious substance whereby to enrich thy selfe out of this masse, it is honey from another hive, though not made so fit for sale in this nation, as it might have beene, but howsoever it is merchantable ware, well conditioned, and for such I commend it unto thee. It must be a great and large feast which must containe dishes to satisifie every appetite: so I know both the Author and Translator shall incurre many evill censures, by such who are nice,[3] *and rather study to finde a fault, then to amend one; howsoever my best wishes shall ever be, that all may hereby receive profit, none prejudice, and chiefest and last, that God may have the praise and glory.* Farewell.

S. DU VERGER

Camus's Epistle to the Reader

The enterprise which I have taken in hand, is to wrastle, or rather to encounter with those frivolous books, which may all be comprized under the name of Romants, which would require the hands which fables attribute unto *Briarius*, or the strength which Poets give unto *Hercules*: the hands of that Gyant to handle so many pens, and the vigour of that *Heros* to undergoe so painefull a labour: but what cannot a courage do, animated by a zeale of pleasuring his neighbour, and provoked by desire to advance the light of vertue, and to lessen vice. O why hath not my pen the vertue to cure the wounds that these wicked books cause in this world! or at least, why cannot it devoure these monsters, which the writers of those aforesaid workes, meere inchanters of mindes cause to appeare in the formes of bookes? or like as an Eagles feather devours all other feathers, so might my pen devour all those other pens. When shall the light of vertue, and verity dissipate the shadowes of vice and vanity?[4]

But let them say on, some good soules (neverthelesse) whose dispositions are inclined to vertue, will be glad to finde profitable admonitions set downe, and sweetly mingled with varieties of pleasures fitting their humour. And therefore I have strove by the helpe of my pen to publish examples worthy to be noted, to the end that wee may grow wise by the good or evill hap of others. This is the marke aymed at by all these Events, which I have gathered in the great field of the world. It is your part, deare Reader, to extract honey out of the hardest stone, oyle out of the flint, studying a reformation of manners in this schoole of humane actions; Remembering alwaies that the secret (and if I may so say) the great worke of prudence and justice, is to avoyd evill, and to imbrace good.

---

3 'nice': fastidious, difficult to please. 4 The narrator then proceeds to discuss the desire to produce books that will be profitable for the reader and lead them to virtue.

The Unlucky Word: *The Eleventh Event.*

Life, and death, are in the power of the tongue, the mouth which tells a lye killeth the soule, much more when it blasphemeth or speaketh rash words, out of a desperate hastinesse, from which the Prophet prayed God that hee would preserve him. This makes St. *James* compare the tongue unto fire, whose least sparke being scattered by carelesnesse causeth great burning and consuming, he calls it likewise an universall iniquity, as being a thing that defiles the whole body and soule, like a tunne full of must[5] or new unrefined wine, which foules it selfe with its owne foame; he addes moreover that it is harder to be tamed then the fiercest beasts, yea worse then Serpents, Tygers, or Lyons, an unquiet evill full of deadly poyson, and the place from whence proceed cursings, and blessings [James 3: 5–6, 8–10]; indeed as there is nothing so light, and slippery, so there is no faculty in us whereunto we ought to take more heed, seeing the greatest part of sinnes come from thence: for very often doth it happen, that men utter so many, and inconsiderate speeches, that they are taken at their word, and they remaine punished for the same, before they can have so much time, as to crave repentance therefore. The history I am about to relate will shew you, that the predictions of the wicked do often turne to their owne ruine.

In a City of *Swisse* which the relation nameth not, a Surgeon as expert in healing bodyes, as he was ignorant in curing his owne soule of the wounds of vice, although he had a faire and very honest wife, not content to quench his concupisence[6] with her alone, had still some giddy passion or other in his soule, which stole away his heart from her, who only had the lawfull right to possesse both it, and his body, he led a most dissolute and deboist[7] life, which abandoned his health bringing it unto shamefull maladies,[8] and his reputation for a prey unto tongues, his wife perceiving his evill courses, laboured at first, by all the gentlest, and most convenient meanes she could devise, to withdraw him from those bottomless pits wherein he was sinking, both soule, body and estate, yet his untractable[9] mind amended not by all these remedies, but on the contrary, as sweet things (according to the Aphorisme) be most easily converted into choller, and as oyle feeds the fire which is quenched by other liquors, so her sweet admonitions made him more chollerick,[10] and the gentler he was handled, the worse he did sting.

Patience leaving this woman, whose head was troubled with a just jealousie, she fell to reproaches, and threates, which more vexed her froward husband, who replyed with sharpe words seconded with such heavy blowes, that the poor woman was half brained thereby. This harsh usage made her complaine to her parents, who made their moane unto the Magistrate, he finding himselfe obliged to redresse this disorder, caused the Chirurgion[11] to be cited before him, and ratled[12] him with so good a lesson, and withall caused him to pay

---

5 'tunne': storage cask, which could contain up to 252 old gallons of wine; 'must': mould. **6** 'concupisence': sexual appetite or lust. **7** 'deboist': debauched. **8** That is, sexually transmitted diseases. **9** 'untractable': stubborn or unchangeable. **10** 'chollerick': hot tempered, angry, irascible. **11** 'Chirurgion': surgeon. **12** 'ratled': frightened or intimidated.

such a fine, that he amended him, if not in effect, at least in shew, and commanded him on paine of imprisonment to leave of his accustomed haunting of such suspitious houses,[13] where if ever hee were knowne, to goe againe, hee would cause him to bee punished as an adulterer.

Here now becomes the sinner humbled, and he who rejoyced in his evill, and gloryed in his fault, endeavoured to hide his dissolutenesse, to avoyde scandall, murmur, and the punishment wherewith the Judge threatened him.[14]

At length having gathered together his affections and rather having setled his infections on a lost creature whose only frequentation had beene sufficient to defame those that resorted unto her, being one, that made an infamous trafficke of her selfe,[15] he made his hearte, and his body one with this woman. This stinking fire could not be kept so secret, but that it shewed it self by its smoke, and blacknes, his wife had already gotten some small knowledge of this matter, and already did the neighbours about the place, where he haunted begin to perceive it, and what veiles soever he invented to cover himselfe withall were meerly as spiders webs which discovered him in covering him.[16]

[Your jealousy] that puts a thousand hammering suspitions into thy head, makes thee imagine that I am now going to some lewd place; but thinke whatsoever thou wilt, I will be my owne master, and free as I list,[17] neither will I give any body account of mine actions.

His wife knew by these speeches that he was going to the place wherunto his unjust concupiscence drew him, for even as ulcerated bodies will not endure to be touched to the quicke, so likewise will guilty minds be netled, and moved unto anger being reprehended for their faults: well she proceeds in her exclamations, railes, and threatens him, he who had hardned himselfe in malice, disputing with this furious woman, rendred her word for word, threat for threat, and at last said unto her, if thy curiosity must needs be satisfied: know then, that in despight of thee, and of thy railing I am going to a bawdy house.

With these words he leapes upon his Mule, and spurring him hard to get from the bawling woman, who began to raise a rumour[18] about her gate by the complaints which she made unto her neighbours. This Mule being something untoward feeling himselfe extraordinarily prest by the spurre, began to kicke, fling, and leape, with such violence that he cast his master from his backe,

13 That is, brothels. 14 However, he could not keep this up for long, and begins to return to his old ways – at night and secretly. He lies to his wife, but she is suspicious of him. She tries to catch him out, but her husband is so successful at hiding his 'naughtines', that her neighbours 'accuse her of causelesse jealousie' (p. 128). 15 That is, a prostitute. 16 His favourite excuse was that he had to go out of town. He would then leave the city but come back at night and visit the 'adulteresse whom he frequented' (p. 129). His wife threatens to go back to the judge, but her husband laughs at her. One night as he is about to set off, his wife questions him about his journey. He replies as follows. 17 as free as I please. 18 'rumour': uproar, tumult, disturbance.

whose foote hanging in one of his stirrups, and the Mule setting himselfe to run with all his force drag'd this adulterer in such a manner on the stones, that his head shattered into many pieces, and his braines lay in the streets, this humorous beast stayed not till shee came before the doore of that infamous house whereunto he had so unluckily said he was going, and where his accustomed haunt was, there did the Mule stay with his unfortunate master who starke dead, and much broken remained there a long on the ground. Thus through divine permission by the death of this miserable man was discovered the commerce, which when he was living, he had kept so secret, and thus was preached on the house tops what he had committed in a close chamber, so was verified what the holy Scriptures teacheth us, that all creatures which breath on the face of the earth fight for Gods justice against those sencelesse persons, that violate his law, and stray from his wayes.

Presently this was bruited[19] all over that part, where this horrid spectacle was, and so farre were any from bewayling this disaster, that contrariwise every one adored and praised the Almighties justice in his chasticement, according to that of the Prophet, that he will make abundent retribution unto the proud, and that the good people rejoycing to see his vengeance, shall wash their hands in the bloud of the sinner [Ps. 59: 10].

ANON.

The Mid-wives Just Petition (1643)

The Mid-wives Just Petition: or, A complaint of divers good Gentlewomen of that faculty. Shewing to the whole Christian world their just cause of their sufferings in these distracted Times, for their want of Trading. Which said complaint they tendered to the House on Monday last, being the 23. of Ian. 1643. *With some other notes worthy of observation.* London: 1642. This petition testifies to the fact that midwives saw themselves as a distinct group or profession that was central to women's fertility and childbirth. Despite their lack of access to the universities and their failure to be allowed by the College of Physicians and the Chamberlen brothers to form a society (in 1616 and 1634 respectively), the petition illustrates nevertheless the distinct collective voice and concerns of midwives during this period. The following extract is from BL, copy text E. 86 (14), sigs. A2r–A4v.

19 'bruited': reported or made known.

The Midwives just Petition, or a complaint of divers Gentlewomen of that faculty, etc

Humbly Shewing,

That whereas many miseries do attend upon a Civill War, there is none greater than the breaking of that conjunction which matrimony hath once confirmed, so that womens husbands being absent at the Wars, they cannot enjoy that necessary comfort and benevolence which they expect from them: this, if well considered, is a shrewd matter and doth give beginning to a naturall depopulation of towns and Cities, when the causes of populous fertillity are any wayes hindered, whereby all places, especially this famous City, must needes become very thin of people, and great want of men fit for employment both for Church and State, and all corporations must necessarily from thence ensue, for men grow not upon a suddain, there must be a seed time before harvest, bearing of children before their birth, as we very well know, who in that kind have been great assistants unto women, and constant deliverers of much good to the Common-wealth.

And whereas we are called Mid-wives by our profession, wee knowing the cases of women better than any other, as being more experienced in what they sensibly suffer since the wars began, living the religious lives of some cloysterd Nuns contrary to their own naturall affections, if they could by any means help it without wronging their husbands: Our Petition shall therfore consist of many branches, whereby the injuries of women in this present age may be cleारely discerned, for it is a great wrong that women should want their husbands and live without comfort, whereby we Midwives are also undone, for as women are helpers unto men, so are we unto women in all their extreamities, for which we were formerly well paid, and highly respected in our parishes for our great skill and mid-night industry, but now our Art doth fail us, and little gettings have we in this age barren of all naturall joyes, and onely fruitfull in bloudy calamities, we desire therefore that for the better propagating of our owne benefit, and the generall good of all women, wives may no longer spare their husbands to be devoured by the sword, but may keep them fast locked within their own loving armes day and night, perfecting their embraces in such a manner as is not to be expressed freely, but may be easily conceived by the strong fancy of any understanding women; We Mid-wives must be as secret as night and close in all conceites, but wee know most assuredly that this would bring about much content, while our selves should feast high at Christnings, and nurses also should more frequently be paid for their monthly keeping of women: we have with much horror and astonishment heard of Kenton-Battayle, wherein many worthy members and men of great ability were lost to the number of 7563, who were buried thereabouts by the Churchwardens, Clerkes, and Sextons of the adjacent Parishes, as they have lately delivered upon their severall oathes, which doth make us humble Petitioners, that blood may not hereafter be shed in such a manner, for many men, hopefull to have begot a race of souldiers, were there killed on a sudden before they had performed any thing to the benefit of Mid-wives, which was a great losse and hinderance to the Common-wealth; whereby some maydes were deprived of promised marriage, and wives by the hand of death were quickly Widdowed, and with them the hope of posterity was also extinguished, it is therefore hereafter to be desired that Warre may not eate up and devoure the youth of this Kingdome, but that men may performe the blessing given to *Adam* by encreasing and multiplying, thereby to repayre the great havock and losse which this unnaturall War doth make in England. Heretofore the happinesse of the English women was compared unto heaven, but now they have just cause to tremble at the report of every gunne, which can send a speedy death to their instruments of conjunction and delight, without whom they are but halfe themselves, and being indeed nothing in themselves, from them they receive perfection, weight, and number, and grow as rich in children as they are in beauty, while wee Midwives shall fare and feede the better for their frequent christnings and gossipings.

We take notice what divellish new Engines for Warre are daily invented by the Cyclops and such like Artists, to destroy one another; namely the Poleax, Petronels, Carbines, Firelocks, Snap-hances, Pistols, nay cases of Pistols, Granadoes, and their hand Granadoes, and the Morter peices, and your terrible two-edged swords, able to affright poor women to see such naked weapons; then the Cavalliers, and your Dragoneers, and your Ingineers, which are those persons which exercised those weapons: such instruments were never used, or scarce seene in England, and all out of jealousies, doubts and feares; because you men will not confide in one another: All these weapons are but to destroy brave man which should be preserved and kept for better uses and purposes: It were farre better for those men that they followed their owne trade, and the old game of England at home with their wives; then for them to runne abroad to be a common souldier, and stand Sentinel two or three hours in the cold for a little Suffolk cheese and a peice of browne bread, and at length kill one another for eight pence a day, with the night to boot too: and it may be lose a limbe or some other good joynt: when indeed and in very good sooth they need not stand at home so long by nineteene parts, and have more thanks (if not reward) for their paines.

It were nothing so irkesome to us poor Midwives that our trade is now decayed, if the sword in the scabbard were used and employed against a Forreigne Enemy, it would not then be halfe so grievous, for the old proverbe saith, what the eye sees not, the heart greives not at. But we poor Midwives both see, and our hearts know it and now our tongues confesse it; that it is a lamentable case when the sonne shall goe out against the father; father against the sonne; brother against brother, and kinsman against kinsman, this wee speake is grievous to bee thought on; and we condole even to the lower-most angle of our triangular hearts.

Wee desire therefore that a period may be set to these unhappy differences, and that the generall and naturall Standard may no longer lye couchant,[1] but

1 'lye couchant': lie down.

that women may be fruitfull vines, that there may be no armes, but such as will lovingly embrace women, and because wee know that some upon different occasions desire to absent themselves from their best beloved, having first plunderd their chests and took away that they have, we desire that such men may be compelled forthwith to return to their wives, or beare on their heads the fortune which they have most worthily deserved, being guilty of that punishment by their long absence.

And whereas all are not Penelopes that can withstand the siege of a strong temptation, but must yeeld up the Fort to the flattering enemie of their long preserved chastity, it is better to keepe then to make that fraile sex honest: let not therefore the drumme wound the ayre no more with false stroakes, nor the pike bee bathed in the bloud of guiltlesse men, let not the sword ravish from our bosomes the delight of our lives: this word husband speaking benefit and comfort both to Wives and Mid-wives, since our felicity cannot subsist without the others fertillity and fruitefullnesse, and therefore let us Mid-wives whom it most nearely concernes, desire that some order may be taken; that the old song of England may not be againe revived, *now men of London*: And that the delicate sex of women may not lye in their bedds like cold marble images cut out by some Artificers hand, but being full of warme spirit and life, they may obliege the world to them by repairing the losses of this War, and have husbands as formerly at their command to maintaine them bravely, and bring them yearely under the delivering power of the Mid-wife, which cannot be done unlesse the Wars cease, and men returne againe unto their wives.

Moreover we have just cause to feare those dreadfull prophesies which point so directly at this age, foretelling that there should be a great scarcity of men, and such abundance of women farre exceeding the other, both in strength and number, so that a hundred should run after one, being a fearefull prodigy in nature, and a dearth to be more feared, then that of Corne or any other commodity:[2] Coals are not so necessary as husbands warme in bed, and comfortable at board, and therefore in this sad age it is fit to take a view of the calamities of women in other nations, for if men be scarce, all other plenty is nothing to women, they consumate our happinesse, and make us richer then all the precious stones of the Indyes, therefore most deplorable with the continuall losse of more Souldiers be, since they might live to comfort us, and declare their undainted valour in the soft and delightfull field of love: And whereas most certaine intelligence brought unto us, that many notorious Papists, doe resort to the Queenes Standard, lately by her erected at Newcastle: we desire likewise that our Standard may once again be set up in our City and Suburbs; for we mid-wives know that women are not so cold or out of soule, but that they can endure a fight bravely under a Standard, and can use a weapon as well as men if they get it in their handling, let their courage therefore teach them to fight for their owne priviledges, and if they prove the

2 Marginal note: 'Mother Shipton's Prophesie' – a number of prophecies between 1641 and 1685 have been attributed to Mother Shipton, or Ursula Shipton (including those prophesying the Civil Wars), although the *Dictionary of National Biography* suggests that she was probably a 'mythical personage'.

weaker vessels, yet wee Mid-wives desire that the distresses of widowed women bee looked upon with a charitable construction, not doubting but by all goodwillers to their sex, their Petition shall be regarded as the publique voyce of their long conceal'd affections, shewing also how greatly necessitated they have bin in their husbands absence, whose happy return shall satisfie their longing, and gives us the Midwives of London great cause to rejoyce. And we shall humbly pray, etc.

LADY BRILLIANA HARLEY

Letters (1642–1643)

Born at Brill in the Netherlands, where her father was Lieutenant-Governor (hence her peculiar name), Brilliana married Sir Robert Harley of Brampton Bryan in Herefordshire, and over the next 20 years wrote copiously to her husband, and later to her son Edward when he was studying in Oxford, then living in London, and finally serving in the Parliamentary army. The letters to her son Ned reproduced here date from 1642, and provide vivid evidence of the impact of the Civil War. While her husband was in London, Brilliana defended Brampton Bryan against Royalist forces during a six-week siege; she died (of the cold mentioned in her last letter) soon after the raising of the siege. The letters are transcribed from Thomas Taylor Lewis's edition for the Camden Society (1854).

For my deare sonne Mr. Edward Harley

My deare Ned – You cannot conceave how wellcome your letters are to me; yet beleeve I give you thankes for them. I receved one by the post and another by the carrier this weake. I see the distance is still keepe betwne the kinge and parlament. The Lord in mercy make them one, and in His good time incline the kinge to be fully assured in the faithfull counsell of the parlament. Our God has doun greate thinges, and I hope He will still glorify Himselfe in exerciseing of His mercy to us His poore sarvants. And, my deare Ned, it is my greate comfort that you have made your God your confidence; and this is most sure, He will never faile you. I purpos, and pleeas God, your sister Brill shall begine her journey to Loundoun on Monday next, and I hope shee will be abell to reache Wickham by wensday night; wheare I hop shee shall meete you at the Catterne wheele;[1]

1 'Catterne wheele': Catherine wheel; here the name of a public house.

shee much longes for this journey. Piner and Hackelet and Prichard goo up with her, and Mr Yeats and his wife. This night Mr Old tells me that Mr Nweport is maried; for my Lady Nweport sent to Shrewsbury to have the bells rounge for it. I wishe, and please God, I had the like ocation of rejoyceing. Your cosen Smith is now well. Doctor Wright stayed with him 3 or 4 dayes, and gave him somethinge, which has doun him much good.

I was ill when docter Wright was with your cosen Smith, and so I have bine sence he went; but I have taken nothing of him sence you went.

Deare Ned, be careful of yourselfe, and I beceach the Lord in much mercy to blles you whith all His bllessings, and I wisch you much joye in your nwe lodging in Lincons Ine. I beleeve your father misess you, and I am sure I doo. I pray you send me word how you like your commons; so I rest,

Your most affectinat mother, Brilliana Harley.

Apr: 29, 1642, Brompton Castell.

Mr Gower is very well pleased that he is chosen on of the ministers.

To her sonne Edward.

My deare Ned – I beleeve some buisines hindered your rwiting this weake or ells I should have promised myself a letter from you; for you know how much I love to have a letter from you. I should wisch you would begine a letter on Monday and take the whoole weake to rwite it in, that so I might know from you how thinges goo, and how your sister Brill pleases my lady Veare. I feare theare will be blowes struck. I pray God prepare us for thos times.

Deare ned, tell your father that the plumer of Woster is now casting the leads; the timber was very rotten; he seems to be an honest man. I wisched you with me to day, to see him cast it. I thanke God your brothers and sisters are well. I pray God blles you, and give you a comfortabell meeting with

Your most affectinat mother, Brilliana Harley.

I hope you doo not forget to spend some time to learne French. I pray you send me word wheather you doo. I hope you have reseaved the letter I sent by Mr Moore.

[no date]

For my deare sonne Mr. Edward Harley.

My deare Ned – Your letter by the post and by the carrier are both very wellcome to me; for besides the knowledge you give me of the publicke affaires, the assurance of your health is very deare to me. We all are ingaged deepely to pray ernestly to our God, that He will give both wisdome and corage to the parlament, and I hope the Lord will so guide them that the mouths of thos that would speake evill of them shall be stoped. I thanke you for desireing me not to beleeve rumors. I doo not; becaus I assure meself I shall heare the truth of thinges from your penn. It is the Lords greate worke, that is now a frameing, and I am confident, it will be finisched with much beauty, so that the very enimyes shall be enforsed to acknowledg it has bine the Lord that has rought for His caus and chillderen; against home they will finde that theare is no devination[2] nor inchantment.

We hard that the Kenttiche peticion was brought by 300 men,[3] and that 300 Loundoners meete them upon Blacke Heath and theare fought, and many weare killed. And now we heare that Sr Francis Wortly drwe his sword and asked whoo was for the king, and so 18 foolowed him. I thinke this later may be true; but for the fight upon Black Heath, I know it is not true.

I am glad our Heariford peticion is come to Loundoun, and I hope delivered before this; your sister, I hope, meet you at Wickcam on wensday last. Deare ned, send me word how my ladey Veere usess her, and how shee carries herself.

I pray God blles you with a large measure of gras and with all the comforts of this life.

Your most affectinat mother, Brilliana Harley.
May 6, 1642.

For my deare sonn Mr. Edward Harley.

My deare Ned – Now I thanke you for your letter by Mr Braughton, whoo brought it this day something late, so that I am shortned in time to rwite to you.

I thinke we must all acknowledeg Gods great mercy that the plot for the takeing of Hull was discovered.[4] I pray God derect the parlement what they ought to doo, for thy have enimyes enough to looke with an evill eye at what theare actions.

At Loudlow they seet up a May pole, and a thinge like a head upon it, and so they did at Croft, and gathered a grate many about it, and shot at it in derision of roundheads.[5] At Loudlow they abused Mr Bauges sonne very much, and are so insolent that they durst not leave theare howes to come to the fast. I acknowledg I doo not thinke meself safe wheare I am. I loos the comfort of your fathers company, and am in but littell safety, but that my trust is in God; and what is doun in your fathers estate pleasess him not, so that I wisch meselfe, with all my hart, at Loundoun, and then your father might be a wittnes of what is spent; but if your father thinke it beest for me to be in the cuntry, I am every well pleased with what he shall thinke beest. I have sent you by this carryer, in a box, 3 shirts; theare is another, but it was not quite made; on of them is not wasched; I will, and pleas God, send you another the next weake, and some handchersher. I rwite yesterday to you by the post of Loudlow, how my thankes was taken at Heariford.

I pray God blles you and keepe you from sinn, and from all other evills, and give you a joyfull meeting with

Your most affectinat mother, BRILLIANA HARLEY.

Your sister Doll is not well, shee has a great weakness upon her; yet I thanke God this day shee is somthinge better than shee was.
June 4, 1642: Brompton Castell.

---

2 'devination': magic. 3 Presenting petitions to Parliament was a common form of political intervention in the Civil War period. 4 A letter from the Parliamentarian Sir John Hotham had been intercepted and revealed a treacherous plot against Hull. 5 'roundheads': Popular nickname for Parliamentarians.

To her son Edward.

My deare Ned – If you beleave how glad I am to have this paper discours with you, you will read it as willingly as I rwite it. Since your father thinkes Hearefordsheare as safe as any other country, I will thinke so too; but when I considered how long I had bine from him, and how this country was affected, my desire to see your father, and my care to be in a place of safety, made me earnestly desire to come up to Loundoun; but since it is not your father's will, I will lay aside that desire. But, deare Ned, as you have promised me, so let me desire you to let me know how thinges goo. This night I hard that my lord Savile was dead. I desire to know wheather it be so or no; and wheather my lord Paget be goon to York. I heare that Mr Mason carride a letter from the justices of this country to the king at York, to let him know that they would sarve him with theare lives and estats. I thought it had bine with the petition they made for the bischops, but they say, it was with a letter. When dr Wright was with Mr James, he toold me you had rwite to him aboute Petters bill, and that it was well if some lords weare spoken to: he desires me to make some means to speake to my lord Brooke, which I promised him I would; thearefore, good Ned, eather speake yourselfe to my lord Brooke, or get somebody to speake to him, that when the bill comes into the lords he may further it. This day Mr. Davis came from Heareford, wheare he went to preach, by the intreaty of some in the town, and this befell him: when he had ended his prayer before the sermon, which he was short in, becaus he was loth to tire them, 2 men went out of the church and cryed "pray God blles the kinge; this man dous not pray for the kinge;" upon which, before he read his text, he toold them that M[in]isters had that liberty, to pray before or after the sermon for the church and state; for all that, they went to the bells and range, and a great many went into the church-yard and cryed "roundheads," and some said, "let us cast stones at him!" and he could not looke out of doors nor Mr Lane but they cryed "roundhead." In the afternoon they would not let him preach; so he went to the cathedral. Thos that had any goodness weare much trubelled and weepe much.

Mr Yats dous much lament doctor Wrights being theare, and says, if he can prevaile with him, he will persuade him to goo to Shreawsbery; which I should be very glad of, becaus he has gained him enemys in standing to geet voices for you. You may see by this how wicked they are growne. I think it beest to let doctor Rogers alone till it pleas God to give a fairer correspondency between the kinge and parlament, and then I wisch he may be soundly punished.

I thanke God I have bine very well, and so well, that I am abell to go abroode, when I am not well as I used to be.

I have sent you a shirt and hafe a dusen handcherchers and some powder for your hair.

I have rwitten so misrabell that I feare you will hardly reade it, but I hope, this will be leagabell to you, that I desire the Lord to blles you, as I desire my own soul should be bllesed: so I rest,

Your most affectinat mother, BRILLIANA HARLEY.

I hope I shall see you this summer; I long for it. I thanke God your brothers

and sisters are well. Deare Ned, send me word wheather my cosen Davis has lost Bucknell or no; he says he has not, and Mr Edwards says he has.
June 20, 1642. Brompton.

For my deare sonne Mr. Edward Harley.

My deare Ned – I longe to see you, but would not have you come downe, for I cannot thinke this country very safe; by the papers I have sent to your father, you will knowe the temper of it. I hope your father will give me full derections how I may beest have my howes gareded, if need be; if he will give the directions, I hope, I shall foolow it.

My deare Ned, I thanke God I am not afraide. It is the Lords caus that we have stood for, an I trust, though our iniquitys testify aganst us, yet the Lord will worke for His owne name sake, and that He will now sheawe the men of the world that it is hard fighting against heaven. And for our comforts, I thinke never any laide plots to route out all Gods chillderen at once, but that the Lord did sheawe Himselfe mighty in saveing His servants and confounding His enimyes, as He did Pharowe, when he thought to have destroyed all Israell [Exod. *passim*], and so Haman [Esther 3: 12–13]. Nowe, the intention is, to route out all that feare God, and surely the Lord will arise to healpe us: and in your God let your Confidence be, and I am assured it is so. One meet Samuell and not knoweing wheare he dwelt, Samuell toold him he was a Darbesheare man, and that he came lately from thence, and so he did in discours; the papis toold him, that theare was but a feawe puretaines in this country, and 40 men would cut them all off.

Had I not had this ocation to send to your father, yet I had sent this boy up to Loundoun; he is such a rogeisch boy that I dare not keepe him in my howes, and as little do I dare to let him goo in this cuntry, least he joyne with the company of vollentirs, or some other such crwe. I have given him no more money than will sarve to beare his charges upe; an becaus I would have him make hast and be sure to goo to Loundoun, I have toold him, that you will give him something for his paines, if he come to you in good time and doo not loyter; and heare inclosed I have sent you halfe a crowne. Give him what you thinke fitte, and I desire he may not come downe any more, but that he may be perswaded to goo to seae, or some other imployment. He thinkes he shall come downe againe. Good Ned, do not tell Martaine that I sent him up with such an intention. I have derected theas letters to you, and I send him to you, becaus I would not have the cuntry take notis, that I send to your father so offten; but when such ocations come, I must needs send to him, for I can rely upon nobodys counsell but his. I pray God blles you and presarve you in safety, and the Lord in mercy give you a comfortabell meeting with

Your most affectinat mother, BRILLIANA HARLEY.
July 19, 1642. Brompton Castell.

My cosen Davis tells me that none can make shot but thos whous trade it is, so I have made the plumer rwite to Woster for 50 waight of shot. I sent to Woster, becaus I would not have it knowne. If your father thinke that is not enoufg, I will send for more. I pray you tell your father that my cosen Robert

Croft is in the cuntry. My cosen Tomkins is as violent as ever, and many thinke that her very words, is in the Heariford resolutions. I beleeve it was Mr Masons pening. He is gone to Yorke, for when he carried the letter from the gentellmen in this cuntry, he was made the kings chapline.

For Mr Edward Harley.[6]

My Deare Ned,

[*When the*] in trihumph [*judges came*] to Worcester [*not to Hearifrd*] then in haste in the more courtly to what purpose lately trained otherwise [*so that theare*] the viccount [*was nothing*] enriching themselfes united under erle Simons and Richards to the hassard of [*doun against me*] or any [*at the bench,*] when I sent [*they sent for*] come protesting which now in feareing fell fomented by the supposed [*the trained*] up in pride [*bands, and have*] not cared to speake as they from him and her, so they goo one [*taken away*] meate colthes [*thearie armes;*] sowords [*some say to*] gaine as much as can be thought and have ended the a greete to [*give the armes*] up and [*to my lord*] Craven so when all is doun it comes all togeather [*Harbreds soulders*] and the [*that wante.*] mony? [*They say*] so when all was sould the mony came short and that was so [*that they gave*] gloves of [*half a crowne*] a peace to comfort them for all loses so they went away [*to every soulder*] howes [*to looke for*] the more [*enimyes*] wheare to the joy of ons hart to the greefe of frends [*every day. They*] went out [*have taken*] fisch good store which may last a greate while [*Mores lad,*] not bine [*and he is in*] a good howes [*prison at*] wheare is a greate many that loves tobacco came to [*Heariford,*] to live a time [*becaus he*] never thought it had bine so hard a matter hogg and dich [*was with*] Poell to [*me. If I had*] hard of the [*mony to*] come to morrow I had then sent it so now they must [*buy corne*] at another place [*and meale*] somewheare elles, or it will not doo well; but it is strange [*and malt*] I should not [*I should hope*] to render it [*to hoold*] as long as any but bravely and beaten and reduced to obedience [*out, but then*] write [*I have 3*] yeares heance will be acknowledged to the joy of all and greefe of [*sheeres against*] which for [*me . . .*]

When you have laught at the nonsense, please your self with this, that is reson; I thanke God we are well, though all would not have it so. I longe to heare from you. Desire your father from me to be carefull of himselfe, and I pray God blles you, and give you a comfortabell meeting with

Your affectinat mother, BRILLIANA HARLEY

Mar: 11, 1642.

To her son Edward.

My deare Ned – I cannot but venture thease lines, but wheather you are at Loundoun or no, I know not. Now, my deare Ned, the gentillmen of this cuntry have affected theair desires in bringing an army against me. What spoyls has bine doun, this barer will tell you. Sir William Vavasor has left Mr Lingen

---

6 This letter was written in a kind of primitive code: a sheet of paper with openings cut into it had to be laid over the paper on which the letter was written, revealing only those words which are here printed in italics.

with the soulders. The Lord in mercy presarve me, that I fall not unto theair hands. My deare Ned, I beleeve you wisch yourself with me; and I longe to heare of you, whoo are my great comfort in this life. The Lord in mercy blles you and give me the comfort of seeing you and your brother.

Your most affectinat mother, BRILLIANA HARLEY.

August 25, 1643.

Mr Phillips has taken a great deale of paines and is full of corage, and so is all in my howes, with honnest Mr Petter and good Doctor Wright and Mr Morre, whoo is much comfort to me. The Lord direct me what to doo; and, deare Ned, pray for me that the Lord in mercy may presarve me from my cruell and blood thirsty enemys.

For my deare sonne Colonell Harley.

My deare Ned – Your short but wellcome letter I receaved by Prosser, and as it has pleased God to intrust you with a greater charge, as to change your trope into regiment, so the Lord in mercy blles you with a dubell measure of abilitys, and the Lord of Hosts be your protector and make you victorious. My deare Ned, how much I longe to see you I cannot expres, and if it be possibell, in parte meete my desires in desireing, in some measure as I doo, to see me; and if pleased the Lord I wisch you weare at Brompton. I am now againe threatned; there are some souldiers come to Lemster and 3 troops of hors to Heariford with Sr William Vavasor, and they say they meane to visit Brompton againe; but I hope the Lord will delever me. My trust is only in my God, whoo never yet failled me.

I pray you aske Mr Kinge what I prayed him to tell you conserning Wigmore.

I have taken a very greate coold, which has made me very ill thees 2 or 3 days, but I hope the Lord will be merciful to me, in giving me my health, for it is an ill time to be sike in.

My deare Ned, I pray God blles you and give me the comfort of seeing you, for you are the comfort of

Your most affectinat mother, BRILLIANA HARLEY.

Octo; 9, 1643.

LADY ELEANOR DAVIES

Her Appeal (1646)

Lady Eleanor is unusual among female prophets of the time: in beginning her career as early as 1625, some two decades before the burgeoning of prophetic writing which marked the Civil War period; in her solitary position, isolated from the sectarian groupings with which most prophets were linked; and in her aristocratic status. Like many of the mid-century prophetesses, though, her writings brought her into conflict with the authorities, and she spent two years in prison in the 1630s. Her career as a prophet lasted until her death in 1652, and she wrote more than 60 pamphlets and petitions, addressing a wide range of personal and public preoccupations. Her father was George Touchet, Lord Audley and Earl of Castlehaven, and she married first Sir John Davies, and later Sir Archibald Douglas; both husbands burned some of her writings. She published under all three names, and constructed puns on her name: 'REVEAL O DANIEL ELEANOR AUDLEY' and 'DAME ELEANOR DAVIES NEVER SOE MAD A LADIE'. The title page of this pamphlet merely identifies her as 'Lady Eleanor', but in the copy text (Bodleian C. 14.11. Linc. (11)) 'Davis' has been inserted by hand. The text is 40 pages long; the extracts reproduced below are from pp. 3–10, 14–17, 25–7, 31–5, 38–40.

Having in the burthen of his precious Word been my self a partaker, made a publique Example, no mean one, concerning the way before the Lords coming to be prepared, Have thought it not unnecessary by what means it came to passe, to impart and publish the same unto your self, in making known some passages, the truth of which unknown not unto the whole world, almost ever since the Year 1625.

Shewing withall about a few dayes before the former Kings departure this life,[1] how first of all there came a Scotish Lad to this City,[2] about the age of Thirteen, one *George Carr* by Name, otherwise cald the dumb Boy or Fortuneteller, so termd, that spake not for some space of time, with whom it was my hap, upon a visit, to meet where some of them would needs send for this Boy, although few more jealous of such acquaintance or sparing, yet able to discern between such a one and Impostures, making bold before my departure thence, to direct him the way to my house, where care should be taken of him, not the lesse because a Stranger, accordingly who there abode, where no simple people, but expert and learnd as any, try'd no few conclusions; some instanced as here:

Sometimes who would take the Bible or a Chronicle, and open it, and close it again, then cause the aforesaid Youth to shew by signs and such like dumb

1 James I of England and VI of Scotland died in 1625 – a personally significant date for Eleanor Davies, as she began her prophetic career in that year. 2 London.

demonstrations, what was contained therein; which things he so to the life exprest and acted, as were it a Psalm or Verse then feignd to sing, though saw not a letter of the Book; and sometime that suddenly behinde him would blow a Horn, whereat never so much as changed his look, seemd so hard of hearing. And again thus, to sound him farther, one must stop his ears fast, and then what two whisperd at the other end of the Gallery, he must declare what they spake in the ear, as often as they pleased several times.

Having by that time gotten a whistling voice, as plain as any can speak, like a Bird; before that had used signs for the space of three Moneths, then no longer dumb or deaf.

To conclude, whatsoever it were he able to manifest it, whether containd in Letters enclosed in Cabinets, or by numbring how many pence or pepper corns in a Bag or Box before it was opened, or any thing of that kind fit for the vulgar capacity too; or when he was brought into any place amongst Strangers, one should write in several papers every ones Name, and he must give them accordingly to each his own Name, at first making as though he were in some doubt which way to bestow himself, where the chief Divines of the City present, some of them bestowing a shilling on him, without farther consideration thought it sufficient, etc. whilest others of that calling as liberal of their slanderous tongues; that no longer might be harbored in our house, likened to Friar *Rush*,[3] Servants had so incensed their Masters, setting all on fire, with Justices of Peace and Church-men, giving out he was a Vagrant, a Counterfeit, or a Witch. Immediately upon which the Spirit of Prophesie falling likewise upon me, then were all vext worse then ever, ready to turn the house upside down, laying this to his charge too: when laying aside Household cares all, and no conversation with any but the Word of God, first by conference with the Prophet *Daniel, cap.* 8 *ver.*13. I found out this place, *Then I heard* ONE *Saint speaking unto another Saint, said unto that certain Saint which* SPAKE (in the Ori[gi]nal (to wit) *The Numberer of Secrets, or the wonderful Numberer* (Hebr. *Palmoni*) *How long the Vision concerning the daily, and the Transgression making desolate, to give the Hoste, etc. And he said unto me, Unto Two thousand three hundred days, then shall the Sanctuary be cleansed.*

The sum of it this, as much to say, Inquired of such a one that spake not at first, How long from the Vision before this Prophesie shall be reveald, or whether I should be able, etc. as now about Two thousand two hundred years complete since the Captivity,[4] as here answered, O *Son of Man, for at the time of the end it shall be: Behold, I will make thee know in the last end of the indignation, for at the time appointed shall be the end, Daniel, cap. 8.*

And thus not only providing for that aforesaid admired Guest, but adored him almost; how it afterward came to pass, like that least of all seeds, how it sprang up, as follows: Here following the Prophets their order in these circumstances, Time, Persons, and Place, observed: Shewing,

3 In *The Historie of Friar Rush* (1620) a devil posed as a friar. 4 The exile and captivity of the Israelites in Babylon, often used as an image of exile and oppression.

In the aforesaid Year, 1625. the first of his Reign, the first of his Name, in the Moneth of *July*, so called after the first Roman Emperor, in *Berks*, the first of Shires, my self whose Father the prime Peer, or first Baron, being at my House in *Englesfield*, then heard early in the Morning a Voice from Heaven, speaking as through a Trumpet these words [Rev. 4: 1];

There is Nineteen years and an half to the Judgment day, and be you as the meek Virgin. . . .

And since prophesies Thundring Reign began, what judgments since the year 1625 *July*, shal give you a list of some of them; beginning at home first, where this Book of mine was sacrificed by my first Husbands hand, thrown into the fire, whose Doom I gave him in letters of his own Name (*John Daves*, Joves Hand) within three years to expect the mortal blow; so put on my mourning garment from that time: when about three days before his sudden decease, before all his Servants and Friends at the Table, gave him passe to take his long sleep, by him thus put off, *I pray weep not while I am alive, and I will give you leave to laugh when I am dead*.

Accordingly which too soon came to pass, for contrary to a solemn Vow within three Moneths married to another Husband, who escaped not scotfree: he likewise burning my Book, another Manuscript, a remembrance to the King for beware great Britains blow at hand, shewd him thus, *Dan.* 12. *And at that time shall Michael the great Prince stand up, and there shall be a time of trouble, such as never was since a Nation*, with the Resurrection in his time to be prophesied: and for a token of the time, *At that time the people shall be delivered*, their oppressors put to flight; where very Parliament-Stars shining for ever, as by such a solemn Oath taken there sworn, etc. the contents of that last chapter verily concluding with the first year of the present Reign, 1625. signified in those no obscure characters, *Blessed is he that waits* [Dan. 12: 12]: And comes to Three hundred thirty five; which being added unto the former reckoning of Two hundred and ninety, amounts to 1625. to wit, when this sealed Vision before the end shall be revealed, witnesse the troublesome time. . . .

And not thus resting, shall give you a passage or two more; shewing the holy Spirit besides speaking with other Tongues [Acts 2: 4], able to speak without a Tongue sometime, as by the Prophet *Ezekiel* to that rebellious Age [Ezek. 2], growing downward, by his portraying and the like: Shewing a few days before my deserting the aforesaid house, coming home, having been forth, and meeting with one seeming dumb, that came along with me, Soldier like, with a long garment or russet Coat, a red Crosse on the sleeve, by signs uttering his minde; where leaving him at door, without other notice, cold welcom, that had watched about the house all day, as they told me, calling to minde what trouble by such a one befel: presently after comes in Sir *Archibald Dowglas* my Husband from *Whitehall*, followed with a Chaplain and some six Servants, affrighted all, protested he had met with an Angel, whose custom always to give something to the poor, saying, He was come with him, a yong man very handsom, about his age, praying me to come forth; the Servants vowing he came out of Heaven, otherwise might (in the open fields) seen him afore suddenly who caught their Master by the arm.

Which man applying himself wholy to Sir *Archibald Dowglas* by such discoursing signs, of his late marriage, and former course of his life; would not a look vouchsafe me, till at last by locking, as it were, and unlocking a door, which I interpreting to presage prison, he assented unto this token bestowed on me; and Sir *Archibalds* back turned, then stept within the door as none should see him but my self, by pointing at him, and bending the fist, looking up as it were to Heaven, as though some heavy hand toward: About a Moneth after that lost both Reason and Speech, by like signs feign to learn his meaning, as he able to impart his minde, formerly shewd. . . .

And though these things not done in corner or remote place, restraind neither city nor court from such violent doings, vain laughter, like the crack of thorns, as the wiseman, *cap. etc.* [Eccles. 7: 6] shews to be regarded as much, of whose high presumption on record, such a blast from *Whitehall*, bearing Date *October*, 1633, *etc.*

From the Court of *Whitehall, etc.*

His Majesty doth expresly Command the Lord Archbishops Grace and his Commissioners, for causes Ecclesiastical, That the Petitioner be forthwith called before them for presuming to imprint the said Books, and for preferring this detestable Petition.

Sidney Montague

Which blasphemous accursed reference thus occasioned was upon their taking away of my Books printed at *Amsterdam*: But pressing to have them restored passages taken out of the Scripture concerning great *Babylons* blow, *Dan. 5. And the Beast ascended out of the Bottomlesse pit, Revel.11.* Applied to Great Britain, with the Hand-writing (*cap.* 5.) *Thou art found wanting, etc.* [Dan. 5: 27] extended from that Marriage feast, ever since 1625. into the year 1645. or from the abomination, etc. *Dan.* 12.

And of the aforesaid reference, thus; save Reverence his Grace the foreman of the Jury,[5] 1633. *Octob.* 23. commanding first a Candle, he that would not be warnd; but said *No more of that;* burnt the Book, saying, *My Lords, I have made you a smoother of Dooms-day, to be in such a year about Candlemas, till then she takes time enough: What shall we do next?* when with one voice, *Let her be fined Three thousand pounds, Excommunicated, no Bible alowed her, or Pen and Ink, or woman Servant; carry her away,* as by a Warrant under twelve Hands, confined to the Gatehouse for ever, where kept a close prisoner for two years, the Lords day unknown from another, the rest for brevity and modesty sake dismissed.

To this day which sentence and remains of the smoked Book remain extant in the Office, Trophees of his Triumph, buried by this *Achan*, this golden wedge or tongue [Josh. 7: 19–26], he sirnamed the *Beast*, from *Oxford* deriving his Name, smothered as other things.

And *Irelands* Massacre, was it not *October* 23? and *Edgehil* fight the 23?[6]

---

5 William Laud, Archbishop of Canterbury, described in these terms because he was head of the Court of High Commission. 6 Irish Catholics engaged in armed rebellion against the government of Charles I in October 1641, and atrocity stories of the massacres of Protestants circulated widely in England. The battle of Edgehill was fought between Royalist and Parliamentary forces in Warwickshire in October 1642; the outcome was inconclusive.

Then *Octobers* Wine-presse trodden; even shewing you a Mystery withal, *Rev.* 17. *The Beast that was, and is not, even he is the eighth, and is of the seven, and goeth into Perdition.* Even Kings and the Beast both put together; as from *H.8. H.7.*[7]etc. with his 7. years complete, and 8. current, the Archbishops lawless term before his going into prison, that Son of Perdition, translated to which place 1633.[8] *September*, his ascending then, etc.

And twelve Bishops at once, were not so many sent to the Tower? hee[9] likewise in the year 1644. *January* on a Friday put to death or killed, according to the tenor of that Petition, stiled in such a probrious maner; composed as follows:

Most humbly shews to Your Majesty,

That the Word of God the first year of Your happy Reign spoken to the Petitioner; upon Friday last did suffer early in the morning, the B. Beast ascended out of the Bottomless Pit, seven Heads having signified seven years his making War, hath overcome and killed them Books sealed with the Prophets Testimony, etc.

ELEANOR. 1633, etc.

For unfolding the mystery of which referring unto *Rev.* 11. . . .

So lastly shewing of that writ served on the Kings house, *Dan.* 5. this also *Zech.* 5. serves for our meridian;[10] *The flying rowl*[11] *twenty Cubits in length, visiting the house of the false swearer, the thief*; appointed for plundring perjured witnesses and Jurors, their whole Estate of it, robbing no few: And with the Coat of the present, displayed too, directed to the sign of the Flying Stork, not unlike the French vertugal[12] like sails, the wind in their wings, mounted into the Air, that fugitive Mother (Sorcerers wickedness) and her Daughter,[13] erecting Castles, old *Babels*, decaid Towers, (besides their *Sedans*) where the leaden weight bids beware the sheet of lead, *Zech.* as by her sitting in the midst of the Ephah carried, etc. So no farther of their cariage, his weighd in the Ballance, as hers measured by the Bushel.[14]

And to like purpose, witnesse our Parliament LIKE-WISE daily visited, though shewd our God a Revealer of secrets, *Daniel* 2. *Sets up Kings, puts down, changes Times and Seasons*, by the great massy Image, as that for ONE piece armed at all points (great Britains figure) points withal to Idolatries downfal for ever; And this although declared unto them aforehand, the *Whitsontide* before the Irish Rebellion brake forth, that the brittle iron feet of the fearful Image broken in pieces, served for the Kingdom of *Irelands* Sad Climat, the first blow to be given there; but so taken up, like the *Athenians*,[15] every one hearing and telling News, passages coming forth every day cry'd, spending their time in nothing else but such Commentaries.

7 Henry VIII, Henry VII. 8 This refers not to the imprisonment of Laud (in 1641) but to his accession to the archbishopric of Canterbury in 1633. 9 Archbishop Laud. 10 An imaginary circle round the earth used in navigation and orientation – loosely, here, guideline. 11 'rowl': roll (of papers) or scroll. 12 'vertugal': farthingale, a wide frame supporting a skirt. 13 Henrietta Maria, Charles I's French Catholic wife and her mother, who fled to the continent in the 1640s. 14 'Ephah' and 'Bushel' are both Biblical units of measurement; the sense seems to be that the King and Queen have both been assessed and found wanting. 15 This refers to the Athenian custom of exchanging news in the market place.

This the sentence of our aforesaid Wisemen, *What will this Babler say* [Acts 17: 18]?

That it might be fulfild, shewd and assurd also by our Savior, *There is nothing so secret and hid which shall be unreveald or not preacht on the house top* [Luke 12: 2–3], from that below, even to that High Court or House, yet asleep all, like that sleeper *Jonah* [Jonah 1: 5], or those bidden *sleep on* [Matt. 26: 45]: So *thank thee, O Father, that hast hidden from them these things* (of thy councel not made) *but to us reveald them*. Dan. 2.19. *Then was the secret reveald to* Daniel, *Ver.* 21. and 28. and 47.

Anagr. { *Reveale O Daniel*
Eleanor Audeley

FINIS.

THOMAS EDWARDS

The First and Second Part of Gangraena: or A Catalogue and Discovery of many of the Errors, Heresies, Blasphemies and pernicious Practices of the Sectaries of this time (1646)

Throughout the 1630s and into the next decade Edwards was a radical preacher; however, he responded badly to the upsurge of radicalism which marked the Civil War period, and *Gangraena* is a violent attack on its proponents. It caused great controversy, going through several editions which were successively revised and enlarged, and prompting numerous published responses. The text does not consist of a single narrative of the sectaries' activities, but is mixed in form; Edwards might be described as its editor as much as its author. The extracts reproduced here come from letters apparently sent to Edwards by various 'godly ministers' who describe encounters such as this one with a group of Anabaptists in Poole. The copy text, BL, 1471. g. 26 (1), is the third edition.

Because we did not allow enough to those bare Revelations, [they] had prepared an Argument (as they conceived) beyond all exception, to convince my Brother and me of the reality and use of them, and therefore invited us after the meeting, to a woman (their Oracle a Supernumary *Sybel*[1] at least) lately delivered of a childe, whose extasies they much confided in. When we came, we found the woman (who it is probable had but lately received some extraordinary comfort, but the Divel had had his Oar too in the Boat) dreamt into *Anabaptism*;[2] but with such Revelations, in which she told us Christ did appear to her gloriously, and perfumed her, (and she would ask those about her, whether they smelt not those perfumes) and told her, her childe must never be baptized. We were loth to trouble her to confute her, then being weakly, but left her with a promise to return when she had gained more strength. Meanwhile, on the next Sabbath, I had occasion to handle the common place of *Revelations*, from Gods appearing to *Abram*: In which Exposition, I told them how easily Satan might deceive under the habit of an Angel in them, with much more to that purpose. After that mornings exercise, these persons sufficiently baited my harmlesse expressions in private, as I heard: But God the next day made the truth of them publique; for the next news which I heard, was that this woman before spoken of, was grown perfectly distracted, which I my self since finde fully verified, for I have talked with her, and now she cryes out of seeing and smelling the Divel in every thing almost. It seems his design being wrought, he thought it fit to resume his proper likenesse. . . .

Among all the confusion and disorder in Church-matters both of opinions and practises, and particularly of all sorts of Mechanicks taking upon them to preach and baptize, as Smiths, Taylors, Shoomakers, Pedlars, Weavers, etc. there are also some women-Preachers in our times, who keep constant lectures, preaching weekly to many men and women. In *Lincolnshire*, in *Holland* and those parts, there is a woman Preacher who preaches, (its certain) and tis reported also she baptizeth, but thats not so certain. In the Isle of *Ely*, (that Island of Errors and Sectaries) is a woman-preacher also: In *Hartfordshire* also there are some woman preachers who take upon them at meetings to expound the Scriptures in Houses, and preach upon Texts, as on *Rom*. 8.2. But in *London* there are women who for some time together, have preached weekly on every *Tuesday* about four of the clock, unto whose preachings many have resorted. I shall particularly give the Reader an account of the preaching of two women, (one a Lace-woman that sells Lace in Cheapside, and dwels in *Bell-Alley* in *Colemanstreet*, and the other a Majors wife living in the *Old Baily*) who about a Moneth ago, the second *Tuesday* in *December* (as I take it) did preach in *Bell-Alley* in *Colemanstreet*, the manner whereof is as follows (as I had it from a godly Minister of this City, who was there present an eye and ear-witnesse of it.) Three women came forth out of an inward room or chamber,

1 In classical mythology, sibyls were wise women with gifts of prophecy and divination. 2 Literally meaning 'baptism again', the term was used as a derogatory description of members of groups which practised adult baptism.

into the room where they used to Exercise, and where some company waited for to hear them; These women came with Bibles in their hands, and went to a Table; the Lace-woman took her place at the upper end; the Gentlewoman the Majors wife sate on one side by her; the third woman stood on the other side of the Table; the Lace-woman at the upper end of the Table, turned her self first to this Gentlewoman, (who was in her hoods, necklace of Pearl, watch by her side, and other apparel sutable) and intreated her to begin, extolling her for her gifts and great abilities; this Gentlewoman refused to begin, pleading her weaknesse; and extolling this Lace-woman who spake to her; then the Lace-woman replied again to the Gentlewoman, this was nothing but her humility and modesty, for her gifts were well known; but the Gentlewoman refused it again, falling into a commendation of the gifts of the Lace-woman; whereupon this Lace-woman turned her self to the company, and spake to some of them to exercise, excusing her self that she was somewhat indisposed in body, and unfit for this work, and said if any one there had a word of exhortation let them speak; but all the company keeping silent, none speaking: Then the Lace-woman began with making a speech to this purpose, That now those dayes were come, and that was fulfilled which was spoken of in the Scriptures, That God would poure out of his Spirit on the handmaidens, and they should prophecy, and after this speech she made a prayer for almost half an hour, and after her prayer took that Text, *If ye love me, keep my Commandements* [John 14: 15]; when she had read the Text, she laboured to Analyze the Chapter as well as she could, and then spake upon the Text, drawing her Doctrines, opening them, and making two uses, for the space of some three quarters of an hour: when she had done she spake to the company, and said, if any had any thing to object against any of the matter delivered, they might speak, for that was their custome to give liberty in that kinde (but though there was a great company both of men and women) yet no man objected, but all held their peace: Then the Gentlewoman that sate at the side of the Table, began to speak, making some Apology that she was not so fit at this time in regard of some bodily indispositions, and told the company she would speak upon that matter her Sister had handled, and would proceed to a Use of Examination, whether we love Christ or no: and in the handling of it, she propounded to open what love was, and what were the grounds of our love, and how we should know it: and as she was preaching, one in the company cried, *speak out*: whereupon she lifted up her voice: but some spake the second time, *speak out*, so that upon this the Gentlewoman was disturbed and confounded in her discourse, and went off from that of love to speak upon 1 *John* 4. *Of trying the spirits*, but she could make nothing of it, speaking non-sence all along: whereupon some of the company spake again, and the Gentlewoman went on speaking, jumbling together some things against those who despised the Ordinances of God, and the Ministery of the Word; and upon that some present spake yet once more, so that she was so amazed and confounded, that she knew not what she said, and was forced to give over and sit down: The Lace-woman who preached first, seeing all this, lookt upon those who had interrupted her Sister with an angry bold countenance, setting her face against them, and she fell upon concluding all with prayer, and in her prayer she prayed to God about them who despised his Ambassadors, and Ministers that he had sent into the world to reconcile the world: whereupon some fell a speaking in her prayer, Ambassadors, Ministers, you Ambassadors! with words to that purpose: and upon those words she prayed expressly that God would send some visible judgments from heaven upon them: and upon those words some of the company spake aloud, praying to God to stop her mouth, and so she was forced to give over: In brief, there was such laughing, confusion, and disorder at the meeting, that the Minister professed he never saw the like: he told me the confusions, horror, and disorder which he saw and heard there, was unexpressible, and so he left them, fearing lest the candles might have gone out and they have faln to kill or mischief one another. The next Tuesday after there came a world of people, to the number of a Thousand first and last to Bell Alley, to hear these women Preach (as an Inhabitant of that Alley related it to me) but these women because of the multitude did not preach there, but preacht in the Old-Baily the same day, and since have Preached in a house near the French Church; where, on Tuesday being the 30 of *December*, another Minister heard them, and related that he saw a great deal of lightnesse and vanity among some that were at that Exercise. And on Thursday the 8 of *January* near the French Church at one Mr. *Hils*, one Mris. *Attoway* (one of the women by all the description of her spoken of before that Preached in Bell-Alley) at three of the clock in the afternoon Preached, where about fifty persons men and women were present. In her Exercise she delivered many dangerous and false Doctrines: As, 1. That it could not stand with the goodnesse of God to damn his own creatures Eternally. 2. That God the Father did raign under the Law; God the Son under the Gospel; and now God the Father and God the Son are making over the Kingdom to God the Holy Ghost, and he shall be poured out upon all flesh. 3. That there shall be a general restauration, wherein all men shall be reconciled and saved. 4. That Christ died for all; with several other Errors and conceits. She told them for her part she was in the Wildernesse, waiting for the pouring out of the Spirit. When her Sermon was done, (which was above an hour) she said, If any one had any exception against what she had delivered, she was ready to give forth her light; and if they could demonstrate that she had Preached any Error, to hear them; she said she was desirous that all the glory should be given to God, and was willing to impart or give out that dram of light the Spirit had given her; that she desired to lay down her Crown at the feet of Christ; and wished that shame and confusion might cover her face for ever if she had any confidence in her self. After she had done speaking, a Sister stood up first and objected what warrant she had to Preach in this manner; the Preaching woman interrupted her and said she knew what she meant, that she ought onely to Preach to those that were under Baptism: and further, she said she disclaimed that she took upon her to Preach, but onely to Exercise her gifts; for, she could not be evinced that any in the world this day living, had any Commission to Preach. Then her Sister asked her what warrant she had to Exercise thus; she Answered, her grounds were 1 *Pet*. 4. 10, 11. *As every man hath received the gifts*, etc. and that in the 10. of the *Hebrews*,

Exhort one another, and in the 3. of *Malachi* the 16. and in *Titus, That the elder women ought to teach the yonger*: Further she professed, That when she and her Sister began that Exercise, it was to some of their own Sex; but when she considered the glory of God was manifested in Babes and Sucklings, and that she was desired by some to admit of all that pleased to come, she could not deny to impart those things the Spirit had communicated to her: but still her Sister insisted upon the former objection, and said she ought not to Preach to the world; and said she would speak more freely, but that there was a multitude there. Then another Sister spake to this second Sister, that truth sought no corners, why should she say so? Then a man stood up and asked the Preaching-woman what she meant by those that were under Baptism: she Answered, under a Gospel order: He Replied, what was that? she said, all that were baptised being not believers. Then a second was objected, Who baptised *Simon Magus, Ananias* and *Saphira* [Acts 5]? Mris. *Attoway* Answered, she doubted whether they did according to their Commission in baptising them. In her prayer this she-preacher prayed God that all those who were present, and did not acknowledge his weak ones that spake for the spirit of God, that he would discover the iniquity of their hearts. She also in her prayer gave thanks for the occasion of their meeting, that they had been quiet without distraction, which they were not the former day: and to the men present that brought an Argument for Infants Baptism, she gave an Answer to it. He asked her what Baptism was? she Answered, she was not very fit to Argue those Questions, and went from the Table to the fire side: and then another Sister said, You have heard what was delivered, and may rest satisfied. I was informed also for certain this week by a Minister who came out of *Kent*, that at *Brasteed* where Mr. *Saltmarsh* is Preacher, there is a woman Preacher, (one at least if not more) in which company besides Preaching, 'tis reported (as this Minister saith, very commonly) that they break Bread also, and every one in their order.

HENRY JESSEY

The Exceeding Riches of Grace Advanced By the Spirit of Grace, in an Empty Nothing Creature, viz. Mris. Sarah Wight (1647)

The remarkable title page of this work is worth quoting in full, in that it epitomises the concerns of a whole body of mid-seventeenth-century texts preoccupied with despair and redemption: *The Exceeding Riches of* Grace Advanced *By the Spirit of Grace, in an* Empty Nothing Creature, *viz. Mris* SARAH WIGHT, *Lately hopeles and restles, her soule dwelling as far from Peace or hopes of Mercy, as ever was any.* Now hopefull, and joyfull in the LORD, *that hath caused* LIGHT *to shine out of* DARKNES; *that in and by this Earthen Vessell, holds forth his Own eternall love, and the Glorious Grace of his dear Son, to the* CHIEFEST OF SINNERS. Who desired that others might hear and know, what the LORD had done for her soul, (that was so terrified day and night:) and might neither presume, nor despair and murmure against God, as shee hath done. *Published for the Refreshing of poor souls, by an* Eye and Ear-witnes of a good part thereof, HENRY JESSE, a servant of *JESUS CHRIST.*, (London, printed by Matthew Simmons for Henry Overton and Hannah Allen, 1647). Copy text is BL, 1418. i. 52, 159pp.

The text records the experiences and sayings of Sarah Wight while, as a teenage girl, she spent more than two months in a state of spiritual ecstasy. Wight's words to her many visitors in this period were apparently recorded by an amanuensis, and the text is written in an unstable mixture of the first and third person. It was widely read, running to eight editions over a period of 20 years. The circumstances surrounding *The Exceeding Riches of Grace* offer an insight into the nonconformist networks of the mid-century: Hannah Allen, who published it, was an important radical publisher and wrote an account of her own spiritual experiences, *Satan his methods and Malice Baffled* (1683); Henry Jessey was a Baptist pastor who worked on a revised translation of the Bible, and supported the rights of the Jews in England. The first extract establishes the context of Sarah Wight's religious experiences (pp. 6–8).

From her childhood she was of a tender heart, and oft afflicted in Spirit: Her Temptations were not so great, till shee was about twelve yeares old; since which, they have continued with more violence till *Aprill* 6. 1647. it being about 4 yeares. (Shee is not *sixteen* yeeres old [as her Mother saith,] till September following.)

The beginning of her more violent Temptations was thus: Her superiour bid her doe a small thing, judging it meet and lawfull: Shee did it, doubtingly, fearing it was unlawfull: and as shee did it, a great Trembling in her hands and body fell upon her: being condemned in her selfe. About a moneth after, returning home, having been abroad, shee had lost her hood, and knew she had lost it. Her Mother asked her, for her hood. She suddenly answered, My Grandmother hath it. Her heart condemned her instantly, and trembled again exceedingly. And these were the first chiefe occasions of her deep despaire: And upon this, shee had cast into her Conscience, that *shee was both a Thiefe, and a lyar*, and was terrified ever since, that shee was shut out of Heaven, and must be damn'd, damn'd.

In the last four yeeres, shee was oft in such extremities, shee could beleeve nothing but Hell and Wrath – to be her Portion; and other times, that there was no heaven, nor hell, but in our Conscience: and that shee was *damn'd already, being an unbeleever*; and therefore if she could dispatch this life of hers, there was an end of her sorrows. A subtle deceit of the old Serpent![1] Hence

1 The devil.

shee oft attempted wickedly to destroy herself, as by drowning, strangling, stabbing, seeking to beat out her braines, wretchedly bruising, and wounding her self. The chiefe cause of *such* weaknes since. . . .[2]

About a moneth before her *great deliverance*, Satan having but a short time so to torment her, her stormes and tempests were greatest of all. Shee was grievously hurried with Temptations; so terrified, shee could not rest at all, for many dayes and nights together. Whilst shee was able to goe abroad, her Mother would have her goe with her to heare Sermons, on the *Lords dayes*, and on the *Lecture*-days there.[3] One *Lecture*-day shee was gone forth before her Mother; who missing her, went to the Assembly, and not finding her there, came forth, and suddenly went, and sent towards *Thames* to seek her: where shee had been, to have cast her selfe in, but was stayd from it by the power and goodnesse of God: and being found, shee had a command on her spirit to goe to heare that Sermon, and her Mother coming to her, shee readily yeelded to goe with her Mother to the *Lecture* there. Where was proved, what favour God will shew towards the stock of the *Jewes*, that he will *graff* multitudes of them *into their own Olive*,[4] pardoning their sinnes against Christ, restoring them to great dignity, etc. He that preached went in to Mris *Wights* house there after the Sermon, and spake with her daughter, asking her, if the Lord spake any peace to her thereby. Shee answered, *shee would not for all the world, but shee had heard that Sermon*. Being asked, why so? Shee said, *That God will shew mercy to the Jewes; and they are the basest people on earth*; that so hate the Name of Christians, and much more Christ himselfe: *and yet that God will call them*; This supported her a little at that present; but it stayed not with her, and shee was againe under horrid Temptations, to beleeve there was *no God, and no Devill: no Heaven, and no Hell, but what shee felt within her.*

One day being strongly carried on in that temptation, *that there was no other Hell, but here in the Conscience*; As that famous Mris *Honywood* had said and done with a *Venice Glasse*,[5] (who said *shee was as sure to be damn'd, as that was to break*; and therewith threw it from her to break it; and yet it brak not;) so did shee with a little white drinking cup, an earthen cup; shee said, *As sure as this cup shall breake, there is no other Hell*: and therewith shee threw the cup with violence, against the far side of the chamber; and though it light against the wood, it brak not. Her mother took it up, and said, *Loe here child, it is not broke*. Shee got it againe, and suddenly said and did it so againe, and again, and once against the edge of the door: thus shee struggled, and did foure or five times, and yet it brake not; but at the fift time a little nip brake out. And now since the Lord hath created peace to her, shee hath desired to drinke still out of that her white cup: till their Water-bearer unawares cast it downe, and then it brake all to pieces.

---

2 Omitted here is a long list of people who tried to comfort her when she was in despair, or visited her after 'her much prayed- and hoped-for *deliverance*' (p. 9), including representatives of Parliament, the nobility and the local community. The extract then resumes with the account of the onset and early stages of Sarah Wight's prophetic state, pp. 10–18. 3 Lecture days were those days other than Sunday on which religious gatherings – often of a less formal nature – took place. 4 Millenarian beliefs among the religious radicals of the seventeenth century favoured a relatively positive attitude towards the Jews: see James Shapiro, *Shakespeare and the Jews* (New York: Columbia University Press, 1996). 5 An elaborate, expensive mirror.

In her despairing fits, shee severall times would turne to the places in *Job*, and in *Jeremy*, where they *cursed the day of their birth*; and shee said to this effect; *Job cursed the day wherein he was borne, and said, Wherefore hast thou brought me forth of the womb? Oh that I had given up the ghost, and no eye had seen me.* Shee turning to the places, *Job* 3.3. *Job* 10.18. *And (Jer. 20.14.* to the end) *Jeremie cursed the man that brought tidings of his birth, with bitter curses, because his mothers womb was not his grave, and said; Wherefore came I out of the wombe, to see toile and sorrow, that my dayes should be consumed with shame?* But shee said, *Have not I much more cause to say so, then they had? for they wre in a blessed condition: but I am curs'd, and must be a fire-brand of Hell for ever.*

These and many other desperate expressions, shee frequently used, especially in the *last moneth* of her sorrowes. When they encreased daily, so that her soule was exceedingly troubled, and shee was as it were all shattered to pieces. And shee was so weary of her life, and of her selfe, and of every thing, shee was never at such a passe, in such extremitie, in all her life before.

Her tender and good *Mother*, attending on her continually day and night, to prevent her mischieveing her selfe; being still upheld with great hopes, that the Lord in his good time would come in to her with his consolations, yea, shee was verily perswaded so. (as was also her *Brother* in *Oxford*,) And this made her sore taske the more easie; which els had been intolerable. Yet when this extremitie had continued long, so that for many dayes and nights together, her mother had taken no rest. At last shee was even wearied out with continuall watchings, and to the end her selfe might enjoy some rest, to prevent harme to her selfe, shee had spoke to a friend, desiring that her daughter might be for a little season with her; which her friend was very willing unto, and her *daughter* was desirous to goe with her, that her *Mother* might enjoy rest. But the *Lord* prevented both in his goodnesse. For when her friend was come, her daughter was taken with such an *exceeding trembling*, and such extremity of sorrow and trouble and *weaknes*, that shee was not able to goe with her. A forerunner of her deliverance.

Then her *Mother* procured a maid that feared God, to help to look to her, who came that same day of her so trembling, being *Tuesday Aprill* 6. When the maid beforesaid came to her, shee found her weeping most bitterly, and wringing her hands grievously saying, *I am a Reprobate, a Castaway, I never had a good thought in all my life. I have been under sinne ever since I can remember, when I was but a childe*, etc.

This heavinesse was greatest, this night was darkest of all, when the day, the joyfull time of her deliverance was neer at hand. And like as at the beginning of her grievous despairing, about foure yeeres agoe, upon those two sinnes beforesaid, a great trembling fell upon her at the beginning of her deep despaire and trouble: so now, at the ending thereof, the like trembling fell upon her, such as shee never had at any other time. And now, thus trembling exceedingly, and weeping, and wringing her hands, shee said to this effect: *My earthly Tabernacle is broken all to pieces; and what will the Lord doe with me? If I should hang on Gibbets, if I should be cut in pieces, if I should dye the cruellest death that ever any did, I have deserv'd it, I would still justifie God; aye if he cast me to hell.* (Thus the Lord caused *Job*, to *humble himselfe*, and *justifie the Lord*, when his restoring was at hand.) Her hands and her feet were clunched, so as shee could not stand. Shee was tempted to blaspheme God and dye. And when shee was urged to speak, her tongue was smitten. Afterward shee being laid down, shee said to her Mother, *Ile lye still, and heare what God will say to me: He will speak Peace, Peace. If God will speak a word of Peace at the last moment, I should be contented.* Then shee desired them that none might trouble her, but that shee might lie in peace. And shee lay still, as in a sleep, or as in a trance rather, from that tuesday night, *Aprill* 6. till the last day of that week (cald Saturday) at night; except when shee cald for a little water to drink, and drunk two or three cups of water. No other sustenance shee took all that time. And this was the time of love, when the exceeding riches of Grace was advanced.

Aprill 10. 1647. that *Saturday* at night, about midnight, or after midnight, shee began to expresse the first expressions of comforts, of such soule-satisfying comforts, that ever shee so manifested: (though her soule enjoyd them for that Tuesday night before; as since her Trances ceas'd shee hath declared.) Even now, when all mans help faild, and when all meanes before used could not doe it; and when now shee was made uncapable that way to receive it, being now struck both blind, and deafe: her eyes being fast closed up, wrapt up together: As *Saul* (who is called *Paul*) when the Lord converted him, *was three dayes without sight, and neither did eat, nor drinke,* Act. 9.9. And thus shee began: *My soule thirsts for the water of life* [John 4: 13–14], *and I shall have it: My soule thirsts for the water of life, and I shall have it,* (foure times in ardency of spirit uttering those words, then adding) *a little water good people, a little water*. So shee drank two or three little cups of water. Then shee sate up, and with a most sweet and chearfull heavenly countenance, and with much brokennesse of heart, in an humble melting manner, Teares sometimes trickling down, shee spake with a low voice, as followeth.

Ah, that Jesus Christ should come from the bosome of his Father, and take the nature of man upon him! and come in such a low estate, and lie in a Manger! There's three sorts of people in the world, a higher sort, and a middle sort, and a lower sort: Christ came to the lowest soule; he lay in a Manger, a contemptible place. Doe you not see an excellency in him? I tell you, there's more excellency in him, in his lowest state, his meanest state, then in the world; ay, then in a thousand worlds. Doe you not see an excellency in him? (twice repeating this question of their seeing this excellency in him.) *Who came he to dye for? for sinners; aye for the greatest sinners, the chiefest sinners, the chiefest sinners. A dying Christ, for a denying* Peter;[6] a *dying Christ, for a denying* Peter; *dying Christ, for a denying* Peter. Peter *denied him, and yet he dyed for him. Goe tell* Peter! *Goe tell* Peter! *Ah* Peter! And then shee paused a while, as admiring it; and proceeded thus: *For a* Peter! *for a* Mary Magdalen![7] *for a Theefe on the Crosse!* [Luke 23: 39–43] *that none should despaire: a crucified* Christ, *for a crucified* Theefe; *a crucified*

6 All the gospels report that Peter, one of the first of the disciples to be called, denied knowing Jesus during the hours preceding the crucifixion. 7 A prominent female follower of Jesus: according to tradition, a former prostitute.

Christ, *for a crucified* Theefe: *A persecuting* Saul, *becomes a beloved* Paul: *for the* chiefest *sinners, the* chiefest *sinners. Not the proud Pharisie, but the poore Publican* [Luke 18: 10–14]. *No sin separates from Christ, but the sin of Unbeliefe. And this is the Faith,* beleeving *a full Christ, to a nothing Creature: a full Christ, to a nothing Creature: a full Christ, to a nothing Creature. To me, the chiefest of sinners: yet I obtained mercy through unbeliefe:*[8] *Christ came not to find faith, but to give faith: Christ came in to me, when I was in my unbeliefe. There's a fountain open, for* Judah, *and for* Jerusalem, *for sin, and for uncleannesse. A fountain open, for* Judah, *and for* Jerusalem, *for sin, and for uncleannesse. A fountain, not streames, but a fountaine: open, an open fountain: if a doore stand shelving, you cannot come in, but you must* thrust *to come in: but if it stand wide open, then there's freedome for you to goe, freedome for you to goe. Its open for* Judah;[9] Judah *that play'd the Harlot, yet God saith to* Judah, *Returne, though thou hast play'd the Harlot with many lovers, returne, for I am married to thee* [Jer. 3: 1]. *For* Judah, *and for* Jerusalem: *and what was* Jerusalem? *her skirts were full of bloud, her streets were full of bloud: Yet the fountain is open for* Judah *and for* Jerusalem, *for sin, and for uncleannesse: for all sin, for the greatest sinne, the chiefest sinne and sinners.*

Who is this fountaine? Jesus Christ, he is this fountaine: a filling fountaine, and never dry; a filling fountaine, and never dry; a filling fountaine, and never dry. . . .

Another Conference *with an afflicted* woman,[10] *that heard of this mercy, and came to her* May 12. *Shee still remaining in Bed, very weak and spent, as beforesaid.*

Woman. Being asked how it was with her: shee said; *I cannot beleeve.*

S. *Its his work to give to beleeve, that dyed for sinners.*

Woman. Its not for me.

S. *Its for chiefe of sinners, for* Mary Magdalen *that had seven Devils.*

Woman. My heart will not be wrought upon.

S. *Is any thing too hard for God? Tis Christs work, and tis his Office, to work on hard hearts; stony hearts.*

Woman. I am oft afraid, I shall never be sav'd.

S. *You are but afraid so. He saith, Ile sustaine thee, Ile save thee, be not afraid. He puts under his everlasting armes. I thought, and said, it was impossible, that ever I should be sav'd. Yet that which was impossible with me, was not impossible with God: But I thought it was impossible with God.*

Woman. How long were you in that affliction?

Another answered, *about foure yeers.*

Woman. But not continually.

S. *Yes continually. But this last halfe yeer, in terror day and night.*

---

8 Marginal note: 'She meant, *being then in unbeliefe*'. 9 Marginal note: 'The house of *David* is of *Judah* Mat. 1: 1; 2: 6'. 10 A substantial proportion of the book consists of dialogues between Sarah Wight and the people – many of them women – who came to her for spiritual advice and comfort: this example comes from pp. 76–9.

Woman. I goe to the meanes,[11] but its to no purpose.

S. *So it was with me: I was worse by the meanes. What may your condition be?*

Woman. I have cursed thoughts of God continually. About three quarters of a yeer agoe, when my husband was dead, I thought, what was become of his soule? and what would become of me, that had made him worse by my perverse words to him, when he was faulty: and one morning, after I was awake, I thought, the roome was full of smoake, and suddenly a fire went in at my mouth, and went downe hot into my belly, and there it went flutter, flutter.[12] Then (said the *woman*) I suddenly flew out of my bed, into the midst of the roome, and a voice said within mee, to my heart, *Thou art damn'd, damn'd*. I felt the smell of brimstone. Thus it began, and I thought the house was full of Devils. Then for six or seven weeks together, I never slept at all, I was so terrified, and have been out of hopes, ever since.

S. *Jesus Christ came to dispossesse the strong man armed, that kept the house, and to possesse it himselfe: The Lyon of the Tribe of* Judah,[13] *hath overcome that roaring Lyon, that seeks to devour you.*

Woman. I can see nothing but damnation.

S. *I could see nothing but Hell, and wrath: I was as desperate, as ever was any: I said, I cared not whether I had mercy or no. I felt my selfe, soule and body in fire and brimstone already. If all the fire and brimstone in* London, *and all the pitch and tarre, should all be in one fire, and I walking in the midst of that fire; this was my condition. I beheld my selfe in hell locally; my terror was so great. And I thought, there was no other Hell, but that which I felt; and therefore I sought to make away my selfe, and many wayes attempted it: But God hath made me see my sin therein, and be ashamed; and mine iniquity, and be confounded. Yet then I could wait no longer: and I said, If God will not save me, let him condemne me: and it terrified me after that I had said so. But were Gods thoughts as my thoughts? were his thoughts ill towards me, because I thought so? Nay, Gods thoughts were not my thoughts: God could withhold possession, and temptation, if he would; but he sees, its for his glory, and for the good of his, that you might love him the more; and that his glory might the more be seen in his delivering of you.*

---

11 That is, 'the means of grace' – a common term in nonconformist circles for a religious gathering.
12 Marginal note: *'Another that lately had been with her, said, this was just her condition, she felt such a fire coming in at her mouth, and so into her belly. But after shee judged it was but a fancy: but remaines in despaire ever since'*.
13 Jesus.

JAMES DALTON

A Strange and True Relation Of a Young Woman Possest with the Devill (1647)

There was a plethora of witchcraft pamphlets printed during this period, often taking the form of letters that sought to replicate the statements of witnesses at witchcraft trials, thereby investing in them authority and validity. The pamphlet printed below is representative of the type of 'report' of possession and it illustrates sharply the gender stereotyping in the interplay of 'woman', female spiritual utterance and the devil. According to the title page, *A Strange and True Relation* 'was certified in a Letter from Mr. *James Dalton* unto Mr. *Tho. Groome,* Ironmonger over-against *Sepulchres* Church in *London*'. The copy texts are BL, B. 58/E. 367 (4), pp. 1–4, printed in London by E. P. for Tho. Vere at the upper end of the Old-Bailey in 1647.

A Letter sent from Mr. *James Dalton* to Mr. *Tho. Groom*, Ironmonger, over against *Sepulchres Church*, London

It is the property of humane nature to desire newes, and therefore having seene the last Diurnall[1] (out of which I could pick but smal crums of comfort) I afterward saw a Letter imparting good Newes, which should come by the Post to *Birmingham*, that the two Kingdomes were reconciled, and a peace concluded. I pray you send me what newes you have, which I shall endeavour to requite by this ensuing Relation, which although I received it but at the second or third hand, yet by such persons, as I nothing doubt the truth hereof: Sir 'tis thus:

At *Bewdley*, seven miles from us, there is a young Woman (by the name *Joyce Dovey*) one who formerly was litle taken notice of for Religion, untill about 4. years since, who after the hearing of a Sermon, seemed to be much wrought upon and dejected, who afterward fell into some passions, and (as was conceived by her friends) Convulsion fits, which in time grew stronger upon her, and observed especially to take her in the time of private prayer, or performance of other pious duties; whereupon they procured a devout religious young man, to be in the house, and to be as a Keeper unto her; the bruit[2] whereof increasing, there came to visit her a Chaplaine of a Regiment, and a Captaine, who by some discourse, and other informations, strongly imagined, that shee was possessed; whereupon about three weeks or a month since, her

1 'diurnall': daily newspaper or news-sheet. 2 'bruit': rumour.

Keeper lift up his heart to the Lord in prayer, without uttering of words, that if she were possessed, the Lord would be pleased to make it manifest, which no sooner conceived, but the Devill answers with swearing, Wounds, Blood, etc. that thou shalt know; and this observe generally, that he makes the womans tongue and organs instruments of speech, but it is in a bigger and grosser tone then her ordinary speech, and when he speaketh, he looketh fiercely with something arising big in her throat, and commonly with swearing, and especially by the life of *Pharoah*. When any discourseth with her about worldly business she will familiarly talk with them, but when any use speech of Divine matters, shee is most troubled.

It is further reported, that M. *Burrowson* Minister there with others came to see her, to whom M. *Bur.* said, thou foule spirit, thy power is limited; to whom was replyed, Thou lyest, my power is over all the world, and my Kingdome is the greatest: To another that said, Thou foule uncleane spirit, what has thou to doe to vex a poore creature, was answered, I have Commission and power to tempt you all. Three Souldiers, (they say,) came to see her, who talking of Papists, Crucifixes, and Crosses, presently appeared in her breast or throat two Crosses, whereupon the Souldiers being agast, began to get away; haw, haw, haw, sayes the Devill: now (sayes her Keeper) they are afraid, and the Devill laughs at them. Shee usually goeth abroad, and comming to the House of an honest religious man, where many came in after her to see her, she began to be so distempered, that she could not goe home that night; and as they were at prayer in an upper Chamber, she was on a sudden caught up into the window, and the greatest part of her body thrust thorow a great casement, but her Keeper having an eye unto her, stept unto her, and caught her by the coats, and took her in again: She is oft thrown against the walls, and into the fire, but all without any hurt: One time being cast into a great fire, some would have taken her out, but her Keeper said, let her alone, and observe the providence of God, and straitway she was snatched out without humane help, not having any hurt, or so much as the smell of fire on her clothes: She hath snatched a pair of Cizzers from a womans girdle, and applyed them to her throat; and another time a knife from another, in an admirable quick way, and strook her breast, yet both without so much as a scarre in either place: She hath throwne a Bible into the fire, which was not burned. On a time one comming into the house, to discourse with her Keeper, and to take some observations in writing concerning her, they went into an inner chamber, and as he came forth with the paper in his hand, shee fell upon him very violently, and would have taken the paper from him, but he contended with her very toughly, and after a long conflict, gave her the repulse, who having kept the paper without tearing, onely a little corner, but not a word torne off, he voluntarily threw it downe on the ground, saying, Devill thou hast not power to take it up, and so took it up himselfe and departed.

It is very like I have not heard of all the passages concerning her, which if any of note come unto my knowledge (as I beleeve I shall shortly see a Catalogue of the particulars) if they come not to publicke view (which I suppose will be ere long) I shall further acquaint you there with (God willing.)

No more at present, but mine and my wives kind remembrance to you, my Sister, and Cousens *Henry* and *Mary*, I rest,*Your very loving and affectionate Brother*,

JAMES DALTON 14. 'Decemb.' 1646.

ELIZABETH POOLE

A Vision: Wherein is Manifested the Disease and Cure of the Kingdome (1648)

This text is the first of two pamphlets written by Poole concerning the hotly debated issue of the execution of King Charles (copy text, BL, E. 537 (24)). Both Christopher Hill and David Underdown discuss the use to which Poole's prophecy was put by Cromwell.[1] On the basis of a complex use of contemporary divorce law and gendered metaphors, Poole advised that Charles I should be punished, but not executed. Ultimately, therefore, Poole's advice was not heeded; undeterred, she wrote her second pamphlet, *An Alarum of War, Given to the Army, And to their High Court Justice (so called) by the will of God* (1649), warning the rulers of their imminent downfall. The text reproduced below is the complete text of the first pamphlet (pp. 1–6).

The Summe of what was delivered to the Councel of War, *Decemb*. 29. 1648

SIRS,

I have been (by the pleasure of the most High) made sensible of the distresses of this Land, and also a sympathizer with you in your labours: for having sometimes read your *Remonstrance*,[2] I was for many daies made a sad mourner for her; the pangs of a travelling woman[3] was upon mee, and the pangs of death oft-times panging mee, being a member in her body, of whose dying state I was made purely sensible. And after many daies mourning, a vision was set before me, to shew her cure, and the manner of it, by this similitude: A man who is a member of the Army, having sometimes much bewailed

1 Christopher Hill, *The World Turned Upside Down* (Harmondsworth: Penguin, 1988), p. 279; David Underdown, *Pride's Purge: Politics in the Puritan Revolution* (Oxford: Clarendon, 1971), p. 183. 2 Oliver Cromwell, *The Remonstrance and Resolution of the Right Honourable and Truly Valiant, Lieut. Gen. Cromwell*, 8 September 1648. 3 'travelling woman': travailling i.e., woman in labour.

her state, saying, *He could gladly be a sacrifice for her*, and was set before mee, presenting the body of the Army, and on the other hand, a *woman crooked, sick, weak and imperfect in body*; to present unto me, the weak and imperfect state of the Kingdom: I having the gift of faith upon me for her cure, was thus to appeal to the person, on the other hand, That he should improve his faithfulnesse to the Kingdom, by using diligence for the cure of this woman, as I by the gift of faith on me should direct him. Neverthelesse it is not the gift of faith in me, say I, nor the act of diligence in you but in dependence on the divine will, which cals me to beleeve, and you to act. Wherefore I being called to beleeve ought not to stagger, neither you being called to act should be slacke: for looke how farre you come short of acting (as before the Lord for her cure) not according to the former rule by men prescribed for cure, but according to the direction of the gift of faith in me, so farre shall you come short of her consolation; and look how farre you shall act, as before the Lord, with diligence for her cure, you shall be made partakers of her consolation.

She being after demanded, *Whether she had any direction to give the Councel?* She answered, no: for the present, for she was in this case presented to her self as the Church, which spirit is in you, and shall guide you.

I am therefore to signifie unto you, that there is but one step between you and restauration, the which whosoever taketh not warily shall stumble, and fall, and be taken, and that is this, you are to stand as in the presence of the Lord, to be dead unto all your own interests, lives, liberties, freedoms, or whatsoever you might call yours: yet pleading for them still with men, speaking to every one in his owne language, for they are your due with them; but except you are as ready to resigne them up to the will of the eternal pleasure, as to plead them with men, you shall surely lose them; *For he that will save his life shall lose it, and he that will lose it shall save it.*[4]

The Lord hath a controversie with the great and mighty men of the earth, with the Captains, and Rulers, and Governours: You may be great and mighty upon the earth, and maintaine his controversie, but against the mighty men of the earth is his controversie held: For as you are the potsherd[5] of the earth, he will surely break you to peeces, till there be not a shred left to carry coals on. The Kingly power is undoubtedly fallen into your hands; therefore my advice is, that you take heed to improve it for the Lord. You have justly blamed those who have gone before you, for betraying their trust therein. I speake not this as you are souldiers, but as the spirit of Judgement and Justice is most lively appearing in you, this is therefore the great worke which lieth upon you, to become dead to every pleasant picture, which might present it self for your delight, that you perfectly dying in the will of the Lord, you might finde your resurrection in him.

She being afterwards asked by some of the chief Officers, *Whether she conceived they were called to deliver up the trust to them committed either to Parliament or People?* She answered, No, for this reason, it being committed to

---

4 The quotation here appears in all three of the synoptic gospels: Matt. 10: 39; Mark 8: 35; and Luke 9: 25.
5 'potsherd': earthenware vessel.

their care and trust, it should certainly be required at their hands, but take them with you as younger brethren who may be helpfull to you: Neverthelesse know you are in the place of watchmen, wherefore slacke not your watch over them, for *the account of the Stewardship shall be required at your hands* [Luke 16: 2].

It was further said unto her, *How then shall we be free from the aspersions of the people, who will be ready to judge that we improve this interest for our own ends?* She answered, Set your selves, as before the Lord, to discharge the trust committed to you, and trust him with your reward: I speake not this that you should bee exalted above your brethren, but that you might stand in faithfulnesse to discharge your duty; *For he that will save his life will lose it, and he that will lose it shall save it.* You have been Noble-men, behaving your selves with much valour and courage (as amongst men) now therefore lose not your reward, for this will be the greatest piece of courage that ever you were made the examples of; if you shall bee as well content to lose house, land, wife and children, or what ever you might call yours in divine will, as ever you were to lay down your lives in the field.

Dear SIRS,

I have considered the agreement of the people that is before you, and I am very jealous lest you should betray your trust in it (in as much as the Kingly Power is fallen into your hands) in giving it up to the people;[6] for thereby you give up the trust committed to you, and in so doing you will prove your selves more treacherous then they that went before you, they being no waies able to improve it without you. You justly blame the King for betraying his trust, and the Parliament for betraying theirs: This is the great thing I have to say to you, Betray not your trust.

I have yet another message to shew you, I know not what acceptance it made finde with you, yet I am content, here it is, let it finde what acceptance it may, I leave it with you.

The Message is as followeth.

Dear SIRS,

Having already found so free admission into your presences it hath given me the greater incouragment (though more peculiarly,[7] the truth perswading me thereunto) to present you with my thoughts in these following lines. I am in divine pleasure made sensible of the might of the affaires which lye upon you; and the Spirit of sympathie abiding in me, constraineth me to groane with you in your paines, you may remember I told you the Kingly power is undoubtedly fallen into your hands, which power is to punish evill doers, and to praise them that doe well: Now therefore my humble advice to you is, that you stand as in the awfull presence of the most high Father, acting your parts before God and

6 This is a reference to *An Agreement of the Free People of England* (1649) written by John Lilburne (leader of the Levellers). 7 'peculiarly': i.e., specifically.

man, you stand in the place of interpreters, for many hard sayings present themselves to you, and will doe, looke for it: wherefore see,

That you give unto men the things that are theirs, and unto God the things that are his,[8] it is true indeed, as unto men (I know I appeale by the gift of God upon me) the King is your Father and husband, which you were and are to obey in the Lord, and no other way, for when he forgot his Subordination to divine Faith hood and headship, thinking he had begotten you a generation to his own pleasure, and taking you a wife for his own lusts, thereby is the yoake taken from your necks (I meane the neck of the spirit and Law, which is the bond of your union, that the holy life in it might not be prophaned, it being free and can not be bound: *For the law of the Spirit of life in Christ Jesus, hath freed us from the law of sinne and of death* [Rom. 8: 2], for the letter of the law, which speaketh to the flesh killeth, therefore you must suffer of men in the flesh, for the Lords sake, that so dying to your own bodies (that is to al selfe interest in divine will) you might also receive your resurrection, for you must dye before you can rise, you must loose your lives, Interests, Liberties, and all (before you can save them) casting your Crowne at the feet of the Lamb, who only is worthy, yet still pleading for them with men, for they are your due with them, a share they may not deny you; *Blessed are the dead which die in the Lord: for they rest from their labours, and their workes doe follow them* [Rev. 14: 13].

From your own labours, I wish you rest in the Lord, that the fruit of your labours, which is the life of your faith may follow you to prison, and to death: know this, that true liberty either is not bound to any thing, nor from any thing, for it is subject to this or that (neither this nor that in divine will) nevertheless as from the Lord you have al that you have, and are so to the Lord, you owe althat you have, and are for his name sake. So from the King in Subordination.

You have all that you have and are, and also in Subordination you owe him all that you have and are, and although he would not be your Father and husband, Subordinate, but absolute, yet know that you are for the Lords sake to honour his person. For he is the Father and husband of your bodyes, as unto men, and therefore your right cannot be without him, as unto men, I know and am very sensible, that no small straight lyeth upon you in respect of secureing his person (for the manifold conceived inconveniences following, and necessities of evill event) in respect of raising more wars, and also other things well known to you which will present themselves unpossible for you to avoid, neverthlesse, this is my humble and hearty prayer to the everlasting Father (which I present to you in words, that you may be edified thereby) Remember I said, everlasting Father, for so we shall best know him for our consolation; that it might please him of his infinite, eternal life and goodnesse to grant you a sure and certaine knowledge of this, that all things which are impossible with men (at the utmost extent of impossibility) are possible with him,[9] who onely saith it, and it cometh to passe, the Lord of hoasts, the God of the whole earth, who

8 An allusion to Matt. 22: 21. 9 Again, this biblical allusion appears in all three synoptic gospels: Matt. 19: 26; Mark 10: 27; and Luke 18: 27.

commandeth all hoasts of men, Angels and Devils, whose eies run to and fro throughout the face of the whole earth; To shew himselfe strong in the behalfe of all those that trust in him: Wherefore put your swords into his hands for your defence, and feare not to act the part of *Abigal*, seeing *Nabal* hath refused it (by Appropriating his goods to himselfe) in relieving *David* and his men in their distresse [1 Sam. 25]; it was to her praise, it shall be to yours, feare it not: Onely consider, that as she lifted not her hand against her husband to take his life, no more doe yee against yours.

For as the Lord revenged his owne cause on him, he shall doe on yours; *For vengeance is mine, I will repay it, saith the Lord* [Rom. 12: 19]; who made him the Saviour of your body, though he hath profaned his Saviour-ship; Stretch not forth the hand against him: For know this, the Conquest was not without divine displeasure, whereby Kings came to reigne, though through lust they tyranized:[10] which God excuseth not, but judgeth; and his judgements are fallen heavy, as you see, upon *Charles* your Lord: Forget not your pity towards him, for you were given him an helper in the body of the people: Which people are they that agreed with him to subject unto the punishment of evill doers, and the praise of them that doe well: Which law is the spirit of your Union: And although this bond be broken on his part.

You never heard that a wife might put away her husband, as he is the head of her body, but for the Lords sake suffereth his terror to her flesh, though she be free in the spirit to the Lord; and he being incapable to act as her husband, she acteth in his stead; and having the spirit of Union abiding in her, she considereth him in his temptations, as tempted with him: And if he will usurpe over her, she appealeth to the Father-hood for her offence, which is the spirit of justice, and is in you; For I know no power in *England* to whom it is committed, save your selves (and the present Parliament) which are to act in the Church of Christ, as she by the gift of faith upon her, shall be your guide for the cure of her body, that you might therefore commit an unsound member to Satan (though the head) as it is flesh; that the spirit might be saved in the day of the Lord (I believe) And accordinly you may hold the hands of your husband, that he pierce not your bowels with a knife or sword to take your life. Neither may you take his, I speake unto you as Men, Fathers, and Brethren in the Lord: (who are to walke by this rule) *Whatsoever you would that men should doe unto you, doe yee the same unto them* [Matt. 7: 12]: I know it would affright you to be cut off in your iniquity; but O, how faine would you have your iniquity taken away! Consider also others in their amazment; I know you have said it, and I believe, that if you could see sutable sorrow for so great offence, you should embrace it: I beseech you in the bowels of love, for there it is I pleade with you, looke upon the patience of God towards you, and see if it will not constraine you to forbearance for his sake: I know the spirit of sanctity is in you; and I know as wel the spirit of bondage holdeth you oft-times, that you cannot but groane for deliverance: Wherfore I beseech you for the Lords sake, whose I am, and whom I serve in the spirit, that you let not goe the

10 According to 1 Sam. 8, the Israelites chose to be ruled by an earthly king.

Vision which I shewed you concerning the cure of *England*, as it was presented to me: Wherein the party acting, being first required to stand, as in the awfull presence of God, and to act for her cure, according to the direction which he should receive from the Church, by the gift of faith upon her: (Act he must) but not after any former rule by men prescribed for cure, but after the rule of the gift of faith) which I humbly beseech the Almighty Lord to establish in you.

I rest,

Your servant in the Church and
Kingdome of Christ.
Elizabeth Poole.

After the delivery of this, she was asked, whether she spake against the bringing of him to triall, or against their taking of his life.

She answered, Bring him to his triall, that he may be convicted in his conscience, but touch not his person.

FRANCES COOKE

Mris. Cookes, Meditations (1649)

The full title of Cooke's text reveals her motivation for writing: *Mris. Cookes, Meditations, Being an humble thanksgiving to her Heavenly Father, For granting her a new life, having concluded her selfe dead, and her grave made in the bottome of the Sea, in that great storme. Jan.* the 5th. 1649. Composed by her selfe at her unexpected safe Arrivall at Corcke. The BL copy text (E. 600 (9)) was published in Cork and London by C. S., in 1649.

Having solemnly promised to the most high God in the great storme, that if his Majesty would be pleased to prolong my dayes, and deliver me from so great a danger, I would studie to prayse and glorifie his name all the dayes of my life, and call upon others that were in the storme so to doe, if I shall neglect to do these broken Meditations may be an evidence against me; written suddenly after my comming to *Corke, Psal.* 118. 17. *verse.* I shall not dye but live and declare the works of the Lord: 66. *Psal.* 16. Come and heare all yee that feare God, and I will declare what he hath done for my soule, 19. *verse*, I cried unto him with my mouth, and he was extolled with my tongue, *Psal.* 56. 12. thy vowes are upon me oh God! I will render prayse unto thee: for thou hast made a path in the great waters for thy redeemed to passe through, and hast brought thy ransomed ones safe to land, therefore blesse the Lord oh my soule, and forget not such mercies, who hast forgiven all my iniquities and saved my life from so great a danger [Ps. 103: 1–4]! oh that I could spend this new life wholly in thy service, and that I might live to the prayse and glory of his grace, wherein he hath made me accepted in his beloved *Eph*. 2. 6. *v*.

Landing in *Kinsale*, I said, am I alive or dead? Doth not the ground move under mee? I have been dying all this storme, and I cannot tell whether I am yet alive; I finding my body much out of frame, and my heart fainting, having been ten dayes at sea without eating, but the next day the Lord made mee more sensible of my new life: and when I came to dive into the mighty depth of the love of God, in granting mee deliverance from so great a danger, my heart was so brim-full with the apprehension of his tender mercies, that I could not containe my selfe, but must needs burst forth in teares, for feare I should not live sutable to so great a mercy, and I said to my friends, that I would gladly be with my Saviour, if it pleased him to take mee: for the mercy I received was so great, that I should never be able to walk answerably in holinesse to the Lord and my care is, that I might not be found a fruitlesse figtree in the garden of my God, when Christ said, I am come into my garden my sister, my spouse, it was but to gather fruit; but when he expected fruit and found none, he was displeased [Mark 11: 12–25].

I know it is a great mercy to blesse God for mercies, and they which have a heart to bless God for mercies, ought to have a tongue to prayse him for the same, and a pen to record them, we being too prone to let them slip out of our memories, which if I shall do, I desire my hand may be brought to testifie against me, my heart and tongue shall not only prayse him, but with my pen also will I stirre up my self, and intreat all others that were in the same storme partakers with me of the same deliverance, to magnifie the Lord for ever. Oh ye couragious Sea-men that said, you were at your wits end, and knew not what would become of you, prayse ye the Lord; O ye that came into the great Cabbin to dye with us, blesse his name for ever. O ye that said you would give all you had to be landed even in your enemies Quarters, that you might fight for your lives, prayse him that is Lord of the Sea, that now we see the faces of our friends in peace, and can joyfully meet together to keep dayes of thanksgiving to the Lord.[1]

God hath granted me the thing I prayed for, although he did not evidence it to my heart then, that it should be granted, but he calmed and contented my heart, by giving me a quiet rest of spirit to submit to my Fathers good wil and pleasure; that living or dying it should goe well with me, and that I was not my owne but bought with a price, I *Cor*. 6. 20. and therefore must glorifie God, both in my body and soule which are his.

---

1 Cooke then refers to the parable of the ten lepers (Luke 17: 15–16) to emphasise the need for thankfulness, and exhorts others to extol God, arguing that 'man' must do what 'angels' do, that is, praise God. She proceeds to discuss what kind of praise God requires, arguing that 'The Lord cares not for burnt-offering and sacrifices' but desires remembrance in song and prayer, praising him for his wonderful works. Cooke then says that she is sure that everyone else on the ship made the same promise, and encourages them to fulfil it by providing more biblical examples: Jonah 1: 16; Ps. 61: 8; Ps. 116: 17; Eccles. 5: 4; Job 22: 27; Num. 30: 2; Deut. 23: 21.

The Lord comes to the quick, and puts me to the tryall, that I might know what temper I was made of, and what was in my owne heart, whether I had improved my talent, and what stock of grace I had gained to support at such a time of need, and if I had a spirit that durst encounter with death, let him appeare never so terrible, and in this trying condition the Lord kept me under water, as I may say, and expostulated the case with me, and put questions to my soule, and pleaded with me about life and death.

I mean onely this temporall death, for I blesse God I know that my Redeemer lives, all the time of the storme the Lord did sweetly smile upon my soule, and I found a strong sensiblenesse of his love and favourable presence in supporting my faith to believe, and in giving me assurance of my eternall salvation, thorough Jesus Christ my Lord and Saviour.

But concerning the being delivered from the power of the waves, the rage of the sea, and the danger of the rocks, the Lord hid it from me, and I could not believe that I should be preserved, neither could I tell whether God would put a period to my life,[2] the Lord revealed it not to me concerning living and dying: but he fitted me for both, in believing that I was his, and I blesse his Name, the Lord kept me all the time of the storme in a submissive, humble, believing and quiet frame of spirit: and he spake to my heart by way of questioning with me, that suppose the Lord should spare my life now, and at another time should call for it: would I be contented to suffer for him by way of being a witnesse to his truth, and the faith of Jesus Christ, if he should call me to it? unto which I found my spirit willingly to submit, and I resolved with all my heart and soule to repay this dying life to my ever living God, whensoever he calls for it, and howsoever he will have me come to him at sea or land. And I will not feare the King of terrors, as *Job* calls death, let him bring me to my Fathers house which way he will, whether through the fire or through the water, I hope I shall be willing to suffer any death that might bring glory to him that hath suffered death to bring me life, believing that Christ would not bring me into any condition but that he would be with me therein, and then I know that I can do any thing through him which strengtheneth me. 4. *Phil.* 13. *v.* For I blesse the Lord, I never once repined all the time, but I patiently lay expecting every houre when I should be dissolved and be with Christ in his glorious and triumphant Kingdome, and after the Lord had searched my heart, and had wrought in me a willingnesse to submit to him, and had shewed me what a solemne action it was to dye, and had made me sensible that there was a cloud of griefe, but faith would pierce thorough that, and see life in the midst of death, and that in finishing my course, and in resigning my spirit to God that gave it, I should find my fraile nature sinking, but the Divine Nature supporting, and that there is a little agony to be gon through about the time of dissolution when the soule will be heavie unto death, notwithstanding a submission to its Fathers will. *Matth.* 26. 38, 39. *v.*

---

2 'period': full stop, end.

After the Lord had given me a taste of death, he gave me life, conditionaly that I should be willing to dye and suffer death for him at another time if he called me to it, whereupon I solemnly promised and covenanted with God, and mad my vowes unto the most high, in the hearing of my dearest friend on earth and others: That if the Lord would deliver me out of this terrible storme and bring me safe to land againe and renew my dayes, I would give up my selfe and my new life wholly to the Lord and that I would walke more closely with him in holy Communion then ever I had done formerly and that I would no more live to my selfe, nor to the world but wholy to the Lord and that I would study to live more Gospel-like, declaring and holding forth to the world: that the Lord had overporw'rd my soul by his free grace and overcome my heart with loving kindnes and many and extraordinary deliverances which cal for extraordinary praises; and if pleased God to mak me partaker of such a singular mercy, I would not only record it in my heart all the dayes of my life, but in all places render thanks unto the Lord while I have any being; and tell all the world, that I have my life from Christ, and therefore must spend it for him.

And the Lord did suddenly accomplish the thing which I had so earnestly prayed for, when the sea had done threatning it was mercifull ere I was aware of it, as if God would surprise me with deliverance, and I could scarce believe that I was come to a harbour when I was told so, the newes was so unexpected and sudden to me, that I was like one of those men that had prayed long for the returne of the captivity of *Babylon*, and it was the conclusion of many prayers, and when they saw that the Lord did accomplish it on a sudden, and the thing was done in a trice, they were as men in a dream *Psal.* 126. 1. *verse.* they could scarce believe it was so, so the Lord wrought deliverance for *Peter* suddenly, when he was fast asleepe, and did not so much as think of it; and so the Lord delivered *Joseph* out of prison on a sudden, which shewed he had heard his prayer; therefore blessed be his Name for ever.

And this the Lord doth to overcome the heart and to draw out the affections unto himselfe, and that he might be admired of his Saints, that they finding him giving in sweet and unexpected deliverances may returne everlasting praises unto him, and glory in the God of their salvation. *Psal.* 40. 10, 11. *verses.* that they may learne alwayes to trust him for we had the sentence of death in our selves; that we should not trust our selvs but in God which raiseth the dead, who delivered us from so great a death and doth deliver, in whom we trust that hee will yet deliver 2: *Cor.* 1. 9, 10.[3]

Where the Lord Jesus is broken forth in spirit, where he is risen forth from the dead there is a glorious appearance of the presence of God which fills the soule with joy, when *Mary* came to *Elizabeth*, shee said, what am I that the mother of my Lord should come unto mee? as soon as the voice of thy salvation sounded in my eares the Babe leaped in my wombe for joy, and she said, *My soule doth magnifie the Lord, and my spirit doth rejoice in God my Saviour* [Luke 1: 46–7], if there be such rejoicing betwixt Babe and his Mother for hearing the voice of the Mother of her Lord, what infinite transcendent

---

3 Here, Cooke provides more biblical precedents: Nahum 2: 3; Job 38: 2, 7; 2 Kings 3: 11; Exod. 19: 18, 9.

happinesse, admirable delight and over-comming and ravishments of joy and abundance of rejoicing wil there be when the *Lord* himself shal apear in his glorious presence to the soule arayed with all his excellent and glorious apparrell, travelling in the greatnesse of his strength and power, having all his artillery of graces following him who is the bright and glittering Morning Star that shineth in such luster and brightnesse, and is the perfection of Beauty that it dazells the beholders; and when the salutations of the Lord Himself are heard thus to a Soule, saying, my lips Oh my Spouse drop as the Honycombe,[4] speaking peace to the Soule, as when Christ appeared unto His Disciples and said, Peace be unto you [John 20: 19], His Voyce is sweete, and His Countenance is comely [Cant. 2: 14], and a Soule that Christ hath taken into Union with Himself, and saith, thou art comely through the comelinesse that I have put upon thee, I have crowned thee in the day of thy Espousall [Cant. 3: 11]: so that in the presence of Christ there is infinite cause of rejoycing, and the Salutations of Christ are but invitations to come above and live aloft in the highest Regions of light. *Revel.* 4. 1, 2. And I heard a voyce saying unto me, come up hither; and immediatly I was in the Spirit.[5]

Hence Christ is overcome with the beauty of a flourishing Soul and admires it, and the Spouse, hearing the voyce of her beloved, ecchoes back again, admiration of her love that he was the chiefest of ten thousand, *Cant.* 5. 20. He is white and ruddy, His Countenance is excellent, His Mouth is most sweet, he is altogther lovely, here the Spouse would, if it were possible, outcrye Christ by way of admiration: here is the displaying the colours of each other, as if they would see which could advance highest in exaltations, and needs must there be joy in such a Soul that is betrothed unto Christ, and made one with Him, very well may it break forth into a singing note; my Beloved spake and sayd unto me; Rise up my love and faire one and come away. *Cant.* 2. 10. For loe the Winter is past, the Raine is over and gone, the Flowers appeare on the Earth, and the time of singing Birds is come, now will I sing unto my well beloved a song of prayses and thanksgiving.[6]

The thoughts of God from everlasting, were thoughts of mercy, love and peace, and when he doth shew mercies by wonderfull deliverances, he doth act but in his own element, for he delights to show mercy unto the sons of Men; I will have mercy on whom I will have mercy; *Gods,* Will and Mercy is the fountaine and spring of our Eternall Salvation and of our temporall deliverances, I remember very well in the middst of the storme, that I fled for refuge to the anchor of Faith, and the Will of *God,* saying to my friend, that the Lord saith, I will never leave thee, nor forsake thee, and I will not cast thee off [Heb. 13: 5], assuring my self, that it was the Will of *God* that I should receive the welcome of my Father pronounced by the Son. Come yee blessed of my Father,

---

4 Cant. 4: 11; today the Book of Canticles is known as the Song of Solomon. **5** Cooke then provides biblical examples of experiences of spiritual ecstasy or ravishment: the transfiguration (Mark 9: 2–8); Stephen (Acts 7: 54–60); John (Revelation); and Moses talking with God on Mount Sinai (Exod. 19); and the effects they have upon the subjects concerned. **6** Here Cooke makes reference to Ps. 47: 6; Ps. 59: 17; Heb. 2: 12; I Chr. 16: 8; Job 29: 13; Ps. 51: 3, 6, and 8.

inherit the Kingdome prepared for you before the foundation of the world [Matt. 25: 34].

Notwithstanding all the comfort and encouragement that my deere Husband gave me, saying, that I had no cause to be troubled at all, in respect of any danger, and bad me sleepe and be still, for all was as well as Heart could wish, and I should land safely, saying he was as sure of safety as if he was on shore, and said; he would not give a farthing to have his life secured him, nay, if the Ship brake in pieces yet we and he should be safe he knew, thereupon I asked him if he knew what he said, surely he was in a Dreame, why would he be so confident of safety when the Captaine and all the rest said, they knew not what would become of them, expecting every minute nothing, but Death; and he replyed, that he had Dreamed, that *Jesus Christ* told him so, and therefore he would believe it. I find that *God* had formerly revealed Himself to His servants by Visions and Dreames[7]. . . . Yet I marvelled at His confidence, and could not believe it, as to assure my self of my life, but my fears were much above my hopes, I confess I had a submissive hope to have life, but no assurance at all of life, *It was enough*, as *Jacob* said, *that my son Joseph is yet alive* [Gen. 45: 28]; it was enough for me that my Soul should ever live with the Lord, and upon this rock he brought me, and set my feet upon that rock that was higher then I, which only is my rock and my salvation, *Psal.* 62. 2. Upon which rock the foundation of my eternal comfort was built, when the rain descended, and the flouds came, and the wind blew and beat upon my soul, my heart fell not from my God, and when we were like to have been split in pieces upon the rocks in the Sea called the 3 *Stags*, I said I would cast my soul and body into the arms of my sweet Saviour, and if I perished I would perish there.[8]

And here do I conclude humbly, spreading before the Lord my earnest desires, that all we Sea-partners may obtain with *Elisha* a double portion of the Spirit of God, and with *Solomon* understanding hearts, that we may understand the Scriptures, for which I shall humbly wait at the feet of my sweet Saviour for a more glorious manifestation of his presence, and for a more enlightning revelation by his blessed Spirit, discovering the hidden Mysteries of the glorious Gospel of Jesus Christ unto my soul, which is life eternal to know God and Jesus Christ his Son whom he hath sent.

Come my fellow-sufferers, we that have had a tryall of ten days tribulation in our Sea Voyage, seeing it hath pleased God to redouble our obligations in miraculous preservations, let us multiply our fervent prayers and praises, and redouble our thanksgiving unto the Lord of Glory, that seeing these dangerous storms, and tempests, and sickness, which we have had, were not unto death, but for the glory of God, and that the Son of God might be glorified thereby, *John* 11. 4. Let us joyn with one consent to give him praise which is due unto his Name all the days of our pilgrimage, which are few and evil. Let us

7 Cooke prays for a double portion of God's spirit: Ps. 27: 4; 2 Kings 2: 9, 3: 9; 1 Kings 3: 5; Luke 24: 45; 1 Kings 3: 14, 15, 28. 8 Here, Cooke stresses the importance of asking God for hard things (1 Kings 3: 10, 14, 15, 28).

exceedingly rejoyce in our God while we are hereupon earth, and cry *Hosanna* to the highest; Let us so run, as we may obtain a never fading Diadem of Glory amongst the Saints of the new *Jerusalem* which is above: Let us be faithful to the death, and we shall have a crown of life, *Rev.* 2. 10. For our God will surely come, and his reward is with him, and he will give to every one according to his works: Therefore God that is rich in mercy to all that call upon him, and a present help in time of trouble, fill your Souls with graces of his most holy Spirit, and accept all our Praises, and help us to perform all our Vows, and grant all our Petititions, so prays,

Your weak Remembrancer in
all Christian Love and Duty,
FRANCES COOK.

ANNA WEAMYS

A Continuation of Sir Philip Sidney's Arcadia (1651)

The Old, the New, and the composite *Arcadia,* 'close' with an invitation from Sir Philip Sidney to continue his work: '[b]ut the solemnities of these marriages . . . the strange continuance of Klaius's and Strephon's desire . . . may awake some other spirit to exercise his pen in that wherewith mine is already dulled'. While Weamys was one of four seventeenth-century writers that took up this challenge, she was the only woman writer to do so explicitly.[1] Although, as Patrick Colborn Cullen points out, Weamys's text seems unaware of Lady Mary Wroth's *Urania,* we have chosen to include the section of her text that deals with Klaius's (in Weamys, 'Claius') and 'Strephon's' struggle for the affections of the character of Urania. Indeed, Cullen notes that, although both Wroth and Weamys 'found in the absence of Urania a site of invention, their Uranias could not possibly be more unlike'.[2] The extract commences at the point where Strephon and Claius are presenting their cases to Pyrocles and Musidorous, asking them to judge which one of them is most worthy of Urania's love. The extracts here are from Strephon's tale. The copy text is BL, E.1288 (2), pp. 159–70; 179–82; 185–94.

1 The other two continuations were Gervase Markham's, *The English Arcadia* (1607/1613) and Richard Belling's, *A Sixth Booke of the Countesse of Pembrokes Arcadia* (Dublin, 1624). See also n. 2, Introduction, p. 17 2 P. Colborn Cullen, ed., *A Continuation of Sir Philip Sidney's 'Arcadia', Anna Weamys*, 'Women Writers in English, 1350-1850' series (New York and Oxford: Oxford University Press, 1994), p. 1.

To recollect *Urania's* virtues, or what surpassing beautie engaged *Claius* and me, to be her servants, would be superfluous, since her divine self is present to merit divine praises from the dullest spectators. Onely first her prettie innocence withdrew our eyes from gazing on the stars, to salute her heavenly spheres that reflected upon us as she passed by. For *Claius* and I having separated our Flocks from our neighbouring shepherds into a fresh and sweet pasture, where none frequented or trode the pleasant grass, but savage Satyrs, and dancing Fairies, we espied a Tree, whose flourishing branches seemed to fortifie themselves against the heat of the sun, and we enticed by the shadow, repaired to it: there we lay down, purposing to trie our skill in describing the pitifull decorums of the shepherds that were inchanted by *Cupids* quiver, to adore the fair beautie of Mortals: but the wonderfull Justice of the highest Powers, taught us to acknowledge our frailtie, by inflicting the like punishment upon us: for as we were reproching their lovesick infirmities, fair *Urania*, enduced by a Sparrow that flew from her when she had courteously bred it up, pursued after it, to take it prisoner, her course bending towards us: but when she had surprized it, she confined it to a Paradise, putting it between the pillows of her Breast, and checking it no otherwise than with her harmless kisses, she went away, leaving *Claius* and my carkass behind her, but our souls cleaved immoveably unto her, and fixing our eyes upon one another, as ashamed of our prodigious censoriousness of our Neighbours, we suffered not our lips to open, till we were acquainted with the subject that did triumph over us; but sounding our Bell, we secured our Flocks, and hastened to repose our selves upon our beds, but our memorie of the most Divine *Urania* taught us a more watchfull lesson than drousiness: her Image, which was engraven in our fancie, disdained to be blurred by our forgetfulness, wherefore the restless night we passed over with sighs, reviling the Fates for burying our felicitie in the depth of adversitie, so hard and explete did we account it ever to obtain *Urania;* and though *Claius* and I were one anothers Rivalls, both aiming at one, yet did it not any way mittigate our friendship, I applauding *Claius* choice, and he mine; neither did we ignorantly admire our judgements, but did enquire, and receive the approbation of a multitude of Swains,[3] who with abundant devotion extolled *Urania's* worth: yet Fortune, that favours not the purest souls, knit her brows, frowning upon our Goddess *Urania*, who mildly strived to wash them away with her Christal tears: the occasion I heard her whisper out one time, when she imagined little, and I resided so near her, in these sweetly expressed, yet dollorous[4] words.

Too great a burden for me to bear oppresses me, *Antaxius* is too offficious in his love, I wish he were more calm; my Parents rigor is too too intollerable, unless my disobedience had been palpable; I have never offended them wilfully, no not in this their desired Match, except they interpret my silence for a refusal, that being the onely symptom of my discontent, nor do I reveal my affection to any but to thee my Sparrow, who canst not discover it with thy chirping, and that note of thine is to me condoling, and chearfull; my discon-

3 'Swains': male servants or, in pastoral romance, lovers. 4 'dollorous': sorrowful, painful.

solate Heart not knowing how to value any other melodious sounds: but alass my incredulitie of the divine Providence may justlie reprove and punish me; yet since I do humbly acknowledge thy alsufficiencie, let thy Mercie chastise me, and deliver me fro the thraldom of *Antaxius*.

Then wiping her bedewed eyes, she arose, as confident her devout Prayers had conjured the Gods to pitie her distress, and beseeching the Deities to make me their instrument; call'd after her. Fair Creature, pardon me if I profane your sacred Title with a feeble one, since your humilitie vouchsafes earthly troubles to perplex you; and believe me, the Fabrick of this world is built upon divers motions, it can boast of no firm foundation; the rarest Beauties in their age seldom escape advers Billows, and boysterous winds, and without relying on a Rock, their perishing is sure: wherefore, sweet Nimph, accept of me to be your Rock, and questionless you shall be preserved from all tempestuous weathers.

Urania trusting in no other Power, than what was celestial, looked up to the Element, where seeing no heavenlie Object, she cast her eyes down, fixing them upon me with such blessedness, as strook me to the ground, not being capable of assisting my self; however I fed upon her voice, which she displayed in this language.

What a presumptuous mortal art thou to frame thy self to be a God, that by such a pretence thou mayst insult over me? For better Powers cannot support me from furious storms. This spoken, she went away, as loathing the sight of such a blasphemous serpent, as she thought me to be. Which I perceiving, and rowsing my self from out of a transe, I began to crie, O stay, stay, stay, but she deaf to my perswasions, hastened beyond the limits of mine eyes; but the rebounding of my words sounded in the ears of the Pastor *Claius*, who was with his and my Flock at a little distance from me. He harkening to my voice, and discerning me to wander out of the close, his jealous brain supposed the reason, and walking as swiftly as his aged leggs would suffer him, he found me out, his inquisitiveness enforcing me not to be niggardly in my answers, which were so tedious, that the Sun vanished from our Horizon, as tired with our unnecessary speeches, and took his farewel, highing him to his Eastern home. But at length *Claius* and I yielding our selves to silence though not to rest, experience had taught us to despair of sleeping, until *Cupids* wounds wear curable.

And early in the morning when the Sheperdesses had driven their Flocks into the Pastures, we lingering with ours, that we might see the place made happie with *Urania's* abiding there, her Enimie *Antaxius* the wealthy Heardsman, driven by a flattering current of his success, approched near us, not scrupulous in asking *Urania's* harbour: we making much of our opportunitie directed him the contrary way from her, to the Island of *Citherea*, her Parents dwelling there, onely they had trusted her with the Flock on this side the River, to feed them with a livelier pasture. But we protested to him, that in the morning we saw the Grass to weep for her departure, and the seas dance with joy that she relyed on their mildness. *Antaxius* easily believed our intilligence, and thanking us for it, he hastened to overtake her: and we pleased with our prosperous subtletie,[5] drove our Flocks to a Pasture adjoyning to *Uranias*, and entreating *Pan* to be their Guardian, we left them to trie Fortunes courtesie.

Urania blushing at our presence, at mine especially, who had before abruptly assaulted her, seemed to rebuke me with it, as in earnest so it did, my trembling witnessed my guiltiness, and my tears and sighs my repentance: my slowness to utterance allowed *Claius* a convenient time to discover his passion to *Urania*, the policie used to *Antaxius*, he forbore to repeat, until my repentance had obtained a pardon, and then he related in what expedition we sent away her undesired suitor; which at first vanished the red from her face, her fears usurping in her tender breast, lest her Parents should doubt her safetie at *Antaxius* report. Yet when she remembred her absence might extinguish *Antaxius* lust, her vermilion came back to mixture, and adorned her, as detesting to be deprived of such an Alabaster shelter.

Claius made Poesies in her praise to please her, dedicating to her service all his studies. My art in framing of Garlands, shewing the flowers natural curiositie in their varietie of shades, a device that sets them forth most perfectly I did teach her; oftentimes presenting her with the choisest of my Flock, when she would accept of them; and if Wolves or other ravenous beasts had happened to lurk that way, I never left hunting them till their hands evidenced me their Conqueror, which I used to lay at *Urania's* feet; other tricks I invented to be admitted into her societie.

Here *Strephon* stopt: but the Princes entreated him to go on. Which happiness of mine, saith he, continued not long without interruption. *Antaxius* learning that *Claius* and I pretended affection to *Urania*, he proudly landed at our haven, rudely carrying her away without resistance. Her commands, that could not be disobeyed, ordained the contrary. Then it was, most gracious Prince *Musidorus* that you escaped the seas, O then it was that *Urania* floted on them, and we bitterly bemoaned our loss. Certainly by the appointment of the Gods the Ocean waxed so calm, yet about where she was embarqued, the waters murmured, and the winds sweetly whistled, combining their voices so harmoniously, that she might really believe, they conspired to crown her with some unexpected blessing; as indeed so they had: for when we had conducted you to my Lord *Kalenders* house, we received a Letter from our adored Goddess. We might have been justly taxed of incredulitie at the first view of it, our rememberance of her uncivil Carrier demollishing all hopefull thoughts; but when we had more believingly read over and saluted those heavenly lines, we taking a short farewel of your Highnes, conformed our pace to our eagerest disposition, and came to the Sands against the Island of *Citherea;* where not caring for any other pass but *Charon's* Boat, we committed our selves to heavens protection, and fixed our eyes upon *Urania's* Island, leaping into the sea, there we had like to have participated of *Leander's* entertainment, but our luckie Stars preserved us to better fortune. . . .

The byest ways, as we conceived, might be the likeliest to find *Urania*, *Lacemon* having many: his felicitie, since he had deprived the Land of its

5 'subtletie': cunning, trickery.

Goddess, and we as deeply ingaged against him, our presumptuous Rival, as any other, searched the most suspitious Corners; but no tidings could be heard of *Urania* up the Island, where we had wandered, except profane ones; for ask the Swains that sluggishly sate nodding by some of their scattered sheep, whose fellows had been devoured by Wolves, through the carelesness of their Shepherds, when we examined them concerning *Urania*, whom we described by her Prayers and tears made to a Knight accoutred in a Martial habit; their reply would be so absurd, nay between sleeping and waking, divers did affirm they saw her, directing us to unseemly Mortals, who indeed had usurped *Urania's* Name, though they came short of her perfections. I cannot judge which was victor in me of Rage and Sorrow; furious I was at the counterfeit *Urania's*, and desperate, despairing of ever finding the real one.

At this passage *Strephon* burst out into floods of tears, which he endeavoured to conceal, excusing his too large rehearsal, and desired to break off; but the Princes earnestness to hear *Urania* rescued from the power of *Lacemon*, induced him to proceed on this manner: My chollerick Passion I vented upon the stupid men, instructing them to entitle their Dames with some meaner Name than *Urania*, under penaltie of their lives, which they dearly valued: and then *Claius* and I renewed our languishing travels.

When we had passed through the publick and remote places of the Island, meeting with no obstacles in the way, either by Freinds or Enemies, we crossed the Ocean, landing at the sands over against the Island, we continued not there, though we could not determin where we had best continue, but a Pilgrims life we resolved on, unless *Urania's* unexpected securitie should forbid it; when therefore we had traced about the Confines of *Arcadia*, without any comfortable reports of her, we rose with the Sun, to take a longer journey, but the tiredness of our legs prolonged the time, and so proved faithfull instruments to further our felicitie, by delaying our haste: Upon a bank we sate down, chafing[6] at the grass for looking fresh and green in *Urania's* absence; and *Claius* folding his arms, and casting his eyes on the ground, as a fit object for him to view, especially when he pitched on such a subject as deserved opposition. . . .

Claius fixing his eyes on the ground, as convinced of his error, sought not to frame an excuse, yet to shew that Age had not deprived him of his senses; he thus spake: An odoriferous[7] scent seems to command me to rest silent, and to bear the blame without controulment, and dreadfulness mixed with hope possess me. O *Strephon*, *Strephon*, faithfully conceal my follie, I beseech thee.

At this suddain Allarm, I gazed about me, an happie sight, though an amazed one approaching near me, *Urania* it was, with her arms spread, and cryes in her mouth, which mentioned murder, her hair contemptibly hung about her, though delicate; and patience and anger seemed to combat in her rosie cheeks for the Victorie; but at the last, abundance of Christal tears became the Arbiter, which when she had vented; she distributed to us these words:

Never was I yet in the Turret of felicitie, but I have stumbled, and fell to the pit of adversitie: *Antaxius*, in the Island of *Citherea* lustfully expects me; and

---

6 'chafing': banter, good-humoured joking. **7** 'odoriferous': fragrant.

here, if I continue, the Furie *Lacemon* will overtake me; O whither shall I flie for safetie? my pitie would not suffer me to retain her in ignorance, wherefore I related *Antaxius* death: her silence seemed to condemn me of rashness, for granting him no time of repentance; but my excuse was prevented by the rage-full coming of *Lacemon*, who with eyes sparkling, and Armour stained with bloud, an Emblem of the Tragedie he had committed, holding in his right hand a spear, and a shield in his left, he mustered up to us; we nothing dreading, but *Urania's* trembling, with our staves,[8] weak instruments (as he imagined) to resist him, made towards him: he disdaining *Claius* age, and my youth, exercised neither vigilance to withstand our blows, nor strength to repay them: I vexed at his so slight regard of my valour, and perswading *Claius* to retire to *Urania*, who willingly yielded to my counsel; I renewed the incounter, and with such fierceness, that *Lacemon* was forced to stand on his own defence; his want of experience might be the cause of his overthrow; for I am certain I can boast but of little that caused it, though the fortune of my blows proved fatal to him, thrusting him off his horse, and beating out his brains: his life was so hatefull, that his death was welcomed by most, and commiserated of none: *Urania* highly commended my action, too large a recompence for so poor a desert, yet I thanked the Gods for giving me such success as she thought worthie of her acceptance; and waiting upon her to the Island of *Citherea*, by the way she yielded to our request, gracefully delivering these words.

The motions of this world I cannot comprehend, but with confusion, so unexpectedly do they surprize me, *Antaxius* by *Lalus* instigations, trusted to the Seas fidelitie, your compulsion forcing them to deceive him, in whose banishment I sent a Letter to you, wherein I acknowledged your sincere affection, and by all the ties of virtuous friendship, conjured you not to denie me your Counsel or Companie in my extremitie; and happening to repose my self upon the Clifts, my harmless Sparrow I set down at a litte distance from me, learning it to come at my inducement,[9] the prettie fool, with shivering wings aspired to mount towards me; but the Tyger *Lacemon*, or Monster, for his disposition could never pretend to humanitie, being prepared in a readiness to commit such a treacherous act, came from a darksom hole, suitable to his practises, and seized on me and my Sparrow for Prisoners, and conveying us to his provided Boat, we were sailed over, and by him conducted to this Countrey of *Arcadia*, where in a Cave he hath enclosed me: and perceiving, that I consorted with my Bird, and delighted in its Innocencie, a virtue which he mortally detested, he unmercifully murdered it, lingeringly tormenting it to death, whilst my Sparrow with its dying looks, seemed to check me, for enduring its sufferance without resistance: thus he endeavoured to terrifie me with his crueltie, but if it were possible, it made me more enflamed to withstand his assaults; neither threats, nor intreaties were wanting to tempt me to his base desires, but I absolutely refused him, till necessitie perswaded me to trie the effect of Policie.[10]

His own reports signifying *Phalantus Helena*, the Queen of *Corinths*

8 'staves': wooden sticks. 9 'inducement': persuasion, influence. 10 'Policie': prudent or politic course of action.

Brothers defiance to the *Arcadian* Knights, his Lance willing to defend his Mistress *Sortesia's* beautie against other Champions; I counterfeited earnestness to *Lacemon*, in exercising his skill to purchase my glorie: he puffed up with hopes of future success, considering it was the first time that I had imployed him, and so publicklie, with all expedition, hasted to the lodge with my Picture, where by a thrust from off his horse, he was made to leave my picture, to reverence *Sortasia's* surpassing one; with a cloudie soul, he returned to me, I being compassed to stay within his bounds, so manie bars and bolts frustrating my escape; but by his muttering I discerned his discontent, an humour that best suited his condition: I strictly examined concerning my Pictures triumph, and his Fortune, he studying to delude me, replied, That business of importance had enforced *Bisilius* to defer the challenge for awhile, out of which regard, he, by the example of other Noble Personages, resigned up my Picture to the custodie of the Governor of *Basilius* lodge, and should be extremelie well pleased, if I would vouchsafe him my companie into the fresh aire; few perswasions served to remove me from that stifling cave, besides the hopes that I relied upon of your encountering *Lacemon;* but little imagined the Shepherd *Lalus* would be the first; kind *Lalus!* it was the least of my thoughts of thy so chearfullie loosing thy life for the preservation of mine; for when *Lacemon* had with boastings, for not being overcome by any of his subjected Rivalls, brought me near the confines of *Arcadia*, swelling with pride, his rough Arms rudely striving with me: then it was that *Lalus* succoured me with his own fatal ruine: for though I was by *Lacemon* desguised, by his suggestion, I knowing no other signe, he discovered me to be *Urania:* his desire to rescue me from *Lacemon*, extinguished the reprehension of his own eminent danger, his courage, though exceeding *Lacemons*, yet his strength and shield was far inferior to him, in the heat of the blows, before conquest, was decided on either side; I fled from dreadfulll *Lacemon*.

His speedie pursuance after me, might be a means to preserve *Lalus* life, yet I doubt it, *Lacemons* bloudie Armour prenominating[11] his wicked action. But I protest, that I had rather my skin should imitate *Pan's*, and my complexion *Vulcan's*, than that any one Tragedie should be committed in its defence.

Fountains running from *Urania's* sparkling eyes, stopped the remainder of her speech. *Lalus* being my assured Rival, mitigated very much my sorrow for him. However, lest I should forfeit *Urania's* favour, I seemed sad, yet strived with it, that I might be a more acceptable instrument to moderate hers. Neither was *Claius* negligent in his love, but with Rhetorical speeches he sought to win on her affections; and the Island of *Citharea* in awhile flourished with her adored Goddess. Her Parents in heavenly raptures welcomed home their dearest Daughter, keeping her watchfully under their eyes, and jealous of our depriving them of her the second time, though we had safely delivered her into their hands. And *Urania* her self suspecting our often resorting to her, might redound[12] to her prejudice,

---

11 'prenominating': forenaming; in this context, giving prior warning of. **12** 'redound': rebound, to one's honour or disgrace.

made excuses to abandon our companie. But death in a short time appeared in his visage to *Urania's* Parents, carrying them to the Elizian fields: she then having the libertie to dispose of her self, which she with confinement did, not delighting in the Pastorals, nor yet in our societie, until this happie Day was nominated. And great Princes, I humbly beseech you to pardon this my tedious Relation.

JOHN ROGERS

Ohel or Beth-Shemesh. A Tabernacle for the Sun (1653)

John Rogers was trained as a Presbyterian minister, but renounced his position and joined the Independents. In 1650, he was sent to Dublin as a minister by Parliament. On his return, however, the quarrel between the Parliament and the army alienated both Presbyterians and Independents, and Rogers became a Fifth Monarchist.[1] *A Tabernacle for the Sun* is an attack on the Presbyterians, but is more Independent in nature than Rogers' later texts. His writing and his sermons eventually landed him in jail. The *Tabernacle* is divided into two parts, the first theoretical (pertaining to Church order) and the second, practical, which includes the testimonies by individual church members reproduced below: Chapter 6; p. 354; p. 392; pp. 402–6; pp. 10–11. (The pagination between pages 412 and 413 is interrupted by pages numbered 1–12. This is where the testimonies of Curtis and Turrant are located.) The copy text (BL, 1488. f. 20) was printed in London for R. J. and G. H. Eversden in 1653.

Chapter 6: *Everyone to be* Admitted, *gives out some* Experimental *Evidences of the* work of Grace *upon his* Soul *(for the Church to judge whereby he (or she) is* convinced *that he is* regenerate, *and* received *of God, which is proved and approved by about forty examples of worth*

Examples of Experiences,

Or *Discourses* and *Discoveries* of the *dead hearing the voice of the Son of God,*

1 For further information about Fifth Monarchists, see Bernard Capp, 'The Fifth Monarchists and Popular Millenarianism', in J. F. McGregor and B. Reay, eds., *Radical Religion in the English Revolution* (Oxford: Oxford University Press, 1984).

and now *living*: As they were *delivered* in *Dublin* by divers *Members* admitted into the *Church*; Being a clear *account* (to the judgement of *Charity*) of the *work of Grace* upon their *hearts*; in *divers ways* and *sundry manners converted*; some *extraordinarily*, and some *ordinarily*. When? Where? and how? with the effects.

But before I begin, I shall premise this, for the godly *Readers* sake, that I must *contract* much their *experiences* as they were *taken*, least they be too *voluminous*: And although in the *choicest* and most *extraordinary* ones, I shall gather the *stalk longer*, least I hurt the *beauty* and *hide* the *excellency* of those *flowers*; yet without *hurt* to the rest, in those which are *ordinary*, I shall be very short, being prevented by *others* (in that little *Treatise of Experiences* newly put out).[2] I shall *gather* out the *flowers* onely, and give you the *sum* of what they said, and so *tie* them up *together* for a *conclusion* of the *whole matter*. The *most* of these are *mens*, and some *womens*, and a very great many more I might adde to them, which I have met with in *England*, *Essex*, and *London*, and in *Ireland*, and at *Chester*, *Holly-Head* in *Wales*, and in my travels; but that, I say, I am (I hope) seasonably (though unexpectedly) prevented; although many more do lie *prepared* by me.

But to the *business*, as comming last from *Dublin* to declare some of those *precious ones* (and which are the greatest *treasure*) that I *brought* with me from thence: The *favor* of which (I hope) will be *attractive*, and encourage others over into *Ireland*, where the *Lord* hath his *Garden* enclosed, and full of *Spices, with the Mandrakes laid up for the Beloved* against his coming (Cant. 7); which is looked for *every day* there, as well as here; and there the *Bride* saith, *O! come Lord Jesus! come quickly* [Rev. 22: 20]*!*

A *Fuller* Testimony *as it was taken from* Elizabeth Avery, *out of her own mouth, and declared by her self to the whole* Church

In this *society* I see much of God, and have a great desire to be one with you. From my *childhood* I have lived under *good education*; my *Father* was a *godly man*. I was always tender and consciencious, but my *conversion* was *wonderful*. On one *Sabbath day* I was playing, but I was soon and soundly *checked* for it in my *spirit*; and went home, but I was a great while troubled, and lay under *bondage* all along: And I was much *distracted* and *confused* for sin a long time, till about *sixteen years* of age; and then I began to be very *strict*, and so retired

2 That is, Mr Powel's, *Spiritual Experiences of Sundry Beleevers*, to which Rogers refers earlier (p. 355). Both earlier in his book and at the very end of Chapter 6, Rogers defines what he means by the terms 'extraordinary' and 'ordinary': 'Those which are the most *extraordinary* of them are uttered in *Dream*, *Trance*, *Voice*, or *Vision*, and Vision is taken two wayes, either first *actually*, by the *senses* of the body, and so in some *visible* bodily shape; or else 2. *potentially* thus (p. 449); 'As for those which are the *ordinary* ones of them, which are call'd home by such means as, *preaching*, *praying*, *reading*, *writings*, or such like; In and by them, if you observe, you shall find a *Call* twofold, *Legal* and *Evangelical*: as to the instance in *Elizabeth Averies* etc. And note further, those who are first *called* by the Word, and *preaching*, are then 2. *confirmed* by the Scriptures and *promises*; and 3. *assured* by the presence of Christ revealed in them' (p. 450).

in my *life*, that many wondered at it: I had an entire *love* to the *preaching of the Gospel;* O how I longed after it! but alas! we had then no good *Preaching-Ministery* to be had or heard about us! and yet my *heart* longed a long time after it, till I came to be *married*. But alas! I was yet under the *Law*, and *Works*, until *God* called me out of *Egypt*; and I could not tell how I was once wrapt up in a *light*, and *hearing* something spoken of *Free-grace*, then I melted. Yet for all these, I had *great afflictions*, and amongst others, by the loss of my *children*, *Gods rod* was laid *heavy* upon me, insomuch, That he struck *three* of them together; and *one childe* above all, a most sweet *childe*, and one that I least thought of them all would have died, was very ill; and we were talking (I, my Husband, and some Friends,) together of comfortable *things*, and amongst others of *David*, when he said of his *childe* (dead) *I shall go to it, it shall not return to me*. Ay sayes one, that is to the *grave*; which word *wounded* me; and I went into the *Garden* to *wail* and *moan* my self; but soon after, my *Husband* came and tolde me my *childe* was dying; at which I was left in an *horror*, as if I were in *Hell*, none could comfort me, nothing could *satisifie* me, no *Friends*, nothing; then it was sad indeed to me, a *Hell* indeed. I sent for the Doctor and others, but to no purpose.

Yet after this the *Lord* wrought on me much; and one, a *Minister of Christ*, that had *power* from *God* to do me good, gave me *much satisfaction* by a *Letter* of his: And after that, me thoughts, I was content to part with all, and to let all go; then God tryed me, and took away another *childe* from me, and I could bear it very well, and was not *troubled*, but rather did rejoyce within me to be thus *tryed*. No cross, nor loss could trouble me then, and I continued in this *strength* (I praise God) pretty long. But after this I was like to have died, and then, to adde to my *great sorrow*, the good *Minister* that did me *so much good*, left the place, and went away, and my *friends* slighted me, and one thing added to another, made me begin to *despair* again; but then I know not how God *quieted me* again, which I wondered at, and was much *comforted*, and *confident*, that *God* would do me *good*, and I hoped and looked for it: And the very *next morning* as I was at *prayer*, God *wonderfully appeared*; and then was it, that *Christ* was *manifested* to my *spirit*, and I was as in a *trance* for a while, but after I awaked *full of joy*; and yet for all this, I was somewhat under *bondage* (me thoughts) but the *Word* and *Means* of *Grace* did *confirm me*, and *comfort me*. In the times of the *Wars* in *England*, I was brought out of *Egypt* into the *Wilderness*. O! I was *much refreshed* by the *Lord* two or three years, and was much *contented*, and had his *teachings within me*, yea, and (many times) *without* his *outward instruments*; for I had his *Spirit*, his *voice* speaking *within me*, and *God* alone was with me, and no *strange god*. But when the *wars* began to cease, my *greatest trouble*, and that at which I took *offence* was, That we were so without the *means*, and without able *Ministers*; for now I could not be *satisfied*, but even *doted* on them, and could not *wait* with *patience*; for I had forgot now how *God* had *taught* me within before, and without them. Yet I *followed* and *hunted* after my *lovers*, having *mens persons in admiration;* and thus *God suffered me* for a while to go on after them.

A while after this, Colonel *Lambert* desired me to go to *Oxford*, and when I was to go, I made ready my self, packt up my cloaths and all, and rid away; most, with *desire* for *communion* with *godly people* there, for (as yet) I could see no futher ———. I heard *their disputes* between Master *Kiffith* and others, very hot, but saw nothing of *God* there, and was troubled at it, and could not after that *hear him* or others; but I went into a *Garden* alone my self mourning, and sat so a while under a *Wall*, and by and by came three men to me (passing that way) and *wondered* to see me so; they asked me many *questions* ———. But a little after I *recovered* my self out of that *passion*, and went and told Colonel *Lambert* how it was with me; but he told me, I should not onely be taken off of *Ordinances*,[3] but off of *believing* too, within a while; at which I was troubled, and went away *unsatisfied*. I was troubled to hear any *Preach*, and being once got to go to the *publick place*, I was so *tormented* that I could not bear it; for I could not *joyn with them*, nor *hear*, nor *pray*, nor had no *rest*, no *comfort*, no *ease*, nor could I *eat* or *drink*, but went (as I was wont) to *bewail* in a *Garden*, where I was *moaning*, when there came *one* unto me, and presently told me, That I was under the *opening* of the *fifth seal*, and very near the *sixth*, in the condition which I was in, and should be in .———

Being thus *afflicted*, I desired to go home again from *Oxford*, and writ to my *Husband*, but the *Letter* was burnt; ——— but I was in such a condition to see *Gods wrath* in every thing against me, as is not to be *expressed*; I was left in *all kindes of troubles* (as it were) at once; but here was all the *comfort* that was left me, and it was my *Heaven* in my *Hell*, that *God would be glorified by my destruction*: And so long I found some *ease*, and *content* (me thought,) and it did *joy* me at my *heart* to think, That all things should *go well* with the *Saints*, and they should be *happy*; though I had no *share with them*, yet these *things* did me *good*. And indeed, I dare boldly say when *my faith was gone*, and *hope gone*, and *all gone*, and *flew from me*, and could not be *seen in me* that I had any; yet *love remained*, and might be *seen*, and *was not gone*; noe, though I were to be cast presently *into Hell*, yet I could *love God*, and *was glad* he was to be *glorified*, though *I were* to be *ruined*; and so *I was glad* at the *welfare* of *Gods people*.

Thus *I was* three quarters of a year, and did not *now care for my self*, what became of me, for the *reasons* said before; but it appeared *my deliverance was near at hand*, though (as yet) I had *no assurance of salvation*; yet at last I was *carried out with a great confidence*, that *light* was near at *hand*, And yet I met *with terrible shakings for all that*, which lit altogether upon *the flesh*, for the *spirit was free*: So that some *three years* agone, *God* came in upon my *spirit*, and gave me *full assurance*, and I heard a *voice* say ———, *And sorrow thou shalt see no more*. Then I *writ down* what *God* had *done* for me, and *writ* about it to *my friends*; but yet I was *struck* in the *flesh* again, *which I wonder at*; and then I heard *the voice* again say, *It was sin that was suffering in me, and the flesh as a punishment of sin*; and so I *found* it was, for the *destruction* of the *flesh*; and ever after that I *found Christ in me*, ruling and reigning, and taking *all power to himself*, and he hath caught the *man-childe* up to God, which I brought forth. *i.e. The flesh*, (by his *incarnation*) and I *have found* in me (and do yet) his

3 'Ordinances': religious observances.

judgement-seat set, to *judge* and *sentence sin*, and *lust*, and *corruption*, and his *throne* is there for *himself* to *sit*, and to *rule* by his own *Laws*: And thus it continues with me at this day, and the *Lord* leads me on, *higher* and *higher* in himself; and for that I see so much of him here in the *midst* of this *Church*, I desire to be *one also with you*.

Experience of Frances Curtis:

I cannot but *Condemn* my self before *I speak*, I am so *unworthy* of this *mercy*. I have lived *wantonly* in my *youth*, forgetting *God*, doing no good, but all evil, till *Gods hand* was *heavy* upon me for about eleven years; and when in my *outward state* I began to *mend*, still in my *inward* I was much *troubled*, and wished that God had *taken* me *away* by my *former afflictions;* these *inward* were so great, *and a troubled spirit, who can bear*? But afterward I was *much comforted* again.

In these *wars* I was stripped by the *Rebels* (being *abroad*) and came home so, thorough *sad tempests*, and since have gone thorough *great troubles*, and very many. A while after, *I heard* my *Husband* was killed by the *Rebels*, which I feared was by my *sins*, and so my troubles were *renewed*; and then the *enemies* came upon us, the *Cannon-bullets* flew over my *head*; and in *few days* I was turned out of *doors*, with *my childe in my arms*. I cannot express what *God* hath done for me, in *saving* my life, and my *Husbands*, in *hearing* my *prayers* and *tears*; and now in *satisfying* my *soul* with himself. I have received much sweet *satisfaction* by Mr. R. and have now the *testimony* within me of *Gods* love to me, which makes me so *unfainedly* to *love him*, and his *ways*, and *desire* to be a *member* with his *people*, in his *Church*.

Experience of Mary Turrant:

I lived till my Twenty third year, and knew not *God*; but after that, *I* came to *religious people*, and received some good, and soon after was brought to the *sight* of my self, and then *I despaired* of *mercy*; and thought I *was damned*, and none of *Gods*, a great while, but was at last *comforted* by *good Ministers*, and the *Word of God*; but *I* was in such a *place* and *condition*, that for *seven years, I* do not know, that I saw so much as a *Religious man*. My *children* were *murthered* by the *Rebels*, and *I* lost my *Husband* by the *sickness*, and yet the *Lord* hath *spared me* in mine *old age*; and now *I* see why? That *I may enjoy* this *great mercy*, which *I* never looked for, to *comfort* me in my *old age*.

I have received great comforts indeed by Master *Rogers*, and *I* must needs say, That *I serve my God with a chearful heart, etc.*

DOROTHY OSBORNE

Letters (1653)

Dorothy Osborne was the youngest child of a large and prominent Royalist family. She met Sir William Temple, who was from a Parliamentarian background, while travelling in France at the age of 21; both families were opposed to their marriage and they conducted a courtship by correspondence (often in secret) for the following seven years, until their relatives finally gave in. Later, Dorothy took an active share of her husband's responsibilities as a diplomat in Brussels, Ireland and London. The copy text is BL, Add. MS 33975; most of the letters are undated in MS, and I have adopted the conjectural datings offered in Parker's edition (Harmondsworth: Penguin, 1987). Extracts from some of the letters were first published as an appendix to a Victorian biography of Sir William Temple; subsequently they have been edited and published in their own right several times, but at the time of writing there is no edition currently in print.

[Thursday 2–Saturday 4 June, 1653]

Sir

I have bin reckoning up how many faults you lay to my Charge in your last letter, and I finde I am severe, unjust, unmercifull, and unkinde; O mee how should one doe to mende all these, 'tis work for an Age and tis to bee fear'd I shall bee soe Old before I am good, that 'twill not bee considerable to any body but my self whither I am soe or not; I say nothing of the Pritty humor you fancy'd me in, in your dream because 'twas but a dream, sure if it had bin any thing Else, I should have rememberd that my Lord L.[1] loves to have his Chamber, and his Bed to himself; but seriously now, I wonder at your Patience, how could you heare mee talke soe sencelessly (though twere but in your sleep) and not bee redy to beate mee, what nice, mistaken points of honnor, I prettended to and yet could allow him a roome in the same bed with mee, well dream's are pleasant things to People whose humor's are soe, but to have the spleen and to dreame upont is a punnishment I would not wish my greatest Enemy, I seldome dream, or never remember them unlesse they have bin soe sad as to put mee into such disorder as I can hardly recover when I am awake, and some of those I am confident I shall never forgett.

You aske mee how I passe my time heer, I can give you a perfect account: not only of what I doe for the present, but what I am likely to do this seven yeare if I stay heer soe long, I rise in the morning reasonably Early, and before I am redy I goe rounde the house til I am weary of that, and then into the

1 Lord Lisle, a member of the Sidney family, whose connections with the Temples went back to the sixteenth century.

garden till it grows to hott for mee about ten a clock I think of makeing mee redy, and when that's don I goe into my fathers Chamber, from thence to dinner, where my Cousin Molle[2] and I sitt in great State, in a Roome and at a table that would hold a great many more. After dinner wee sitt and talk till Mr B[3] com's in question and then I am gon, the heat of the day is spent in reading or working and about sixe or seven a Clock, I walke out into a Common that lyes hard by the house where a great many young wenches keep Sheep and Cow's and sitt in the shade singing of Ballads; I goe to them and compare theire voyces and Beauty's to some Ancient Sheperdesses that I have read of and finde a vaste difference there, but trust mee I think these are as innocent as those could bee, I talk to them, and finde they want nothing to make them the happiest People in the world, but the knoledge that they are soe; most Comonly when wee are in the middest of our discourse one looks aboute her and spyes her Cow's goeing into the Corne and then away they all run, as if they had wing's at theire heels I that am not soe nimble stay behinde, and when I see them driveing home theire Cattle I think tis time for mee to retyre too, when I have supped I goe into the Garden and soe to the syde of a small River that runs by it where I sitt downe and wish you with mee, (You had best say this is not kinde neither) in Earnest tis a pleasant place and would bee much more soe to mee if I had your company I sitt there somtimes till I am lost with thinking and were it not for some Cruell thoughts of the Crossenesse of our fortun's that will not lett mee sleep there, I should forgett there were such a thing to bee don as going to bed. Since I writt this my Company is increased by two, My Brother Harry, and a faire Neece, the Eldest of my Brother Peyton's Daughter's,[4] she is soe much a woman, that I am almost ashamed to say I am her Aunte, and soe Pritty that if I had any designe to gaine a Servant[5] I should not like her company. but I have none, and therfore, shall indeavour to keep her heer as long as I can perswade her father to spare her, for she will Easily consent to it haveing soe much of my humor (though it bee the worst thing in her) as to like a melancholy place, and litle company My Brother John is not come down againe nor am I certaine when hee will bee heer, hee went from London into Gloucestershyr to my Sister[6] who was very ill, and his youngest Girle of which hee was very fonde is since dead, but I beleeve by that time his wife has a litle recoverd her sicknesse and the losse of her Childe, hee will bee comeing this way, My father is reasonably well but keeps his Chamber still, and will hardly I am affrayde Ever bee soe perfectly recoverd as to come abroade againe;

I am sorry for Poore Walker, but you need not doubt of what hee has of yours in his hands, for it seems hee do's not use to do his worke himself, (I speake seriously) hee keeps a french man that setts all his Seal's and Ring's[7]

---

2 Henry Molle, though a distant relative, was a regular visitor. He was a Fellow of King's College, Cambridge. **3** Levinus Bennet, sheriff of Cambridgeshire; Molle hoped that Dorothy would marry him, but she was not enthusiastic. **4** Evidently, Dorothy sometimes wrote her letters in instalments. Her niece, child of her older sister Elizabeth and Sir Thomas Peyton, was also called Dorothy. **5** 'Servant': suitor. **6** Her sister-in-law, Eleanor. **7** In January, Dorothy had asked Sir William if he could get some seals for her, to use on her letters to him; Walker was the man who set them. It is not clear why he is to be pitied.

if what you say of my Lady Lepington bee of your owne knoledge I shall beleeve you, but otherwise I can assure you I have heard from People that prettend to know her very well, that her kindenesse to Compton was very moderate, and that she never liked him soe well, as when hee dyed and gave her his Estate[8] but they might bee deceived, and tis not soe strange as that you should imagin a Coldenesse and an indifference in my letter where I soe litle meant it, but I am not displeased you should desyre my kindenesse, Enough to aprehende the losse of it, when it is safest, Only I would not have you aprehende it soe farr as to believe it possible, that were an injury to all the assurances I have given you and if you love mee you cannot think mee unworthy, I should think myself soe, if I founde you grew indifferent to mee, that I have had soe long and soe perticuler a freindship for, but sure this is more then I need to say, you are Enough in my heart to know all my thoughts, and if soe, you know better then I can tell you how much I am

Yours

[Saturday 25 or Sunday 26 June 1653]

Sir

You amaze me with your story of Tom Cheek,[9] I am certaine hee could not have had it where you imagin, and tis a miracle to mee that hee remembers there is such a one in the world as his Cousin D.O. I am sure hee has not seen her this sixe yeare, and I think but once in his life. If hee has spred his opnion in that Famely I shall quickly heare on't, for my Cousen Molle is now gon to Kimolten[10] to my Lord Manchester and from thence hee goe's to Moore Parke[11] to my Cousen Franklins and in one, or both, hee will bee sure to meet with it. The matter is not great for though I confesse I doe naturaly hate the noise and talk of the worlde and should bee best pleased never to bee knowne int upon any occasion whatsoever, yet since it can never bee wholy avoyded one must sattisfye on's selfe by doeing nothing that one need care whoe know's, I doe not think it (a propos) to tell any body that you and I are very good friends, and it were better sure, if nobody knew it but wee our selves, but if in spight of all our Caution it bee discoverd, tis no Treason, nor any thing Else that's ill, and if any body should tell mee that I had a greater kindnesse and Esteem for you, then for anyone besydes I doe not think I should deny it. howsoever you doe oblige mee in not owning any such thing, for as you say, I have noe reason to take it ill that you indeavour to preserve mee a liberty,

8 This refers to a discussion initiated in the previous letter about the consequences of a duel fought between George Brydges, Lord Chandos, and Henry Compton over Mary Carey, Lady Lepington. Compton was killed and Chandos was subsequently convicted of manslaughter. 9 Thomas Cheke was a distant relative of Dorothy and a first cousin of Henry Molle. A complex web of family relationships connects all the people and places mentioned in the next few lines. 10 Kimbolton in Cambridgeshire, the seat of the Earl of Manchester. 11 Moor Park was the house in Hertfordshire where Dorothy and William were to spend their honeymoon; later they named their own house after it. The gardens at the original Moor Park were designed by Lucy Harington, Countess of Bedford (1581–1627), an important patron of the arts.

though I am never likely to make use on't, besydes that I agree with you too, that certainly tis much better you should owe my kindenesse to nothing but your owne merritt and my inclination then that there should lye any other Necessity upon mee of makeing good my worde to you.

for god sake doe not complaine soe that you doe not see mee, I beleeve I doe not suffer lesse in't then you, but tis not to bee helpt if I had a Picture that were fitt for you, you should have it, I have but one that's anything like and that's a great one, but I will send it some time or other to Cooper or Hoskins,[12] and have a litle one drawne by it, if I cannot bee in Towne to sitt my selfe.

you undoe mee by but dreaming how happy wee might have bin, when I consider how farr wee are from it in reality, Alasse, how can you talk of deffyeing fortune, noe body lives without it, and therfore why should you imagin you could; I know not how my Brother coms to bee soe well informed as you say but I am certaine hee know's the utmost of the injury's you have received from her, tis not possible she should have used you worse then hee say's, wee have had another debate, but much more calmly 'twas just upon his goeing up to Towne and perhaps hee thought it not ffitt to parte in Anger, not to wrong him hee never sayed to mee (what Ere hee thought) a word in prejudice of you, in your owne person and I never heard him accuse any thing but your fortune, and my indiscretion, and wheras I did Expect that (at least in Complement to mee) hee should have sayed wee had bin a Couple of Fooles well mett, hee says by his Troath hee do's not blame you, but bids mee not deceive my self to think you have any great passion for mee.

If you have done with the first Part of Cyrus[13] I should bee glad Mr Hollingsworth had it, because I mentioned some such thing in my Last to my Lady.[14] but there is noe hast of restoreing the other unlesse she should send to mee for it which I beleeve she will not, I have a third Tome heer against you have done with that second, and to Encourage you let mee assure you that the more you read of them you will like them still better.

O mee whilest I think ont, let mee aske you one question seriously, and pray resolve mee truely; doe I look soe Stately as People aprehende, I vowe to you I made nothing on't when Sir Emperour[15] sayed soe, because I had no great opinion of his Judgment, but Mr Freeman[16] makes mee mistruste my self Extreamly (not that I am sorry I did apeare soe to him since it kept mee from the displeasure of refuseing an offer, which I doe not perhaps deserve), but that it is a scurvy quality in it self, and I am affrayd I have it in great measure if I showed any of it to him, for whome I have soe much of respect and Esteem, if it bee soe you must need's know it, for though my kindnesse will not let mee look soe upon you, you can see what I doe to other People, and besydes there was a time when wee our selves were indifferent to one another, did I doe soe then or have I learn't it since. for god sake tell mee that I may try

12 Miniaturists working in London. 13 *Artamène; ou, Le Grand Cyrus*, a lengthy romance by Madeleine de Scudéry, published in instalments 1645–53; it was extremely popular in both France and England. 14 Diana Rich, one of Dorothy's closest friends. 15 Sir Justinian Isham, one of Dorothy's suitors – her nickname for him alludes to the Roman Emperor Justinian. 16 In the previous letter, Dorothy had denied a rumour that Ralph Freeman was her 'Servant'.

to mend it. I could wish too, that you would lay your commands on mee to forbeare fruite, heer is Enough to kill a 1000 such as I am, and soe Exelently good that nothing but your power can secure mee, therfor forbid it mee that I may live to bee

Yours

[Sat 17 or Sun 18 Sept 1653]

Sir

All my quarrells to you are kinde on's, for sure tis alike impossible for me to bee angry, as for you to give mee the occasion; therefor when I chide (unlesse it bee that you are not carefull Enough of your selfe and hazarde too much a health that I am more concerned in, then in my owne), you need nott studdy much for Excuses, I can Easily forgive you any thing but want of kindenesse. the Judgement you have made of the fower Lovers[17] I recommended to you do's soe perfectly agree with what I think of them, that I hope it will not Alter when you have read their Story's L'Amant Absent has (in my opinion) a Mistresse, soe much beyonde any of the rest that to bee in danger of Loosing her, is more then to have lost the others, L'Amant non Aimé was an Asse under favour, (notwithstanding the Princesse Cleobulines letter), his Mistresse had Caprices that would have suited better with our Amant Jaloux then with any body Else; And the Prince Artibie was much too blame that hee outlived his belle Leontine. but if you have mett with the beginning of the story of Amestris and Aglatides, You will find the rest of it in this part I send you now, and tis to mee one of the Prittiest I have read and the most Naturall; they say the Gentleman that writes this Romance[18] has a Sister that lives with him a Mayde and she furnishes him with all the litle Story's that come between soe that hee only Contrives the main designe and when hee wants somthing to Entertaine his company withall hee call's to her for it, shee has an Exelent fancy sure, and a great deal of witt, but I am sorry to tell it you, they say tis the most ilfavoured Creatur that Ever was borne, and it is often soe, how seldome doe wee see a person Exelent in any thing but they have some great deffect with it that pulls them low Enough to make them Equall with Other People, and there is Justice in't; those that have fortunes have nothing Else, and those that want it deserve to have it; that's but small comfort though you'le say, 'tis confess't but there is noe such thing as perfect happynesse in this world, those that have come the nearest it had many things to wish, and – O mee whither am I goeing, sure tis the Deaths head I see stand before mee putts mee into this grave discourse, (pray doe not think I meant that for a conceite[19] neither) how idly have I spent two sydes of my paper and am affrayde besydes I shall not have time to write two more, therfor i'le make hast to tell you, that my

---

17 The four lovers, identified in what follows, are characters in Book 3 of *Le Grand Cyrus*. 18 On first publication, Georges de Scudéry was named as the author. 19 She means her unconscious juxtaposition of 'Deaths head' and 'grave'.

friendship for you, makes mee concern'd in all your relations, that I have a great respect for Sir meerly as hee is your Father, and that tis much increased by his Kindnesse to you, that hee has all my Prayers and wishes for his safety and that you will Oblige mee in letting mee know when you heare any good news from him; hee has mett with a great deal of good company I beleeve.

My Lady Ormonde I am told is wayting for a passage and divers others, but this winde (if I am not mistaken) is not good for them; In Earnest 'tis a most sad thing that a person of her quality should bee reduced to such a fortune as she has lived upon these late year's and that shee should Loose that which she brought as well as that which was her husbands; yet I heer she has now gott some of her owne Lands in Ireland granted her, but whither she will gett it when she com's there is I think a question;[20] Wee have a Lady new come in to this Country that I pitty too Extreamly shee is one of my Lord of Valentia's daughters and has marryed an old fellow that is some threescore and ten whoe has a house that is fitter for the hoggs then for her, and a fortune that will not at all recompence the least of these inconveniency's; Ah tis most Certain I should have chosen a handsome Chaine to Leade my Apes in, before such a husband but marryeng and hanging goe by destiny they say;[21] it was not mine it seem's to have an Emperour the spitefull man, meerly to vexe mee has gon and Marryed my Country Woman my Lord Lee's daughter what a multitude of willow garlands shall I weare before I dye,[22] I think I had best make them into fagotts this cold weather, the flame they would make in a Chimny would bee of more use to mee then that which was in the hearts of all those that gave them me and would last as long.

I did not think I should have gott thus farr, I have bin soe persecuted with Vissetts all this week I have noe time to dispatch any thing of businesse soe that now I have don this I have 40 letters more to write how much rather would I have them all to you then to anybody else, or rather how much better would it bee if there needed none to you and that I could tell you without writeing

how much I am Yours

20 Lady Ormonde was a member of an important Royalist family in Ireland; she was experiencing financial difficulties because of the political situation. 21 Leading apes in hell was proverbially the fate of spinsters: cf. Shakespeare, *The Taming of the Shrew*, II. i. 34; another proverb cited by Shakespeare is alluded to in the notion that 'hanging and wiving goes by destiny', *Merchant of Venice*, II. ix. 83. 22 Willow garlands were traditionally worn by abandoned lovers.

ANNA TRAPNEL

Strange and Wonderfull Newes from White-Hall (1654)

This is one of the four texts published in 1654 attributed to Anna Trapnel: the texts vary in length and, to a certain degree, in form and content (her other texts also contain poetry and are more autobiographical in nature), but *Strange Newes* shares an important characteristic with the others: it is an account of her prophecies uttered in a trance-like state that has been taken down by a 'Relator'. *Strange Newes* is reproduced in full below. Trapnel fell into a trance at Whitehall during the trial of Vavasor Powell, a Fifth Monarchist leader. Powell, along with Christopher Freake and John Simpson, had been arrested for prophesying and preaching against Cromwell after the dissolution of the Barebones Parliament in 1653. Trapnel's prophetic utterances clearly criticise Cromwell's rule, identifying it as the fourth 'Horn' of Daniel's prophecy (see Daniel 7), which had to be overthrown before the arrival of the personal rule of Christ ('the Fifth Monarchy'). The copy text is BL, E. 224 (3), pp. 3–8, which was printed in London for Robert Sale.

Upon the 7 day of the 11 month called *Janu.* being the 6 day of the week, or Fryday, Mr. *Powel* Minister of the Gospel in *Wales*, being brought before the Council at Whitehall, to give an account of some things by him delivered in his publike Exercises: Among many other friends who came to see what would be done with him, there came a maid, Mrs. *Anna Trapnel* by name, who waiting in a little room neer the Council door, where there was a fire; amongst many others she staid for Mr. *Powels* coming forth, and then intending to return home, she was beyond her own thoughts or intentions, having much trouble in her thoughts; and being as it were seized by the Lord, she was carried forth in a Spirit of prayer and singing from noon till night, and went down into Mr. *Roberts* Lodging, who kept the Ordinary in White-Hall, and finding her natural strength going from her, she took her bed about eleven of the clock in the night, where she lay from that day being the 7 day of the month, to the 19 day of the same month, in all 12 dayes together: the first five dayes she neither eat nor drank; and the rest of the time, once in 24 ho: sometimes a very little toast in small beer; sometimes onely chewed it, and took down the moysture; sometimes she drank of the small beer, and sometimes onely washt her mouth therewith, and then cast it forth, lying in bed with her eyes shut, and her hands seldom seen to move: She delivered in that time many and various things, speaking every day 3 or 4 hours, and sometimes praying both night and day, and singing spiritual songs; which many eminent persons hearing of, amongst the rest, came Col. *Sydenham* (a member of the Council), Col. *West*, Col. *Bennet*, with his wife, Col. *Bingham*, the Lady *Dercy*, the Lady *Vermuden*, and divers others; who heard her declare as followeth, to wit, That 7 years since she being sick of a Feaver, and given over by all her friends as one not like to live, the Lord then gave her faith to believe from that Scripture, After two dayes I will revive thee, and the 3d day I will raise thee up, and thou shalt live in my sight; which two days I understood to be two weeks that I shold lye in that feaver; and at that very time and hour that it took her, that very hour it left her; and according from which time, the Lord made use of her for refreshing of afflicted ones, and such as were under temptation: and when that time was ended, she being in her chamber, desired of the Lord to know whether she had done that which was off, and from himself, Reply was made to her, That she should approve her heart to God, and for that she had been faithful in a little, she should be made an instrument of much more; for particular soules shal not onely have benefit by her, but the Universality of Saints shal have discoveries of God through her: whereupon shee prayed that she might be led by the still waters, and honour God secretly, being conscious to her self of the deceitfulness of her own heart, looking upon her self as the worst amongst Gods flock: whereupon the Lord told her, that out of the mouthes of babes and sucklings he would perfect his praise [Ps. 8: 2]. After which she had many Visions, and Revelations touching the Government of the Nation, the Parl. Army, and Ministry, and having fasted nine days, nothing coming within her lips, she had a most strange Vision of horns [Dan. 7–8]; she saw four Horns which were 4 Powers: the first was that of the Bishops, which first Horn she saw broken in two, and thrown aside: then appeared the second Horn, and joyned to it an head, and although it seemed to bee more white then the first, yet it endeavouring to get aloft it was suddenly pulled down and broken to pieces. The third Horn had many splinters joyned to it, like to the skales of a fish, and this was presented to be a Parl. consisting of many men, having very fair and plausible pretences of love: yet this Horn she saw broken to pieces, and so scattered, that not so much as one bit remained. Then she saw the 4. Horn, and that was very short, but very sharp, and full of variety of colours sparkling red and white; and it was said to her, that this last *horn* was different from the other three, because of great proud and swelling words, and great promises of kindness should go forth to it from all people, like unto that of *Absolom*, speaking good words to the people in the gate to draw their affections away from honest *David* [2 Sam. 15]. After this she had a Vision, wherein she saw many Oaks, with spreding branches full of leaves; and presently she saw a very goodly tree for stature and compleatness every way, before which great Tree the rest of the Oaks crumbled to dust; which she perceiving, desired Scripture to make known to her the Vision: whereupon Reply was made in the first of Isaiah, –They shall be confounded in the Oakes which they have chosen [Isa. 1: 29].

Another Vision she had two nights before the Lord Protector was proclaimed; at which time she saw a glorious Throne with winged Angels flying before the throne, and crying, Holy, holy, holy, unto the Lord; the great one is coming down with terror to the enemies, and glory and deliverance to the sincere, and them that are upright in the earth. In another Vision she saw a great company of little children walking on the earth, and a light shining round about them, and a very glorious person in the midst of them, with a Crown on his head, speaking these words: These will I honour with my Reigning presence in the midst of them, and the Oppressor shall dye in the wilderness.

When she was at White-hall she saw as it were great darkness on the earth, and a marvellous dust like unto a thick mist, or smoak, ascending upward from the earth; and at a little distance a great company of cattel, some like Buls, some like Oxen, and some lesser cattel, their faces and heads like men, having on either side their heads a horn: for the foremost, his countenance was perfectly like unto ——s, and on a sudden there was a great shout of those that followed him, he being singled out alone, and the foremost and he looking back, they bowed themselves unto him, and leaped up from the earth; and shewed much joy that he was become their Supream; and immediatly they fawning upon him, he seemed to run at her; and as he was neer to her breast with his horn and hand an arm grasped her round, and a voice said to her, I will be thy safety; and then he run at many precious Saints that stood in his way, and that durst look boldly in his face, he gave them many pushes, scratching them with his hornes, and driving them into several houses: he ran along still; at length there was a great silence, and suddenly there brake forth great fury in the earth, and they were presently scattered, their horns broken, and so tumbled into graves: With that she brake forth, and sang praise, and the Lord said to her, Mark that Scripture, three horns shall arise, and a fourth shall come out different from the former, which shall be more terrible to the Saints then others that went before: though like a Lamb, as is spoken in the Revelations, in appearance a Lamb; but pushing with his horns, like a Beast: being not onely one, but many, and much strength joyned together [Rev. 13: 11–18].

Upon the tenth of *Feb.* or eleventh month, the Relator came into the chamber where she lay, where he heard her making melody with a spritual Song, and after she had done singing, she brake forth into these and the like words: It is not all the force in the World that can strike one stroke against thine, but thou sufferest them to come forth to try thine, Oh that thine could believe thee for the breaking of thine enemies as well as for the binding up of thine own people, all things under the Sun, all things before, in or round about you, shal work for your good, when you come to know more of the mystery and life of the Scriptures, how will you praise his Highness? the Enemy is strong, Satan is strong, Instruments are strong, Temptations are strong: but what strengths are against thy flock, they cannot be without the Lyon, and Lyon-like Creatures: But oh! if thy servants suffer, let them not suffer through passion, or rash words, but as Lambes: there is a zeal which is but from Nature, that a mans own Spirit may prompt him to: but the zeal of God is accompanied with meekness, humility, grief for Christ: and seeing thou hast taken thine Handmaid into the Mount, who can keep in the rushing wind, who can rule the influence of the Heavenly Orizon; yea, who can stop thy Spirit; it is good to be in the Territories, in the Regions, where thou walkst before thy servant: Oh, how glittering, how glorious are they: what sparklings are there. Thou hast yet a great Gust to come upon the earth, a great Wind that shal shake the Trees, that now appear upon the Earth, that are full of the leaves of Profession; but they have nothing but outward beauty and outward flourish; but thy Trees, Oh Lord, are full of sap. A great number of people have said, O let our Oaks stand, let them not be cut down. But sayes the Lord, I will make you ashamed in the Oakes that ye have chosen [Isa. 1: 29]; and because ye will have those, I will now give you other Oaks: and what are they? a first, a second, and a third Power, and they are broken one after another: But oh thine own have had a great hand in these things: thine have said, We will have Oaks and Gardens, how have they run to and fro, saith the Lord? and now I will give you Gardens, but they shall have no Springs in them; but they shalbe as dry chopt ground; yea, as Fallow-ground: What lovelyness is there, to walk upon Fallow-ground? you may have stumbling walkings upon them: you shal have no green grass in these Gardens: what have all the Gardens of the Earth been? they have been as stumbling blocks to thine: But oh, thou wilt by these strange wayes, draw up thine into thy upper and nether Springs: thou hast deceived thy Saints once more about these Gardens, let them now run after them no more: but be ashamed, and abashed, we have hankered from Mountain to Hill; We have said Salvation is in this Hill, and in that Mountain; but let us not say so any longer: When we shalbe drawn up to thee, then we shal prosper; and thou wilt give us a Vinyard, and Gardens, and fruitful Trees of thine own, which shall abide.

And after some repose she sang divers Hymnes, or spiritual Songs; and among other things, spake as followeth:

Lord, let it be sounded in their Ears, and let them mark, it will be as great superfluity as ever, as great lust, as great wickedness, as great enmity as ever; yea, and greater then before. Oh, they are all for themselves; and doth not *Sathan* appear in their Feasts, and in their Garments, and in their Locks: yea, O Gideon, when in thine own Family there are those that are naked and wanton, Oh let not this be found in thy Family. *David* had not such in his Family; and if thou must rule the Nation, then be sure to look into thine own Family, and rule that; but perhaps thou mayst say, *thou canst not rule them*: O then remember what God said to *Ely* of old, because of his Sons, *How can any go and cry out to King Jesus, if he have him not in his own bosome.* But oh, he is a sealed One; then how beautiful will his Walks be; and if the Spirit of Christ reign in his soul, then he may reign for Christ. Otherwise not. Therefore, you doubting *Christians*, have a care that you have courage given into your harts, before you go out to plead against Antichrist, the Devil and Wickedness, and come you Army-men, and acquaint your selves with the *Lord Jehovah*, for if you have not acquaintance with him, then all you have is nothing. Oh do justice, and do it for Justice-sake, and not for by ends or respects: And thou, Oh *Gideon*, who art in the highest place, thou art not onely to do justice thy self, but thou art to see justice done in all Places, Courts, or councels, and Committees, that they may not feed upon the Poor. Thou art not onely to receive pleasures at home, but to establish Righteousness abroad. Oh by your diligence, make it manifest that you love justice and mercy, as you seem to do. Oh remember *Absolom*, who was of a fair and gentle courage, and of a lovely nature, but it was to steal away the hearts of the People from his Father *David*. But God forbid your Honour should be stain'd with the least Guilt thereof. And thus soon after she ended in prayer and singing, having lain in bed 11 dayes and 12 nights together. After which time, she rose up in the morning and the same day travelled on foot from White-hall to Hackney; and from thence back to *Mark-Lane* in *London* in health and strength.

ELINOR CHANNEL

A Message from God, By a Dumb Woman (1653/4)

In order to legitimise Channel's prophecy, the title page of this text cites Proverbs 31: 8, 'Open thy mouth for the Dumb in the ca[u]se of all such as are appointed to destruction'. The extract below was published and mediated by Arise Evans, who is succinctly described as a 'fanatic' in the *Dictionary of National Biography* and became notorious for his claim to be Christ and his publications urging the Restoration of Charles II. The title page makes a point of stressing the date of publication 'Printed in the year 1653. Or as the Vulgar think 1654', and the text discusses the drawbacks of the Julian and Gregorian calendar systems. Despite this, as Evans makes direct reference to Anna Trapnel, which suggests that *A Message* was published after *Strange and Wonderful Newes*, we have placed it after Trapnel's prophecy. The copy text is BL, G. 16132, pp. 1–7.

To his Highness the Lord Protector Oliver Crumwel. *The humble Petition of* Elenor Channel

May it please your Highness to understand, That your Petitioner is an inhabitant at Cranley in *Surrey*, who upon a Sabbath day about two Months agone, at night, as she was in bed in a slumber, had a Blow given her upon her heart, which blow awaked her. And immediately with that, the thoughts of her heart were changed, and all the corruption thereof taken away, that from that day to this, she could think of no evil. And then she heard an audible voice, which said unto her, *Come away, I will send thee on my message to* London, *fear not to go, for I thy Lord am with thee.* And the thoughts of your Petitioners heart was so directed, that she was given to understand, *how that the Spirit of the Lord had called her;* to the end that she should be sent to your Highness: and by the same *Holy Spirit*, inwardly though she be but a weak woman in expression, she was taught in brief how to express her message from God to your Highness. And your Petitioner being three times hindered by her Husband, who is a very poor man, and hath many small children, three of them very young ones, her mind was sore troubled that her sleep went from her; and at sometimes she was speechless: whereupon your Petitioners Husband seeing her restless condition, consented to let her come to *London*, that she might express her mind to your Highness and have rest in her spirit. The premises being considered, and further to give your Highness to understand the Petitioners message to you, which she hopes will not onely be accepted of you, but will also be effected by you.

The words of her Message are these that follow:

1. She is to say upon her Coming to you, *Peace be to this house, and peace be to the whole Kingdom, and the peace of God be with us evermore. Amen.*

2. She is to say to you, *The God of* Abraham, *the God of* Isaac, *and the God of* Jacob *hath opened the mouth of the* Dumb *to speak for peace.*[1] *The sword must be stayed. The world draweth toward an end, and the knots of peace and love must be made in all Christian lands.*

3. She is to say to you, *Sir, you have taken upon you to be a Protector of your Lords* Vine-yard,[2] *but he requireth that you should make the Hedges and the Walls of it; which is Peace and Love, and the true* Gospel.[3] *And that you should protect the* Steward *to plant his vin-yard.*

4. She is to say unto you, *If a man fall into the hands of a Creditor, if his Creditor be one of Gods servants, he will not take Bodie and Goods; if his* Bodie *pays the* Debt, *his* Heir *shall have the Inheritance.*[4]

Be it known to your Highness, that your Petitioner is a true Member of the Catholick and Apostolick Faith, as it was Reformed and Established in the Church of *England*, by King *Edward* the 6. and continued by Queen *Elisabeth*, King *James*, and King *Charles*.[5] And though the Petitioner can say or dispute but little for it, yet she believeth that to be the true and onely way of salvation, which in due time shall prevail over all the earth.

Amen.

Elenor Channel

April 19. 1654

1 Marginal note explains that 'By the *Dumb* she meaneth her self, cause she had been dumb'. 2 Marginal note: 'By the *Vine-yard* she meaneth the *Church* & *Kingdom*'. 3 Marginal note: 'By the *True Gospel* she meaneth that worship we had once. By the *Steward* she means the *King*'. 4 Marginal note: 'By the *Bodie that paid the debt*, she means the *late King* that died. By the *Heir* his *Son*'. 5 'Catholick and Apostolick Faith': this phrase is still used in Church of England services today and should not be read as a reference to Roman Catholicism; rather, it refers to the notion of an all-encompassing, pre-schismatic Church. In this context, it signifies Channel's Anglicanism.

This poor woman came to the Court upon the 17. day of last *April*, and thought immediately to have spoken with his Highness the Lord Protector, and to return again the same day: but alas she found it other ways. And some of the Guard about the Court told her, if she had but five pounds to give them, they would help her to the presence of the Lord Protector. Whereupon, after two days waiting in vain at Court, being much troubled that she could not come before his Highness, to discharge her conscience, she came to the Citie of *London*, and wandered up and down to see if she could get any body to take it from her mouth, and publish it in Print, that she might get some ease that way: but of a long while, she being a stranger, she could get none to hear or regard her. At last she met with some compassionate bodie that talked with her, and sent her with a note to me, who took all the Report from her mouth, as you have it above, and then sent her away, promising to get it Printed, if she could not get the Copie delivered to his Highness, which she had to give him, and have sen her no more since.

But hearing now that such a like woman is about the Citie, and that she is Dumb, and that she was in *Fleet-street* on Sunday *June* 18. where she stood mute for a long while, and as it is said, the cruel Bedles dragged her to Bridewel,[6] and wounded the poor soul for nothing, but because she stood harmlesly in the street: and that they refused her at Bridewel, and turned her out among the wanton mad crew, who flocked about her and abused her; when indeed, if there had been any charitie in them at Bridewel (as some pretend the house is for that use) there was for them a fair object to shew their charitie upon: but she stayed thereabouts until night; and what is become of her since, God knows, we hear nothing more of her.

Now this woman was very sensible and profound in what she spake to me, but as she said, when she is Dumb, all her sences are taken up, and then the matter which troubles her mind, is dictated and made plain to her by the Spirit of God; so that when she comes to her self, she has it by heart. And though it be but short, yet you shall find more truth and substance in it, than all *Hana Trampenels* songs or sayings, whom some account of as the *Diana* of the English, *Acts* 19. 34.[7] as may appear by this that was written for her.

---

6 'Bedles': parish officers with the power to punish petty offenders; 'Bridewel': a house of correction. 7 I.e., Anna Trapnel; the biblical reference here is to the story of the destruction of the pagan goddess Diana's temple. Thus Evans is identifying Trapnel with paganism and idolatry, in opposition to Channel's 'true' Christianity.

PRISCILLA COTTON AND MARY COLE

To the Priests and People of England we Discharge our Consciences, and Give them Warning (1655)

Cotton and Cole were Quakers from Plymouth in Devon. They composed this text while imprisoned in Exeter as a result of their religious activities. Its primary focus is on challenging abuses which the authors perceive within the Christian community, but it has considerable interest for modern readers as an unusual intervention in the debate about whether women could be permitted to speak or before religious gatherings, a debate also addressed by Margaret Fell (see below, pp. 217–20), with whom Cotton corresponded. Priscilla Cotton was the author of several other works, including *A Visitation of Love unto All People* (1661). The text (BL, E. 854. (13)) is about 3000 words long, and is mainly a challenge to those Christians who are absorbed in their own 'learning and self-conceitedness' instead of 'hearken[ing] to the light of Jesus Christ'. The final section is reproduced below.

Come down then thou therefore that hast built among the stars by thy arts and learning; for it's thy pride and thy wisdom, that hath perverted thee, thou hast gone in the way of *Cain*,[1] in envy and malice, and ran greedily after the reward of *Balaam* [Num. 23], in covetousness, and if thou repent not, shalt perish in the gainsaying of *KORE*:[2] for if a Son or a Daughter be moved from the Lord, to go into the Assembly of the people, in a message from the Lord God, thou canst not endure to hear them speak sound Doctrine, having a guilty Conscience, and fearing they would declare against thy wickedness, thou incensest the people, telling them, that they are dangerous people, Quakers, so making the people afraid of us: and incensest the Magistrates, telling them that they must lay hold on us, as troublers of the people, and disturbers of the peace, and so makes them thy drudges to act thy malice, that thy filthiness may not be discovered, and thy shame appear; but God will make them in one day to forsake thee, and leave and fly from thee, though for the present thou Lordest it over Magistrates, people, meeting house and all, as though all were thine: and thou sittest as a Queen and Lady over all,[3] and wilt have the pre-eminence and hast got into the seat of God, the consciences of the people, and what thou sayest must not be contradicted: if thou bid them fight and war,

1 The son of Adam and Eve, who was jealous of his brother Abel, and murdered him: see Genesis 4. 2 Jude 11; more often spelt Korah. 3 Cotton and Cole seem here to appropriate the seventeenth-century identification of the Roman Catholic Church with the Whore of Babylon mentioned in Revelation 17. Hilary Hinds notes in *God's Englishwomen* (Manchester: Manchester University Press, 1996) that this is an important move in the identification of priests with 'the woman'.

they obey it; if thou bid them persecute and imprison, they do it; so that they venture their Bodies and Souls to fulfil thy lusts of envy and pride, and in thy pride thou contemnest all others, thou tellest the people Women must not speak in a Church, whereas it is not spoke only of a Female, for we are all one both male and female in Christ Jesus [Gal. 3: 28], but it's weakness that is the woman by the Scriptures forbidden, for else thou puttest the Scriptures at a difference in themselves, as still its thy practice out of thy ignorance; for the Scriptures do say, that all the Church may prophesie one by one [I Cor. 14: 31], and that women were in the Church, as well as men, do thou judge; and the Scripture saith, that a woman may not prophesie with her head uncoverd [I Cor. 11: 5], lest she dishonour her head: now thou wouldst know the meaning of that Head, let the Scripture answer, I Cor. 11.3. *The head of every man is Christ*. Man in his best estate is altogether vanity, weakness, a lie [Ps. 39: 5]. If therefore any speak in the Church, whether man or woman, and nothing appear in it but the wisdome of man, and Christ, who is the true head, be not uncovered, do not fully appear, Christ the head is then dishonoured. Now the woman or weakness, that is man, which in his best estate or greatest wisdom is altogether vanity, that must be covered with the covering of the Spirit, a garment of righteousness, that its nakedness may not appear and dishonour thereby come. Here mayst thou see from the Scriptures, that the woman or weakness whether male or female, is forbidden to speak in the Church; but its very plain, *Paul*,[4] nor *Apollo* [Acts 18: 26], nor the true Church of Christ, were not of that proud envious Spirit that thou art of, for they owned Christ Jesus in Man or woman; for *Paul* bid *Timothy* to help those women that laboured with him in the Gospel [Phil. 4: 3], and *Apollo* hearkened to a woman, and was instructed by her, and Christ Jesus appeared to the women first,[5] and sent them to preach the Resurrection to the Apostles, and *Philip* had four Virgins that did prophesie [Acts 21: 9]. Now thou dost respect persons I know, and art partial in all things, and so judgest wickedly, but there is no respect of persons with God. Indeed, you yourselves are the women, that are forbidden to speak in the Church, that are become women; for two of your Priests came to speak with us, and when they could not bear sound reproof and wholesome Doctrine, that did concern them, they railed on us with filthy speeches, as no other they can give to us, that deal plainly and singly with them, and so ran from us. So leaving you to the light in all your consciences to judge of what we have writ, we remain Prisoners in *Exeter* gaol for the word of God.

4 A crucial figure in the early dissemination of Christianity, Paul was the author of most of the New Testament Epistles, which are extremely important texts for the nonconformist tradition. 5 Matthew 28, Mark 16, Luke 24, John 20.

MARGARET CAVENDISH, DUCHESS OF NEWCASTLE

Nature's Pictures, Drawn by Fancies Pencil to the Life (1656)

Margaret Cavendish, Duchess of Newcastle, was an enormously prolific writer, producing poetry, drama, prose, fiction, science fiction, autobiography, biography, letters, orations and philosophical treatises. *Natures Pictures,* of which there were two editions, in 1656 and 1671, was her fifth book to be printed in three years. At nearly 400 pages, the book contains six prefatory addresses to the reader (one of which is printed below) and in Cavendish's words, the material consists of 'several feigned Stories of Natural Descriptions, as Comical, Tragical, and Tragi-Comical, Poetical, Romancical, Philosophical, and Historical, both in Prose and Verse, some all Verse, some all Prose, some mixt, partly Prose, and partly Verse. Also, there are some Morals, and some Dialogues . . . and a true Story at the latter end, wherein there is no feigning'. The latter refers to her own autobiography and the book includes the fictions, 'Assaulted and Pursued Chastity', 'The Contract' and 'The She Anchoret'. Thus, the prefatory material and the comical tales reproduced below represent only a fraction of her work in this one collection. The copy text is BL, G. 11599, printed in 1656 for J. Martin and J. Allestrye, sig. 4r; pp. 109–13; pp. 114–17; pp. 144–8.

To the Reader

As for these Tales I name Romanticall, I would not have my Readers think I write them either to please, or to make foolish whining Lovers, for it is a humor of all humors, I have an aversion to; but my endeavour is to express the sweetness of Vertue, and the Graces, and to dress and adorn them in the best expressions I can, as being one of their servants, that do unfeignedly, unweariedly, industriously, and faithfully wait upon them: Neither do I know the rule or method of Romancy Writing; for I never read a Romancy Book throughout in all my life, I mean such as I take to be Romances, wherein little is writ which ought to be practised, but rather shunned as foolish Amorosities, and desperate Follies, not noble Loves discreet Vertues, and true Valour. The most I ever read of Romances was but part of three Books, as the three parts of one, and the half of the two others, otherwise I never read any; unless as I might by chance, as when I see a Book, not knowing of what it treats, I may take and read some half a dozen lines, where perceiving it a Romance, straight throw it from me, as an unprofitable study, which neither instructs, directs, nor delights me: And if I thought those Tales I call my Romanticall Tales, should or could neither benefit the life, nor delight the minde of my Readers, no more than these pieces of Romances I read, did me, I would never suffer them to be printed;

but self-partiality perswades me otherwise, but if they should not, I desire those that have my book to pull out those tales and burn them: Likewise if I could think that any of my writings should create Amorous thoughts in idle brains, I would make blotts insteed of letters; but I hope this work of mine will rather quench Amorous passions, than inflame them, and beget chast Thoughts, nourish love of Vertue, kindle humane Pitty, warme Charity, increase Civillity, strengthen fainting patience, encourage noble Industry, crown Merit, instruct Life; and recreate Time. Also I hope, it will damn vices, kill follies, prevent Errors, forwarne youth, and arme the life against misfortunes: Likewise to admonish, instruct, direct, and perswade to that which is good and best, and in so doing, I the Authoress have my wishes and reward.

The Tobacconist[1]

There were two maides talking of Husbands, for that for the most part is the theame of their discourse, and the subject of their thoughts;

Said the one to the other, I would not marry a man that takes Tobacco for any thing.

Said the second, then it is likely you will have a fool for your husband, for Tobacco is able to make a fool a wise man: for though it doth not always work to wise effects, by reason some fools are beyond all improvement, yet it never failes where any improvement is to be made.

Why, said the first, how doth it work such wise effects?

Said the second, it composes the mind, it busies the thoughts, it attracts all outward objects to the mindes view, it settles and retents the senses; it cleeres the understanding; strengthens the Judgement, spyes out Errors; it evaporates Follyes, it heates Ambition, it comforts sorrow, it abates passions, it excites to Noble actions; it digests conceptions, it inlarges knowledge, it elevates imaginations, it creates phancies, it quickens wit, and it makes reason Pleader, and truth Judge in all disputes or Controversies betwixt Right and Wrong.

Said the first, it makes the breath stinke.

Said the second, you mistake, it will make a stinking breath sweet.

It is a beastly smell, said the first.

Said the second, Civet is a beastly smell, and that you will thrust your nose to, although it be an excrement, and for anything we know, so is Amber-Greece,[2] when Tobacco is sweet and pleasant, wholesom and medicinable hearb.

The Loving Cuckhold[3]

There was a Gentleman that had marryed a Wife, beautifull, modest, chaste, and of a milde and sweet disposition; and after he had been marryed some

1 From 'Her Excellencies Comical Tales in Prose. The first Part'. 2 'Amber-greece': ambergris, a substance used in making perfume. 3 From 'Her Excellencies Comical Tales in Prose, The second Book'.

time, he began to neglect her, and make courtship to other Women; which she perceiving, grew very melancholy; and sitting one day very pensive alone, in comes one of her Husbands acquaintance to see him; but this Lady told him, her Husband was abroad.

Said he, I have been to visit him many times, and still he is gone abroad.

Said she, my Husband finds better Company abroad than he hath at home, or at least thinks so, which makes him go so often forth.

So he, discoursing with the Lady, told her, he thought she was of a very malancholy disposition.

She said, she was not naturally so, but what her misfortunes caused.

Said he, can Fortune be cruel to a Beautifull Lady?

'Tis a sign, said she, I am not Beautifull, to match me to an unkinde Husband.

Said he, to my thinking it is as impossible for your Husband to be unkinde, as Fortune to be cruel.

Said she, you shall be Judge whether he be not so; for first, said she, I have been an obedient Wife, observed his humours, and obeyed his will in every thing; next, I have been a thrifty, cleanly, patient and chaste Wife; thirdly, I brought him a great Portion;[4] and lastly, my Neighbours say I am handsome, and yet my Husband doth neglect me, and despise me, making courtships to other Women, and sometimes, to vex me the more, before my face.

Said he, your Husband is not worthy of you; therefore if I may advise you, I would cast aside the affection I had placed upon him, and bestow it upon a Person that will worship you with an Idolatrous Zeal; and if you please to bestow it on me, I will offer my Heart on the Altar of your Favours, and sacrifice my Services thereon; and my Love shall be as the Vestal Fire that never goeth out, but perpetually burn with a Religious Flame.

Thus speaking and pleading, made courtship to her, but she at first did not receive it; but he having opportunity by reason her Husband was much from home, and using importunity,[5] at last corrupted her, and she making a friendship with this Gentleman, began to neglect her Husband as much as he had done her; which he perceiving, began to pull in the bridle of his loose carriage: but when he perceived his Acquaintance was her courtly Admirer, he began to wooe her anew to gain her from him; but it would not be; for she became from a meek, modest, obedient, and thrifty Wife, to be a ranting, slanting, bold, imperious Wife.[6]

But her Husband grew so fond of her, that he sought all the wayes he could to please her, and was the observants Creature to her that might be, striving to please her in all things or wayes he could devise; insomuch as observing she was never pleased but when she had Gallants to Court her, he would invite Gentlemen to his House, and make Entertainments for them; and those she seemed to favour, he would make dear Friendships with; and would often be

---

4 'Portion': i.e., dowry. **5** 'importunity': pestering in seeking a response. **6** 'slanting': dishonest or devious.

absent, to give them opportunities to be with his Wife alone, hoping to get a favourable look, or kiss for his good services, which she would craftily give him to encourage him.

But the other Gentleman that made the first adresses to her, being a maryed Man, his Wife hearing her Husband was so great a Lover of that Lady, and that that Ladyes Husband was reformed from his incontinent[7] life, and was become a doting fond Wittal,[8] loving and admiring her for being courted and made love to, esteeming that most that others seemed to like well of; she begain to imitate her; which her Husband perceiving, gave her warning not to do so, but she would take no warning, but entertained those that would address themselves; whereupon her Husband threatned her: but at last she was so delighted with variety, that she regarded not his threats; whereupon he used her cruelly, but nothing would reclaim her, onely she would make more secret meetings, wherewith she was better pleased; for secret meetings, as I have heard, give an edge to Adultery; for it is the nature of Mankinde to be most delighted with that which is most unlawfull. But her Husband finding no reformation could be made, he parted with her, for he thought it a greater dishonour to be a Wittal than a Cuckhold, although he was very much troubled to be either; for though he was willing to make a Cuckhold, yet he was not willing to be one himself. Thus you may see the different natures of Men.

The Travelling Spirit[9]

There was a Man when to a Witch, whom he treated to aid his Desires; for, said he, I have a curiousity to travel, but I would go into those Countryes, which, without your power to assist me, I cannot do.

The Witch asked him, what those Countryes were.

He said, he would go to the Moon.

Why, said she, the Natural Philosophers[10] were the onely Men for that Journey, for they travel all the Planets over; and indeed, study Nature so much, and are so diligent and devout in her services, that they despise our great Master the Devil, and would hinder our wayes very much, but that they travel most by Speculation.

Then, said he, I would go to Heaven.

Truly, said she, I cannot carry you thither, for I am as unpracticed in those wayes, and have as little acquaintance there, as the Natural Philosophers have, for they belive there is no such Kingdome.

But if you desire to travel to that Kingdome, you must go to the Divines,[11] who are the onely Guides; yet you must have a care in the choyce; for some will carry you a great way about, and through very troublesome and painfull

7 'incontinent': lacking restraint. 8 'Wittal': a man who is aware of and complaisant about the infidelity of his wife; a contented cuckold. 9 From 'Her Excellencies Comical Tales in Prose. The Third Book'. 10 'Natural Philosophers': natural philosophy was the knowledge and study of nature, or of natural objects and phenomena. 11 'Divines': theologians.

places; others, a shorter, but a very strait, narrow way; others, through wayes that are pleasant and easy; and you will finde, not onely in the Natural Philosophers, but also Divines, such Combats and Dissentions amongst them, that it is both a great hindrance and a trouble to the Passengers, which shews they are not very perfect in their wayes; for many Travellers go, some a quarter, and some half, and some three parts of the way, and then are forced to turn back again, and take another Guide; and so from Guide to Guide, untill they have run them all over, or out of breath, and yet be as far to seek of their way as when they first set out.

Why then, said the Man, carry me to Hell.

Truly, said the Witch, I am but a Servant extraordinary, and have no power to go to my Masters Kingdome untill I dye; although the Way be broad and plain, and the Guides sure; so that I am but his Factor to do him service on the Earth: but yet I can call forth any from thence, although it were the King himself.

Why then, pray, said he, carry me to the Center of the Earth.

That I can do, said she, and so obscurely, that the Natural Philosophers shall never spye us. So she prayed to him to come into her House; for, said she, it is a great Journey, therefore you must take some repast before you go. Besides, said she, your Body will be too cumbersome; wherefore we will leave that behinde, that you may go the lighter, as being all Spirit. So she went out, and came and brought a Dish of *Opium*, and prayed him to eat well thereof; so he eat very heartily; and when he had done, his Senses grew very heavy, insomuch as his Body fell down, his Spirit stole out, and he left his Body asleep.

So the Witch and he took their Journey; and as they went, he found the Climate very untemperate, sometimes very hot, and sometimes very cold: but there were great Varieties in the way; and in some places, monstrous great and high Mountains of the Bones of Men and Beasts, which lay alltogether with one another. Then he saw a very large Sea of Blood, which had issued from slain Bodyes, but those Seas seemed very rough, whereupon he asked what was the reason; she answered, because their Deaths were violent. And there were other Seas of Blood, which seemed so smooth, that there was not a wave to be seen; said he, how comes this to be so smooth and calm? she said, it was the Blood of those that dyed in peace. Then he asked her, where was the Blood of other Creatures, as Beasts, Birds, Fish, and the like. She said, amongst the Blood of Men; for, said she, the Earth knows no difference. And as they went along, they came through a most pleasant place, which she said was the Storehouse of Nature, where the shapes and substances of all kinds of Fruits and Flowers, Trees, or any other Vegetables, but all were of a dusky colour. Then he gathered some Fruit to eat, but it had not tast; and he gathered some Flowers, and they had no smell; whereupon he asked the reason; she said, that the Earth gave onely the form and substance, but the Sun was the onely cause of the tast, smell and colours. And as they went, they saw great Mines, Quarries, and Pits; but she, being vers'd, and knew the way well, did avoyd them, so that they were no hindrance in their Journey, which otherwise would have been. But going down further, it began to grow very dark, being far from the face of the Earth, insomuch that they could hardly see the plainest way; whereupon he told the Witch, that the Hill was so hideously steep, and the place began to grow so dark, that it was very dangerous.

No, said she, there is no danger, since our Bodyes are not here; for our Spirits are so light, that they bear up themselves. So they went; and they went a great length, untill the place grew so strait, as began to be a pain even to their Spirits; whereof he told the Witch, his Spirit was in pain; she said, he must endure it, for the Center of the Earth was a Point in a small Circle. So when he came to the Center of the Earth, he saw a Light like Moonshine: but when he came near, he saw the Circle about the Center was Glow-worms Tails, which gave that Light; and in the Center was an old Man, who neither stood nor sit, for there was nothing to stand or sit on; but he hung as it were in the Air, nor never stirred out of his place, and had been there ever since the World was made; for he having never had a Woman to tempt him to sin, never dyed; and allthough he could never remove out of that place, yet he had the power to call all things on the Earth unto him by degrees, and to dispose of them as he would.

But when they were near the old Man, the Witch excused her coming, and prayed him not to be offended with them; for there was a Man desired Knowledge, and would not spare any pains or industry thereunto; for which he praised the Man, and said, he was welcome; and any thing he could inform him of, he would.

But the old Man asked him about the Chymists[12] that lived upon the face of the Earth.

The Man answered, they made much choyse in talk, and took great pains, and bestowed great costs, to finde the Philosophers Stone,[13] which is to make the Elixar, but could never come to any perfection.

Alas, said the old Man, they are first too unconstant to bring any thing to perfection, for they never keep to one certain ground or track, but are allwayes trying of new Experiments; so they are allwayes beginning, but never go on towards an end. Besides, said he, they live not long enough to finde the Philosophers Stone, for, said he, 'tis not one nor two Ages will do it, but there must be many Ages to bring it to perfection: but I, said he, living long, and observing the course of Nature strictly, and much, I am arrived to the height of that Art; for all the Gold that is digged out of the Mines was converted by me; for in the beginning of the World there was very little Gold to be found; for my Brother *Adam* said, he nor his Posterity after him for many Ages knew no such thing: but since I have attained to the perfection of that Art, I have caused so many Mines, that it hath caused all the outward part of the World to go together by the ears for it: but I will not make so much as to have it despised.

As for my Stills, said he, they are the Pores of the Earth; and the Waters I distill, said he, are the sweet Dews which issue out of the Earth; the Oily

12 'Chymists': alchemists. 13 'Philosophers Stone': a reputed substance that was supposed by alchemists to possess the property of changing other metals into gold or silver.

part is the Amber-greece that is cast upon the Earth; and they know not how, or from whence, or from what it comes; for some say, from Trees; others, that it is the spawn of some kinds of Fish; so some think it one thing, some another.

And also the saltness of the Sea comes from [my] Chymistry; and the Vapour that arises from the Earth, is the Smoke that steems from my Stills. But, said he, the World is not to continue long as it is, for, said he, I by my Art intend to turn it all into Glass; for as my Brother *Adam* transplanted Men from Earth by his sin, as some to Heaven, some to Hell, so I will transplant the World from Earth to Glass, for that is the last act of Chymistry.

Then the Man observing a great concourse of Waters that went with a violent force close by the Center, he asked the old Man how came that Water there; he answered, it was the Gutter and Sink of the Earth; for whatsoever Water the Sun drank from the Sea, and spued upon the Earth, run through the Veins into the Sea again by the Center, all little Pipe-veins meeting there, or else, said he, the World would be drowned again; for at *Noah's* Flood those Pipe-veins were commanded by *Jove* to be stopp'd, and after such a time to be opened again. I wonder, said the Man, that all the weighty Materials in the World do not fall upon your Head, and so kill you; why so they would, said he, if they lay alltogether on a heap; but as everying hath a several motion, so everything hath a proper place; for Gold and Iron never dwell together in the Earth; neither are all kinds of Stones found in one Quarrie, nor do all the Mines or Quarries joyn together, but some are in one place, and some in another, which poyses the weight of the Earth equal, and keeps it from falling.

Said the Man, you have but a melancholy life, being none but yourself.

O, said the Man, the Riches of the Earth, and all the Varieties thereof, come in to my Compass; this place is the Heart or Soul of Plenty; here have I sweet Dormice, fat Moals, nourishing Worms, industrious Ants, and many other things for Food; here are no Storms to trouble me, nor Tempests to disorder me, but Warmth to cherish me, and Peace and Quiet to comfort and joy me; the drilling Waters are my Musick, the Glow-worms my Lights, and my Art of Chymistry my pastime. So when he had done speaking, they took their leaves, craving pardon for their abrupt visit, giving him thanks for his gentle entertainment. But the old Man very kindly prayed them to have care of themselves as they returned; for, said he, you must go through cold, crude, anguish, and hot burning and pestilent places; for there are great damps in the Earth; also, a great Heat and Fire in the Earth, allthough it gives not Light like the Sun; for the heat of the Earth, said he, is like the Fire in a Coal; but the heat of the Sun is like that of a Flame, which is a thinner part or substance set on fire, which is a weaker or fainter Heat: but the Sun, said he, gives Heat more by his quick motion, than that the Heat gives motion; and though, said he, the Fire be the subtillest of all Elements, yet it is made slower and more active, by the substance it works upon; for Fire is not so active upon solid Bodyes, as it is upon lighter and thinner Bodyes.

So the Witch and the young Mans Spirit gave him thanks, and departed. But going back, they found not the wayes so pleasant as when they went; for some wayes were deep and dirty, others heavy and clayie, some boggy and sandy, some dry and dusty; and great Waters, high Mountains, stony and craggy Hills, some chalky and limy.

But at last arriving where they set out, he found his Body where he left it: so putting on the Body as a Garment, gave thanks to the Witch, and then went home to rest his weary Spirits, *etc.*

C. B. (trans.)

Anna Maria Van Schurman, *The Learned Maid; or, Whether a Maid may be a Scholar? A Logick Exercise* (1659)

Anna Maria van Schurman was Dutch; her brief, schematic treatise was originally written in Latin, and published in Leyden in 1641. It has been included here because of its importance in the debate about women's education, and because of Anna Maria van Schurman's significance in an international network of erudite women (she is mentioned by Mary More, for example: see p. 248). The opening passages are extracted here: the bulk of the work consists of formal logical proofs designed to show, both by argument and example, women's fitness for intellectual activity. The translator was probably Clement Barksdale: his preface suggests that there had been an earlier edition, indicating considerable interest in the treatise. Copy text, BL, E. 1910. (3), pp. 1–6.

The Learned *Maid*. A Logicall Exercise upon this Question. *Whether a* Maid *may be a Scholar?*

We hold the *Affirmative*, and will endeavour to make it good.

These *Praecognita*[1] we premit: First on the part of the *Subject*,[2] and then of the *Predicate*.[3]

By a *Maid or Woman*, I understand her that is a *Christian*, and that not in Profession onely, but really and indeed.

By a *Scholar*, I mean one that is given to the study of *Letters*, that is, the knowledge of *Tongues* and *Histories*, all kinds of Learning, both superiour entitled *Faculties*; and inferiour, call'd *Philosophy*. We except onely *Scriptural*

1 'Praecognita': things already known. 2 'Subject': in logic, the thing about which an argument or judgement is made. 3 'Predicate': statement made about the subject.

Theology properly so named, as that which without Controversie belongs to all Christians.

When we enquire, *whether she may be*, we mean whether it be *convenient*, that is, expedient, fit, decent.

The *words* being thus distinguished, the *Things* are to be distinguished also.

For some *Maids* are *ingenious*,[4] others *not so*: some are *rich*, some *poor*: some *engaged* in Domestick cares, others *at liberty*.

The studies of a *Scholar* are either *universal*, when we give our selves to all sorts of Learning: or *particular*, when we learn some one Language or Science, or one distinct Faculty.

Whereof we make use of these Limitations:

First, of the *Subject*; and first, that our *Maid*[5] be endued at least with an indifferent good *wit*, and not unapt for learning.

Secondly, that she be provided of necessaries, and not oppressed with want: which exception I therefore put in, because few are so happy to have Parents to breed them up in studies, and Teachers are chargeable.

Thirdly, that the condition of the Times, and her quality be such, that she may have sparciall Calling, that is, from the exercises of Piety and houshold Affairs. To which end will conduce, partly her immunity from cares and employments in her yonger years, partly in her elder age either celibate, or the Ministry of handmaids, which are wont to free the richer sort of Matrons also from Domestick troubles.

Fourthly, let her end be, not vain glory and ostentation, or unprofitable curiositie: but beside the generall end, Gods Glory and the salvation of her own soul; that both her self may be the more vertuous and the more happy, and that she may (if that charge ly upon her) instruct and direct her Family, and also be usefull, as much as may be to her whole Sex.

Next, *Limitations* of the *Predicate*, *Scholarship*, or the study of *Letters* I so limit, that I clearly affirm all honest Discipline, or the whole ιγχυχλοϖαιδεια'[6] the Circle and Crown of liberal Arts and Sciences (as the proper and universal Good and Ornament of Mankind) to be convenient for the *Head* of our *Christian Maid*: yet so, that according to the Dignity and Nature of every Art or Science, and according to the capacity and condition of the Maid herself, all in their order, place and time succeed each other in the learning of them, or be commodiously conjoyned. But especially let regard be had unto those Arts which have neerest alliance to *Theology* and the *Moral Virues*, and are Principally subservient to them. In which number we reckon *Grammar, Logick, Rhetorick*; especially *Logick*, fitly called *The Key of all Sciences:* and then, *Physick, Metaphysicks, History*, etc. and also the knowledge of Languages, chiefly of the *Hebrew* and *Greek*. All which may advance to the more facile and full understanding of *Holy Scripture*: to say nothing now of other Books. The rest, i.e. *Mathematicks* (to which is also referred *Musick*) *Poesie, Picture,*

---

4 'ingenious': naturally intelligent. 5 Marginal note: *Of the erudition of Maids you may read in* Liv. 3. Plin. Epist. 17. l. 1. Athen. 1. Plutarch. de educ. lib. Gord. l. 16. de Negat, Fornar. ad Cas. 6 'ιγχυχλοϖαιδεια': each time Schurman uses Greek an explanation follows in the text.

and the like, not illiberal Arts, may obtain the place of pretty Ornaments, and ingenious Recreations.

Lastly, those studies which pertain to the practice of the Law, Military Discipline, Oratory in the Church, Court, University, as less proper and less necessary, we do not very much urge. And yet we in no wise yield that our *Maid* should be excluded from the Scholastick knowledge or Theory of those; especially, not from understanding the most noble Doctrine of the *Politicks* or Civil Government.

And when we say a Maid may be a Scholar, it is plain we do not affirm Learning to be a property, or a thing requisite, and precisely needfull to eternall salvation: no, nor as such a good thing which maketh to the very *Essence* of Happiness in this life: but as a mean and very usefull, conferring much to the integrity and perfection thereof: and as that, which by the contemplation of excellent things will promote us to a higher degree in the Love of God, and everlasting Felicity.

HENRY WILKINSON

'The Life and Death of Mrs. *Margaret Corbet,* who dyed *Anno Christi,* 1656', from Samuel Clarke, *Lives of Ten Eminent Divines* (1662)

This exemplary biography is included in Samuel Clarke's *A Collection of the Lives of Ten Eminent Divines* (1662). Altogether this book contains 16 biographies, four of which are of women: Mrs Jane Ratcliffe, Mrs Margaret Ducke, Mrs Elizabeth Wilkinson and Mrs Margaret Corbet. Corbet's 'Life' is reproduced in full below (pp. 501–11); at the end of the biography, Clarke states that '[t]his Life was drawn up by my Reverend and worthy Friend Dr. *Henry Wilkinson,* principal of *Magdalen* Hall, *Oxon.*'. The copy text (BL, 491. c. 12) was printed in London for William Miller in 1662.

If we enquire into the Relations of this Gentlewoman, either by Affinity or Consanguinity,[1] on both sides, the Families are ancient, of renown, and good reputation. Concerning the Family from whence she was descended, her Father was Sir *Nathaniel Brent,* late Warden of *Merton* College, a learned Knight, whose great pains, and dangerous adventures to procure the *History of*

1 'Affinity': relationship through marriage; 'Consanguinity': relationship by descent from a common ancestor (blood relation).

the Councel of Trent (which he translated into *English*) are to be remembred with an honourable mention, and for his faithful discovery of *Jesuitical* juglings, his name will be had in honour, when the names of the *Popish* party will rot.

Her Mother, the Lady *Martha Brent*, was a Lady of a Gracious spirit, abounding in love, meekness, humility, love to Gods Ordinances, and Gods children. Her delight (with *David*) was in the society of Saints. She imitated her worthy Father in the sweetness of disposition, who was Dr. *Robert Abbot*, that learned and godly Bishop of *Sarum*, who was *Malleus Papism and Armianismi*, the Hammer of *Popery* and *Arminianisme*: His excellent Works or Monuments of his Honourable memory.[2]

To be born of a godly Family, and to be well descended, is a mercy not to be neglected. Mr. *Philpot*, a zealous Martyr, being a Knights Son, and an *Archdeacon*, told his adversaries that he was a Gentleman. *Anabaptistical* parity, and *Levelling* designs are worthily to be abhorred, and looked upon as a ready way to confusion, rapine, and violence.[3] So then we see that she was a Gentlewoman every way well descended. Her Ancestors were persons of Honour, and from them she had the benefit of an ingenuous and liberal Education. This is much, but its more, when I say that she came of a godly stock, and of praying Relations; and indeed, this is that which ennobles Nobility it self.

God in mercy began with this Gentlewoman betimes, even about the fourteenth year of her age. Then God gave her a willing minde, and purpose of heart to serve him in the dayes of her youth: Insomuch as she was *swift to hear* the word of God, *she waited diligently at the posts of Wisdomes Gate*. She wrote the Sermons which she heard (a practice used by King *Edward* the sixth, that rare *English Josiah*) and she left many volumes of Sermons of her own handwriting, taken with great dexterity, and these are as so many choise Monuments of her Industry. She was much conversant in reading of the holy Scriptures (which can *make us wise unto salvation* [2 Tim. 3: 15]) and she joyned with her reading, prayer, and meditation. Her delight was in the word of God: It was (as with *Jeremy*) the *joy and rejoycing* of her soul; and with the reading of Scriptures she searched Expositors, and *Practical Divines*, and attained thereby to such a measure of Divine knowledge, as enabled her to state some Questions of controversie for her better use, and help of her memory, and to discourse very soundly upon the most material points of Religion, and even above her age and sexe, to maintain the truth, as occasion was offered, with strength of Argument against gain-sayers.

She was eminent for the grace of *Humility*; and when I have said that she was of an humble spirit, what can be said more? This the Apostle would have us *to be cloathed withall*, I Pet. 5. 7. Humility is the ornament of all Graces: Its that Salt that seasons the best parts and graces. So humble was the spirit of this

2 'Arminianism': sect whose beliefs were based upon the doctrines of James Arminius, a Protestant Dutch theologian, who opposed Calvin's doctrines (especially on the question of predestination) and whose own doctrines were condemned by the synod of Dort 1618–19. 3 'Anabaptism': second baptism: one who baptises over again, whether once or regularly as a point of ritual (as opposed to the Anglican practice of christening just after birth).

excellent Gentlewoman, that the poorest might have free access unto her, and receive curteous language from her mouth, and liberal almes from her heart and hand, both being opened wide for their relief. The observation of this humble deportment from her child-hood, gained the heart of her dear Husband unto her, long before she was ripe for her Marriage: Her humble spirit evidently appeared by her condescending *to them of low estate*: the servants in her Family, the poorest, and meanest in the Parish where she lived, will bear witness to the truth of this particular.

She was of a *meek and quiet spirit*, which (as the Apostle saith, I *Pet. 3. 3.*) *is in the sight of God of great price*. All her Relations will attest her meek deportment, and how much she hated brawls and contentions: Her very enemies (if they would speak their consciences) can testifie her readiness to pass by injuries. So far she was from *rendring reviling for revilings*, that she endeavoured to *recompence evil with good*, and prayed for such as despitefully used her, professing that it was the desire of her soul to do her very enemies all the Christian offices of love which lay in her power.

Special notice ought also to be taken of her Wisdome and Gravity in the ordering of her conversation. Her discourses were savoury, administring *Grace to the hearers*, and tending to edification. Her behaviour was modest, and grave; though she was of a cheerfull spirit, yet it was without levity: She was no tatler, busie-body, no medler in the affairs of others: She was no gadder up and down from house to house, hearing, and telling of news (as too many do to the wounding of the reputations of others). The vain and frivolous discourse of some who came to visit her, was an heavy burden, and affliction to her spirit. The discourses of such as tended to the defaming and blasting others reputation, were a great grief and trouble unto her; and when she heard such discourses, she would endeavour to turn the stream another way, and move such discourse as might be profitable for the souls good.

Her Love was very eminent towards all those that feared God, she was with *David*, a *Companion* to such, a lover of their acquaintance, who were the Saints, the *excellent ones*, Psal. 16. 3. Insomuch as when she apprehended any thing of God, though in persons inclining to separation, and of a contrary judgement from her, she was so compassionate, as to labour with much sweetness and candour, to convince them of their errours, and to win them to the truth; imitating herein the holy practice of learned *Musculus*, who gained some *Anabaptists* and *Sectaries* by kindness, and benefits, and overcame them as much by love as by arguments.[4]

Her holy Courage deserves special notice; for though she was humble, meek, and loving, yet she was stout and couragious in declaring her judgement upon just occasions, before those whom she knew to be contrary minded, hating compliance against conscience, and doubting alwayes the soundness and sincerity of those who durst not own their opinions. She was much of her wor-

4 'persons inclining to separation': those who advocated ecclesiastical separation; in the seventeenth century it applied chiefly to Independents, but became a term of abuse covering all Protestant dissenters; 'Sectaries': members of a sect. In the seventeenth century this included Independents, Baptists and Quakers.

thy Fathers temper in that particular, who hath often been heard to say, that a Coward can hardly be an honest man; and much of *Esters* resolution, desiring rather to suffer her self than sluggishly, and silently to see the truths of God to suffer.

She was a praying Christian: She was much in prayers and tears; much in a sacred acquaintance, and holy communion with God: Her gift in prayer was very great: She was much in her Closet alone, and there much upon her knees: An excellent patern for womens imitation, which by no means should suffer that great duty to be omitted. It was a Character of *Paul*, when converted, *Act.* 9. 11. *Behold he prayes*. Praying Christians are the best Christians, they are prevailing Christians; and as Reverend and holy Mr. *Dod* was used to say, *Never despair of that person who can but pray.*

She was fixed and stedfast in Religion, having frequently read the Scriptures, and many sound, orthodox, and practical *Divines*, she became settled, rooted and grounded in the truth. She was one that held *fast her profession without wavering*. She was not carried about with *every wind of Doctrine*, Eph. 4. 14. neither was she of their humours, who for politick ends comply with all companies in their opinions. She kept close to the publick Ministry where she lived, there she heard the word faithfully dispensed. She neither was of their opinion, or practice, who out of I know not what kinde of singularity, separate from the Ministry of a godly Pastor and Husband. Her delight was very great in Gods Ordinances, and she was glad when they said, *Let us go to the house of the Lord in company* [Ps. 122: 1]. She had such an high esteem of, and longing desire unto the house of God, that when her strength failed her, she would be carried thither; by reason of lameness, the feet of her body were weak, but the feet of her soul, her affections, were strong, nimble, and vigorous.

Look upon her in her Relations, as a Wife, a Mother, and Mistress, and you shall see she was mindefull of her duty to God in them all: Her great care and endeavour was to set up God in her Family; in order whereunto she bestowed great pains in *Catechising* of her children, and other near Relations committed unto her charge. Her great design was to bring them all up in the fear and admonition of the Lord, and to inculcate again and again, that main and needfull lesson of *Remembring their Creator in the dayes of their youth* [Eccles. 12: 1]. Much pains she took in *Catechising*, and instructing her servants, especially before they were to receive the Sacrament of the Lords Supper. She used to examine them of the Sermons they heard, and she customarily read over those Sermon Notes to them which she had taken at Church, that so they might be the better prepared to give an account thereof to her Husband. God was pleased to give her several *Olive branches round about her Table*, well bred, well *Catechised*, and well governed, and of very great hopes. As *Eunice* and *Lois* instructed young *Timothy*, so she instructed those hopefull little ones in the holy Scriptures, and acquainted them with the knowledge of God in their tender years. Thus according to *Solomons* counsel, they were trained up in the way wherein they should walk, *Prov.* 21. 6. and that even from their childhood; insomuch as one of them (though very young) hearing a neighbour using the name of the Lord upon a sleight occasion, reproved him for it, alleadging the

Commandement of God against it, *Thou shalt not take the Name of God in vain* [Exod. 20: 7]. And another of them reasoning with his fellows about God and the Devil, professed that he had rather be in hell with God, than in heaven with the Devil. And a third, who by reason of her age could not speak distinctly, said in some discourse with her Father, that God Almighty would not bless them who tell Fibbs (meaning Lies) and that she had rather dye than tell a Fibb; so far had their Mothers instructions prevailed with them.

She was eminent for a charitable and bountifull spirit; she was another *Dorcas*, full of *good works*, and *Alms-deeds*. That high *Elogium*[5] that *Solomon* gives a vertuous woman, may properly be applied unto her, *Many Daughters have done vertuously, but she excelled them all*, Prov. 31. 29. Many there are that come far short of her, but very few that went beyond her in the acts of Charity. God gave her a liberal and plentifull estate, and that was a great mercy; but it was a far greater mercy that gave her a liberal heart *to do good, and to distribute: To cast her bread on the waters*, and to *honour God with her substance*. That protestation which *Job* makes for his own vindication, may fitly be applied unto her, *Job* 31. 16, 19. He would not *with-hold the poor from their desire, nor cause the eyes of the widow to fail*. He would not *see any to perish for want of cloathing, nor any poor without covering*. The whole Country round about where she dwelt, will bear her witness, that she visited and relieved the sick, and cloathed the naked, fed the hungry, and healed the wounded. Her purse, her hand, her heart, were all open for their relief. She bought many precious Drugs, and cordial waters: She made several precious salves, and gave them all away to such as were in need of them. She spared not her best pains, being never aweary of well doing; insomuch that in the extremity of her greatest sickness (such bowels of compassion yearned in her) she compounded several Medicines with her own hands, and applied them. Thus will her works praise her in the Gate, and *being dead, she yet speaketh*, Prov. 31. 31. Heb. 11. 4. For her precious name liveth. The Lord will have the name of the Righteous to be in *everlasting remembrance*, Psal. 112. 6. and the *memory of the just is blessed*, Prov. 10. 7. And *precious in the sight of the Lord is the death of his Saints*, Psal. 116. 15. Now this rare Gentlewoman reaps the fruit of her serving of God, and the whole harvest, whereof she received onely the first fruits in this present world.

The usual saying is, *All is well that ends well:* Come we therefore to speak of her end. Her life was holy, and therefore her death must needs be happy. It pleased the Lord to exercise her with a long and lingring sickness; and amidst the weakness of the outward man, God gave her great strength in her inward man; though her limbs and outward strength failed her, yet God was her *strength and portion*, and he never failed her. A few dayes before her distemper waxed high (her Husband being from home) she sent for all her Family both young and old, to come in unto her chamber, with whom she prayed near two hours, with such pathetical, heavenly, Scripture-language, as drew admiration and tears from those that were present. She blessed her children, counselled

5 'Elogium': a biographical summary of a person's character, usually an expression of praise.

her servants, heartily and affectionately commended her Husband unto God; she wept and prayed, and prayed and wept, and could not easily part with the company, nor yet leave off praying, and weeping.

Upon the encrease of her distemper, her spirit was much disturbed, and some impertinent speeches did fall from her, yet in the middest of all her impertinencies, Grace, and the Spirit of God, did eminently declare their Power and Sovereignty in her, by many savoury and choice speeches, and sweet breathings of her soul; some of which are these that follow, *I was in the Devils claws, but Jesus Christ, the sweet Bridegroom of my soul, the sweet Bridegroom of my soul* (these words she often reitered) *the sweet Bridegroom of my soul hath delivered me.* At another time, *I am safe, for Jesus Christ is at my heart, and I would not part with him for ten thousand worlds.* Again, *Come Lord Jesus the Captain of my salvation, ride on gloriously conquering, and to conquer for me Satan, Sin, Hell, Death, and all mine enemies.* Afterwards again, *I was in Hell, but now I am in Heaven; I am in Heaven indeed, indeed I am in Heaven; I am in Heaven eternally; I am in Heaven the habitation of Gods glory unto all eternity.* Much of this nature she did speak, even when her understanding was so disturbed, that she scarce did know her near Relations, and those who did attend upon her in her Chamber.

And now all these things are worthy to be transmitted unto posterity, and to be had, in perpetual remembrance. She was an eminently godly Gentlewoman, being but little above Eight and twenty years of age when she dyed, which was in the beginning of *March, Anno Christi 1656.* But though she was young in years, yet she was old in Grace: She had lived long in a little time: She was a mirror of her age, and a renown of her sexe, a pattern worthy of imitation. She was the beloved faithfull wife of as an intirely loving and faithfull Husband. She was a tender affectionate Mother to her own, and no less carefull of those pledges committed to his charge. She was a most dear Sister, an affectionate Mistress, carefull both of the bodies and souls of her servants, that they should neither want corporal, nor spiritual food. Her profession was with *Joshua*, Chap. 24. 15. *Choose you this day whom you will serve; But as for me, I and my house, we will serve the Lord*. She was not onely a friend to her friends, but a friend to her enemies, even unto such as despitefully used her. All the Country round about could not but look upon her, whilst living as a publick gain, and when dead, as a publick loss: She was very usefull whilst she lived, and will be much missed now she is dead. Two things were very eminent in her: Setledness in Religion, and holiness of conversation. By her death the poor have lost a liberal *Almoner*; the sick have lost a good *Physitian*; the wounded have lost a good *Chirurgion*;[6] the Husband hath lost a faithful *Wife*; the children a tender *Mother*, the servants a gracious *Mistress*: and not any that knew her of all her neighbours and friends, but they will finde a great loss, and miss of her. All that knew her loved her, but[7] onely such whose love is not worth the having. She lived much desired, and dyed much lamented: For her *to live was Christ, and to die was gain*, Phil. 1. 21. She was honoured in her life,

6 'Chirurgion': surgeon. 7 I.e., 'except'.

and she was honoured at her death, by a confluence of many persons of quality, of the Gentry, Ministry, and Neighbourhood round about, who by their concourse at her Funeral, shewed plainly in what an high estimation she was amongst them, and that her *good Name was like a precious Oyntment powred forth* [Eccles. 7: 1]. The hope of Glory was that soverign Cordial which abundantly revived, and satisfied her spirits whilst she lived, and now her hope is turned into fruition, and her faith into vision. All her sorrows and sighings are turned away, and her imployment is without the least tediousness, without interruption, and intermission to sing *Hosannahs*, and *Allelujahs* to him that sitteth upon the Throne, and to the Lamb for evermore.

MARGARET FELL

Womens Speaking Justified, Proved and Allowed of by the Scriptures (1666)

The copy text, BL, 855. f. 4 (2), is the first edition, printed in London in 1666; a further edition, also printed in London, followed in 1667. Like Priscilla Cotton and Mary Cole, Margaret Fell was being held in jail because of her controversial religious activities (she was imprisoned in Lancaster Castle from 1664 to 1668) when she wrote her contribution to the debate on women's public speech on religious matters. She was a powerful figure in the Society of Friends and published more than 20 works on Quaker issues. The extract given here (pp. 12–16) constitutes a kind of postscript to the main body of the tract, where Fell constructs her argument through detailed exegesis of key scriptural passages – many the same as those discussed by Mary More (see pp. 247–53). The text is mostly calm and moderate in tone, but on pp. 9–11 a more apocalyptic passage conveys Fell's sense – shared with many of her contemporaries – that the 'night of Apostacy draws to an end, and the true Light now shines' (p. 10).

A further Addition in Answer to the Objection concerning Women keeping silent in the Church; For it is not permitted for them to speak, but to be under obedience; as also saith the Law, If they will learn any thing, let them ask their Husbands at home, for it is a shame for Woman to speak in the Church: *Now this as* Paul *writeth in* I Cor. 14. 34. *is one with that of* I Tim. 2. 11. *Let Women learn in silence, with all subjection*. To which I say, If you tie this to all outward Women, then there were many Women that were Widows which had no Husbands to learn of, and many were Virgins which had no Husbands; and *Philip* had four Daughters that were Prophets [Acts 21: 9]; such would be despised, which the Apostle did not forbid: And if it were to all Women, that no Woman might speak, then *Paul* would have contradicted himself; but they were such Women that the Apostle mentions in *Timothy*, That *grew wanton, and were busie-bodies, and tatlers, and kicked against Christ* [1 Tim. 5: 13]: For Christ in the Male and in the Female is one [Gal. 3: 28], and he is the Husband, and his Wife is the Church, and God hath said, that his *Daughters* should Prophesie as well as his *Sons*: And where he hath poured forth his Spirit upon them, they must prophesie, though blind Priests say to the contrary, and will not permit holy Women to speak.

And whereas it is said, *I permit not a Woman to speak, as saith the Law*: but where Women are led by the Spirit of God, they are not under the Law, for Christ in the Male and in the Female is one; and where he is made manifest in Male and Female, he may speak, for *he is the end of the Law for Righteousness to all them that believe* [Rom. 10: 4]. So here you ought to make a distinction what sort of Women are forbidden to speak, such as were under the Law, who were not come to Christ, nor to the Spirit of Prophesie: For *Hulda*, *Miriam* [Exod. 15: 20], and *Hanna*,[1] were Prophets, who were not forbidden in the time of the Law, for they all prophesied in the time of the Law: as you may read, in 2 *Kings* 22 what *Hulda* said unto the Priest, and to the Ambassadors that were sent to her from the King, *Go*, saith she, *and tell the Man that sent you to me, Thus saith the Lord God of Israel, Behold, I will bring evil upon this place, and on the Inhabitants thereof, even all the words of the Book which the King of* Judah *hath read, because they have forsaken me, and have burnt Incence to other Gods, to anger me with all the works of their hands: Therefore my wrath shall be kindled against this place, and shall not be quenched. But to the King of* Judah, *that sent you to me to ask counsel of the Lord, so shall you say to him, Thus saith the Lord God of Israel, Because thy heart did melt, and thou humblest thy self before the Lord, when thou heardest what I spake against this place, and against the Inhabitants of the same, how they should be destroyed; Behold I will receive thee to thy Father, and thou shalt be put into thy Grave in peace, and thine eyes shall not see all the evil which I will bring upon this place.* Now let us see if any of you blind Priests can speak after this manner, and see if it be not a better Sermon then any of you can make, who are against Womens speaking? And *Isaiah*, that went to the Prophetess, did not forbid her Speaking or Prophesying, *Isa*. 8. And was it not prophesied in *Joel* 2. that *Hand-maids should Prophesie*? And are not Hand-maids Women? Consider this, ye that are against Womens Speaking, how in the *Acts* the Spirit of the Lord was poured forth upon Daughters as well as Sons. In the time of the Gospel, when *Mary* came to salute *Elizabeth in the Hill Country in* Judea, *and when* Elizabeth *heard the salutation of* Mary, *the Babe leaped in her Womb, and she was filled with the Holy Spirit; and* Elizabeth *spoke with a loud voice, Blessed art thou amongst Women, blessed is the fruit of thy Womb; whence is this to me, that the Mother of my Lord should come to me? for lo, as soon as thy Salutation came to my ear, the Babe leaped in my Womb for joy, for blessed is she that believes, for there shall be*

---

1 1 Samuel 1–2. Hannah's prophetic song in Chapter 2 prefigures the Magnificat, which Fell quotes below.

a performance of those things which were told her from the Lord [Luke 1: 42–5]. And this was *Elizabeths* Sermon concerning Christ, which at this day stands upon Record: And then *Mary* said, *My soul doth magnifie the Lord, and my Spirit rejoyceth in God my saviour, for he hath regarded the low estate of his Hand-maid: for behold, from henceforth all Generations shall call me blessed; for he that is mighty, hath done to me great things, and holy is his Name; and his Mercy is on them that fear him, from Generation to Generation; he hath shewed strength with his Arm; he hath scattered the proud in the imaginations of their own hearts; he hath put down the mighty from their Seats, and exalted them of low degree; he hath filled the hungry with good things, and the rich he hath sent empty away: He hath holpen his Servant* Israel, *in remembrance of his mercy, as he spake to his Father, to* Abraham, *and to his Seed for ever* [Luke 1: 46–55]. Are you not here beholding to the Woman for her Sermon, to use her words to put into your Common Prayer? and yet you forbid Womens Speaking. Now here you may see how these two women prophesied of Christ, and Preached better then all the blind Priests did in that Age, and better then this Age also, who are beholding to women to make use of their words.[2]

Likewise you may read how *Judith* spoke, and what noble acts she did, and how she spoke to the Elders of *Israel*, and said, *Dear Brethren, seeing ye are the honorable and elders of the People of God, call to remembrance how our Fathers in time past were tempted, that they might be proved if they would worship God aright; they ought also to remember how our Father* Abraham, *being tryed through manifold tribulations, was found a friend of God; so was* Isaac, Jacob, *and* Moses, *and all they pleased God, and were stedfast in Faith through manifold troubles.*[3] And read also her prayer in the Book of *Judith*, and how the Elders commended her, and said, *All that thou speakest is true, and no man can reprove thy words, pray therefore for us, for thou art an holy Woman, and fearest God.* So these elders of *Israel* did not forbid her speaking, as you blind Priests do; yet you will make a Trade of Womens words to get money by, and take Texts, and Preach Sermons upon Womens words; and still cry out, Women must not speak, Women must be silent; so you are far from the minds of the Elders of *Israel*, who praised God for a Womans speaking. But the *Jezebel*,[4] and the Woman, the false Church, the great Whore, and tatling women, and busiebodies, which are forbidden to Preach, which have a long time spoke and tatled, which are forbidden to speak by the True Church, which Christ is the Head of; such Women as were in transgression under the Law, which are called a Woman in the *Revelations*.[5] And see further how the wise Woman cryed to *Joab* over the Wall, and saved the City of *Abel*, as you may read, 2 *Sam*. 20. how in her wisdom she spoke to *Joab*, saying, *I am one of them that are*

---

2 Omitted is a passage of some 600 words where Fell adduces further instances from the Old Testament to support her argument, naming Ruth, Hannah, the Queen of Sheba and Esther as precursors of the preaching women of her time. **3** Judith 8. The book of Judith is one of the Apocrypha, books which were not accepted as part of the canon of the Bible; they were more widely known in the early modern period than today. **4** Jezebel appears in 1 Kings: here, as with the allusion to Revelation 17 in Cotton and Cole, the figure of a sinful woman is being used to symbolise religious corruption. **5** Revelation 17.

peaceable and faithful in Israel, *and thou goest about to destroy a city and Mother in* Israel; *Why wilt thou destroy the Inheritance of the Lord? Then went the woman to the people in her wisdom, and smote off the head of* Sheba, *that rose up against* David, *the Lords Anointed: Then* Joab *blew the Trumpet, and all the People departed in peace.* And this deliverance was by the means of a Womans speaking; but tatlers, and busie-bodies, are forbidden to preach by the True Woman, whom Christ is the Husband, to the Woman as well as the Man, all being comprehended to be the Church; and so in this True Church, Sons and Daughters do Prophesie, Women labour in the Gospel; but the Apostle permits not tatlers, busie-bodies, and such as usurp authority over the Man would not have Christ Reign, nor speak neither in the Male nor Female; Such the Law permits not to speak, such must learn of their Husbands: But what Husbands have Widows to learn of, but Christ? And was not Christ the Husband of *Philips* four Daughters? And may not they that learn of their Husbands speak then? But *Jezebel*, and Tatlers, and the Whore that denies Revelation and Prophesie, are not permitted, which will not learn of Christ; and they that be out of the Spirit and Power of Christ, that the Prophets were in, who are in the Transgression, are ignorant of the Scriptures; and such are against Womens speaking, and Mens too, who Preach that which they have received of the Lord God; but that which they have preached, and do preach, will come over all your heads, yea, over the head of the false Church, the Pope; for the Pope is the Head of the False Church, and the False Church is the Popes Wife: and so he and they that be of him, and come from him, are against Womens speaking in the True Church, when both he and the false Church are called *Woman*, in *Revel.* 17. and so are in the Transgression that would usurp authority over the Man Christ Jesus, and his Wife too, and would not have him to Reign; but the Judgment of the great Whore is come. But Christ, who is the Head of the Church, the True Woman which is his Wife, in it do Daughters Prophesie, who are above the Pope and his Wife, and a top of them; And here Christ is the Head of the Male and Female, who may speak; and the Church is called *a Royal Priesthood*; so the Woman must offer as well as the Man, *Rev.* 22. 17. *The Spirit saith, Come, and the Bride saith, Come*: and so is not the Bride the Church? and doth the Church only consist of Men? you that deny Womens speaking, answer: Doth it not consist of Women as well as men? Is not the Bride compared to the whole Church? And doth not the Bride say, *Come*? Doth not the Woman speak then? the Husband Christ Jesus, the *Amen*, and doth not the false Church go about to stop the Brides Mouth? But it is not possible for the Bridegroom is with his Bride, and he opens her Mouth. Christ Jesus, who goes on Conquering, and to Conquer, who kills and slayes with the Sword, which is the words of his Mouth; the Lamb and the Saints shall have the Victory, the true Speakers of Men and Women over the false Speaker.

LADY ELIZABETH DELAVAL

Memoirs and Meditations (1662–1671)

The title heading the Bodleian Library MS Rawl. D. 78, 'Mrs. Delaval's Memoirs and Meditations' is not Delaval's own choice; nor is her manuscript complete. Although the text is contained within 332 numbered pages there are over 100 blank pages at the end of the large quarto volume. As Delaval's text exists only in manuscript, current critical opinion tends to view her work as 'private', but this view is contested by Margaret J. M. Ezell who points out that her 'manuscript volume received lavish attention in terms of presentation techniques' (Ezell, *Writing Women's Literary History*, p. 224). One of the most striking characteristics of her manuscript is the fact that she capitalises the first letter of the first word on every line, which, at first sight, makes her text appear to be poetry. Many of Delaval's meditations concern her relationship with particular suitors. The extract below indicates her struggle to come to terms with her arranged marriage, and highlights her difficult relationship to her father. However, much of the rest of the manuscript details the strong influence of women (especially her aunt, her grandmother and a servant (Mrs Carter)) upon her, partly due to the early death of her mother and her father's absence (he fled from England when his correspondence with the exiled Charles II was discovered).

Meditations in the same yeare [1670] Conserning my Father some months before I maryed Mr. DeLaval

I am positively commanded by God to honnour My Father, and yet without any regard at all to This Law of God (which has the bleseing of long Life anex'd to it) I faile not with bitternesse to sensure him for all his faileings and to discourse of them to many heareurs, which I am now senceible is a Great wickednesse. The Lord in much mercy pardon me. I will now begin to lesen his faults in the estime off Others, and that way begin to honnour him; And what ever he dos amiss to me in, I will no more strive to turn his heart from; but by my prayers to Allmighty God and by my paying of any humble and a constant Respectfull duty to him, even when he most of all crosses my mind I will represent to my selfe all the exelent qualitys he has, which has justly gained him so many Friends, in the first place, his great loyallty and true courage, of which he has given many profes and particularly a most convinceing one since the king came home, when he went against the Rebells in Scotland,[1] it being at a time that he had the gout so violently upon him that he cou'd not stand upon his feet, but was forced to be lifted up a Horse backe, which was a reasonable

1 Possibly the Pentland Rising, November 1666.

excuse for him to have declined commanding the Kings Life Guard that day, but he wou'd not make use of it; and God blesed the performance of his duty with victory, as he has been pleased also to blese his steadynesse to his friends upon all ocations, with a generall estime in the world, he has a most compassionate good nature to all people, and has imployed his interist at court much more to serve others, who have made there Aplycations to him, then to do good to himselfe and his Family; which is a temper very rarely to be found at Court.

Christmasse Eve, 1670, the first meditation writ after my maryage with Mr. DeLaval

Since my state of life is changed, tho I cannot say I mete with joyes to destract me in the performance of holy Duty's, or that I have entertained a violent passion in my heart; yet something or other dos incline me to tryfle away my time yet more in this new condition of life, I have so lately enter'd into, then formerly; and yet I have often thought that cou'd scarcely be.

But now I find that evill pursues me continually the evill of sin more then the Evill of punishment, and I (Alass) am ready to imbrace the first with gredynesse, of which the second must be a consequent.

Since I am not dazell'd with the luster of great Riches, nor burthen'd with honnours (which might perhapes increase my Pride), nor charmed with so much love for my husband as might make mine grow cold to my God, why is it, O my soul, that thou art dayly overtaken with new mischefes.

Why hast thou no Courage left to bear an injury with patience, and why are my tear's so often shed for ill humour's I mete withall but nether cause nor can avoid.

Certenly this must be because I am as it were amaized in a new world, and haveing quited my Beloved vergin state of life, I scarce yet know where I am; and all the Evills I feele come upon me are for want off alowing my selfe that due time of consideration which I ought to do.

That pleaseing word of liberty, being now no more to be pronounced by me as what I have a right too, I cannot but at the first puting on of shakells find there weight heavy; so to put of that thought, I fly solitude and seek busynesse; or devertions, any thing which may take up that time I use to thinke in.

But now I will no longer run on in this Evill, here will I make a full stop, and dayly alow my selfe one houer at least, of retierment; besides my usuall Morning and Evening devotions, least my Love to God grow not only cold but dead also, and I forget my Vow's.

These folowing meditations will but too planely prove how much reason I have never to let a day slip without observing those times of private devotions, which I have set my selfe; for haveing neglected them now of late, my former resolations and Vows have been banished out of my memory, and without scruple I have broke so many of them that now I begin to recolect my selfe and weigh my actions, I am amaized and confounded at the intollerable number of my sins; and Cheifly at my horible inniquity in breakeing those resolutions I made not 3 months ago of paying allway's an humble duty to my father. O miserable wretch that am, I have so far broke them that, quite contrary, I have scarce payed him any duty at all, but out of a wicked revengefull spirit, even in his sicknesse, nay what is yet more haineous upon his very Death bed, have I pevishly expressed my sence of his unkindnesse to me in things which I had reason to beleive he bitterly repented of; yet I then slighted him and stuck to the Interist of a Father in Law who dayly flatter'd me, and did not only neglect to visit my father the last 8 or 10 day's of his life, but did also neglect some of those days so much as to send and inquier after his health; tho I cou'd not be ignorant that my undutyfull behaveour wou'd grive his soul, which certenly it did to the very quick.

I knew he had so much naturall affection for me, and withall I may say (with truth) so much estime, that he wou'd readily have hearken'd to me in any thing, but rashly and inconsiderately I suffer'd the height of my spirit to sway me and did not endeavour to do the least servise, to his decaying body, ruined fortune, or aflicted soul; and now whilest I am meditateing upon my unworthy neglect of the last duty's I shou'd have pay'd him, and my unexpressable loss in not being neer him to receive a Blessing from him in his last houers, he is resting in his grave, and tis (Alass) to late for me to beg his pardon for faults, which I am but newly senceible of.

Tis only to my God that I can fly for mercy whom I have also offended in the breach of his laws, and in the breakeing of my Vows, and to whom I can never make any recompence for the least of those sins I have commited against his infinit Majestie, and much less for all the transgretions of my whole life heaped up together. But what I can do now, which may loke well to my Fathers memory (thro the grace of God asisting me) I will not faile to do, and that is to excuss what I have thought great unkindnesse to me as well as posibly I can, to put the best construction that may be upon all his Actions, and to condemn my selfe to others for haveing resented them so ill; and to my Heavenly Father I will humbly pray that all my iniquities may be bloted out and my transgresstions no more remember'd, for his sake who came into the world to save sinners, even Christ Jesus my Blesed Lord and Saviour.

Christmasse holy day's, 1670

Tis not enough for our actions to be inocent unless they be provident also, since our Saviour has commanded us to be wise as serpents, as well as harmlesse as doves, that so we may every way be secured against the subtleties of that Old serpent which deceived our first Parents [Matt. 10: 16]. Ffor this reason I find it now nesesary to deny my selfe the sight of the Comte Dona,[2] who

2 An earlier suitor to Lady DeLaval.

is now returned to England and much grived that he was not hear time enough to prevent my maryage.

Nether the seeing him nor the heareing him speake is a thing criminall; for never did I hear him say a word contrary to the strictest Vertu, but because his visits to me disturbs the peace of a Family which I am now a part of, I chuse rather to punish my selfe then them; and yet to own the truth off my weakenesse, did not his Interist joyne with there's that it shou'd be so, I thinke they wou'd scarce have prevaled, since my Husband who is the only one of them to whom I ow a duty is not uneasy at his seeing me but has the justice to believe me faithfull.

But my leaveing this Towne being the only way I can thinke of, to change his passion for me into Friendshipe, tis high time for me to chuse absence, which may worke that cure upon his heart that I wish, which indeed deserves better from me then to suffer any paine, that tis in my power to remedy. he is now an Eldest Brother, and yet for all that he is not very easy in his fortune, but being extreamly hansome (as all people alows who have ever seen him) and a most acomplished gentellman in all things, had he but shaked of a foleish hopelesse Love that torments him; he might soon be much at his ease, for there is a Lady who has 3000 pound a yeare land of Inheritance, that his relations presses him every day to mary, and I am sure I will do all I can that he may do so. I will not only argu with him upon this subject before I go, but I will also be gone very soon.

What He begs of me with earnestnesse dos not seem Criminall. Tis but only that I will give him leave to see me, as others of my Friends do, without ever hearing him once speake of Love, and this he has beged of me with tear's. Ffor my own sake, as well as his, I find it nesesary to refuse him, what he askes (tho it seems to be only a harmelesse request), for tho I have hetherto kept my selfe from giveing him any other love then what a sister may have for a Brother, yet I know not how long I may so well defend my Heart, if I often loke upon those charmes that are in youth, Grife, and Beauty, joyn'd with a respectful love.[3]

I will therefore fly those objects which cause a pleaseing paine and which allready seaze my thoughts to much when they shou'd be otherwise imployed, and since I was never yet so much my own Mistresse as to give my selfe to him but have been destined for another, I will carefully avoid what ever may incline me to wish the decrees of Gods Providence had been otherwise order'd for me then they are.

I was at that time liveing in London with my Father and Mother in Law, and it was intended we shou'd have pased that whole winter all together in Towne, it being then but 4 months after my maryage. But upon the Comte Dona's comeing into England along with the Prince of Orange, to whom he had the honnour to be related, and by whose interist he hoped my father might be prevaled withall to give consent that I shou'd be maryed to him; since he came too late for those flatering hopes to signify any thing, I toke the resolution of not staying in Towne; and I prevaled with Mr. DeLaval to go with me to my

---

3 Marginal note: 'the Comte Dona was then but 22 Yeares old'.

Aunt Stanhopes at Nocton where we stayed till the Winter was done, that Sir Ralph DeLaval and my Lady Ann DeLaval came to cary us with them into the North; all the court was surprissed that I made so short a stay amongst my Friends and relations as only 6 weekes, for they were at that time of my life very fond of me; and they wonder'd the more at my going away because my Father and Mother in Law stay'd behind us, but none knew the true cause: I have allway's loke'd upon it as a great blessing of God Allmighty's that I was then mistresse enough of my selfe to let reason get the better of my inclenation; it cannot be denyed but that it was very naturall for a person of my Age, to have liked better staying in a place where I was every day much courted by people of the best quality, and where I was much favour'd by the queen my Mistresse, then to retier to a Contry House; where notwithstanding the prospect of a hapy, peacefull dwelling for a time which I had figured to myselfe, and the pleasures I proposed to have in receiveing the dayly profes of a sincere kindnesse from my Aunt, I did not scape the haveing many uneasy houers for I had not been there a weeke before the Earle of Rutland came to his Hunting House and haveing never spoke to me of love at all (my father haveing maryed me to Mr. DeLaval before the act off Parlement was past, which gave him leave to mary), I cou'd not but live friendly with him and receive his visits as I use to do. My Aunts Friendshipe and his continued to be the same it was, and so did his kindnesse for me. Mr. DeLaval being a very sickly young man, there was a sort of Deboach'd crew about my Lord Rutland that to make there court to him, dayly made it there busynesse to be intimate with Mr. DeLaval and had resolved amongst themselves to drinke him to death (as I was informed some time afterwards) one of them who was more abominably wicked then the rest, braged to his companions that he had like to have done Mr. DeLavals busynesse all at once, for that he very narowly scaped the[4] last day tumbleing him downe Horse and all a great precepice over the Edge of the Clife Hills; for he said, catching him there he rid against him with all his force and pretended that his Horse run away with them. After this they ticed him out to go and be mery at the Towne of Lincolne for one night, which was about 6 miles from my aunts house, where he stayed with them 3 nights and at last came home very much disorder'd, which put him into a cruell fit of Asmah that being a distemper which use to trouble him very often, which I knew nothing of before I was his wife. I was so foleish at that time of my life as to beleive t'was in my power to change any custume he had that I did not like; and to be very much disoblidged when I found my selfe mistaken, so that this begining of a maryed life was very disagreable to me, but I knew there was no remedy and therefore resolved to suffer it with the most patien[ce], and so when Sir Ralph DeLaval and my Lady Ane DeLaval came from London in the spring, I went away with them into Northumberland very willingly where at Seaton DeLaval I writ the folowing Meditation.

---

4 Marginal note: 'Hunting'.

May the 12, 1671

The life of a Christian if led as we are oblidged by our high calling to lead it, is no state of slothfull rest, no condition free from cares, but on the contrary tis a state in which our most diligent watchfullnesse is nesesary to preserve us from entering into temptation, and when enter'd (as at some time o[r] other the best of us all may do) to prevent our falling.

In all the varyous accidents of our lives new dangers asault us, and therefore upon every change, we have reason to seek out still stronger Guards to defend us.

Our Saviour's blest command, watch, and pray [Matt. 26: 41], ought to be the constant practise of our lives: for he gave us no precept but what was given with the designe of a reward attending our obedience, a gloryous reward far above all we can wish for or imagine, and certenly the biding us watch as well as pray was not the least of his mercy's, since generally we are to much inclined to thinke our duty done when we have offer'd up our prayers and prayses to God.

Yet we shou'd thinke it madnesse to see a husbandman expect corn to spring up in his ground, at the same time it dos in his neighbour's field: shou'd he only morning and evening knell downe and beg God's bleseing upon it and ofer him thanks for all the seazonable wether that he sends: whereas his neighbour leaves not those duty's undon, but add's to them others also: his own dayly labour, which God bleses with a joyfull harvest, whilest the other man (suposeing there can be such a creature in the world) get's nothing but scorn's from his companions for his folly and justly gaines the reputation of being a madman.

And yet when we give our selves leave to consider, the conclution is very easy to be made, that a far worse madnesse posesses all the children of men who do not faile to acknowledge God by praying to him, and yet at the same time disobey his command by neglecting to watch: thus owning his Devinity without practiseing his Doctrine, and yet vainely hopeing to be deliver'd out of dangers, and protected by him whilest we sit idle and set no Guards upon our selves.

Tis true that except the Lord keepe the Citty the Watchman watcheth but in vaine, and tis as true that there ought to be a watchman, or rather many watchmen to every Citty, and that they are oblided to watch and not to slepe.

All our passions if rightly corected may severally helpe us in our watch, as for example:

Iff our love be fixed upon God with all our Heart's with all our soul's and with all our minds, t'will force us to watch with unwearyed diligence, least we shou'd be so unhappy as to displease our Beloved (who is all faier and has no spot in him).[5]

5 Marginal note: 'see the Song of Solomon Chap. 4. vers. 7'.

If our feare be of Eternall torments, iff we dread the abideing in everlasting burnings, we shall certenly by our feare be moved to watch against all sin, for they who are guilty of iniquity, for them was Tophet[6] prepared of old, and lastly if we delight in joy, our desier to have a large share of it for our portion will make us watch against all sin; which we are sure will banish us eternally from his presence where there only is a fullnesse off joy, and at whose right hand there are pleasures for Evermore [Ps. 16: 11].

Thus may our passions when subdue'd by grace prove all of them nesesary to assist us in our watch, and in every change off our life we have reason to set a new watch upon our selves, for the same Actions are not alike inocent in every condition of life.

As for example the Gayety of my humour, and the harmelesse mirth in my conversation, was pleaseing to those I formerly kept company withall, and what was estimed by them to be Wit, in this part of the world is look'd upon to be a Gidynesse[7] unbecomeing a wife and want of a prudent sober temper.

Therefore since in what we can we ought to avoid giveing ofence, I must anew watch my words and check my mirth not only takeing care to speake such words as are no way sinfull, but also I must speake in such a style as is most agreable to the tempers of those people amongst whom my lot is cast.

JANE SHARP

The Midwives Book (1671)

The full title to this text is given in order to provide readers with a sense of the enormous scope of Sharp's text: The Midwives Book Or the whole Art of Midwifry Discovered. Directing Childbearing Women how to behave themselves In their Conception, Breeding, Bearing, *and* Nursing of Children. In Six Books, Viz. I. An Anatomical Description of the Parts of Men and Women. II. What is requisite for Procreation: Signes of a Womans being with Child, and whether it be Male or Female, and how the Child is formed in the womb. III. The causes and hinderance of conception and Barrenness, and of the paines and difficulties of Childbearing with their causes, signes and cures. IV. Rules to know when a woman is near her labour, and when she is near conception, and how to order the Child when born. V. How to order women in Childbirth, and of several diseases and cures for women in that condition. VI. Of Diseases incident to women after conception: Rules for the choice of a nurse; her office; with proper cures for all diseas incident to young Children. *By Mrs.* Jane Sharp *Practitioner in the Art of Midwifery*

6 'Tophet': name of a place near Gehenna, south of Jerusalem where, according to Jer. 19: 4, the Jews made human sacrifices to strange gods. Symbolically, as here, it signifies the torments of hell. 7 'Gidynesse': frivolousness or fickleness.

above thirty years. London, Printed for *Simon Miller,* at the Star at the Well end of St. *Pauls,* 1671. 418 pp (copy text BL, 1177. b. 19). The following extracts (pp. 18–21; 33–6; 41–6; 102–5; 166–9; 170; 176–8) illustrate Sharp's concern with disseminating anatomical information as well as that solely concerned with the business of childbirth. This two-fold approach was crucial since midwives were denied access either to the universities or to register for apprenticeships that would teach midwifery.

Book I. Chap. II. Of the Seed-preparing Vessels

The Yard[1] is as it were the Plow wherewith the ground is tilled, and made fit for production of Fruit: we see that some fruitful persons have a Crop by it almost every year, only plowing up their own ground, and live more plentifully by it than the Countryman can with all his toil and cost: and some there are that plow up other mens ground, when they can find such lascivious women that will pay them well for their pains, to their shame be it spoken, but commonly they pay dear for it in the end, if timely they repent not. The Yard is of a ligamental substance, sinewy and hollow as a spunge, having some muscles to help it in its several postures. The Yard and the Tongue have more great Veins and Arteries in them than any part of the Body for their bigness; by these porosities,[2] by help of Imagination the Yard is sometimes raised, and swels with a windy spirit only, for there is a natural inclination and force by which it is raised when men are moved to Copulation, as the motion is natural in the Heart and Arteries; true it is that in these motion is alwayes necessary, but the Yard moves only at some times, and riseth sometimes to small purpose. It stands in the sharebone in the middle as all know, being of a round and long fashion, with a hollow passage within it, through which passe both the Urine and Seed; the top of it is called the Head or Nut of the Yard, and there it is compact and hard, and not very quick of feeling, lest it should suffer pain in Copulation; there is a soft loose skin called the foreskin which covers the head of it, and will move forward and backward as it is moved; this foreskin in the lower part only in the middle, is fastned or tyed long ways to the greater part of the Head of the Yard by a certain skinny part called the string or bridle. It is of temperament hot and moist, and it is joined to the middle of the share bone, and with the Bladder by the Conduit pipe that carrieth the Urine, and with the brain by Nerves and Muscles that come to the skin of it, to the Heart and Liver by Veins and Arteries that come from them. The Yard hath three holes or Pipes in it, one broad one and that is common to the Urine and Seed, and two small ones by which the Seed comes into the common long Conduit pipe; these two Arteries or Vessels enter into this pipe in the place called the *Perinaeum,* which in men is the place between the root of the Yard and the Arsehole or Fundament, but in a woman it is the place between that and the cut of the neck of the womb; from those holes to the Bladder, that passage is called the neck of the Bladder, and from thence to the head of the Yard is the common pipe or channel of the Yard. The Yard hath four Muscles, two towards

1 'Yard': penis. 2 'porosities': porous areas.

the lower part on both sides, one of them near the channel or pipe of the Yard, and these are extended in length, and they dilate the Yard and raise it up, that the Seed may with ease pass through it: two other muscles there are that come from the root of it near the share bone that comes slanting toward the top of the Yard in the upper part of it, when these are stretched the Yard riseth, and when they slacken then it falls again, and if one of these be bent and the other be not, the Yard bends to that muscle that is stretched or bent.

If the Yard be of a moderate size, not too long, nor too short, it is good as the Tongue is, but if the Yard be too long, the spirits in the seed flee away; if it be too short, it cannot carry the Seed home to the place it should do.

Chap. X. Of the Generation or Privy parts in Women

Man in the act of procreation is the agent and tiller and sower of the Ground, Woman is the Patient or Ground to be tilled, who brings Seed also as well as the Man to sow the ground with. I am now to proceed to speak of this ground or Field which is the Womans womb, and the parts that serve to this work: we women have no more cause to be angry, to be ashamed of what Nature hath given us than men have, we cannot be without ours no more than they can want theirs. The things most considerable to be spoken to are, 1. The neck of the womb or privy entrance. 2. The womb it self. 3. The Stones. 4. The Vessels of Seed. At the bottom of a womans belly is a little bank called mountain of pleasure near the well-spring, and the place where the hair coming forth shews Virgins to be ready for procreation, in some far younger than others; some are more forward at twelve years than some at sixteen years of age, as they are hotter and riper in constitution. Under this hill is the springhead, which is a passage having two lips set about with hair as the upper part is: I shall give you a brief account of the parts of it both within and without, and of the likeness and proportion between the Generative parts in both sexes.

Chap. XI. Of the Womb

The Matrix or Womb hath two parts, the great hollow part within, and the neck that leads to it, and it is a member made by Nature for propagation of children. The substance of the concavity of it is sinewy, mingled with flesh, so that it is not very quick of feeling, it is covered with a sinewy Coat that it may stretch in time of Copulation, and may give way when the Child is to be born; when it takes in the Seed from Man the whole concavity moves towards the Center, and embraceth it, and toucheth it with both its sides. The substance of the neck of it is musculous and gristly with some fat, and it hath one wrinkle upon another, and these cause pleasure in the time of Copulation; this part is very quick of feeling. The concavity or hollow of it is called the Womb, or house for the infant to lie in. Between the neck and the Womb there is a skinny fleshy substance within, quick of feeling, hollow in the middle, that will open and shut, called the Mouth of the Womb and it is like the head of a Tench,[3] or of a young Kitten; it opens naturally in Copulation, in voiding menstrous blood, and in child-birth; but at other times, especially when a woman is with Child, it shuts so close, that the smallest needle cannot get in but by force.

The neck is long, round, hollow, at first it is no wider than a mans Yard makes it, but in maids, much less. About the middle of it is a Pannicle[4] called the Virgin Pannicle, made like a net with many fine ligaments and Veins, but a woman loseth it in the first act, for it is then broken. At the end of the neck there are small skins which are called foreskins; within the neck, a little toward the share bone, there is a short entrance, whose orifice is shut with certain fleshy and skinny additions, whereby, and by the aforesaid foreskin, the air coming between, they make a hissing noise when they make water.

Chap. XIII. Of the secrets of the Female sex, and first of the privy passage

. . . The Lips, or Laps of the Privities are outwardly seen, and they are made of the common coverings of the body, having some spongy fat, both are to keep the inward parts from cold, and that nothing get in to offend the womb; some call this the womans modesty, for they are a double door like Floodgates to shut and open: the neck of the womb ends in this, and it is as it were a skinny addition, for covering of the neck, answering to the foreskin of a Mans yard. These Lips which make the fissure of the outward orifice, are long, soft, of a skinny and fleshy substance; in some kind spongy and like kernels, with a hard brawny fat under them, and they are covered with a thin skin; but in those women that are married, they lye lower and smoother than in maids; when maids are ripe they are full of hair that grows upon them, but they are more curled in women than the hair of Maids. They that have much hair and very young are much given to venery.[5]

The wings appear when the Lips are parted, and they are made of soft spongy flesh, and the doubling of the skin, placed at the sides of the neck, these compass the Clitoris, and are like a Cocks Comb. These wings besides the great pleasure they give women in Copulation, are to defend the Matrix from outward violence, and serve to the orifice of the neck of the womb as the foreskin doth to a mans Yard, for they shut the cleft with lips as it were, and preserve the womb from cold air and all injuries: and they direct the Urine through the large passage, as between two walls, receiving it from the bottom of the cleft like a Tunnel, and so it runs forth in a broad stream and a hissing noise, not so much as wetting the wings of the Lap as it goes along; and therefore these wings are called *Nymphs*, because they joyn to the passage of the Urine, and the neck of the womb, out of which as out of Fountains, whereof the *Nymphs* were called Goddesses, water and humours do flow, and besides in them is all the joy and delight of *Venus*. . . .

The *Clitoris is* a sinewy hard body, full of spongy and black matter within it,

---

3 'tench': a thick-bodied freshwater fish, related to the carp. 4 'pannicle': hymen. 5 'venery': the practice or pursuit of sexual pleasure; indulgence of sexual desire.

as it is in the side ligaments of a mans Yard, and this *Clitoris* will stand and fall as the Yard doth, and makes women lustfull and take delight in Copulation, and were it not for this they would have no desire nor delight, nor would they ever conceive. Some think that *Hermaphrodites* are only women that have their Clitoris greater, and hanging out more than others have, and so shew like a Mans Yard, and it is so called, for it is a small exuberation in the upper, forward, and middle part of the share, in the top of the greater slit where the wings end. It differs from the Yard in length, the common pipe, and the want of one pair of the muscles which the Yard hath, but is the same in place and substance; for it hath two sinewy bodies round, without thick and hard, but inwardly spongy and full of holes, or pores, that when the spirits come into it, it may stretch, and when the spirits are dissipated it grows loose again; these sinews as in a Mans Yard, are full of gross black vital blood, they come from both the share-bones and join with the bones of the Hip, they part at first, but join about the joining of the share-bones, and so they make a solid hard body of the Yard; and the end is like the Nut, to which is joined a small muscle on each side. The head of this counterfeit Yard is called *Tertigo*, and the Wings joining cover it with a fine skin like the foreskin; it hath a hole, but it goes not through, and Vessels run along the back of it as upon a Mans Yard; commonly it is but a small sprout, lying close hid under the Wings, and not easily felt, yet sometimes it grows so long that it hangs forth at the slit like a Yard, and will swell and stand stiff if it be provoked, and some lewd women have endeavoured to use it as men do theirs. In the *Indies*, and *Egypt* they are frequent, but I never heard but of one in this Country, if there be any they will do what they can for shame to keep it close.

The *Clitoris* in Women, as it is very small in most, serves for the same purpose as the bridle of the Yard doth, for the womans stones lying far distant from the Mans Yard, the imagination passeth to the spermatical Vessels by the Clitoris moving and the lower ligatures of the Womb, which are joyned to the carrying Vessels of the Seed, so by the stirring of the Clitoris the imagination causeth the Vessels to cast out that Seed that lyeth deep in the body, for in this and the ligaments that are fastened in it, lies the chief pleasure of loves delight in Copulation; and indeed were not the pleasure transcendently ravishing us, a man or woman would hardly ever die for love.

Book III. Chap. II. Of great pain and difficulty in Childbearing, with the Signs, and causes, and cures

I have done with that part of *Anatomy*, that concerns principally us Midwives to know, that we may be able to help and give directions to such women as send for us in their extremities, and had we not some competent insight into the *Theory*, we could never know how to proceed to practice, that we may be able to give a handsome account of what we come for.

The accidents and hazards that women lye under when they bring their Children into the world are not few, hard labour attends most of them, it was that curse that *God* laid upon our sex to bring forth in sorrow, that is the general cause and common to all as we descended from the same great Mother *Eve,* who first tasted the forbidden fruit; but the particular causes are diverse according to several ages, and constitutions, and conformations, or infirmities. For sometimes Maids are married very young at twelve or fourteen years of age, and prove so soon with Child, when the passage is very little dilated, but is very strait and narrow; in such a case the labour in Child-bearing must needs be great for the infant to find passage, and for the Mother to endure it; and it must of necessity be much greater if some diseases go along with it, which happens oft in those parts, as Pushes, and Pyles, and Aposthumes,[6] that Nature can hardly give way for the Child to be born. Sometimes the Bladder or near parts are offended, and the womb is a sufferer by consent, and this will hinder delivery: And so if her body be bound that she cannot go to stool, the belly stopt with excrement will make the pain in travel the greater, because the womb hath not room to enlarge it self. So if women be too old as well as too young, or if they be weak by accident, or naturally of feeble constitutions, if they be fearful, and cannot well endure pain: be they too lean or too spare bodies, too gross or too fat, or if they be unruly and will not be governed, they will suffer the greater pain in Child-birth; and it is not without reason maintained also, that a Boy is sooner and easier brought forth than a Girle; the reasons are many, but they serve also for the whole time she goes with Child, for women are lustier that are with Child with Boys, and therefore they will be better able to run through with it: the weaker they are the greater the pain, because they are less able to endure it; and the strength of the Child is much, for it will sooner break forth, than when it is weak though it be of the same sex; if the Child be large, and the passage strait, as it is alwayes, though not alike in all, she must look for a great deal of pain when the time of delivery comes; but none more painful and dangerous than Monstrous births. Sometimes the Child doth not come at the time appointed by Nature, or it offers not it self in such a posture as that it may find a passage forth, as when the feet first present themselves to the neck of the womb, either both feet together, or else but one foot, and both hands upwards, or both knees together, or else more dangerous yet, lying all upon one side thwart the womb, or else backward or arselong; or two Children offer themselves at once with their feet first, or one foot and one head; the postures are so many and strange, that no woman Midwife, nor man whatsoever hath seen them all.[7]

A single birth, and a Boy, which is easier labour as I said, than of a Girle, and a young woman who had born one child before; yet Child-bearing is so dangerous that the pain must needs be great, and if any feel but a little pain it is commonly harlots who are so used to it that they make little reckoning of it, and are wont to fare better at present than vertuous persons do, but they will one day give an account for it if they continue impenitent, and be condemned to a torment of hell which far supasses all pains in Child birth, yet these doubtless are the greatest of all pains women usually undergo upon Earth.[8]

---

6 'Pushes': pimples, boils; 'Pyles': haemorrhoids; 'Aposthumes': large deep-seated abscesses. 7 Sharp goes on to cite scriptural examples of difficult births: Judah and Tamar, Gen. 38: 26; and Rachel and Jacob, Gen. 35: 17, 18. 8 There then follows a description of the pain of miscarriage and stillbirth.

There being then so many causes, and accidents whereby women usually fall into such mishaps, 'twill be profitable for women with child to observe some good rules beforehand, that when her time of delivery is at hand, she may more easily undergo it, and not so soon miscarry. But as there are diverse causes of miscarriage, so the times are diverse that we are to provide for, either before or after conception. And before she be conceived with child, let her use means both by diet and physick to strengthen her womb, and to further conception: Drink wine that is first well boyled with the mother of Tyme, for it is a pretious thing. If the womb be too windy, eat ten Juniper berries every morning, if too moist, the woman must exercise, or sweat in a Stove, or Hot-house, or else take half a dram of *Galingal*[9] and as much Cinnamon mingled in powder and drink it in Muskadel every morning, but if she use moderate labour, perhaps she may have no need of this: but the most frequent cause of barrenness in young lusty women that are of a cholerick complexion, is driness of the Matrix, and this is easily known by their great desire of copulation. It is to be corrected by cooling drinks, and emulsions made of barley-water, blanched Almonds, white poppy seeds, Cucumber, Citrons, Melons, and Gourds,[10] and to drink frequently of this; all violent exercise drinking of wine, or strong waters must be forborn.[11]

I grant that sometimes *God* is the cause of barrenness, who shuts up the womb, and will not suffer some women to conceive; we have multitudes of examples in Scripture for it, *Rachel* doubtless was not barren of her self, and she was angry with *Jacob*, that she said unto him, *Give men Children or else, I die*, but he acknowledgeth *God* to be the chief cause of it, *And he said unto her, Am I God, who hath withheld the fruit of the womb from thee?* And again he makes the barren women to keep house and be a joyful mother of Children.

Prayer is then the chief remedy of their barrenness, not neglecting such natural means to further conception and to remove impediments that *God* hath appointed, and those means are chiefly, either by a well ordering of the body and mind, or else when need requires by taking of Physick.

SUSANNA BELL

The Legacy of a Dying Mother (1673)

This text was published posthumously by Thomas Brooks, Bell's church minister, who wrote its extensive dedicatory epistle that eulogises Bell's exemplary life and character. Bell's 'Legacy to her Mourning Children' is a testimony of her experiences in New

9 'Galingal': a form of mild ginger. 10 'Gourds': the large fleshy fruit of the trailing plants of the N.O. Cucurbitaceae (OED). 11 Sharpe also recommends 'Oyle of Nightshade' and the 'seeds of mandrakes' (poisonous but used medicinally for their emetic and narcotic properties).

England. According to the title page, it was 'taken from her own Mouth by a near Relation of hers a little before her death', which problematises its autobiographical status. It could be described as a conversion narrative, but, as Hobby notes, Bell 'uses her text to work out the requirements of wifely duty'.[1] The copy text is University of Cambridge Library, Dd*. 5. 22. (9), published by John Hancock Senior and Junior in 1673; the extracts are from pp. 47–62. The asterisked biblical citations in the extract below denote the fact that the original text quoted the complete scriptural verses but in this edition they have been omitted for the sake of space.

A True Relation of some of the Experiences of Mrs. Susannah Bell

It pleased the Lord to order it so, that in my young days I was cast into a Family that feared the Lord. And going to hear Mr. *White*, preaching from those words, *Prov.* 15. 15 *But he that is of a merry heart hath a continual Feast*. From those words he did shew, how happy a thing a good conscience was, and what a sad thing it was with *Judas* to have a bad conscience; and what a blessed thing it was to have a good conscience. From that of *Hezekiah, Isa.* 38. 3. *And he said, Remember now, O Lord, I beseech thee, how I have walked before thee in truth, and with a perfect heart, and have done that which is good in thy sight*. This Sermon God made useful to me, and after this, it pleased the Lord to order it so, that I changed my condition, and the Lord provided for me a good Husband, one that feared him. And some troubles being here, many of the people of God went for *New England*, and among them my Husband desired to go, but I and my friends were very averse unto it. I having one childe, and being big with another, thought it to be very difficult to cross the Seas with two small children, some of my Neighbours advising me to the contrary, living so well as I did. But I told them that what the Lord would have me to do, that I would willingly do; and then it pleased the Lord to bring that Scripture to my mind, *Eph.* 5. 22. *Wives submit your selves unto your own Husbands, as unto the Lord*. And then my heart was brought off to a quiet submission.

But after this, I being well delivered, and the Child well; It pleased the Lord soon after to take my Child to himself: Now upon this, so far as it pleased the Lord to help a poor wretch, I begged earnestly of him, to know why he took away my Child, and it was given to me, that it was because I would not go to *New England*. Upon this the Lord took away all fear from my spirit, and then I told my husband I was willing to go with him. For the Lord had made my way clear to me against any that should oppose. And then my husband went presently upon the work to fit to go. And the Lord was pleased to carry us as upon Eagles wings, according to that *Deut.* 32. 10, 11. We were eight weeks in our passage, and saw nothing but the Heavens and Waters. I knew that the Lord was a great God upon the shore: But when I was upon the Sea, I did then see more of his glorious power then ever I had done before, according to that

1 Elaine Hobby, *Virtue of Necessity*, p. 69.

of the Psalmist, *Psal.* 107. 23, 24. And when the Lord was pleased to bring us in safety on shore, his people gave us the best entertainment they could, and then I thought I could never be thankful enough to the Lord for his goodness in preserving us upon the Sea, I being big with Childe, and my Husband sick almost all the Voyage. After this my Husband would have gone by water higher into the Countrey. But I told him, the Lord having been so good in bringing us safe ashore amongst his people, I was not willing to go again to Sea. And it was a good Providence of God we did not; for most of them that went were undone by it.

The first Sermon that I heard after I came ashore was out of *Jer.* 2. 13. *For my people have committed two evils; They have forsaken me the Fountain of living waters, and hewed them out* Cisterns, *broken* Cisterns *that can hold no water.* Now the Minister did shew, that whatever we did build on short of Christ, would prove but a broken Christ, would prove but a broken Cistern; and by that Sermon the Lord was pleased to shake my foundation: but I being a poor ignorant creature thought if I could but get into the fellowship of the People of God, that that would quiet my spirit, and answer all my Objections; And I did accordingly attempt to joyn with the Church, but they were very faithful to the Lord, and my soul, and asked me what Promise the Lord had made home in Power upon me. And I answered them, *Jer.* 31. 3. *Yea, I have loved thee with an everlasting love, therefore with loving kindness I have drawn thee.* But they told me that that was a general Promise: that I must look to get some particular Promise made home in Power upon me, and perswaded me to wait a little longer to see what God would further do for my poor soul, which accordingly I did.

And going to hear Mr. *Cotton*, who did preach out of *Rev.* 2. 28. *To him that overcometh I will give the Morning-star*; from which words he did observe, that the Star was Christ. And this he came to shew, how a soul might know whether it had an interest in Christ or no, and that was by the Lords giving out such precious Promises as these to the poor soul, *viz.* That God was in Christ reconciling the world to himself, 2 *Cor.* 5. 19. and that *John* 16. 21.* And *Isa.* 54. 22.* and that *Isa.* 43.5. which Promises afterwards God made sweet to my soul. After this I went to hear Mr. *Shepherd*, and he was preaching out of the Parable of the ten Virgins *Matth.* 25. 1–13. In his discourses he shewed that all were Professors, but the foolish had nothing, but Lamps without oyle, a Profession without grace in their hearts: but that the wise had got grace in their hearts, and so were ready prepared to meet the Bridegroom when he came. Now, by that discourse of his the Lord was pleased to convince me that I was a follish Virgin, and that I made a Profession, but wanted the oyle of grace in my heart, and by this means I was brought into a very sad condition. For I did not experimentally know what it was to have oyle in my Lamp, grace in my heart, nor what it was to have union with Christ, that being a mystery to me: And then I did think my self guilty of breaking all the Commandments of God except the sixth. For I thought I had neither desired, wished or endeavoured any mans death. But then the Lord shewed me, that if I were saved by Christ, my sins had murdered him, according to that *Acts* 3. 15. *chap.*

And this did aggravate my sin the more into me. Now one of my neighbors observing that I was in a distressed condition told me that she had been a hearing; and that the Minister she heard was a shewing that the Lord had more glory in the salvation then in the damnation of sinners. For in their salvation, his Mercy and his Justice were both glorified, but in their destruction only his justice was glorified. Hearing of this, the Lord was pleased to draw out my heart to plead with him. That if he might receive more glory in my salvation then in my destruction, that then his Mercy might be manifested to me. For I thought, although I had many worldly comforts, yet had I no interest in Christ, and that if I should die presently, Hell would be my portion; and in this sad and sore distress, the Lord was please to imprint that Scripture upon my mind.[2]

After this it pleased God, that Mr. *Elliott*, and some other of the people of God, seeing me in this sad condition, told me the Church would have me come in to be a Member with them; but I did reply, that all Church-fellowship would do me no good. Then Mr. *Elliott* asked me, What would do me good? and I told him, Nothing but an interest in Christ. His Answer was, That I was already in the pangs of the New Birth; and he did believe it would not be long before the Lord spoke peace to my poor soul. After that, reading a book of Dr. *Prestons*, where he did shew, *that when the Lord joyned himself to a believer, he did first comprehend the soul, and then enabling the soul by faith to apprehend him*. Which double Act of faith I then knew not. About fourteen days after, considering what a distressed condition I was in, I was bemoaning my self before the Lord; and the Lord was pleased to bring that Scripture to my remembrance in *John* 16. *I will give you that joy, that no man taketh from you.*

And then I thought with myself that it was Christ that I did want, and not joy. But the Lord brought that Scripture to me, *that Christ was tidings of great joy*, Luke 2. 10, 11. And I thought how could this be to such a poor wretch as I was, and the Lord was pleased to bring that Scripture to my mind, That he looked not as man looked, I *Sam*. 16. 7. And that he was God and not man, *Hos*. 11.9. And by this means he took away all my fears. And then the Lord did help me to discern that this was a mystery indeed, and did so quiet my heart, that all the World seemed as nothing unto me. For I never heard such a voice before, blessed be his Name.

And then the people of God would have me come into fellowship with them. And soon after I was admitted a Babe in Christ among them: Afterwards being to hear Mr. *Cotton*, on I *Pet*. 2.2. *As new-born Babes desire the sincere milk of the Word, that you may grow thereby.* And from thence he shewed, that if it were a living Babe it would cry out for nourishment, and that that soul that did once really taste of Christ was never satisfied, but would still be crying out for more and more of Christ; when such a soul came to any Ordinance, as Hearing, Prayer, the Lords Supper, and did get nothing of Christ, they were all as lost Ordinances to it.

2 The 'scriptures' Bell received were Job 10: 2; Job 40: 2; Rom. 9: 20–1.

It so fell out, that the next Lords day was the day of sitting down at the Lords Table. And the Lord did put it into my thoughts, that if we received nothing but a piece of bread and a sip of wine, it would be but a poor empty thing, and so the Lord did help me to beg, that if what he had pleased to speak to my soul before were a true manifestation of himself, that he would be pleased to speak again unto my soul. For a threefold cord is not easily broken, *Eccles.* 4. 12.

Being at the Ordinance. the bread and wine coming about, I was thus sighing unto the Lord: what shall I have nothing but a bit of bread and sip of wine this day? And the Lord was pleased to bring that Scripture to my minde, *John* 6. 55.* And so the Lord was pleased to give something more of himself to my poor soul at that time. After this, a sad Providence attended one of my Neighbors, I was full of fears that her condition might be mine. But the Lord brought that Scripture to my mind, *Jer.* 29. 11.* And thereby the Lord stayd my heart in trusting upon himself, and giving me a safe delivery. And being up again, I went to hear Mr. *Cotton*, and he was shewing what Assurance was, and how happy that soul was that could say as *Job* did, *Job* 19. 25. And with *David Psal.* 119. *For ever Lord thy Word is setled in the Heavens*; and so the Lord was pleased to shew me what a mercy I had that had Assurance. Then I went to speak to Mr. *Cotton*, to ask him what he thought of the work of God upon my poor soul. And he told me, that he was satisfied that it was a real work of God. And he did councel me to walk humbly and thankfully, and to take heed of grieving that the Spirit of God by which I was sealed up to the day of Redemption, and to walk humbly towards those that God had not revealed so much of himself to as he had to me. And then the Lord was pleased by his Providence to call my husband to come for *England*, and he did tell me, that he should so order his business that I should have less of the world to trouble me; I was glad to hear it from him, and desired him to go. And then the Lord was pleased to help me to consider whether I had not got a better Husband, my soul being espoused to him, 2 *Cor.* 11. 2. After he was gone from me, we did hear of a War broke forth in *England*, and friends told me my Husband would be in danger of his life if taken. I told them the best I knew, and the worst I knew; and that if God should take my Husband out of the world, I should have a Husband in Heaven, which was best of all. And Mr. *John Elliott* did visit me in his absence, and asked me how the Lord did bear up my heart in my Husbands absence: And I did tell him, that the Lord was as well able to bring him to me in safety, as he did to carry him out. And he answered me, I believe the Lord will say unto thee as he did to the *Canaanitish* woman, *Matth.* 15. 28. Be it unto thee according to thy faith. And the Lord was pleased to keep me and all that I had, and to preserve him, and to bring him home in safety unto me. And then instead of having less of the world which I desired, the Lord did cast in more of it. After this, my Husband told me, That he must go again to *England*, and I was very unwilling to it; but he told me, if he did not the Name of God would suffer. To prevent which, I consented, and it pleased God to bring him home in safety to me. And in a few years after he brought me over to *England* and God shewed much of his goodness to me.

After it had pleased God to bring me back to my Native Countrey. I was much troubled that there was no better observation of the Lords day, it being our Practice in *New-England* to begin it at Sunne-set the Evening before, as it is Recorded in *Genesis, That the Evening and the Morning was the first day*, and that Scripture was brought to my Memory, *Prov.* 14. 10. *The heart knows its own bitternesse, but no man intermeddles with its joy: Many trials the Lord hath been pleased to exercise me with, but in the midst of all God hath made that Word sweet to my soul*, Isa. 54. 10. For the Mountains shall depart and the Hills be removed, but my kindness shall not depart from thee, neither shall the Covenant of my Peace be removed, saith the Lord that hath mercy on thee.[3]

After this it pleased the Lord to visit one of my Daughters with a great sickness, upon which my heart was drawn out to seek the Lord on her behalf, then that Scripture was brought to my mind, *John* 11. 21. *Then said* Martha *unto Jesus, Lord, if thou hadst been here, my Brother had not died. But I know that now whatever thou wilt ask of God, God will give it to thee.* Jesus *saith unto her, thy Brother shall rise again.* Martha *saith unto him, I know that he shall rise again at the last day.* Jesus *saith unto her, I am the Resurrection and the Life, and he that believeth in me shall never die.* And it pleased the Lord to give me her life as an Answer of prayer. It pleased the Lord after this to visit this Land with the Pestilence, a severe stroak of his, that swept away many thousands; and under that sad Providence of his the Lord did help me to rely alone upon himself, from that Scripture, *Psal.* 91. 7. *A thousand shall fall at thy side, ten thousand at thy right hand, but it shall not come nigh thee.* And according to my faith, it pleased the Lord to preserve both my self and all my Relations from that sad stroak, though some of them were often in the midst of danger, blessed be his Name. The next year after the Lord did again (for our sins) visit us, and that by a dreadful fire, which reduced to ashes many thousand houses, and yet his love was then manifeste to me in the preservation of my habitation, when many better than my self were burnt out. Therefore unto my God shall I, (who am less then the least of all his mercies) render that praise which is due unto his Name.

Since that, whilst I was upon a languishing bed, and Death even knocking at the door, it pleased the Lord once again to alarme me in that weak condition by a dreadful fire which brake out very near unto us, and at that time it pleased God to support and strengthen my spirit with that Scripture, *Isa.* 43. 2. *When thous passest through the waters, I will be with thee; and through the Rivers, they shall not overflow thee: when thou walkest through the fire thou shalt not be burnt, neither shall the flame kindle upon thee.* And that Scripture, *Isa.* 54. 5. *For thy Maker is thy Husband, the Lord of Hosts is his Name, and thy redeemer the Holy One of* Israel, *the God of the whole Earth shall be called.* And this second time also the Lord was gratiously pleased to preserve me and my House from that amazing stroke which did so threaten us; And O that all these new and old

3 Bell records a period of physical weakness, the cause of which is unspecified, during which she receives scriptures from God, which encourage her: Isa. 50: 8; Job. 15: 11; Zech. 9: 12; Ps. 116: 7; 1 John 5: 12; John 8: 36.

Experiences might be high obligations upon me and mine to holiness and fruitfulness all our days.

Whilst I remained in *New-England* there hapned a great earthquake which did shake all in the house, and my son being by me, asked me what it was, I told him, our Neighbours were all amazed at it, and knew not but that the world might be at an end; and did run up and down very much affrighted at it; but I sate still, and did think with my self what a Christ was worth to my poor soul at that time. And then God made these Scriptures sweet refreshings, supporting and quieting my soul.[4]

BATHSUA PELL MAKIN

An Essay to Revive the Antient Education of Gentlewomen (1673)

Makin's defence of women's education is presented in epistolary form and, although written by a woman, the narratorial voice is gendered male: the *Essay* poses as one man's defence of women in direct, point by point response to another man's objections. Initially, Makin resorts to history to make her points: 'Women have formerly been educated in Arts and Tongues' (pp. 8–9), and 'have been eminent in them' (pp. 9–11). She provides evidence of women's abilities in languages, oratory, logic, philosophy, mathematics (pp. 13–16), and lays special emphasis upon women's poetic abilities (pp. 16–21). The extracts below are from the latter part of Makin's *Essay*, which focuses on how women should be educated and in what subjects. The copy text (BL, 1031. g. 19) was printed in London by J. D. in 1673. The extracts reproduced below are from pp. 3–4; 21–3; 24; 25; 26; 35–6; 42–3.

To all Ingenious and Vertuous Ladies, more especially to her Highness the Lady Mary, *Eldest Daughter to his Royal Highness the Duke of* York

Custom, when it is inveterate, hath a mighty influence: it hath the force of Nature it self. The Barbarous custom to breed Women low, is grown general amongst us, and hath prevailed so far, that it is verily believed (especially amongst a sort of debauched Sots)[1] that Women are not endued with such

---

4 Ps. 18: 46; Heb. 11: 13; Rev. 7: 9.   1 'Sots': drunkards.

Reason, as Men; nor capable of improvement by Education, as they are. It is lookt upon as a monstrous thing, to pretend to the contrary. A Learned Woman is thought to be a Comet, that bodes Mischief, when ever it appears. To offer to the World the liberal Education of Women is to deface the Image of God in Man, it will make Women so high, and men so low, like Fire in the House-top, it will set the whole world in a Flame.

These things and worse then these, are commonly talked of, and verily believed by many, who think themselves wise Men: to contradict these is a bold attempt; where the Attempter must expect to meet with much opposition. Therefore, Ladyes, I beg the candid Opinion of your Sex, whose Interest I assert. More especially I implore the Favour of your Royal Highness, a Person most Eminent amongst them, whose Patronage alone will be a sufficient Protection. What I have written is not out of humour to shew how much may be said of a trivial thing to little purpose. I verily think, Women were formerly Educated in the Knowledge of Arts and Tongues, and by their Education, many did rise to a great height in Learning. Were Women thus Educated now, I am confident the advantage would be very great: The Women would have Honour and Pleasure, their Relations Profit, and the whole Nation Advantage. I am very sensible it is an ill time to set on sort this Design: wherein not only Learning but Vertue it self is scorn'd and neglected, as pedantick things, fit only for the Vulgar. I know no better way to reform these Exorbitancies, than to perswade Women to scorn those Toyes and Trifles, they now spend their time about, and to attempt higher things, here offered: This will either reclaim the Men; or make them ashamed to claim the Sovereignty over such as are more Wise and Vertuous than themselves.

Were a competent number of Schools erected to Educate Ladyes ingenuously, methinks I see how asham'd Men would be of their Ignorance, and how industrious the next Generation would be to wipe off their Reproach.

I expect to meet with many Scoffes and Taunts from inconsiderate and illiterate Men, that prize their own Lusts and Pleasure more than your Profit and Content. I shall be the less concern'd at these, so long as I am in your favour; and this discourse may be a Weapon in your hands to defend your selves, whilst you endeavour to polish your Souls, that you may glorify God, and answer the end of your Creation, to be meet helps to your Husbands. Let not your Ladiships be offended, that I do not (as some have wittily done) plead for Female Preeminence. To ask too much is the way to be denied all. God hath made the Man the Head, if you be educated and instructed, as I propose, I am sure you will acknowledge it, and be satisfied that you are helps, that your Husbands do consult and advise with you (which if you be wise they will be glad of) and that your Husbands have the casting-Voice, in whose determinations you will acquiesce. That this may be the effect of this Education in all Ladyes that shall attempt it, is the desire of

Your Servant.

It may now be demanded, by those studious of Antiquity, why the Vertues, the Disciplines, the Nine Muses, the Devisers, and Patrons of all good Arts, the

Three Graces; should rather be represented under the Feminine Sex, and their Pictures be drawn to the Portraictures of Damosels, and not have Masculine Denominations, and the Effigies of Men? Yea, why Christians themselves, in all their Books and Writings, which they Commit to Posterity, still continue the same practice? Why Wisdom is said to be the Daughter of the Highest, and not the Son? Why *Faith*, *Hope*, and *Charity*, her Daughters, are represented as Women? Why should the seven Liberal Arts be expressed in Womens Shapes? Doubtless this is one reason; Women were the Inventors of many of these Arts, and the promoters of them, and since have studyed them, and attained to an excellency in them: And being thus adorned and beautified with these Arts, as a testimony of our gratitude for their Invention, and as a token of honour for their Proficiency; we make Women the emblems of these things, having no fitter Hieroglyphick to express them by. I shall add this one thing, worthy observation, to the great honour and commendation of the Feminine Sex.

The parts of the World have their denomination from Women, *Asia*, is so called from the Nymph *Asia*, the Mother of *Japethius* and *Prometheus*. *Europe*, from *Europa* the Daughter of *Agenor*. *Lybia* (which is *Africa*) from *Libia* the Daughter of *Epaphus*. *America* (lately discovered) bears the same Female Figure.

It is usual for men to pride and boast themselves in the Wisdom, Valour, and Riches of their Ancestors; what wise Men their Fore-fathers have been, what great things they have done, and what large possessions they have had, when they themselves are degenerated and become Ignorant, Cowardly, beggarly, debauched Sots.

I hope Women will make another use of what I have said; instead of claiming honour from what Women have formerly been, they will labour to imitate them in learning those Arts their Sex hath invented, in studying those Tongues they have understood, and in practising those Virtues shadowed under their Shapes; the knowledge of Arts and Tongues, the exercise of Virtue and Piety, will certainly (let men say what they will) make them honourable.

Care ought to be taken by us to Educate Women in Learning

That I may be more distinct in what I intend, I shall distinguish of women,

Women are of two sorts,	RICH	*Of good naturall Parts.*
	POOR	*Of low Parts.*

I do not mean, that it is necessary to the *esse*, to the *subsistence*, or to the Salvation of Women, to be thus educated. Those that are mean in the World, have not an opportunity for this Education: Those that are of low Parts, though they have an opportunity, cannot reach this; *Ex quoris Ligno non fit Minerva*: My meaning is, Persons that God hath blessed with the things of this World, that have competent natural Parts, ought to be educated in Knowledge; That is, it is much better they should spend the time of their Youth, to be compentently instructed in those things usually taught to Gentlewomen at Schools, and the overplus of their time to be spent in gaining Arts, and Tongues, and useful Knowledge, rather than to trifle away so many precious minutes meerly to polish their Hands and Feet, to curl their Locks, to dress and trim their Bodies; and in the mean time to neglect their Souls, and not at all, or very little to endeavour to know God, Jesus Christ, Themselves, and the things of Nature, Arts and Tongues, subservient to these. I do not deny but Women ought to be brought up to a comely and decent carriage, to their Needle, to Neatness, to understand all those things that do particularly belong to their Sex. But when these things are competently cared for, and where there are Endowments of Nature and leasure, then higher things ought to be endeavoured after. Meerly to teach Gentlewomen to Frisk and Dance, to paint their Faces, to curl their Hair, to put on a Whisk,[2] to wear gay Clothes, is not truly to adorn, but to adulterate their Bodies; yea, (what is worse) to defile their Souls. This (like *Circes* Cup) turns them to Beasts; whilst their Belly is their Godd, they become Swine; whilst Lust [is their God], they become Goats; and whilst Pride is their God, they become very Devils. Doubtless this underbreeding of Women began amongst Heathen and Barbarous People; it continues with the *Indians*, where they make their Women meer slaves, and wear them out in drudgery. It is practised amongst degenerate and Apostate Christians, upon the same score, and now is a part of their Religion; it would therefore be a piece of Reformation to correct it; and it would notably countermine them who fight against us, as Satan against *Adam*, by seducing our Women, who then easily seduce their Husbands.

Had God intended Women onely as a finer sort of Cattle, he would not have made them reasonable. Bruits, a few degrees higher than Drils[3] or Monkies, (which the *Indians* use to do many Offices) might have better fitted some mens Lust, Pride, and Pleasure; especially those that desire to keep them ignorant to be tyrannized over.

God intended Woman as a help-meet to Man, in his constant conversation, and in the concerns of his Family and Estate, when he should most need, in sickness, weakness, absence, death, etc. Whilst we neglect to fit them for these things, we renounce God's Blessing, he hath appointed Women for, are ungrateful to him, cruel to them, and injurious to our selves.[4]

If any desire distinctly to know what they should be instructed in?

I Answer, I cannot tell where to begin to admit Women, nor from what part of Learning to exclude them, in regard of their Capacities. The whole *Encyclopedia* of Learning may be useful some way or other to them. Respect indeed is to be had to the Nature and Dignity of each Art and Science, as they are more or less subservient to Religion, and may be useful to them in their station. I would not deny them the knowledge of Grammar and Rhetorick, because they dispose to speak handsomly. Logick must be allowed, because it is the Key to all Sciences. Physick, especially Visibles, as Herbs, Plants, Shrubs,

2 'Whisk': fashionable neckerchief. 3 'Drils': West African species of baboon. 4 Here, the narrator cites an example from Erasmus detailing men's anxiety that if women were educated they would surpass them, and provides biblical examples of women 'eminently employed in the great Transactions of the Church', including Deborah, Judith, Anna and Eunice.

Drugs, etc. must be studyed, because this will exceedingly please themselves, and fit them to be helpful to others. The Tongues ought to be studyed, especially the *Greek* and *Hebrew*, these will enable to the better understanding of the Scriptures.

The Mathematicks, more especially Geography, will be useful; this puts life into History. Musick, Painting, Poetry, etc. are great ornament and pleasure. Some things that are more practical, are not so material, because publick Employments in the Field and Courts, are usually denyed to Women: Yet some have not been inferior to many men even in these things also.[5]

This kind of Education will be very useful to Women.

1. The profit will be to themselves. In the general they will be able to understand, read, write, and speak their Mother-Tongue, which they cannot well do without this. They will have something to exercise their thoughts about, which are busie and active. Their quality ties them at home; if Learning be their Companion, Delight and Pleasure will be their Attendants: for there is no pleasure greater, nor more sutable to an ingenious mind, than what is founded in Knowledge; it is the first Fruit of Heaven, and a glymps of that Glory we afterwards expect. There is in all an innate desire of knowing, and the satisfying this is the greatest pleasure. Men are very cruel that give them leave to look at a distance, only to know they do not know; to make any thus to tantalize, is a great torment.[6]

More particularly, persons of higher quality, for want of this Education, have nothing to imploy themselves in, but are forced to Cards, Dice, Playes, and frothy Romances, meerly to drive away the time; whereas knowledge in Arts and Tongues would pleasantly imploy them, and upon occasion benefit others.[7]

We cannot be so stupid as to imagine, that God gives Ladies great Estates, meerly that they may Eat, Drink, Sleep, and rise up to Play. Doubtless they ought not to live thus. God, that will take an account for every idle thought, will certainly reckon with those Persons that shall spend their whole lives in idle play and chat. Poor Women will make but a lame excuse at the last day for their vain lives; it will be something to say, that they were educated no better. But what Answer Men will make, that do industriously deny them better improvement, lest they should be wiser than themselves, I cannot imagine.[8]

Object. Solomon's *vertuous Woman*, Prov. 31. *is commended for good Housewifery, not for Arts and Tongues; yet her Husband was a Person of Quality, he sat amongst the Elders of the Land in the Gate.*

---

5 Provides examples, including the Queen of Sheba, Catherine de Medici and Elizabeth I. 6 Another reason for educating women is to stop them from being led astray by heretical ideas and, like Eve, 'seducing' their families into wrong beliefs. 7 There follows an example from Seneca. 8 The *Essay* then moves on to discuss the purpose of women's education, and provides answers to a number of objections, of which the following is one example.

Answ. It seems Persons of Quality were more industrious in those times than now they are. Our Ladies would count it a great disparagement to them to do as she did; to seek Wool and Flax, and to work willingly with their own hands, *vers.* 13. to lay their hands to the Spindle, and to take hold on the Distaffe, *vers.* 19. to rise while it is Night, and to give Meat to her Houshold, and a Portion to her Maids, *vers.* 15. It's like the necessities of those times were greater, and the way of living far different from that which is now in use. The Duke of *Florence* is a great Merchant; Noblemen in *England*, and Gentlemen in *France*, think it disparagement to them to be so.

Answ. 2. I plead that our Ladies should have but the same Abilities this vertuous Woman had; not to labour as she did, but to understand as she did. I am sure to do all those things well that she performed, so as to be reverenced of her Servants, that her Children should rise up before her, and call her Blessed, and that her Husband should praise her, requires knowledge in Arts and Sciences, which were hardly got in those dayes without knowledge of Tongues; if they then were, or can be now, I am contented without them.

To buy Wooll and Flax, to die Scarlet and Purple, requires skill in Natural Philosophy. To consider a Field, the quantity and quality, requires knowledge in Geometry. To plant a Vineyard, requires understanding in Husbandry: She could not Merchandize, without knowledge in Arithmetick: She could not govern so great a Family well, without knowledge in Politicks and Oeconomics: She could not look well to the wayes of her Houshold, except she understood Physick and Chirurgery: She could not open her Mouth with Wisdom, and have in her Tongue the Law of kindness, unless she understood Grammar, Rhetorick and Logick. This seems to be the description of an honest, well-bred, ingenious, industrious Dutch-woman.[9] I desire our Women (whose condition calls them to business) should have no other breeding, but what will enable them to do those things, performed by this Woman.

As for those that are above these, I am sure the highest breeding imaginable will be useful to them. I believe the men of our times would say, it's a pitty any Woman should have so much Authority as this Woman had, she would be so masterly there would be no living with her.

Postscript

If any enquire where this Education may be performed; such may be informed, That a *School* is lately erected for Gentlewomen at *Tottenham-high-Cross*, within four miles of *London*, in the Road to *Ware*; where Mris. *Makin* is Governess, who was sometimes Tutoress to the Princess *Elizabeth*, Daughter to King *Charles* the First; Where, by the blessing of God, Gentlewomen may be instructed in the Principles of *Religion*; and in all manner of Sober and Vertuous Education: More particularly, in all things ordinarily taught in other Schools:

9 'Dutch-woman': Anna Maria van Schurman.

As { *Works of all Sorts,* / *Dancing,* / *Musick,* / *Singing,* / *Writing,* / *Keeping Accompts,* } Half the time to be spent in these Things.

The other half to be imployed in gaining the *Latin* and *French* Tongues; and those that please, may learn *Greek* and *Hebrew*, the *Italian* and *Spanish*: In all which this Gentlewoman hath a competent knowledge.

Gentlewomen of eight or nine years old, that can read well, may be instructed in a year or two (according to their Parts) in the *Latin* and *French* Tongues; by such plain and short Rules, accommodated to the *Grammar* of the *English* Tongue, that they may easily keep what they have learned, and recover what they shall lose; as those that learn Musick by Notes.

Those that will bestow longer time, may learn the other Languages, aforementioned, as they please.

Repositories also for Visibles shall be prepared; by which, from beholding the things, Gentlewomen may learn the Names, Natures, Values, and Use of *Herbs, Shrubs, Trees, Mineral-Juices, Metals* and *Stones.*

Those that please, may learn *Limning, Preserving, Pastry* and *Cookery.*

Those that will allow longer time, may attain some general Knowledge in *Astronomy, Geography*; but especially in *Arithmetick* and *History*.

Those that think one Language enough for a Woman, may forbear the Languages, and learn onely *Experiemental Philosophy*; and more, or fewer of the other things aforementioned, as they incline.

The Rate certain shal be 20*l. per annum*: But if a competent improvement be made in the Tongues, and the other things aforementioned, as shall be agreed upon, then something more will be expected. But the Parents shall judge what shall be deserved by the Undertaker.

Those that think these Things Improbable or Impractical, may have further account every *Tuesday* at Mr. *Masons* Coffe-House in *Cornhil*, near the Royal Exchange; and *Thursdayes* at the Bolt and Tun in *Fleetstreet*, between the hours of three and six in the Afternoons, by some Person whom Mris. *Makin* shall appoint.

MARY MORE

The Woman's Right (*c.* 1674–1680)

Mary More's proto-feminist critique of inequality in marriage is known to exist in only one copy, in a small manuscript volume in the British Library containing fair copies of a number of diverse texts (BL, Harleian MS 3198). This suggests that although the work was not published, it circulated beyond her own private circle by means of scribal publication – the response by Robert Whitehall, an extract from which follows, bears this out. In *The Patriarch's Wife: Literary Evidence and the History of the Family* (Chapel Hill: University of North Carolina Press, 1987), Margaret Ezell dates *The Woman's Right* to the late 1670s, and provides rich contextual information, noting that More had links with the social and intellectual circles surrounding the Royal Society, and that she first came to public attention as an artist: a painting by her, a copy of Holbein's portrait of Sir Thomas Cromwell, is still in the Bodleian Library. Whitehall, a minor poet and fellow of Merton College, Oxford (and therefore obliged to remain unmarried, like all university Fellows at that time) exchanged verses with More on the subject of her presentation of this picture to the Bodleian in 1674: these verses are reprinted by way of introduction to the extract from Whitehall which follows.

To My little Daughter Elizabeth Waller

At first view of this following discourse it may seem strange to thee that I thy Mother of all Women should concern my self in a Subject of this Nature, having never had any Reason as to complain of the least Ill Cariage of my Husbands to me, nor hath any occasion or action in my whole life ever offered any thing, wherein the Power and Will of my husband hath been disputed on mee, for we finding it our Interests to be embarked in one bottom, and so must be guided and steered one way, have (I hope I may say it without Vanity) so ordered our affairs and actions to the utmost of our Power and Skill, to tend to the Comfort and good liking of both.

So then that which made me more then ordinary to consider this Subject, hath been from a trouble in me observing the sad consequences and events that have fallen on men and their Wives, through this mistake of mens pretending a Power over their wives, that neither God nor nature doe allow, and I dare be confident that if any unbiassed person observe it, they must conclude this to bee the first and great cause of most breaches between men and their Wives. If thou my Child shall live to years fitt, and thou purposes to marry

1 First I advise thee to seek God by earnest and frequent prayers, for direction and a blessing on this so great a work, as the choice of a Husband which is as the hinges whereon hangs and turns all wordly Comfort to thee. And first in thy Choice (as far as is possible for thee to know) choose a man that fears and serveth God, tis usually the want of grace and the not knowing the Scriptures, that is the principall cause of the Ill carriage of men to their wives.

2 Secondly choose a wise and understanding man, for as Solomon saith of a ffoolish Wife, she is as rottenness in a mans bones which will soon destroy and ruine him I am sure may be truly said of a foolish Husband, for the Laws of our Country giving a Man after marriage a greater Power of their Estate than the Wife, unless the Wife take care before hand to prevent it (which I advise thee to doe) I say an unwise husband doth for the most part destroy and bring to nought what is in his power.

3 Thirdly (so far as thou canst discover it) choose one of a good naturall disposition and temper, I mean one that is free from the harshness and morosity that is sometimes naturally in men. Like Ishmael against all and all against him, a wife will find hard work and against the grain to live comfortably with such an Husband.

4 Lastly choose a Person whom thou dost love and affect and that loves thee, (for love hides a multitude of faults) but rather marry a man for his love to thee, than thine to him, for I seldome find the Wife fail on this part if the Husband love her.

But my Child if God shall see fitt to cross thee in all or any of these, in thy choice of a Husband, then I advise thee

To a patient Submission to the hand of God on thee, take up thy Cross and Bear it for in Mariage you are joyned, as it were in a Yoke, and if either strive to get free, or loosed from their unruly yokefellow, they do but Gall and tire themselves. Prudently hide it from the World, for I do not believe that ever Husband or Wife that complained of each other found comfort or releif in it, it being a complaint against ones self.

Nor do thou ever study to requite him in his kind, if he be vicious be thou the more Virtuous, if he be a Spend-thrift, be thou the more frugall. And remember to bear thee up, that God will take thy part sooner or later: it being Gods usuall manner when we bear afflictions patiently (and leave him to revenge) to doe it for us and retaliate it on the offender in some answerable punishment, we often reading the Sin by the Punishment.

That thou my Child maist be blest with a Religious, Wise, good tempered and loving husband is the earnest and constant prayers of thy faithfull and affectionate Mother M:M:

The Womans Right
The Argument

It is one end (among others) in writing to doe something either as to the thing or manner that is new and not commonly known; of this I am sure not to miss in this little treatise, for the truth that I shall here endeavour, and doubt not to prove, is so unknown at this time in England that I find they do, as is said of the Inventors of untruths, that they tell them so long untill they bring themselves into the beleif of their truth; so is it grown between husbands and their Wifes in our time, by a long practising of Power towards Wives, (impowered to it by laws of their own making) I say they are by practise grown into a beleif of their

Right to that, which I do not find allowed neither by the laws of God nor Nature.

That which I shall principally aim at in this discourse shall be to prove a greater equality between Husbands and Wives then is allowed and practised in England.

And God said let us make man in our own Image after our likeness, and let them bear dominion over the fish of the Sea and over the fowl of the Air, and over all the Earth (Gen. 1. v. 26.).

So God created man in his own Image, in the Image of God created he him, male and female created he them (v. 27).

And God blessed them and God said unto them, be fruitful, and multiply, and replenish the earth and subdue it and have dominion over the fish of the Sea, and over the fowl of the Air, and over Every living thing that moveth upon the Earth (v. 28).

Let us make man: the word man here comprehend both sexes, or mankind, for in the next verse we read God created him, male and female created he them (v. 29).

And God blessed them and gave them dominion over all the Creatures in the earth, to subdue them, from whence I lay down this as a Truth, that before the fall Man and Woman, Adam and Eve had equally power over each other and over the Creatures; finding noe difference: onely Adams being created first in order of time, and his naming the Creatures, and not Eve; neither of which seemes to me to be a signe of superiority in Adam (v. 30).

For first Adams being made before Eve, is but as beasts were made before Adam, for the Evening and the Morning were the first day, none will from thence think the night better, wch rather shows the contrary for God in the work of Creation went on Gradually higher and higher, creating the choisest and best last; so that if I would be criticall I might say that Eve was the most curious peice of nature in the whole creation being left till last, untill all things were fitted to receive and entertain her, besides she was made of the most refined part of the Creation, Adam. Adam was made of the earth refined Eve of Adam.

For the man is not the Woman (but of the earth) but the woman of the Man; but all things of God (I Cor. 11. v. 8). So that doubtless Eve was, and all (or most) women ever since are of a finer mould and mettall than most men are: nor do I see any Reason why we may not on good Grounds argue from thence; that the bodys of women being more fine, which body is the Organ that Acts and declares the soul, the souls of Women are acted more serene and agile then mens are: our common experience shewing us then when ever Women give themselves to study etc. they prove as learned and good proficients, and with as much (or more) ease then men, but the same hath been done by Women: What hath been done may be done is a rule in Philosophy.

A Prophetess and a Scholar bred up in the Colledges, Huldar, and Eusebius quotes out of Philo, that the Women had their studys and conferences severally from the Men (2 Kings v. 22). A Schollar. Anna Maria a Shurman, and the Lady Jane Gray both great Scholars.

Valiant. Deborah, and Boadicea in England etc (Jud[ges]).

Prudence to rule and Courage to maintain it: Queen Elizabeth of England who was also so expert in Tongues and languages, that she heard and gave answer to all Embassadours herself and had the Greek and Latine so fluent that she frequently spake verses in those languages extempore.

As for the Salique Law in France it is known to be made at first, onely as to a particular place Sala; for the faults of some dishonest Women who lived there, but after was falsly expounded to be for the whole nation of France, onely to debar the English Kings from the claime of the ffrench Crowne, tho the ffrench Kings themselves derive their Rights often from the heirs female.[1] By the Law made by God the Lawgiver the Daughters are to inherit their ffathers Inheritance alloted to them in the tribe of Manasses, God telling them that if a man had noe Sons then the Daughters should inherit, and if he hath no Daughter, then the inheritance should go to his Brethren [Num. 27: 6–8; Josh. 17: 3–6].

And Sheshomes Daughter was sole heir to her fathers Patrimony tho she married an Egyptian, and her posterity had their possesions amoung the tribes of Judah to the Captivity of Babylon (2 Cron: 2.54).

The second seeming difference between Adam and Eve before the fall is that Adam named the Creatures, it appears to me that Adam named them before Eve was created (tho they were both created in one day) but if Adam did name the beasts when Eve was there Eve named her Children when Adam was there, and gave them as Significant names as Adam did her, or the rest of the Creatures, it being the practise of the Women in the Scriptures to name their Children significantly (Gen. 2: 22). Eve was made of Adams Rib, not his head, nor foot, but middle, his equall and meet helper, flesh of his flesh, and bone of his bone (Gen. 3. 1).

This equall and happy man and his Wife envied by the Devil came in the Serpents shape, who was the most subtle of all the beasts, and assaulted Eve to break the Command, that God had newly enjoyned Adam and her, Thou in the singular number includes both, for Eve tells the Serpent, Wee may eat of the fruit of the trees of the Garden, but this God hath said thee shall not eat of etc. So then as they were equall partners in the power that God first gave them so were they equally concernd in the Command and in the Penalty for the breach of it, so I find the 10 Commandments afterward given by God to Moses for the People, are given in the singular number, Thou Shalt; yet there God commands a man and his Wife equally, they being one as appears by the 4th Command, Thou and Thy Son and Thy Daughter; not thou and thy wife, or thou and thy husband. By the Devils assaulting Eve and not Adam, it seems clear to me that she had the most high and strong soul, and so hardest to be overcome else would the Devil (the subtlest of the three) have fallen upon Adam, and not have left Adam the stronger to have been tempted by Eve the weaker, the interests of each others affections being (no doubt) of equall prevalence, Eve being as ready to have been perswaded by Adam, As Adam was by Eve.

But unhappy were those her better parts, and that she was first in the transgression, for she being first in the Sin, was in some respect higher in the punishment though I shall prove man and Woman more equall after the fall, then is beleived and practised.

1 The Salic Law prevented anyone from ascending to the throne of France if their claim could only be made through the female line; it was not always observed in practice.

Eve being first tempted to Sin, and perswading her husband, Gods just hand of punishment (who is ever most just) took the transgressours to task, according to their order in offending, first the Serpent, then the Woman, then the Man.

The seed of the Woman shall bruise the serpents head, from whence I observe, that before the Woman had her Sentence of Sorrow, she hath a promise (the greatest that was ever made to mankind) to support her, where I cannot but take notice of the high and unparalel Honour that God hath done to Women above men: that Christ God-man should be born of a Woman without a man, Christ having no mans flesh (Gen. 3: 15).

Then comes Eves Sentence of Sorrow (though not till the Support to bear her up) I will greatly multiply thy sorrows in conception, in sorrow shall thou bring forth children, and thy desire shall be to thy Husband and he shall rule over thee (Gen. 3:16); which words do shew something of a subjection to her husband after the fall, tho not much, for I find the sence of these words mistaken by most readers, they being the very same in the Originall, and are rendered in the very wordes in our Bibles; which God said to Cain when God saw Cains countenance fallen at his Brothers being better accepted than he (Gen. 4. v. 16). God comes to him as it were to expostulate the case with Cain, if thou dost well shalt thou not be accepted, and unto thee shall be his desire, and thou shalt rule over him, which are the very same words that God said to the Woman, so that I make it (at most) but a superiority of Eldership, which God seems to tell Cain was his due, if he did well. So then tho there were no Superiority in Adam before the fall by being made first, that after the fall because Woman first sind she lost that perfect equality.

Therefore the Apostle (after the fall) argues a difference between man and woman from his being first made.

The Man is the glory of God, and the Woman the glory of the man, which indeed is a Syllogysticall proof that the woman is the Glory of God (I Cor: 11. v. 7).

Man is the glory of God
The Woman of the Man
Ergo The Woman is the Glory of God.

Wee find indeed after the fall that when the thoughts of men grew altoghether evil, they found out many inventions, as to take many Wives, and to abuse them for which hardness of their hearts Moses was forced to write them bills of divorce so to part them (Gen. 6. v. 5), but our Saviour saith from the begining it was not soe (Mar[k] 10): I say we do find that the most wicked thus sind yet the good men and their Wives ruled equally. Which is plain in the whole Story of the Shunamite and divers others that were holy, and Solomons Mother tells us, the good wife considereth a field and buyeth it etc (Prov. 31. v. 11).

She perceiveth that her Merchandise is good, and we read Luke 8. v. 3. that the believing Women (when their husbands were alive) ministered to Christ of their substances, the holy Ghost calling it theirs as well as their husbands, nor surely would Christ have taken it, had it not been their right to have disposed of it.

And Joanna the Wife of Chuza Herods Steward, and Susanna, and many others which minstred to him of their substance (v. 3).

Last of all God comes to Adam, and to make his curse the Greater, curseth the ground with barrennesse, that hereby he with the harder labour should make it bear fruit or else he must have none. In the sweat of thy face shalt thou eat bread, which reacheth to all men, plainly shewing it their duty in some calling or employment that they ought to labour, whereby to provide for their family, and is as really their duty, as it is the Womans to bear children, he being worse than an Infidell that provideth not for his family. He in the Masculine Gender, which cannot include the Woman (Cor.).

Well then we find after the fall, the works different that God hath laid out for men and Women, neither have cause to brag, nor I am sure to oppress each other, by adding that to either which I am sure God never intended, but to help and ease each others burdens: Therefore are they called Yokefellows from a Yoke of Oxen drawing equally through the cloddy troubles of this life. The man carefully providing a maintenance for his Wife and family the best he can leaving no Lawful way untried, and with all tender affections comfort and cherish his wife. And the wife on the other part with all love and affection to her husband patiently submitt to the decree of God in her sorrowfull child-bearing, and frugally use the estate her husband so carefully gets, they both endeavouring the promotion of Gods Glory and their own salvation, forsaking all other Persons and Interests. This I conceive is their whole duty.

And here I cannot but take notice of the Practise of men in our time, who make it their business to raise themselves by estates with Wives, which seems to cross the command and curse of God laid on fallen man: whereas if men while they are young would take half the pains and Industry in lawfull callings as they do betray women (and children sometimes) to be their Wives, they would find it thrive better then now it doth: And sure our Laws are cruel to Women in this case (as many others more than in other Countrys) it being lawfull in England for a girle of 12 years of age to marry, thereby giving her husband all her estate, it being often very considerable, none can beleive any one marrys that child but for her Estate, nor can any Reason be given for that Law, but to empower the Man and enslave the Woman.

To return to our happy man and wife each doing their duty, which is the true honourable mariage this is the emblem of Christ and his Church, for whom he laid down his life. Christ hath but one wife, one spouse, which leads me to take notice of Polygamy.

Marriage is the indivisible conjunction of one man and woman onely, God created one man and one woman, And we find our Saviour tells his desciples, therefore must a man cleave to his wife, and they twaine shall be one flesh, not they 3 or they 4. And in this Christ makes no new Law, but revives the first made by God, Poligamy doubtless was a Sin in the Patriarchs yet not a known sin, because we do not read of their particular repentance for it. The World wanted replenishing, besides their great desire that the Messias might descend on their Line.

Lamech was the first that so Sind, Abram the first holy man, but sure in Abram it was Sarahs fault tho her end was good, for She knowing the promise was made to Abram, considered not that tho that promise was made to Abram alone, that he then having a wife, it could not be fulfild but by being her Sonn too, the

Command and the promises (as I proved before) being made to one, includes both. I say Sarah knowing the promise not the full meaning of God in it, thought that if Abram had a Son it was enough, so after she had waited till she was past children herselfe she propounds her maid: but this would not do, it must be Sarah and Abrams son that must fulfill Gods promise made to Abraham [Gen. 20–1].

Let us now look into the New Testament and see what that declares concerning Men and their Wives. First from our Saviour who when he was asked about this matter, makes no difference in the Power of man and wife.

And he said unto them whosoever shall put away his wife and marrieth another committeth adultery and if a Woman shall put away her husband, and be married to another she committeth adultery (Mark 10: 11–12); now Christ using the same words in the Womans case as in the Mans sheweth their equal power over each other, nor do we read in any of the Evangelists (who wrote of what Christ did and said) that ever Christ commanded a Subjection from the wife to the Husband, or gave power to the Husband over the wife, but shewed them as much love and honoured them as high as he did men, both before he was crucified, and after he was risen he first appearing to Women etc.

And it seems to me that women did preach the Gospell after Christs death. Saint Paul writing to the Corinthians saith every man prophesiing or preaching ought not to have his head covered, and every woman prophesiing should be covered (2 Cor: 22). Indeed I find the same Apostle advises women to be in the Churches (Rom. 16. v. 5).

When he sent his Epistles to the Romans by Phoebe he calls her his Assistant (Rom. 16. v. 5).

Saint Paul there speaks of the Women that laboured with him in the Gospell, Whose names are in the book of life (Phil. 4. v. 13).

We read of Priscilla that she taught the eloquent Apollos, and expounded the ways of God to him more perfectly (Acts 18).

And Anna the Prophetess continued in the Temple prophesiing [Luke 2: 36–8].

I confess the Apostles in their Epistles to the severall Churches leave not any argument untryed to perswade the holy Women to endeavour the promotion of the Gospell, pressing it hard on them to submitt to their husbands, to that end.

The Apostle in the first of Peter cap. 2. urging men to a patient bearing with, and submitting to each other, saith it was thank worthy if a man for conscience towards God endured greif, suffering wrongfully instancing in Christ who did no sin, that when he was reviled, reviled not again etc. The Apostle goes on in the next verse (though it be divided into another chapter so to break the sense) saith likewise the wives be in subjection to your own husbands, that if any obey not the word they also without the word may be wonn by the conversation of the wife which word 'Likewise' joyns the sence.

So that I find the Apostle seeing more Women brought over to the faith (and I believe are more still) perswades the women (thereby to winn their husbands) to a greater subjection to them, then I find commanded by God in the old Testament, or by our Saviour in the new.

And here I cannot but take notice of our Translators who are not contented with our Apostles advice to women which is hard enough on them, and (I doubt not) was endited by the holy Ghost, I say our Translators[2] do render severall places falsly (2 Cor. 22).

The Apostle there perswading the beleiving husband to dwell with the unbeleiving wife, saith let him not put her away: and in the next verse perswading the beleiving wife to dwell with the unbelieving husband, we read it let her not leave him, when the word is the same in both places in the original viz αφιετω, surely the difference of putting away or leaving is very considerable, leaving implies leaving him in possession, put away to keep possession.

The 2d Titus 5 and I Cor. 14. v. 34 there we read it obedience speaking to the Wives, which is there false rendred the word in the original being υποτατλω not υπαχοω, the first signifing submission, the last obeience, the word υποτατλω comes from υπο and τατλω certo ordine subjicio: that is to be a degree lower and connot be rendred to be obedient to a Command. The word υπαχοω comes from υτ and αχοω audio to hear, and so to do what we hear is commanded us, wch word the holy Ghost useth where ever this obedience is required as from children to parents, servants to masters etc. but is not any where used to wives thro out the whole bible.

Objection υποτατλω and υπαχοω will both bear a double interpretation, to obey, or to be subject, and we find them in Greek Authors so used.

I answer that the Holy Ghost God himself the first and great Author of all Languages and Tongues hath thought fit to use the word υπαχοω wherever he requires the greater duty as in obedience to himself and his commands, and of Children to Parents, and Servants to Masters. but the word υποτατλω in scripture we find still used when the lesser duty is required as from the younger to the elder etc. and tho the word υποτατλω be often used to wives in scripture yet it is but twice rendred obey I Cor. 14.34, 2 Tit. 5 and pray observe that in I Cor. where the word υποτατλω they render to obey to the Wife, in the verse but one before that the same word υποτατλω is rendred subject or submit speaking of the Prophets.

The Apostle there encouraging Women to an humility or submissiveness (still aiming at what I said before to draw their husbands to an holyness like theirs) instancing in the holy Women of Old (I Pet. 3.1), as he calls them and in particular Sarah, telling them that she obeyed Abram calling him Lord, which saying of the Apostle is an hyperbolical expression he well knowing that Sarahs calling him Lord was a small sign of her obedience, Lord being Abrams title, as Sarah was Lady or Empress, being the true signification of both their names, after God had equally blesst them, so that we must beleeve the expression of Saint Peter as an earnest desiring to have good Women do more than their duty (as is plain in the verses before it being thank worthy) that so they may win their husbands to the faith, nor can he mean in instancing in Sarahs obedience further then what he speaks, for in a serious examination of the Story we shall find that Abram obeyed Sarah far higher than Sarah did Abram, she said turn out the bond woman and her Son, and tho the thing greived Abram, yet he did it with nothing but a bottle and a bag.

2 This refers to the translators of the 1611 Authorised Version of the Bible.

Objection, it may be objected in Luke We read the word θποτατλφ is there rendred subject, and yet spoken of Christ to his Parents, and do you not think Christ obeyed his Parents (Luke 2)?

Answer, yes I do beleive Christ obeyed his earthly Parents, else had he not fulfilled the whole Law, but because Christ Submitted to his Parents, whom he also obeyed, must I therefore argue that a wife who must submitt must obey, arguing from the lesser to the greater here is incongruous, as for example, I am commanded to obey God, I am commanded to love God, I am also commanded to love my neighbour, shall I therefore argue, that because I am to love God and to love my neighbour, that therefore I must obey my neighbour?

Just so it is in the case of the Wife, I am commanded to obey my Parents, I am also to submit to my Parents and I am also to submitt to my husband shall I therefore argue, that because I am to submitt to my Parents and to my Husband that therefore I must obey my husband?

Indeed had I been commanded to obey my husband I must have submitted, the greater would have encluded the less, but being onely to submitt the less cannot include the Greater, if I can carry one hundred pound, I can carry one, but I may carry one and not one hundred.

Besides the word which we read subject in Luke, speaking of Christ is the same in the Originall that is used to Wives and to Wives is twice rendred obey, as if they would adventure to stretch the sence to Wives, which they durst not do to Christ.

Pray observe that the Translation of the Bible which was made by the Protestants in Queen Marys days was done at the City of Geneva by the most holy and laborious divines of England, flying to that city for Refuge, where they were labouring more than two whole year day and night to translate the Bible into English, and it was finished in the year 1560 and afterward presented to Queen Elizabeth and was received with the approbation of her and her people, and that translation hath been printed by her and her rightfull sucessors above thirty times. Now this translation done thus carefully and thus approved hath not translated the word υποτατλω obedient or obey, through the whole Bible, but rendred it to wives submitt, not obey, they not finding Gods Autority for it, but our modern Writers will have the Geneva translation read with the Spectacles of their Marginal notes, where they make that which they render subject, to be obedient, and this onely to wives.

I shall conclude that it is the want of learning, and the same education in women, that men have, which makes them loose their right. Men always held the Parliament and have enacted their own wills, without hearing them speak, and then how easy is it to conclude them guilty. Were this Errour in Parents amended in their not bringing up their Daughters learned, then I doubt not but they would as much excel men in that as they do now in Virtue. And of bad Women, of whom I know but few, I say Optima Corrupta, pessima.[3]

Finis

3 The best fate, for the worst is destruction.

ROBERT WHITEHALL

The Womans Right Proved False in which the True Right is Easily Discerned (1674–1680)

Whitehall's reply to *The Woman's Right* and the verses he addressed to More are also in BL, Harleian MS 3198; her response is in Bodleian MS Rawl. D. 912. Whitehall wrote:

To the No Less Virtuous than Ingenious Mris Mary More; upon her Sending Sr Thomas More's Picture[1] (of her own drawing) to the Long Gallery at the Publick Schools in Oxon

Madam:
Your Benefaction has been such,
That few can think it is a Womans touch:
So to the Life was Issa drawn (the Bitch)
That the beholder doubted which was which:
Seldom so Rare an Artist hath theere bin,
Yet every Lady Knows to draw Man In.
Since your Pencil far exceeds your Pen,
Let it be said I was the first of Men
Could stop in Scribling – know we study thrift
And fancy this a Richer new yeares-Gift.
When one in Shadows, and other deals in Rime,
Painters and Poets should knock off in Time.
Janus will knit both Brows too, if I trouble You
Longer, or interrupt his.

Yours

R:W:

More responded:

Sr.
Jear your Benefactress thats but Just
And I can bear't, but why no Woman must
An Artist bee in Painting, cause you see
I'm none, make the whole Sex Suffer for me.

---

1 As Ezell notes in *The Patriarch's Wife*, Whitehall is mistaken here – the picture was of More's antagonist, Sir Thomas Cromwell.

It made me Dogged Martials Bitch to read,
Besides I find his baudy Steps you tread.
Fellow and Batchelour, it must be soe
Hide yours sixt line, sure't speaks more than you know.
The Holb[e]in Coppyer yeilds, lets Pencils fall,
Scarce knows her poet from's Originall.
Three for our selves and six for friends beside
Nine ways at once, what the Muse squint eyde.
Ile close them then, for the vein I fear
May prove catching, I wish yould do so there:
Just what I thought, Oxford I knew before
How ere take Jear for Jear from
Mary More.

Madam,

If the entire body of your Ingenious Discourse had been drawn with as apparent and legible Features of Truth, as your Argument, my Pen has never moved but in Justification of the Womans Right. I must confess the Virtue, Prudence, Ingenuity, Sweet disposition, Meekness, Affableness etc this Constellation of Perfections, characterized with Sun-beams in some of your Sex, force me to entertain so great an Honour, Service and Respect for them, that sometimes I dispute sharply with my self and others, whether the Right hand be theirs onely by Virtue of a Modish Complement or due uncontrovable[2] Right. Tis one Article of my belief, that many Imperious Priests and Fathers in Ancient times made the Pulpit emitt a corrupt and passionate Sound (especially when Women were the Subjects of their discourse) where by the gratified ears of their Auditt have bribed their Judgement to Inconsiderate Embracing [of] Painted Errour. I scorn that Baseness of Spirit, which prompts but to the least thought of robbing a *Woman of Her Right*, that acted by a Generous Principle, I could readily grant all you Ladiships Reasons and Ingenuity plead for, add some grains of Redundance to your Treatise, and increase the Number of your Arguments to fortifie your Assertion. But beleeving my Opinion is single (tho I never met with strong Reason to oppose it) because most preach Contrary Doctrine, I chuse rather to abett an Ancient Faith, than introduce a New Creed. Moreover, suppose your Maxime not unsound, your Topick most proper, your Arguing not Sophisticall, yet if any Brave Virago will enter the Field, sound a Defiance, make the first Assult to release the Womans Right prisoned by Ancient Tradition, let Her fight every Inch of ground she advances and by force of Arms deliver it out of the hands of *Usurping Autority*, that so regaining by strength of Reason, they may assure

2 I.e., incontrovertible.

the World they know how to manage it with highest Prudence: and that if the Victory after a sharp Contest be won by their hands, they may with Greatest Triumph wear a Crown of Immortal Praise on their Heads: Or that if this New Generation can keep still in their Possession *this Patrimony*, which their fathers took with their Sword and with their Bow, with their Craft and their Cunning, and to which they are born Heirs; yet being convinced of injustice in detaining what was got by Subtle usurpation, tho conveyed by unquestioned Succession, may Galantly restore the Daughters of Zelophehad[3] to their rightfull Inheritance to their content, and their own Honour, that Women may be constrained to beleeve, Every Age grows more Generous as well as Wise. Again because your treatise boasts of demonstrating a *Truth New and not commonly known*, and Novelty is commonly pregnant with Errour, none can be reputed blameworthy for bringing it to the Test, weighing it in the Balance of Discretion, and propounding his Objections, that these vanishing by an ADDITIONAL LIGHT, it may shine with such Meridian Splendour,[4] that every one that runs may read it and acknowledge it Legitimate. These and some other Incentives not here nor now to be revealed, provoke me to resist your Charge that so famous a Conquest may not be gained by one Single Stroke of a Womans Hand: and to play the Defendant that the Plaintiff may not carry so momentous a Cause with a *Nemine contradicente*.[5]

What Power Husbands have over their Wives I am Utter Alien to by experience, (having never practised any over mine own) therefore can form my Conception of it onely by Reason, Observation, and Report. That some of them exceed the Bounds of their Empire is undeniable; but where their Province terminates is rightly questionable: and he must be as famous in metaphisicks as those 7000 Archers, who could direct an Arrow to a hairs bredth, were in the Art of Shooting, who can exactly determine this Controversy, and prescribe the limits of the Husbands oeconomy:[6] for such an one must be sure to remember, it is dangerous to remove ANCIENT LANDMARKS: and that when EVIL SPIRITS have once got Possession its not every EXORCIST can cast them out.

That many Women are more than ready to snatch at the Reins of Government, and surrogate a Power allowed neither by the Laws of God or Nature, is so certain, that to prove it would be to suspect the Sun shines at Noon day; to whome Should an Inch be given they would presently take more than an Ell, whose Brains being intoxicated with proud desire and ambition after Rule, were they admitted to co-equal sway in a Domestick Kingdome, would presently begin to aspire at Absolute monarchy, then to challange an equall Autority in State, to make Laws, bear Offices, vote as Members in Parliament, and afterwards presume to sit in Moses his Chair pretending they

3 Numbers 27: 7: because Zelophehad had no sons, his daughters were allowed to inherit from him. 4 The sun shines most brightly when it is at the meridian. 5 Latin: no-one disagreeing. 6 Deriving from Greek, the term 'economy' originally meant household management.

have power to TEACH as well as RULE: and then what can we expect but to see those things which our fathers dreaded to see, but saw not: and to hear those things which they dreaded to hear but heard not: viz to see all things post to Confusion, Princes {Men, Husbands} running on foot, Servants {Women, Wives} riding on Horseback, and to hear such Doctrines as never Heretick taught and so the last Errours and Age would be infinitely worse than *all the former.*[7]

ANON.

Murther Will Out, Or, A True and Faithful Relation of an Horrible Murther commited Thirty Three Years ago, by an Unnatural Mother (1675)

Popular pamphlets containing 'reports' or eyewitness accounts of the actions of ordinary men and women were prolific during this period and they were permeated with cultural and gender stereotyping that invariably had a didactic intent. This example of just such a pamphlet presents the stereotypes of 'woman' with reference to maternity, femininity and witchcraft, and the text raises questions about the cultural threat that such references register and the authority of narrative voice. The copy text is BL, 1132. 1. 42, and was licensed, 30 November by Roger L'Estrange, and printed for C. Pasinger in 1675. The extract is from pp. 1–6.

Murther will out

To religious hearts there is nothing so distastful as Sin, nor any Sin so odious and execrable as Murther: for it being contrary to Nature and Grace; the very thought, much more the act thereof strikes horrour to their Hearts and Consciences; Wherefore if this foul and bloody sin be so displeasing to godly Men, how infinitely more detestable is it then to God himself; who made all Living creatures for to serve Man, and onely created Man and Woman to serve himself; but as chollar proceeds from the passions of a man or Wom[an], so doth Murther from the Devil, for else we should not so often and frequently see it perpetrated in most Countries of

7 In the remainder of his text, Whitehall goes on to oppose More's claims and arguments point by point.

the World; A mournful but true example I here produce to your serious consideration: in the parish of *Stephney* lived a Widdow Woman, whose name I shall forbear to name, upon the account of a Son of hers living in *Redrisse* Parish: This Widdow being left with one small child, about half a year old, seemed to be satisfied at the loss of her husband, and well contented that she had of his seed left her which she hoped would prove a comfort to her after some trouble and cost in bringing him up: which she resolves within her self should not be wanting from her, though she worked her fingers to the bone; and in this mind she continued for some time after the disease of her dear husband; but the child being visited by the hand of Almighty God with a lingering distemper, made it very froward both by night and day; and so continued for a long time pining away, and with its continual crying a nights made its Mothers life very uncomfortable, but this poor Woman bore up under it as well as could be expected for a weak Vessel, but at last having laid out most of what she had upon the Doctors for cordials for her child, she began to murmur at the hard providence as she thought it, that had brought her into so sad a condition, and this was the way Satan began to work upon this poor Woman, first to think hardly of God who thus afflicted her, telling her that she got by her hearing of these good men as she called them; and so by degrees those subtile temptations of the Devil wrought so much upon the Woman; being oft alone, and being kept awake when that nature should have been a refreshing with sleep, I say upon her pillow, she ruminated upon what Satan had suggested to her, and giving way to this grand enemy of her salvation, she soon was made a slave to him; he having got such strong hold and good footing never lets her alone but follows her from place to place, in her out-goings he is with her, and is not this sad to be lead by the Devil, to have him for ones Companion, to walk with, to have this fiend to be by us, nay, in us, and a counsellour to us, as this poor miserable soul had, who was so hurried about by him that she could have no rest till she had done what he required, which he told her would be fore her ease and comfort: for now says he you are unhappy onely in this child of yours, which as long as it lives you will never enjoy a good day: and besides it hinders your preferment; you are young and handsome, and might have a husband or two more if this childs head was but laid, but who do you think will come to wooe you as long as this froward Child is with you: and therefore it is your best way to rid your hands of it: These and the like thoughts the Devil continually filled her heart with: insomuch that she could have no quietness: at last she begins a parley with the Devil: and, Oh sad is it when we stand and parley with him in our own strength: If she had gone to Christ when she was tempted: and cryed, O Lord Satan seeks to make a prey of my Soul, he tempts me to have hard thoughts of thee night and Day, and never gives me rest, but would have me lay violent hands upon the fruit of my Womb, promising me happiness in so doing, and pronouncing me miserable if I do it not: Now Lord I come to thee for supporting grace, I am a weak creature and not able to resist this adversary of my soul, much less to overcome him, but I come to thee for thou art able to tread Satan under thy foot, do it Lord for thy names sake; I say, if this poor tempted soul had upon the first temptation of Satan gone to Christ, and in the like manner laid open her case before him, doubtless she had found him ready to help and deliver her, but the not doing of this will of God be not infinite merciful in the blood of his son will be her undoing. For Satan at last prevailed on her to lay violent hands upon the poor innocent Babe, in the manner and form as followeth: She resolves that she will not lead such an uncomfortable life any longer and therefore thinks of many wayes how she may send her child out of the World, so as not to be mistrusted that she killed it, whereupon she being to go to the Bake-house, takes her Child and lays it upon the Bed, and lays a pillow upon the mouth of it, and not questioning but that would dispatch it before she came again, but returning she found it alive; thinks of another way; for now the Devil who had brought it so far was resolved to help her to finish it, and accordingly another way is thought of: Viz. To put the Child under a Tub, so whelmed down the Tub close to the ground: This Stragedem proved effectual, she haveing put it under in an hours time takes it up to see if the Child was Dead, found it to be almost cold: whereupon to blind the Eyes of her Neighbours she runs out and cryed that her Child was Dead, and that it Dyed while she was gone to the Bake-house; the Neighbours all believe that it went away in a Fit: and all appeared to be well, that Woman soon afterwards Marryed and had a brave Boy, which is now grown to Mans estate, she hath lived above this thirty years with her husband that now is, and nothing known.

But mark how the Wise All-seeing and sin-revenging God brings this bloody crime to light. About a fort-night ago this Woman was visited with a Cold that was a common distemper, and with that a Feaver succeeded that appeared to be mortal, not onely to those that were about her, but her self apprehended the Danger; Upon which she was exceedingly Disquieted at the Remembrance of her former bloody crime, and could not rest till she had revealed it in a manner as before, for which she was though in a very weak condition, carried in a Coach to Prison; she further told that she cannot nor shall not dye till she be hanged.

HANNAH WOOLLEY

The Gentlewomans Companion (1675)

Hannah Woolley was an established writer of advice books for women that provided information about a number of subjects, including cookery, physic and letter-writing. However, as Elaine Hobby explains, the attribution of *The Gentlewomans Companion* to her is doubtful.[1] Hobby points out that in *A Supplement To The Queen-like Closet*, Woolley objects to a book having been published under her name, and one of her objections is that it contains a false biography (which is reproduced below). Despite this, and the fact that the biography contradicts many of the known facts about her life (see Hobby, pp. 166–7), its 'spurious' contents have been used in modern biographical accounts of her. Nevertheless, some of the material in the book is plagiarised from Woolley's earlier works, and some is from books by other (male) writers in this genre; thus, this text raises interesting questions about authorship and authorial 'intent'. The copy text is BL, 1037. e. 15; extracts, pp. 10–14; 109–13; 117; 121–2.

A Short account of the life and abilities of the Authoress of this Book

I would not presume to trouble you with any passages of my life, or relate my innate qualifications, or acquired, were it not in obedience to a Person of Honour, who engag'd me so to do, if for no other reason than to stop the mouths of such who may be so maliciously censorious as to believe I pretend what I cannot perform.

It is no ambitious design of gaining a Name in print (a thing as rare for a Woman to endeavour, as obtain) that put me on this bold undertaking; but the meer pity I have entertain'd for such Ladies, Gentlewomen, and others, as have not received the benefits of the tythe of the ensuing Accomplishments. These ten years and upwards, I have studied how to repair their loss of time, by making publick those gifts which God hath bestow'd upon me. To be useful in our Generation is partly the intent of our Creation; I shall then arrive to the top of the Pyramid of my Contentment, if any shall profit by this following Discourse. If any question the truth of what I can perform, their trial of me I doubt not but will convince their infidelity.

The things I pretend greatest skill in, are all works wrought with a Needle, all Transparent works, Shell-work, Moss-work, also cutting of Prints, and adorning Rooms, or Cabinets, or Stands with them.

1 Elaine Hobby, *Virtue of Necessity*, p. 166.

All kinds of Beugle-works upon Wyers, or otherwise.
All manner of pretty toyes for Closets.
Rocks made with Shells, or in Sweets.
Frames for Looking glasses, Pictures, or the like.
Feathers of Crewel for the corner of Beds.[2]
Preserving all kind of Sweet-meats wet and dry.
Setting out of Banquets.
Making Salves, Oyntments, Waters, Cordials; healing any wounds not desperately dangerous.
Knowledg in discerning the Symptomes of most Diseases, and giving such remedies as are fit in such cases.
All manner of Cookery.
Writing and Arithmetick.
Washing black or white Sarsnets.[3]
Making sweet Powders for the Hair, or to lay among Linnen.
All these and severall things beside, too tedious here to relate, I shall be ready to impart to those who are desirous to learn.

Now to the intent I may increase your wonder, I shall relate how I came to the knowledge of what I profess. When I was fourteen years old, I began to consider how I might improve my time to the best advantage, not knowing at that age any thing but what reason and fancy dictated to me. Before I was Fifteen I was intrusted to keep a little School, and was the sole Mistress thereof. This course of life continued till the age of Seventeen, when my extraordinary parts appear'd more splendid in the eyes of a Noble Lady in this Kingdom, than really they deserv'd, who praising my works with the appellation of curious pieces of Art, was infinitely pleas'd therewith. But understanding withal, that I understood indifferently the smoth *Italian*, and could sing, dance and play on several sorts of Musical Instruments, she took me from my School, and greedily entertained me in her house as Governess of her only Daughter. Unto this honourable Person I am indebted for the *basis*, or groundwork of my Preserving and Cookery, by my observation of what she ordered to be done. By this Ladies means I came acquainted with the Court, with a deportment suitable thereunto.

The death of this Lady gave me a fit opportunity to be entertain'd by another no way inferiour to the former, with whom I lived seven years. At first I was Governess to those of her Children, whose forward virtue sufficiently declared the goodnes of the stock from whence they came. Time and my Ladies good opinion of me, constituted me afterwards her Woman, her Stewardess, and her Scribe or Secretary. By which means I appear'd as a person of no mean authority in the Family. I kept an exact account of what was spent in the house. And as I profited in Externals; so I treasured up things necessary for my understanding, having an happy opportunity so to do, not only by hearing that ingenious and agreeable discourse interfac'd between my Lady

2 'Crewel': a thin worsted yarn of two threads used for tapestry and embroidery, and formerly for making fringes, laces and hosiery. 3 'Sarsnets': very fine and soft silks.

and Persons of Honour, but also by inditing all her Letters; in the framing and well fashioning of which (that I might increase my Ladies esteem) I took indefatigable pains. There were not any who both wittily and wisely had publisht their Epistles to the view of the world, whom I had not read, and on all occasions did consult: those which I placed in my greatest esteem were the Letters of Mr. *Ford*, Mr. *Howel*, Mr. *Loveday*, and Monsieur *Voiture*.[4]

But that which most of all increast my knowledg was my daily reading to my Lady, Poems of all sorts and Plays, teaching me as I read, where to place my accents, how to raise and fall my voice, where to lay the *Emphasis* of the expressions. Romances of the best sort she took great delight in; and being very well verst in the propriety of the *French* tongue, there was not any thing published by the *Virtuosi* of *France*, which carefully and chargeably she procur'd not; this put me upon the understanding of that Language, she was so well experienc'd therein as those learned Tongues, of which the Academical *studioso* boasts a more than common understanding.

Here as I learned hourly courtly phrases and graces, so how to express my self with the attendancy of a becoming air. And as I gather'd how to manage my tongue gracefully, and discreetly; so I thought it irrequisite to let my hands lye idle. I exercised then daily in carving at Table. And when any sad accident required their help in Physick and Chyrurgery, I was ready to be assisting; in those two excellent arts in this place I acquired a competent knowledg.

In short time I became skilful, and stayed enough to order an house, and all Offices belonging to it; and gained so great an esteem among the Nobility and Gentry of two Counties, that I was necessitated to yield to the importunity of one I dearly lov'd that I might free my self from the tedious caresses of a many more.

In the time I was a Wife, I had frequent occasions to make use of all, or most of my aforenamed qualities; and what I exercised not within my own roof, I used among my neighbours, friends and acquaintants.

That which qualified me as a Governess for Children as well as any thing yet I have mention'd, was the great knowledg I had in the humours, inclinations, and dispositions of Children, having often had at one time above threescore in number under my tuition.

Besides, as I have been the Mistris of many Servants, so I have qualified them with my instructions to be Mistress to others; the major part of them living very comfortably in a married condition.

As I have taken great pains for an honest livelihood, so the hand of the Almighty hath exercised me in all manner of Afflictions, by death of Parents when very young, by loss of Husband, Children, Friends, Estate, very much sickness, by which I was disenabled from my Employment. Having already given you an account of the duty, and requisite, endowments which ought to be in a Governess, and how qualified I was my self in that troublesome concern, I shall

4 *Les Lettres de M. de Voiture*, were published in two editions (1657, 1660; first translated into English in another edition in 1657) and there were over 11 editions of his *Oeuvres* (1654–85), which contained some of his letters; Robert Loveday's letters were published in five editions by 1673 (edited by Anthony Loveday); James Howell, historiographer to Charles II, had published four editions of his *Epistolae Ho-Elianae . . . Familiar Letters domestic and forren* by 1673; the only 'letter' attributed to a Mr Ford that I could locate from about this period was Simon Ford, *A Sober Answer to an Angry Epistle* (1656).

now proceed in giving young Ladies such Rules which long experience and observation have taught me, which may be as their perfect guide in all ages and conditions, the practise whereof will assuredly imbalm their names here: let their stedfast faith in Jesus Christ only crown them with glory hereafter.

Of Womens behaviour to their Servants, and what is to be required of them in the house, or thereunto appertains

If by a thorough inspection and experience, you find you have a faithful Servant, give her to understand you are not insensible thereof by your loving carriage, and in acknowledgement of her fidelity, and frequently find out some occasions to give her some little encouragments to engage her continuance therein; do not dishearten her in her duty, by often finding fault where there is little or none committed, yet be not remiss in reproving where she does amiss.

If you find you have a bad or unfaithful Servant (as now adays there are too many, more than ever) whom you cannot either by fair means or foul reclaim: Vex not nor fret at what you see is remediless, but first making her thoroughly sensible of her errors, give her fair warning to provide for her self, and convenient for your own affairs; and do not (as a great many much to blame) give too ill a character of her, which will raise you little benefit, although it may lay the basis of her utter ruin; but rather be silent if you cannot speak good, which course I should think was sufficient of work on the greatest stupidity for a future amendment. Though a bad Servant detain not the wages, nor any part that is justly due, *for the Labourer is worthy of his hire*.

Be not too passionate with your Servants; and look narrowly to them, that they waste or lavish nothing, lest thereby you impair your estate, and so purchase the repute of a careless and indiscreet Woman.

If you find that they affect bravery too much, and presume to wear what misbecomes their present condition, rebuke them mildly into a moderation for their future advantage, and the credit of the Family wherein they are.

Let not the business of the House take them clearly off of service of God, but let them so relieve one the other in their duties, that they may be sometimes hearers of a good Sermon; and do not forget to make enquiry how they improve by what they hear at Church, and in your own house.

Let every Servant, Men and Women have their daily work appointed them, which must be duly exacted, and taken account of, either by your self, or some superior servant constituted by you for that purpose, and let not your constant and painful care of your worldly affairs exclude your greatest concern, the things of Heaven; and therefore appoint certain hours, Morning and Evening for publick prayers for the Family, and let not any Servant be absent, unless some extraordinary occasion hinder.

As near as you can, keep one set and certain time with good orders observed for the Table, in which be free, yet frugal. Let there be a competent allowance for the Servants, that they may have no just cause to complain; nor so much superfluity as that they may entertain a sort of loose Gossips in corners, the very bane and spoil of Servants.

Invert not the course of Nature (as too many do of late) by converting day into night, and night into day; but keep good hours for your repose, that your Servants may be the better disposed for the next days labour. Observe due times for washing and smoothing up the Linnen quickly, that it may not be thrown up and down and be mildewed and spoil'd, and so be fit for nothing but the wash again, and forget not to dearn or mend it every week, that it may not run to tatters before it be half-worn; and do not suffer any Servant to be idle.

If you have a Dairy, see it be kept clean and neat. Let not the Corn in the Granary muste and spoil for want of skreening[5] and turning.

Let your Servant see that your Beasts and Poultry be fatted in their due season; and that your Stable keep no more Horses than your own.

In the Brew-house, that the first Wort[6] be not drunk up by idle people, and so the smallness of your Beer become a disparagement to your Family.

In the Bake-house, that your Dough which should be for the finest Bread at your Table, be not half consumed in making of Cakes. That there be always Bread enough for the Servants before hand, for it is a point of ill Huswifry to eat hot or very new Bread.

In the Kitchen, that there be no Necessaries wanting, nor no waste or spoile made, but that the Meat be salted, and spent in due time.

In the Parlour, let the Fire be made, and the Cloth laid in due time, that the Cook may have no excuse for the spoiling of his Meat.

In the Chambers, that every thing be kept cleanly; the Beds often turned, the Furniture often beaten in the Sun, and well brushed.

In the Buttery and Cellars, that the Butler be careful of not making every idle fellow drunk that comes to the House, and so squander away without credit the Wine, Ale, and Beer.

Now because you will have frequent occasions for Banquets, in the entertaining of persons of Quality, I think it not unfit for a Gentlewoman to learn the art of Preserving and Candying, of which I shall, according to the Profession I make thereof, give you an ample account or instruction in some Chapters following. Frugality will perswade you to learn these excellent Arts, for in the constant use of the product thereof, you will save much for Sweetmeats, you will make much cheaper than you can buy them, and more commendable.

Other things you will meet withal worthy of your observation, of which this is no mean one, most requisite and in no wise dishonourable, that is, your understanding how to dress Meat as well as eat it that your Servants may be guided by you, and not you by them.

Gentlewomen, I will appeal to you as persons competent to judg whether the right understanding of these things be not altogether requisite and necessary; and as to your divertisements, none carries in it more profit than Cookery.

---

5 'skreening': i.e. screening. **6** 'Wort': unfermented beer.

LADY ANNE HALKETT

Memoirs (*fl.* 1677)

Halkett's *Memoirs* were written *c.* 1677. The manuscript is held at the British Library (BL, Add. MS. 32376): it is clearly legible, shows signs of revision, and is only very lightly punctuated. In the following extract small gaps at the end of sentences have been taken as an indication of paragraph breaks; however, some extra paragraphs have been inserted. Halkett also does not always use capital letters at the beginning of new sentences. Her *Memoirs* were published in 1701 in a collection of her works, including her *Meditations upon the 25. Psalm,* and *Instructions for Youth.* Much of Halkett's text is devoted to her various romantic liaisons, and this extract is no exception. However, in addition to her (ultimately doomed) entanglement with 'C. B.' this brief excerpt also narrates her involvement in the Duke of York's escape from St James's Palace. Unless otherwise indicated, square brackets in this extract denote the insertion of the enclosed text above the main text in the manuscript.

This Gentleman [C. B.] came to See mee Sometimes in the company of Ladys who had beene my Mother's Neibours in St Martins Lane and sometimes alone. butt when ever hee came his discourse was Serious, handsome, and tending to imprese the advantages of Piety Loyalty and Vertue and these Subjects were so agreeable to my owne inclination that I could nott butt give them a good reception especially from one that seemed to bee so much an owner of them himselfe. After I had beene used to freedome of discourse with him I told him I aproved[1] of his advise to others butt I thought his owne Practise Contradicted much of his proffesion, for one of his aquaintance had told mee hee had nott Seene his wife in a twelvemonth and itt was imposible in my opinion for a good Man to bee an ill husband and therfore hee must defend himselfe from one before I could beleeve the other of him. Hee Said itt was nott nesesary to give every[one] that might Condemne him the reason of his beeing so Long from her yett to Satisfy mee hee would tell mee the truth which was that hee beeing ingaged in the Kings Service, hee was oblieged to bee att London where itt was nott Convenient for her to bee with him, his stay in any place beeing uncertaine besides, she Lived amongst her friends who though they were kind to her yett were nott so to him for most of that Country had declared for the Parleament and were enemys to all that had or did Serve the King and therfore his wife hee was Sure would not Condemne him for what hee did, by her owne Consentt. This seeming reasonable, I did insist noe more upon that Subject.

1 The word 'much' has been crossed out here.

Att this time hee had frequent letters from the King who imployed him in Severall affaires butt that of the greatest Concerne which hee was imployed in was to Contrive the Duke of Yorkes escape outt of St James (where his Highnese and the Duke of Glocester and the Princese Elizabeth Lived under the Care of the Earle of Northumberland and his Lady). The dificultys of itt was representted by coll B butt his Majestie still pressed itt, and I remember this expresion was in one of the letters: *I beleeve itt will bee dificult and if hee Miscary in the attempt itt will bee the greatest afliction that can arive to mee butt I Looke upon James escape as Charles's preservation and nothing Can Content mee more therfore bee Carefull what you doe.* This letter amongst others hee shewed mee and where the King aproved of his choice of mee to intrust with itt for to gett the Dukes cloaths made [and] to drese him in his disguise. So now all C.B. busynese and Care was how to Manage this busynese of so important Concerne which Could not bee performed withoutt Severall persons Concurrence in itt. For hee beeing Generally Knowne as one whose stay att London was in order to Serve the King few of those who were intrusted by the Parliamentt in puplicke Concernes durst owne Convearse or hardly Civilitty to him, lest they should have beene Suspect by there party. which made itt deficult for him to gett accese to the Duke butt (to bee short) having Comunicated the designe to a Gentleman attending his Highnese who was full of honor and fidelity by his meanes hee had private accese to the Duke to whom hee presented the Kings letter and order to his Highnese for Consenting to act what C.B should Contrive for his escape which was so cheerefully intertained and so readily obayed that beeing once designed there was nothing more to doe then to prepare all things for the Execution.

I had desired him to take a ribban with him and bring mee the bignese of the Dukes wast and his lengh to have cloaths made fitt for him. In the meane time C.B was to provide Mony for all nesesary expence which was furnished by an honest Cittisen. When I gave the measure to my Tailor to inquire how much Mohaire would Serve to make a petticoate and wastcoate to a young Gentlewoman of that bignese and stature hee Considered it a Long time and said hee had made many Gownes and Suites butt hee had never made any to Such a person in his Life. I thought hee was in the right butt his Meaning was hee had never Seene any woman of so Low a stature have so big a Wast. However hee made itt as exactly fitt as if hee had taken the Measure himselfe. It was a Mixt Mohaire of a light haire Couler and blacke and the under petticoate was scarlett. All things beeing now ready upon the 20 of Aprill 1648 in the evening was the time resolved on for the Dukes escape. And in order to that itt was designed for a weeke before every Night as soone as the Duke had Suped, hee and those Sarvants that attended his Highnese (till the Earle of NorthumberLand and the rest of the howse had Suped) wentt to a Play called hide and seeke, and sometimes hee would hide himselfe So well that in halfe an howers time they Could not find him. his Highnese had so used them to this that when he wentt really away they thought hee was butt att the usuall Sport. A litle before the Duke wentt to Super that night hee Called for the Gardiner (who only had a treble key, besides that which the Duke had) and bid him give him that key till his owne was mended which hee did. And after his Highnese had Suped hee imeadiately [called to goe to the play, and] went downe [the] privy staires into the Garden and opened the Gate that goes into the parke treble Locking all the doores behind him. And att the Garden Gate C. B waited for his Highnese and putting on a cloake and perewig huried him away to the parke gate where a Coach waited that Caried them to the watter Side and taking the boate that was apointed for that Service they rowed to the staires next the Bridge. where I and Miriam[2] waited in a private howse hard by that C. B had prepared for dresing his Highnese where all things were in a readinese.

Butt I had many feares, for C. B had desired mee if they Came nott there prescisly by ten a clocke to shift for my Selfe for then I might Conclude they were discovered and so my stay there Could [doe] noe good butt prejudice my Selfe: yett this did nott make mee leave the howse though ten a clocke did strike and hee that was intrusted, offten wentt to the Landing place and saw noe boate Comming, was much discouraged and asked mee what I would doe. I told him I came there with a resolution to Serve his Highnese and I was fully determined nott to Leave that place till I was outt of hopes of doing what I came there for and would take my hazard. hee left mee to goe againe to the watter Side and while I was fortifying my Selfe against what might arive to mee I heard a great Noise of many as I thought Comming up staires which I expected to bee Soldiers to take mee butt itt was a pleasing disapointmentt for the first that Came in was the Duke who with much joy I tooke in my armes and gave God thankes for his Safe arivall. His Highnese called quickely, quickely, drese mee and putting off his cloaths I dresed him in the wemens habitt that was prepared, which fitted his Highnese very well and was very pretty in itt. Affter hee had eaten Some thing I made ready while I was Idle, lest his Highnese should bee hungry and having sentt for a Woodstreet Cake (which I knew hee Loved) to take in the Barge, with as much hast as Could bee his Highnese wentt Crose the Bridge to the staires where the Barge Lay, C. B Leading him and imediately the boatemen plied the oare so well that they were soone outt of Sight having both wind and tide with them. Butt I affterwards heard the wind changed and was so Contrary that C. B told mee hee was terribly afraid they should have beene blowne backe againe. And the Duke said Doe any thing with mee rather then lett mee goe backe againe which putt C. B to Seeke helpe where itt was only to bee had and affter hee had most fervently Suplicated assistance from God presently the wind blew faire and they Came Safely to there intended Landing place. Butt I heard there was some deficulty before they gott to the ship att Graves-End which had Like to have discovered them had nott Collonell Washingtons Lady assisted them.

Affter the Dukes barge was outt of Sight of the Bridge I and Miriam wentt where I apointed the Coach to Stay for mee and made drive as fast as the

2 Halkett's servant.

Coachman Could to my brother's howse where I staid. I mett none in the way that gave mee any aprehension that the designe was discovered nor was itt noised abroad till the next day. for (as I related before) the Duke having used to play att hide and seeke and to Conceale him Selfe a Long time when they Mist him att the Same play, thought hee would have discovered himselfe as formerly when they had given over Seeking him. butt a much Longer time beeing past then usually was spentt in thatt deverttisementt some began to aprehend that his Highnese was gone in earnest past there finding which made the Earle of NorthumberLand (to whose Care hee was Committed) affter strict Scearch made in the howse of St James and all theraboutts to noe purpose, to send and aquaint the Speaker of the howse of Commons that the Duke was gone butt how or by what meanes hee knew nott butt desired that there might bee orders Sent to the Cinque Ports for stoping all Ships going outt till the passengers were examined and scearch made in all Suspected places where his Highnese might bee Concealed. Though this was gone aboutt with all the vigillancy immaginable yett itt pleased God to disapoint them of there intention by so infatuating those Severall persons who were imployed for writting orders, that none of them were able to writt one right butt ten or twelve of them were Cast by before one was according to there mind. This accountt I had from Mr. N., who was Mace bearer to the Speaker att that time and a wittnese of it. This disorder of the Clarkes Contributed much to the Dukes Safety for hee was att Sea before any of the orders came to the Ports and so was free from what was designed if they had taken his Highnese. Though Severalls were Suspected for beeing accesory to the escape, yett they Could nott charge any with itt butt the person who wentt away and hee beeing outt of there reach they tooke noe notice as either to examine or imprison others.

Affter C. B had beene so Succesfull in Serving the Duke The Prince imployed him and Commanded him backe againe to London with severall instructions that might have beene Serviceable to the King had nott God Allmighty thought fitt to blast all indeavers that might have Conduced to his Majesty's Safety. As soone as C. B Landed beyond the Tower hee writt to desire I would doe him the faver as to come to him as beeing the only person who att that time hee Could trust and when hee should aquaint mee with the occation of his Comming hee doupted nott butt I would forgive him for the Liberty hee had taken. I knowing hee Could Come upon noe accountt butt in order to Serve the King I imediately sentt for an honest hackney Coachman who I knew might bee trusted and taking Miriam with mee I wentt where hee was who giving mee a short information of what hee was imployed aboutt and how much Secrisy was to bee used both as to the Kings interest and his owne Security, itt is nott to bee doupted butt I Contributed what I could to both and taking him backe in the Coach with mee left him att a private Lodging nott very farre from my brothers howse that a Sarvantt of his had prepared for him. The earnest desire I had to Serve the King made mee omitt noe opertunity wherin I could bee usefull and the zeale I had for his Majesty made mee not See what [inconveniencys] I exposed my Selfe to, for my intentions beeing

Just and inocentt made mee nott reflect what Conclusions might bee made for the private visitts which I could nott butt nesesarily make to [C. B][3] in order to the Kings service. for what ever might relate to itt that came within my knowledge I gave him accountt of and hee made Such use of itt as might Most advance his designe. As long as there was any posibility of Conveying Letters Secrettly to the King hee frequently writt and receaved very kind letters from his Majesty with Severall instructions and letters to persons of honour and Loyalty butt when all access was debarred by the strict Guard placed aboutt the King all hee Could then doe was to keepe warme those affections in Such as hee had influence in till a Seasonable opertunity to evidence there Love and duty to his Majesty. Though C. B discovered himselfe to none butt such as were of knowne integrity yett many Comming to that place where hee Lay made him thinke itt Convenient for his owne Safety to goe sometime into the Country and att his returne to bee more private.

One evening when I wentt to See him I found him Lying upon his bed, and asking if hee were nott well hee told mee hee was well enough butt had receaved a visitt in the morning from a person that hee wondred much how hee found him outt. hee was a Solicittor that was imployed by all the gentlemen in the County where hee Lived which was hard by where his wife dwelt and hee had brought him word shee was dead and named the day and place where shee was buried. I Confese I saw him nott in much greefe and therfore I used nott many words of Consolation but left him after I had given him accountt of the busynese I wentt for. I neither made my visitts lese nor more [to him] for this news; for Loyalty beeing the principle that first led mee to a freedome of Converse with him, so still I Continued itt as offten as there was occation to serve that interest. Hee putt on Mourning and told the reason of itt to Such as hee Conversed with. butt had desired the Gentleman who had first aquainted him with itt nott to make itt puplicke lest the fortune hee had by his wife and shee injoyed while shee Lived should bee sequestred. To bee short affter a Litle time hee on a day when I was alone with him began to tell mee that now hee was a free Man hee would say that to mee which I should have never knowne while hee Lived if itt had beene otherways which was that hee had had a great respect and honour for mee since the first time hee knew mee butt had resolved itt should die with him if hee had nott beene in a Condittion to declare itt withoutt doing mee prejudice. for hee hoped if hee could gaine an interest in my affection itt would nott apeare so unreasonable to marry him as others might representt itt. for if it pleased God to restore the King of which hee was nott yett outt of hopes hee had a promise of beeing one of his Majesty's Bedchamber and though that should faile yett what hee and I had together would bee aboutt eight hundred pound [sterling] a yeare which with the Lords blesing might bee a Competency to any Contentmentt minds.

Hee so offten insisted on this when I had occation to bee with him that att Last hee prevailed with mee and I did Consentt to his proposall and resolved

3 In the manuscript, the word 'him' is crossed out, and the initials 'C. B.' inserted above the main text.

to Marry him as soone as itt apeared Convenientt. but wee delayed itt till wee Saw how itt pleased God to determine of the Kings afaires. I know I may bee condemned as one that was too easily prevailed with butt this I must desire to bee Considered. hee was one who I had beene Conversantt with for Severall yeares before; one that proffesed a great friendship to my [beloved] brother Will; hee was unquestionably Loyall, handsome, a good Skollar, which gave him the advantages of writting and speaking well, and the cheefest ornamentt hee had was a devoutt life and Conversation. att least hee made itt apeare Such to mee. and what ever Misfortune hee brought upon mee I will doe him that right as to acknowledge I learnt from him many excellentt Lessons of Piety and vertue and to abhorre and detest all kind of vice. this beeing his Constantt dialect made mee thinke my Selfe as Secure from ill in his company as in a Sanctuary. from the prejudice [which] that opinion brought upon mee, I shall advise all, never to thinke a good intention Can Justify what may bee Scandalous, for though ones actions bee never So inocentt yett they Cannott blame them who Suspect them guilty when there is apearance of there deserved reproach. and I Confese I did Justly Suffer the scourge of the toung for exposing my selfe upon any Consideration to what might make mee Liable to itt. for which I Condemne my Selfe as much as my Sevearest enemey.

The King's misfortune dayly increasing and his enemys rage and Malice; both were att Last determined in that execrable murder, never to bee mentioned withoutt horror and detestation.[4] This putt Such a dampe upon all designes of the Royall party that they were for a time Like those that dreamed. butt they quickely roused up themselves and resolved to Leave noe meanes unesayed that might evidence there Loyalty. Many excellentt designes were Laid butt the Lord thought fitt to disapoint them all that his owne power might bee the more magnified by bringing home the King in Peace when all hostile attempts failed.[5]

ANNE BATHURST

Meditations and Visions (1679)

Anne Bathurst's *Meditations and Visions* is a diary-style account of spiritual experiences for the period from March 1679 to June 1693; a second, smaller volume resumes the diary in June 1693 and goes on until October 1696 (Bodleian MS Rawl. D. 1263). It is prefaced by a brief autobiographical account, focusing on the author's recurrent

4 The execution of Charles I in 1649. **5** The Restoration of Charles II in 1660.

experiences of despair and anxiety, and on the transformative role of religious faith in her life. Bathurst seems to have been a significant figure in the Philadelphian Society, a group which was devoted to mystical principles, focusing on the notion of divine wisdom, but did not dissent from conventional religious and political authority. The Reverend Richard Roach, head of the Philadelphians in the early eighteenth century, wrote an account of the communication he claimed to have had with the spirits of both Bathurst and her friend and fellow writer Jane Lead after their deaths (see MS Rawl. D. 833), and a second copy was made of portions of her diary for June–September 1679, presumably to allow wider circulation (MS Rawl. D. 1338). Copy text (Bodleian MS Rawl. D. 1262) runs to 607 pages; the extracts reproduced below are from pp. 45–7.

September 9, 1679
[marginal note: The Nuptial with the Transports of Love and Divine Union then enjoyed]
I found my heart much enflamed this morning, and I awaked also in his arms, and seeing the Glorified person of Christ behind me, I considered what it meant; Sure I wanted his driving power, He hath seen me slack or remiss: and I begged his strength, for I had now seen Him thrice behind me, but not taking then such observation. And I looked and said, let Him kiss me with the kisses of his mouth [S. of S. 1: 2]; and there came like to firey streams, one out of one side of his mouth, the other out of the other; and compassed my Head, with the two other ends in my mouth; so that it seemed like *a Ring* of firey gold held between his lips, circling round my Head, and the other part of the Ring between my Lips, he being behind me: I said, This is more than Isaiah desired, which was that God would touch his lips with a Coal from his Altar [Isa. 6: 6–7]; but God has touched me with fire from his Lips, a pledge of his Love: and then *The Nuptial*; for so it was, that I turned to see Him again, being very desyrous of His enjoyment; and He removed coming to me, expressing great Love, delight and joy, which caused in me admiration, what manner of Communication this was, even for the Holy Ghost to come to me, and the power of the Highest to overshadow me. O the Love of God! O Jesus! I am thine, thou hast ravished me, thou hast taken away my Heart; I am full, wanting words to vent! O the Sweetness and full Satisfaction! having such Love as is better than wine [S. of S. 1: 2; 4: 10]! That night I was pressing for the same Enjoyment that I had had the night before, being swallowed up of the Father, and taken into Him, being like all one Glory; (this morning I was in Christ's embraces, even the Nuptial after the King of Glory) and then the Glory of the Father came, I Lying in it as in a Cloud, – It came filling with Love, Life, Vertue and Power, joy, delight and praise. Then I thought of the Glory of the Son, that I had enjoyed so much love from, and desyred the Glorified Person of Christ and the Glory of the Father, so that I was swallowed up with this joy and felicity, holding them with great filling joy; sometimes we were all one, sometimes as three, sometimes I taken into Them, other times They filling me [marginal note: A Sweet Embleme of Eternal Bliss!], even the whole Man with such Transports, that though all the senses were delighted, yet not as in this Body; but a Body fitted for such an Union for surmounting all Earthly delights, which

are not in the least to be compared to it. And having some indisposition of Body, some times when at leasure to take notice, or else when the pain permitted to make use of my familiarity with Him that was in me, I could goe also to ease me (for whatever I desired as to Union and Communion that I had) so He could the same doe; what I desired for the Body was as soon answered as desired. Sometimes He would seem to go so stilly away, as I might not feel Him; but my earnest reaching desires soon caused his return, even to take Him fully into Me; so that I was full with the Glory of the Father, Son and H. [*sic*] Ghost; who being come to take their abode in Me, their Influences did so remain as I felt they had taken possession, whipping the Buyers and Sellers out of the Temple of my Heart [John 2: 15]: but who can express it? It is so great that I at present think, one cannot desire mor than I feel; only I desyre to be capable to express; but what I could declare, cannot be conceived nor believed but by those that hath it felt: but it doth fully satisfy me that I have had and have such freedom of converse and familiarity as with ones self. O such endearing Love! well may he be called a God of Love, whose Love hath outdone the most nearest and dearest Relation. These are but shady representations of what hath been acted and manifested to the Life by Himself who is Life and Power; and thus I was filled with such expressions. Then said I again, Now I feel him filling me so full, as at present I can desire no more: and what can be more? for when I look inward, there I see the Father, Son and Spirit: if I look about me, there He surrounds me so that I feel His Embraces, the Kisses of his mouth are allwise remembered by me: I have often groan'd at this State of absence, thus to be cabin'd in flesh, that I could not take my flight and be with Him. But now I have seen Him come running to Me. He comes and abides with me, and is close cabin'd in Me; so that this is Heaven where His Presence is. . . .

September 12 1679

[marginal note: The Beauty of Christ's Ear, with the great advantages of having it] In the morning I waked being very carefull to see and observe, whether the Beloved of my Soul lay by me, as I left Him asleep; and I said, Oh Thou the delight of my Soul! Thou fair one come away! But soon was staid, not to awake my Love till He please. And when I lookt to admire Him, I was caused admire his Ear with great delight and admiration; which made me enquire why seeing He was altogether lovely, why should the chief delight be directed to his Ear, when it might rather seem less lovely than his Cheeks, and the other beautifull parts of his face? *I was told* that was his Right Ear, which had been so often ready to hear and to come and answer with Communion and Union and friendly visits which I had had, He hath heard my requests and fully answered above what I could conceive; accordingly as it is said, He giveth above what we can ask or think. And one spake to me saying further, His Ear hears the Groans which we would desire, could we declare what we would have, so that his Ear hath not only heard what we have asked many times, and have often been answered; but He hath heard and given what you understand not to ask, but would have asked if you had knowen it. And further said to me, 'tis accounted a great favour from an Earthly King, to be so esteem'd as to have his Ear; but what is it then to have that of the King of Kings.

[marginal note: He shews his Hand that had miraculously healed Her] Then I desired to see *his Hand* which he had laid some years ago on my Head, that passed all over me, removing a long illness before it, as it went over me, of which I was immediately well, going forth the next day being Lord's day, and no more a return of that distemper, to admiration, when the Physitian could tell no more what to doe than He had done: This Hand I saw, which was his Right Hand of Power that had healed me. Great were the Delights and several were the Comforts of this day. At night I saw his glorified Person asleep by me, and desired to see his Crown on his head, and I did: after, it was laid by Him, he being still asleep: I touched his Hand and drew near Him, but some thing drew him further from me: He seem'd to be in a deep sleep even like one in a sound,[1] no motion; but His head hung looking pale. I was much troubled lest I had done anything to estrange him, and to cause that drawing away; and examin'd my Self of my demeanour that day as to the world, having some little thing to charge my self with I was greatly concerned. At length I perceived he was not fully asleep and nearer me than before; I said, O thou Beloved that sleepest, but thy heart waketh; and there arose a Crimson blushing colour in his Cheeks, and He begun to awake, and drew back his head to look on Me, and lookt a little strange, like not fully awake, as if he did not know me; at which I was more troubled: and so again, even three or four times, till I became much grieved. I entreated the Lord for his wonted favours, and that if he saw any thing in me that was not becoming a Spouse betrothed to so Dear and glorious a Saviour as Himself, that He would be pleased to cure me and keep me; and He at length came near, though far off at first, then nearer and nearer, till he laid his mouth to my mouth; [marginal note: She is taught to receive the Law at his Mouth and not to look into the Creature] and there was a Book laid betwixt his mouth and mine open, He touching the leaves with his mouth, and the leaves touched my mouth; *it was said*, that I might receive the Law at his mouth. That which I read in it was, *vilis facies*; and I was told, that was the book of the Creature, *a vile face*, which I must not look into, but wholly delight in Him; which I did, greatly desiring pardon if He had seen any thing amiss. Then great was the delight in Christ, being admitted to behold and admire whole Christ, his beauty being altogether lovely.

---

1 'sound': swoon, faint.

MARY ROWLANDSON

A True History of the Captivity and Restoration of Mrs. Mary Rowlandson (1682)

Mary Rowlandson's narrative of her capture by native Americans in Lancaster, Massachusetts on 10 February 1675 was incredibly popular, both in 'New England' and Britain (there were at least 30 editions of her text). Rowlandson's narrative is accompanied by her husband's last sermon, 'of the possibility of God's Forsaking a People that have been near and dear to him'. Her narrative begins with an account of the attack upon their garrison and Rowlandson's capture, continues by describing her nomadic existence among the 'Indians' (as she calls them), and culminates in her return to her husband. There is an early twentieth-century edition of this text (edited by Henry Stedman Nourse and John Eliot Taylor in 1903 (BL, 10880. i. 16)), which praises the text in imperialist terms. I have, however, made some use of their annotations in the footnotes to the extracts from Rowlandson's narrative. The copy text is BL, 4745. bb. 18, first printed in New England and reprinted in London, 1682; the following extracts are from pp. 1–3; 15–17; 33–6 (page 36 should read 34).

A Narrative of the Captivity and Restoration of Mrs. *Mary Rowlandson*

At length they came and beset our own House, and quickly it was the dolefullest day that ever mine eyes saw.[1] The House stood upon the edge of a Hill; some of the *Indians* got behind the Hill, others into the Barn, and others behind anything that would shelter them: from all which Places they shot against the House, so that the Bullets seemed to fly like Hail: and quickly they wounded one Man among us, then another, and then a third. About two Hours (according to my observation in that amazing time) they had been about the House, before they could prevail to fire it, (which they did with Flax and Hemp which they brought out of the Barn, and there being no Defence about the House, onely two Flankers,[2] at two opposite Corners, and one of them not finished.) They fired it at once, and one ventured out and quenched it; but they quickly fired it again, and that took. Now is that dreadful Hour come, that I have often heard of, (in the time of the War, as it was the Case of others) but now mine Eyes see it. Some in our House were fighting for their Lives, others wallowing in their Blood; the House on fire over our Heads, and the bloody

1 The opening paragraph describes the attack on the garrison in general. 2 'Flanker': a projected fortification which has a defensive purpose.

Heathen ready to knock us on the Head if we stirred out. Now might we hear Mothers and Children crying out for themselves, and one another, *Lord, what shall we do!* Then I took my Children (and one of my Sisters, hers) to go forth and leave the House: But as soon as we came to the Door and appeared, the *Indians* shot so thick; that the Bullets ratled against the House, as if one had taken an handful of Stones and threw them; so that we were fain to give back.[3] We had six stout Dogs belonging to our Garrison, but none of them would stir, though another time, if an *Indian* had come to the Door, they were ready to fly upon him, and tear him down. The Lord hereby would make us the more to acknowledge his Hand, and to see that our Help is always in him. But out we must go, the Fire increasing, and coming along behind us roaring, and the *Indians* gaping before us with their Guns, Spears, and Hatchets, to devour us.

No sooner were we out of the House, but my Brother-in-Law (being before wounded (in descending the House) in or near the Throat) fell down dead, whereat the *Indians* scornfully shouted, and hallowed,[4] and were presently upon him, stripping off his Clothes. The Bullets flying thick, one went thorow my Side, and the same (as would seem) thorow the Bowels and Hand of my dear Child in my Arms. One of my elder Sisters Children (named *William*) had then his Leg broken, which the *Indians* perceiving, they knock'd him on the head. Thus were we butchered by those merciless Heathen, standing amazed, with the Blood running down to our Heels. My elder Sister being yet in the House, and seeing those woful Sights, the Infidels haling Mothers one way, and Children another, and some wallowing in their Blood, and her elder Son telling her that (her Son) *William* was dead, and my self was wounded; she said, And *Lord, let me die with them*: Which was no sooner said, but she was struck with a Bullet, and fell down dead over the Threshold. I hope she is reaping the Fruit of her good Labours, being faithful to the Service of God in her Place. In her younger years she lay under much trouble upon Spiritual accounts, till it pleased God to make that precious Scripture take hold of her Heart, 2 *Cor.* 12. 9. *And he said to me, My grace is sufficient for thee.* More than twenty years after I have heard her tell, how sweet and comfortable that Place was to her. But to return: The *Indians* laid hold of us, pulling me one way, and the Children another, and said, *Come, go along with us:* I told them, they would kill me: They answered, *If I were willing to go along with them, they would not hurt me.*

O the doleful Sight that now was to behold at this House! *Come, behold the Works of the Lord, what desolation he has made in the Earth* [Ps. 46: 8]. Of thirty seven Persons who were in this one House, none escaped either present Death, or a bitter Captivity, save onely one, who might say as he, *Job* 1. 15. *And I onely am escaped alone to tell the News.* There were twelve killed, some shot, some stabb'd with their Spears, some knock'd down with their Hatchets. When we are in prosperity, Oh the Little that we think of such dreadful Sights, and to see our dear friends and Relations lie bleeding out their Heart-blood upon the Ground! There was one who was chopp'd into the Head with a Hatchet, and stripp'd naked, and yet was crawling up and down. It is a solemn Sight to see

3 'fain': obliged. **4** 'hallowed': shouted or cried loudly.

so many Christians lying in their Blood, some here, and some there, like a company of Sheep torn by Wolves. All of them stript naked by a company of hell-hounds, roaring, singing, ranting and insulting, as if they would have torn our very hearts out, yet the Lord by his Almighty power, preserved a number of us from death, for there were twenty four of us taken alive: and carried Captive.

I had often before this said, that if the *Indians* should come, I should chuse rather to be killed by them, than taken alive: but when it came to the trial my mind changed: their glittering Weapons so daunted my Spirit, that I chose rather to go along with those (as I may say) ravenous Bears, than that moment to end my daies. And that I may the better declare what happened to me during that grievous Captivity, I shall particularly speak of the several Removes we had up and down the Wilderness.

The first Remove. Now away we must go with those Barbarous Creatures, with our bodies wounded and bleeding, and our hearts no less than our bodies. About a mile we went that night; up upon a hill within sight of the Town where they intended to lodge. There was hard by a vacant house (deserted by the English before, for fear of the *Indians*) I asked them whether I might not lodge in the house that night? to which they answered, what will you love *English-men* still? this was the dolefullest night that ever my eyes saw. Oh the roaring, and singing, and dancing, and yelling of those black creatures in the night, which made the place a lively resemblance of hell: And as miserable was the waste that was there made, of Horses, Cattle, Sheep, Swine, Calves, Lambs, Roasting Pigs, and Fowls (which they had plundered in the Town) some roasting, some lying and burning, and some boyling, to feed our merciless Enemies; who were joyful enough though we were disconsolate. To add to the dolefulnes of the former day, and the dismalness of the present night, my thoughts ran upon my losses and sad bereaved condition. All was gone, my Husband gone (at least separated from me, he being in the Bay; and to add to my grief, the *Indians* told me they would kill him as he came homeward) my Children gone, my Relations and Friends gone, our house and home, and all our comforts within door, and without, all was gone (except my life) and I knew not but the next moment that might go too.

There remained nothing to me but one poor wounded Babe, and it seemed at present worse than death, that it was in such a pitiful condition, bespeaking Compassion, and I had no refreshing for it, nor suitable things to revive it. Little do many think, what is the savageness and bruitishness of this barbarous Enemy! even those that seem to profess more than others among them, when the *English* have fallen into their hands.[5]

The thirteenth Remove. Instead of going toward the Bay (which was that I

5 Rowlandson continues by describing her life among the native Americans, placing a great deal of emphasis upon their eating habits; she herself cannot stomach their food until her hunger eventually forces her to eat. The 'wounded Babe' dies in her arms, but she manages to acquire a Bible, which helps to sustain her. Their journey leads them to 'King Philip', leader of the Quabaug tribe. At this point, Rowlandson tries to see her son, who has been separated from her, but gets lost; and she asks her 'master' (Quanopin or Quinnapin of the Narraganset tribe) to sell her back to her husband, but this is refused. Despite this, Rowlandson identifies her 'master' as her best friend; certainly, she seems to have a better relationship with him than with the squaws, as the end of the next extract illustrates.

desired) I must go with them five or six miles down the River, into a mighty Thicket of Brush: where we abode almost a fortnight. Here one asked me to make a shirt for her Papoos, for which she gave me a mess of Broth, which was thickened with meal made of the Bark of a Tree: and to make it the better she had put into it about a handful of Pease, and few roasted Ground-nuts. I had not seen my Son a pretty while, and here was an *Indian* of whom I made inquiry after him, and asked him when he saw him? he answered me that such a time his Master roasted him; and that himself did eat a piece of him, as big as his two fingers, and that he was very good meat: but the Lord upheld my Spirit, under his discouragement; and I considered their horrible addictedness to lying, and that there is not one of them that makes the least conscience of speaking the truth.

In this place on a cold night as I lay by the fire, I removed a stick which kept the heat from me, a Squaw moved it down again, at which I lookt up, and she threw an handful of ashes in my eyes; I thought I should have been quite blinded and have never seen more: but lying down, the Water run out of my eyes, and carried the dirt with it, that by morning, I recovered my sight again. Yet upon this, and the like occasions, I hope it is not too much to say with *Job, Have pity upon me, have pity upon me, Oh ye my Friends, for the hand of the Lord has touched me* [Job 19: 21]. And here I cannot but remember how many times sitting in their Wigwams, and musing on things past, I should suddenly leap up and run out, as if I had been at home, forgetting where I was, and what my condition was: But when I was without, and saw nothing but Wilderness, and Woods, and a company of barbarous Heathen; my mind quickly returned to me, which made me think of that, spoken concerning *Sampson*, who said, *I will go out and shake my self as at other times, but he wist not that the Lord was departed from him* [Judg. 16: 20].

About this time, I began to think that all my hopes of Restoration would come to nothing. I thought of the *English* Army, and hoped for their coming, and being retaken by them, but that failed. I hoped to be carried to *Albany*, as the *Indians* had discoursed, but that failed also. I thought of being sold to my Husband, as my Master spake; but instead of that, my Master himself was gone, and I left behind: so that my spirit was now quite ready to sink. I asked them to let me go out, and pick up some sticks, that I might get alone, and pour out my heart unto the Lord. Then also I took my Bible to read, but I found no comfort here neither: yet I can say, that in all my sorrows and afflictions, God did not leave me to have my impatience work towards himself, as if his ways were unrighteous; but I knew that he laid upon me less then I deserved. Afterward, before this doleful time ended with me, I was turning the leaves of my Bible, and the Lord brought to me some Scriptures, which did a little revive me, as that *Isai.* 55. 8. *For my thoughts are not your thoughts, neither are your ways my ways, saith the Lord*. And also that, *Ps.* 37. 5. *Commit thy way unto the Lord, trust also in him, and he shall bring it to pass.*

About this time they came yelping from *Hadly*, having there killed three *English-men*, and brought one captive with them, *viz. Thomas Reid*. They all gathered about the poor Man, asking him many Questions. I desired also to go and see him; and when I came he was crying bitterly: supposing they would kill him. Whereupon I asked one of them, whether they intended to kill him? he answered me, they would not: He being a little cheared with that, I asked him about the welfare of my Husband, he told me he saw him such a time in the *Bay*, and he was well, but very Melancholy. By which I certainly understood (though I suspected it before) that whatsoever the *Indians* told me respecting him, was vanity and lies. Some of them told me, he was dead, and they had killed him: some said he was Married again, and that the Governour wished him to Marry; and told him he should have his choice, and that all perswaded him I was dead. So like were these barbarous creatures to him who was a liar from the beginning.

As I was sitting once in the Wigwam here, *Philips* Maid came in with the Child in her arms, and asked me to give her a piece of my Apron, to make a flap for it, I told her I would not: then my Mistress bad me give it, but still I said no. The Maid told me, if I would not give her a piece, she would tear a piece off it: I told her I would tear her Coat then: with that my Mistress rises up: and takes up a stick big enough to have killed me, and struck at me with it, but I stept out, and she struck the stick into the Mat of the Wigwam. But while she was pulling of it out, I ran to the Maid and gave her all my Apron, and so that storm was over.[6]

I can remember the time, when I used to sleep quietly without working in my thoughts, whole nights together: but now it is otherwise with me. When all are fast about me, and no eye open, but his who ever waketh, my thoughts are upon things past, upon the awful dispensations of the Lord towards us: upon his wonderful power and might in carrying us through so many difficulties, in returning us in safety, and suffering none to hurt us. I remember in the night season, how the other day I was in the midst of thousands of enemies, and nothing but death before me: it was then hard work to perswade my self, that ever I should be satisified with bread again. But now we are fed with the finest of the Wheat, and (as I may so say) with honey out of the rock [Ps. 81: 16]: instead of the husks, we have the fatted Calf: the thoughts of these things in the particulars of them, and of the love and goodness of God towards us, make it true of me, what *David* said of himself, *Psal.* 6. 6. *I water my Couch with tears.* Oh the wonderful power of God that mine eyes have seen, affording matter enough for my thoughts to run in, that when others are sleeping, mine eyes are weeping.

I have seen the extream vanity of this World: one hour I have been in health, and wealth, wanting nothing: but the next hour in sickness, and wounds, and death, having nothing but sorrow and affliction.

Before I knew what affliction meant, I was ready sometimes to wish for it. When I lived in prosperity; having the comforts of this World about me, my Relations by me, and my heart chearful: and taking little care for any thing; and

---

6 Despite Rowlandson's fears and discouragement, news of plans for her and the other captives' 'redemption' reaches her as they are crossing the Baquaug river. Rowlandson is asked to set her own price for her redemption; she vacillates, trying not to either set a price that is too high or too low, but settles on 20 pounds. Eventually, she was allowed to return to her husband, and they then set about rescuing their daughter, for whom, by accident rather than design, they do not have to pay to 'redeem'. The final extract is Rowlandson's conclusion.

yet seeing many (whom I preferred before my self) under many trials and afflictions, in sickness, weakness, poverty, losses, crosses, and cares of the World, I should be sometimes jealous least I should have my portion in this life; and that Scripture would come to my mind, *Heb.* 12. 6. *For whom the Lord loveth he chasteneth, and scourgeth every Son whom he receiveth*: but now I see the Lord had his time to scourge and chasten me. The portion of some is to have their Affliction by drops, now one drop and then another: but the dregs of the Cup, the wine of astonishment, like a sweeping rain that leaveth no food, did the Lord prepare to my portion. Affliction I wanted, and Affliction I had, full measure (I thought) pressed down and running over [Luke 6: 38]: yet I see when God calls a person to any thing, and through never so many difficulties, yet he is fully able to carry them through, and make them see and say they have been gainers thereby. And I hope I can say in some measure, as *David* did, *it is good for me that I have been afflicted* [Ps. 119: 71]. The Lord hath shewed me the vanity of these outward things, that they are the *Vanity of vanities, and vexation of spirit* [Eccles. 1: 14], that they are but a shadow, a blast, a bubble, and things of no continuance; that we must rely on God himself, and our whole dependence must be upon hm. If trouble from smaller matters begin to arise in me, I have something at hand to check my self with, and say when I am troubled, It was but the other day, that if I had had the world, I would have given it for my Freedom, or to have been a Servant to a *Christian*. I have learned to look beyond present and smaller troubles, and to be quieted under them, as *Moses* said, *Exod.* 14. 13. *Stand still, and see the salvation of the Lord.*

ELIZABETH GAUNT

Mrs Elizabeth Gaunt's Last Speech (1685)

Gaunt, an Anabaptist and shopkeeper, was tried at the Old Bailey, indicted for high treason and burnt at Tyburn for harbouring a Mr Burton in her house. Burton, outlawed for his part in the Rye House Plot (a conspiracy to murder the King and the Duke of York in 1683), had returned to London following the defeat of the Duke of Monmouth's Protestant revolt at Sedgemoor in 1685. He had callously gained his own pardon by informing on Elizabeth Gaunt, and the night before her execution she wrote the following tract that expressed her sense of betrayal and which protested her innocence. Gaunt was the last woman to be executed in England for a political offence and her 'execution speech' appeared in both English and Dutch in Amsterdam in 1685. The full speech, printed below, is from BL, copy text 8052. i. 1(29).

Not knowing whether I shall be suffered, or able, because of weaknesses that are upon me, thro my hard and close imprisonment, to speak at the place of Execution, I have wrote these few Lines, to signify that I am reconciled to the wayes of my God towards me, tho it be in ways I looked not for, and by terrible things, yet in righteousness; for having given me life, he ought to have the disposing of it, when and where he pleases to call for it; and I desire to offer up my all to him, it being but my reasonable service, and also the first terms Christ offers, that he that will be his disciple, must forsake all and follow him: and therefore let none think hard, or be discouraged at what hath happened unto me; for he doth nothing without cause in all that he hath done unto us, he being holy in all his wayes, and righteous in all his works; and it is but my Lott in common with poor desolate *Zion* at this day; neither do I find in my heart the least regret for any thing that I have done in the service of my Lord and Mr. C. Jesus, in securing and succouring any of his poor sufferers, that have shewed favour to his righteous cause, which cause, tho it be now faln and trampled on, as if it had not been anoynted, yet it shall revive, and God will plead it at another rate than ever he hath done yet, with all its opposers and malicious haters; and therefore let all that love and fear him, not omit the least duty that comes to hand, or lyes before them, knowing that now Christ hath need of them, and expects they should serve him; and I desire to bless his holy name, that he hath made me usefull in my generation, to the comfort and relief of many desolate ones, that the blessing of those that were ready to perish hath come upon me, and been helpt to make the heart of the widow to sing; and I bless his holy name, that in all this, together with what I was charged with, I can approve my heart to him, that I have done his will, tho it doth cross mans will; and the scriptures which satisfy me are *Esay.* [Isaiah] 16. 3, 4. *Hide the Out-casts, bewray not him that wandreth; be thou a covert to them from the face of the spoyler.* And *Ob.* 12, 13, 14. *Thou shouldest not have delivered up those of his that did remain in the day of distress*: but men say, you must give them up, or you shall dye for it; now who to obey, judge ye; so that I have cause to rejoyce, and be exceeding glad, in that I suffer for righteousness sake, and that I am accounted worthy to suffer for well-doing, and that God hath accepted any service from me, which hath been done in sincerity, tho mixt with manifold infirmities, which he hath been pleased for Christs sake to cover and forgive. And now as concerning my crime, as it is called, alas! it was but a little one, and might well become a Prince to forgive. (But he that shews no mercy, shall find none.) And I may say it in the language of *Jonathan, I did but taste a little hony, and lo I must dye for it*; I did but relieve an unworthy, poor, distressed family, and lo I must dye for it; well, I desire in the Lamb-like nature of the Gospell to forgive all that are concerned, and to say, Lord, lay it not to their charge; but I fear it will not; nay I believe, when he comes to make inquisition for blood, it will be found at the door of the furious Judge, who because I could not remember things through my dauntedness at *Burton's* wife and Daughter's witness, and my ignorance, took advantage thereat, and would not hear me when I had call'd to mynd that which I am sure would have invalidated the evidence; and tho he granted something of the same kind to another, he denyed it to me at that tyme: my blood will also be found at the door of the unrighteous Jury, who found me guilty upon the single oath of an out-lawd man; for there was none but his Oath about the mony, who is no legal witness, tho he be pardoned, his outlawry not being reversed, the law requiring 2 witnesses in poynt of Treason, and then about by going with him to the place mentioned (*viz* the *Hope*) it was by his own word before he could be out-lawd; for it was but about 2 monthes after his *absconding*, so that tho he was in a *Proclamation* yet not high Treason, as I am informed, whereby I am clearly murdered; and also bloody Mr. *Atterbury*, who hath so unsatiably hunted after my life, tho it is no profit to him, yet thro the ill will he bears me, left no stone unturned, as I have ground to believe, till he brought it to this, and shewed favour to *Burton*, who ought to have dyed for his own fault, and not to have bought his life with mine: and Captain *Richardson*, who is cruell and severe to all under my circumstances, and who did at that time, without all mercy and pity, hasten my sentence, and held up my hand that it might be given; All which, together with the great one of all, by whose power all these and multitudes more of cruelties are done, I do heartily and freely forgive as against me, but as it is done in an implacable mind against the Lord Christ and his righteous cause and followers, I leave it to him, who is the avenger of all such wrong who will tread upon Princes as upon mortar, and be terrible to the Kings of the earth; and know this also, that tho you are seemingly fixed, and because of the power in your hands, are weighing out your violence, and dealing with a despiteful mind, because of the old and new hatred, by impoverishing and every way destressing those you have got under you, yet unless you can secure *Jesus Christ* and all his holy Angells, you shall never do your business, nor your hand accomplish your enterprizes; for he will be upon you ere you are aware; and therefore that you would be wise, instructed, and learn, is the desire of her that finds no mercy from you.

APHRA BEHN (trans.)

J. V. Brilhac, *Agnes de Castro: Or, the Force of Generous Love* (1688)

Aphra Behn has been acclaimed as the first Englishwoman to earn her living by the pen. While the accuracy of this is debatable, she has been established as one of the first women to write on a professional basis. Today, Behn is most famous for her plays, poetry and short stories; however, she also produced a number of translations. The text extracted here was initially written by a French 'Lady of Quality', J. B. de Brilhac; it was also turned into a play by another famous English female Restoration playwright, Catherine Trotter. The story is set in Portugal and, like other of Behn's works, it focuses on complex relationships of love and desire. The story centres on Don Pedro, prince and heir to the Portuguese throne; his second wife, Constantia; her maid, Agnes de Castro; and Elvira, a courtly lady with whom Don Pedro had had a liaison during his first marriage. The extract below commences just after the point where Elvira has heard Don Pedro talking in his sleep about the woman he loves; finding that he has written a poem on this subject, Elvira adds a verse naming his beloved (Agnes de Castro) and leaves the poem in Constantia's room. The copy text is BL, 1073. e. 25, printed in London by R. P. for William Canning, 1688; pp. 9–16; 25–7; 48–51; 61–3.

As soon as *Constantia* was return'd she enter'd into her Cabinet and saw the Book open, and the Verses lying in it, which were to cost her so dear: she soon knew the hand of the Prince which was so familiar to her, and besides the information of what she had always fear'd, she understood it was *Agnes de Castro*, (whose friendship alone was able to comfort her, in her Misfortunes) who was the fatal cause of it; she read over the Paper an hundred times, desiring to give her Eyes and Reason the Lye, but finding but too plainly she was not deceiv'd, she found her Soul possesst with more Grief than Anger: when she consider'd as much in Love as the Prince was, he had kept his Torment secret. After having made her moan, without condemning him, the tenderness she had for him made her shed a Torrent of Tears, and inspir'd her with a resolution, of concealing her resentments.

She wou'd certainly have done it, by a Virtue extraordinary, if the Prince, who missing his Verses when he wak'd, and fearing they might fall into indiscreet hands, had not enter'd the Palace, all troubled with his loss, and hastily going into *Constantia's* Apartment, saw her fair Eyes all wet with Tears, and at the same instant cast his own on the unhappy Verses that had escap'd from his Soul, and now lay before the Princess.

He immediately turn'd pale at this sight, and appear'd so mov'd, that the Generous Princess felt more pain than he did: Madam, said he, (infinitely Alarm'd) from whom had you that Paper? it cannot come, but from the hand of some Person, answer'd *Constantia*, who is an Enemy both to your repose and mine; it is the work, Sir, of your own hand, and doubtless the sentiment of your Heart. But be not surpris'd, and do not fear, for if my tenderness should make it pass for a crime in you, the same tenderness, which nothing is able to alter, shall hinder me from complaining.

The moderation and calmness of *Constantia*, serv'd only to render the Prince more asham'd and confus'd: How Generous are you Madam, persu'd he, and how unfortunate am I. Some Tears accompanied his words, and the Princess, who lov'd him with extream Ardor, was so sensibly touch'd at it, that it was a good while before she cou'd utter a word. *Constantia* then broke silence, and showing him what *Elvira* had caus'd to be written, you are betray'd Sir, added she, you have been heard speak, and your secret is known. It was at this very moment that all the forces of the Prince abandon'd him, and his condition was really worthy of Compassion; he cou'd not pardon himself the unvoluntary crime he had committed, in exposing of the Lovely and the Innocent *Agnes*: and though he was convinc'd of the Virtue and Goodness of *Constantia*, the apprehensions he had that this modest and prudent Maid might suffer by his conduct, carryed him beyond all consideration.

The Princess, who heedfully survey'd him, saw so many Marks of Dispair in his Face and Eyes, that she was affraid of the Consequences; and holding out her Hand, in a very Obliging manner to him, she said, I promise, you Sir, I will never more complain on you, and that *Agnes* shall always be very dear to me; you shall never hear me make you any reproaches. And since I cannot possess your Heart, I will content my self with endeavoring to render my self worthy of it. *Don Pedro* more confus'd and dejected, than before he had been, bent one of his Knees at the Feet of *Constantia*, and with respect kist that fair kind Hand she had given him; and perhaps forgot *Agnes* for a moment.

But LOVE soon put a stop to all the little Advances of *Hymen*, the fatal Star that presided over the Destiny of *Don Pedro*, had not yet vented its Malignity; and one moments Sight of *Agnes* gave new Forces to his Passion.

The Wish and Desires of this charming Maid had no Part in this Victory; her Eyes were just, though penetrating, and they searched not in those of the Prince, what they had a Desire to discover to her.

As she was never far from *Constantia*, *Don Pedro* was no sooner gone out of the Closset, but *Agnes* entred; and finding the Princess all Pale and Languishing in her Chair, she doubted not but there was some sufficient Cause for her Affliction; she put her self in the same Posture the Prince had been in before, and expressing an Inquietude, full of Concern, Madam, said she, by all your Goodness, conceal not from me the Cause of your Trouble: Alas *Agnes*, replyed the Princess, What would you know? And what should I tell you? The Prince, the Prince, my dearest Maid is in Love; the Hand that he gave me was not a Present of his Heart; and for the Advantage of this Alliance, I must become the Victim of it. – What! the Prince in Love, replyed *Agnes* (with an Astonishment mixt with Indignation) What Beauty can dispute the Empire over a Heart so much your due? Alas, Madam, all the Respect I owe him, cannot hinder me from murmuring against him. Accuse him of nothing, interrupted *Constantia*, he does what he can; and I am more obliged to him for desiring to be Faithful, than if I posssest his real Tenderness. It is not enough to Fight, but to Overcome; and the Prince does more in the Condition wherein he is, than I ought reasonably to hope for: In fine, he is my Husband, and an agreable one; to whom nothing is wanting, but what I cannot inspire, that is a Passion which wou'd have made me but too Happy. Ah, Madam, cry'd out *Agnes*, transported with her Tenderness for the Princess, he is a blind and stupid Prince, who knows not the pretious Advantages he possesses. He must surely know Something, reply'd the Princess, modestly; but, Madam, reply'd *Agnes*, Is there any thing, not only in *Portugal*, but in all *Spain*, that can compare with you? And, without considering the Charming Qualities of your Person, can we enough admire those of your Soul? My dear *Agnes*, interrupted *Constantia*, Sighing, she who robs me of my Husband's Heart, has but too many Charms, to plead his Excuse, since it is thou, Child, whom Fortune makes use of, to give me this Killing Blow. Yes, *Agnes*, the Prince loves thee; and the Merit I know thou art possest of, puts Bounds to my Complaints, without suffering me to have the least Resentment.

The delicate *Agnes* little expected to hear what the Princess told her, Thunder wou'd have less surprised her, and less oppress her: She remained a long time without speaking, but at last fixing her Looks all frightful on *Constantia*, What say you, madam? (cry'd she) And what Thoughts have you of me? What, that I should betray you? And coming hither only full of Ardor to be the Repose of your Life, do I bring a fatal Poyson to afflict it? What Detestation must I have for the Beauty they find in me, without aspiring to make it appear? and how ought I to curse the Unfortunate Day in which I first saw the Prince? – but, Madam, it cannot be me, whom Heaven has chosen to torment you, and to destroy all your Tranquillity: No, it cannot be so much my Enemy, to put me to so great a Tryal: And if I were that odious Person, there is no Excuse or Punishment to which I would not Condemn my Self; it is *Elvira*, Madam, the Prince loves, and lov'd before his Marriage with you, and also before his Devorce from *Bianca*: And some Body has made an indiscreet Report to you of this Intriegue of his Youth; but, Madam, what was in the time of *Bianca*, is nothing to you. It is certain that *Don Pedro* loves you, answered the Princess; and I have Vanity enough to believe that none besides your Self cou'd have disputed his Heart with me; but the Secret is discover'd, and *Don Pedro* has not disowned it; What, interrupted *Agnes*, (more surprised than ever) Is it then from Himself you have learnt his Weakness? The Princess then shew'd her the Verses, and there was never any Dispair like to hers.[1]

It was in her own Chamber that *Agnes* examining more freely this adventure found it as cruel as Death: She lov'd *Constantia* sincerely, and had not till then any thing more than an Esteem mixt with Admiration for the Prince of *Portugal*, which indeed none cou'd refuse to so many fine Qualities. And looking on her self as the most unfortunate of her Sex, as being the cause of all the suffering of the Princess to whom she was oblig'd for the greatest Bounties, she spent the whole Night in tears, and complaints sufficient to have revenged *Constantia* of all the Griefs she made her suffer.

The Prince, on his side, was in no greater Tranquillity; the Generosity of his Princess encreas'd his Remorse, without diminishing his Love, he fear'd, and with Reason that those who were the Occasion of *Constantia's* seeing those Verses should discover his Passion to the King, from whom he hop'd for no Indulgence, and he would most willingly have given his Life to have been free from this Extremity.

In the mean time the afflicted Princess languisht in a most deplorable Sadness, she found nothing in those who were the Cause of her Misfortunes,

1 At this point, Elvira enters the room, seeking to find out whether her plan has worked. When the Princess asks her to leave, Elvira does so, satisfied that her plan has worked. Agnes also leaves.

but things fitter to move her Tenderness than her Anger; it was in vain that Jealousy strove to combate the Inclination she had to love her fair Rival; nor was any Occasion of making the Prince less dear to her, and she felt neither Hatred, nor so much as Indifference for Innocent *Agnes*.[2]

What ails you, *Agnes*? said the Princess to her, in a soft Tone, and her ordinary Sweetness; and what new Misfortune causes that Sadness in thy Looks? Madam, reply'd *Agnes*, shedding a Rivulet of Tears, The Obligations and Ties I have to you, put me upon a cruel Tryal; I had bounded the Felicity of my Life in hope of passing it near your Highness; yet I must carry, to some other part of the World, this unlucky Face of mine, which renders me nothing but ill Offices: And it is to obtain that Liberty, that I am come to throw my Self at your Feet; looking upon you as my Sovereign.

Constantia was so surpris'd and touch'd with the Proposition of *Agnes*, that she lost her Speech for some moments; Tears, which were sincere, exprest her first Sentiments: And after having shed abundance, to give a new Mark of her Tenderness to the Fair afflicted *Agnes*, she with a sad and melancholoy Look, fixt her Eyes upon her, and holding out her Hand to her, in a most obligng manner, Sighing, cry'd – you will then, my dear *Agnes*, leave me? And expose me to the Griefs of seeing you no more? Alas, Madam, interrupted this lovely Maid, hide from the Unhappy *Agnes* a Bounty, which does but increase her Misfortunes. It is not I, Madam, that wou'd leave you, it is my Duty, and my Reason that orders my Fate. And those Days which I shall pass far from you, promise me nothing to oblige me in this Design, if I did not see my Self absolutely forc'd to it: I am not ignorant of what passes at *Coimbra*; and I shall be an Accomplice of the Injustice there committed, if I should stay there any longer. – ah, I know your Virtue, cry'd *Constantia*, and you may remain here, in all Safety, while I am your Protectress, and let what will happen, I will accuse you of nothing. There's no answering for what's to come, reply'd *Agnes*, sadly; and I shall be sufficiently Guilty, if my Presence cause Sentiments, which cannot be innocent. Beside, Madam, the Importunities of *Don Alvaro* are insupportable to me; and though I find nothing but Aversion for him, since the King protects his Insolence, and he's in a Condition of undertaking any thing, my Flight is absolutely necessary; but, Madam, tho' he has nothing but what seems odious to me. I call Heaven to witness, that if I cou'd cure the Prince by marrying *Don Alvaro*, I wou'd not consider of it a moment; and finding in my Punishment the Consolation of Sacrificing my Self to my Princess, I wou'd support it without murmuring. But if I were the Wife of *Don Alvaro, Don Pedro* wou'd always look upon me with the same Eyes: so that I find nothing more reasonable for me than to hide my Self in some Corner of the World; where, though I shall most certainly live without Pleasure, yet, I shall preserve

2 Elvira informs her brother, Don Alvaro, about the prince's passion for Agnes. Don Alvaro has a secret desire for Agnes, so he tells the king about it; as he suspected, the king heartily disapproves of his son's actions and promises to help Don Alvaro (who is one of his favourites) to marry Agnes. Alvaro then persists in forcing his unwelcome attentions upon Agnes, who decides that the only thing she can do is leave the court, so she goes to see Constantia.

the Repose of my dearest Mistris. All the reason you find in this Design, answered the Princess, cannot oblige me to approve of your Absence: Will it restore me the Heart of *Don Pedro*? And will he not fly away with you; his Grief is mine, and my Life is ty'd to his; do not make him despair then, if you love me. I know ye, I tell you so once more; and let your Power be never so great over the Heart of the Prince, I will not suffer you to abandon us.

Though *Agnes* thought she had perfectly known *Constantia*, yet did she not expect to find so intire a Virtue in her, which made her think her self more Happy, and the Prince more Criminal. Oh! Wisdom! Oh Bounty without Example! (cry'd she) Whay is it that the cruel Destinies do not give you all you deserve? You are the Disposer of my Actions, continued she (in kissing the Hand of *Constantia*) I'll do nothing but what you'll have me: But consider, weigh well the Reasons that ought to counsel you in the Measures you oblige to take.[3]

The Prince ran to *Constantia*, whom he found dying; and *Agnes* in a swoon, in the Arms of some of the Ladies. What caus'd this double Calamity was, that *Agnes*, who cou'd suffer no longer the Indifferency of the Princess, had conjur'd her to tell her what was her Crime, and either to take her Life from her, or restore her Friendship.

Constantia, who found she must die, cou'd no longer keep her secret Affliction from *Agnes*; and after some Words, which were a Preparative to the sad Explanation, she shew'd her that fatal Billet which *Elvira* had caus'd to be written. 'Ah, Madam!' (*cry'd out the fair* Agnes, after *having read it*;) 'Ah, Madam! How many cruel Inquietudes had you spar'd me, had you open'd your Heart to me with your wonted Bounty: 'Tis easie to see that this Letter is counterfeit, and that I have Enemies without Compassion. Cou'd you believe the Prince so imprudent, to make use of any other Hand than his own, on an Occasion like this? And do you believe me so simple, to keep about me this Testimony of my Shame, with so little Pre-caution? You are neither betray'd by your Husband, nor me; I attest Heaven, and those Efforts I have made, to leave *Coimbra*. Alas, my dear Princess! How little have you known her, whom you have so much honour'd? Do not believe, that when I have justify'd my self, I will have any more Communication with the World. No, no; there will be no Retreat far enough from hence for me. I will take care to hide this unlucky Face, where it shall be sure to do no more harm'.

The Princess, touch'd at this Discourse, and the Tears of *Agnes*, press'd her Hand, which she held in hers; and fixing Looks upon her, capable of moving Pity in the most insensible Souls, 'If I have committed any Offence, my dear

---

3 When Constantia tells Don Pedro of Agnes's plan, he decides that it should be he who leaves. While he is gone, the king tries to force Agnes to marry Don Alvaro, but she stoutly refuses to do so. Don Alvaro arranges for her to be kidnapped, but she is eventually rescued by Don Pedro. On their return to the court, Elvira writes a letter, supposedly from Don Pedro, which she persuades a maid to give to Constantia, telling her to say that she saw it fall from Agnes's pocket. When she receives this letter, Constantia does not talk to Agnes about it, and becomes dangerously ill.

Agnes,'(answered she,) 'Death, which I expect in a Moment, shall revenge it. I ought also to protest to you, that I have not ceas'd loving you, and that I believe every thing you have said; giving you back my most tender Affections'.

'Twas at this time that the grief, which equally oppres'd 'em, put the Princess into such an Extremity, that they sent for the Prince. He came, and found himself almost without Life or Motive at this Sight: And what secret Motion soever might call him to the Aid of *Agnes*, 'twas to *Constantia* he ran. The Princess, who finding her last Moments drawing on, by a cold Sweat that cover'd her all over, and finding she had no more Business with Life, and causing those Persons she most suspected to retire, 'Sir', (*said she to* Don Pedro,) 'if I abandon Life without Regret, it is not without Trouble that I part with you. But, Prince, we must vanquish when we come to die; and I will forget my self wholly, to think of nothing but of you. I have no Reproaches to make against you, knowing that 'tis Inclination that disposes Hearts, and not Reason. *Agnes* is beautiful enough to inspire the most ardent Passion, and vertuous enough to deserve the first Fortunes in the World. I ask her once more Pardon for the Injustice I have done her, and recommend her to you, as a Person most dear to me. Promise me, my dear Prince, before I expire, to give her my Place in your Throne; it cannot be better fill'd: You cannot chuse a Princess more perfect for your People, nor a better Mother for our little Children. And you, my dear, and my faithful *Agnes' (pursued she;)* 'listen not to a Vertue too scrupulous, that may make any Opposition to the Prince of *Portugal*: Refuse him not a Heart, of which he is worthy; and give him that Friendship which you had for me, with that which is due to his Merit. Take care of my little *Fernando*, and the two young Princesses: Let 'em find me in you, and speak to 'em sometimes of me. Adieu; live both of you happy, and receive my last Embraces'.

The afflicted *Agnes*, who had recover'd a little her Forces, lost 'em again a second time: her Weakness was follow'd with Convulsions so vehement, that they were afraid of her Life; but *Don Pedro* never remov'd from *Constantia*. 'What, Madam', (*said he;*) 'you will leave me then; and think you 'tis for my Good. Alas, *Constantia*! if my heart has committed any Out-rage against you, your Vertue has sufficiently reveng'd you on me, in spight of you. Can you think me so 'barbarous? –' As he was going on, he saw Death shut the Eyes of the most generous Princess ever; and he was within a very little of following her.

But what Loads of Grief was this for *Agnes*, when she found that in that Interval, when Life and Death were struggling in her Soul, that *Constantia* was newly expire'd: She wou'd then have taken away her own Life, and have her Despair fully appear.[4]

Agnes lov'd everything that gave the Prince satisfaction, but a secret trouble made her apprehend some Misfortune in this unhappy Journey. 'Sir', (*said she*)

4 After numerous vacillations, Don Pedro and Agnes marry secretly. Eventually, however, the king and Don Alvaro discover this, and Don Alvaro persuades the king 'to consent to the death of Agnes' (p. 60). Unaware of this, Don Pedro prepares to go out hunting.

to him alarm'd without knowing the reason why, 'I tremble, seeing you to day, as it were design'd the last of my Life. Preserve your self my Dear Prince, and though the Exercise you take be not very dangerous, beware of the least hazards, and bring me back all that I trust with you'. *Don Pedro* who had never found her so handsome and so charming before embraced her several times, and went out of the Palace with his followers with a design not to return till the next Day.

He was no sooner gone but the Cruel *Don Alvaro* prepared himself for the Execution, he had resolv'd on; he thought it of that importance, that it required more hands than his Own; and so chose for his Companions *Diego Lopes Pacheo*, and *Pedro Cuello*, two Monsters like himself, whose Cruelty he was assur'd of by the presents he had made 'em.

They waited the coming of the Night, and the lovely *Agnes* was in her first sleep, which was the last of her Life, when these Assassins approach'd her Bed. Nothing made resistance to *Don Alvaro*, who cou'd do every thing, and whom the blackest furies introduc'd to *Agnes*, she waken'd, and opening her Curtains, saw by the Candle burning in her Chamber, the Poniard with which *Don Alvaro* was Arm'd, he having not his Face cover'd she easily knew him, and forgetting her self to think of nothing but the Prince. 'Just Heaven', (*said she*) lifting up her fine Eyes, 'If you will revenge *Constantia*, satisfie your self with my Blood only, and spare that of *Don Pedro*'. The Barbarous Man that heard her, gave her not time to say more; and finding he cou'd never (by all he cou'd do by love) touch the heart of the fair *Agnes*, he pierc'd it with his Poniard; his Accomplices gave her several Wounds, though there were no Necessity of so many to put an end to an innocent Life.

What a sad Spectacle was this for those who approach'd her Bed the next Day, and what dismal News was this to the Unfortunate Prince of *Portugal*. He return'd to *Coimbra*, at the first report of this Adventure, and saw what had certainly cost him his Life, if Men cou'd Die of grief; after having a thousand times embrac'd the bloody Body of *Agnes*, and said all that a just Dispair cou'd inspire him with, he ran like a Mad-man into the Palace, demanding the Murderers of his Wife, of things that cou'd not hear him, in fine he saw the King, and without observing any respect, he gave a loose to his Resentment; after having rav'd a long time, overwhelm'd with grief he fell into a Swound,[5] which continued all that Day; they carried him into his Apartment, and the King believing that this Misfortune wou'd prove his cure, repented not of what he had permitted.

Don Alvaro, and the two other Assassins, quitted *Coimbra*, this absence of theirs, made 'em appear guilty of the Crime, for which the afflicted Prince vow'd a speedy vengeance to the Ghost of his lovely *Agnes*, resolving to pursue them to the uttermost part of the Universe; he got a considerable Number of Men together, sufficient to have made resistance, even on the King of *Portugal* himself, if he shou'd yet take the part of the Murderers, with these he

5 'Swound': swoon, faint.

ravag'd the whole Country, as far as the *Duero* Waters, and carried on a War, even till the Death of the King; continually mixing tears with Blood which he gave to the revenge of his dearest *Agnes*.

Such was the deplorable end of the unfortunate Love of *Don Pedro* of *Portugal*, and of the fair *Agnes de Castro*, whose remembrance, he faithfully preserv'd in his heart even upon the Throne, to which he mounted by the right of his Birth, after the Death of the King.

Select bibliography

Books/essay collections

Barbour, Hugh, *The Quakers in Puritan England* (New Haven: Yale University Press, 1964)

Barnard, Toby, *The English Republic, 1649–1660* (Harlow: Longman, 1986)

Beilin, Elaine V., *Redeeming Eve: Women Writers of the English Renaissance* (Princeton: Princeton University Press, 1987)

Bell, Maureen, George Parfitt and Simon Shepherd, eds., *A Biographical Dictionary of English Women Writers, 1580–1720* (New York and London: Harvester Wheatsheaf, 1990)

Brant, Clare and Diane Purkiss, eds., *Women, Texts, Histories, 1575–1760* (New York and London: Routledge, 1992)

Cerasano, Susan and Marion Wynne-Davies, eds., *Gloriana's Face: Women, Public and Private, in the English Renaissance* (New York: London and Harvester Wheatsheaf, 1992)

Chedgzoy, Kate, Melanie Hansen and Suzanne Trill, eds., *Voicing Women: Gender and Sexuality in Early Modern Writing* (Keele: Keele University Press, 1996)

Crawford, Patricia, *Women and Religion in England, 1500–1720* (London and New York: Routledge, 1993)

Cressy, David, *Literacy and the Social Order: Reading and Writing in Tudor and Stuart England* (Cambridge: Cambridge University Press, 1980)

Evans, Robert C. and Anne C. Little, eds., *'The Muses Females Are': Martha Moulsworth and Other Woman Writers of the English Renaissance* (West Cornwall, CT: Locust Hill, 1995)

Ezell, Margaret J. M., *Writing Women's Literary History* (Baltimore and London: Johns Hopkins University Press, 1993)

Farrell, Kirby, Elizabeth H. Hageman and Arthur F. Kinney, eds., *Women in the Renaissance: selections from 'English Literary Renaissance'* (Amherst, MA: University of Massachusetts Press, 1990)

Ferguson, Margaret, Maureen Quilligan and Nancy J. Vickers, eds., *Rewriting the Renaissance: The Discourses of Sexual Difference in Early Modern Europe* (Chicago and London: University of Chicago Press, 1986)

Goreau, Angeline, *Reconstructing Aphra, A Social Biography of Aphra Behn* (Oxford: Oxford University Press, 1980)

Grundy, Isobel and Susan Wiseman, eds.,*Women, Writing, History, 1640–1740* (London: Batsford, 1992)

Hall, Kim F., *Things of Darkness: Economies of Race and Gender in Early Modern England* (Ithaca: Cornell University Press, 1995)

Hannay, Margaret P., *Philip's Phoenix: Mary Sidney, Countess of Pembroke* (New York and Oxford: Oxford University Press, 1990)

Hannay, Margaret P., ed., *Silent But For the Word: Tudor Women as Patrons, Translators, and Writers of Religious Works* (Kent, OH: Kent State University Press, 1985)

Harvey, Elizabeth D., *Ventriloquized Voices: Feminist Theory and English Renaissance Texts* (New York and London: Routledge, 1992)

Haselkorn, Anne M. and Betty S. Travitsky, eds., *The Renaissance Englishwoman in Print: Counterbalancing the Canon* (Amherst, MA and London: University of Massachusetts Press, 1990)

Hendricks, Margo and Patricia Parker, eds., *Women, 'Race,' and Writing in the Early Modern Period* (New York and London: Routledge, 1994)

Hill, Christopher, *The World Turned Upside Down: Radical Ideas during the English Revolution* (Harmondsworth: Penguin, 1988)

Hinds, Hilary, *God's Englishwomen: Seventeenth-Century Radical Sectarian Writing and Feminist Criticism* (Manchester and New York: Manchester University Press, 1996)

Hobby, Elaine, *Virtue of Necessity: English Women's Writing, 1646–1688* (London: Virago, 1988)

Hull, Suzanne, *Chaste, Silent and Obedient: English Books for Women, 1475–1640* (San Marino: Huntingdon Library, 1985)

Hutson, Lorna, *The Usurer's Daughter: Male Friendship and Fictions of Women in Sixteenth-Century England* (New York and London: Routledge, 1994)

Jones, Ann Rosalind, *The Currency of Eros: Women's Love Lyric in Europe 1540–1620* (Bloomington, IN: Indiana University Press, 1990)

Krontiris, Tina, *Oppositional Voices: Women as Writers and Translators of Literature in the English Renaissance* (New York and London: Routledge, 1992)

Lamb, Mary Ellen, *Gender and Authorship in the Sidney Circle* (Madison, WI and London: University of Wisconsin Press, 1990)

Lewalski, Barbara K., *Writing Women in Jacobean England* (Cambridge, MA. and London, Harvard University Press, 1993)

Lucas, Caroline, *Writing for Women: The Example of Woman as Reader in Elizabethan Romance* (Milton Keynes: Open University Press, 1989)

Mack, Phyllis, *Visionary Women: Ecstatic Prophecy in Seventeenth-Century England* (Berkeley: University of California Press, 1992)

Maclean, Ian, *The Renaissance Notion of Woman: A Study in the Fortunes of Scholasticism and Medical Science in European Intellectual Life* (Cambridge: Cambridge University Press, 1980)

McGregor, J. F. and B. Reay, eds., *Radical Religion in the English Revolution* (Oxford: Oxford University Press, 1984)

Miller, Naomi J. and Gary Waller, eds., *Reading Mary Wroth: Representing Alternatives in Early Modern England* (Knoxville: University of Tennessee Press, 1991)

Pollard, A. W. and G. R. Redgrave, *A Short Title Catalogue of Books Printed in England, Scotland and Ireland, and of English Books Printed Abroad, 1475–1640,* 2nd edn., revised by W. A. Jackson, F. S. Ferguson and K. F. Pantzer (London: Bibliographical Society, 1986), 3 vols.

Prior, Mary, ed., *Women in English Society, 1500–1800* (London: Methuen, 1985)

Rose, Mary Beth, ed., *Women in the Middle Ages and the Renaissance: Literary and Historical Perspectives* (Syracuse, NY: Syracuse University Press, 1986)

Smith, Hilda L., *Reason's Disciples: Seventeenth-Century English Feminists* (Urbana: University Press of Illinois, 1982)

Solt, Leo F., *Church and State in Early Modern England, 1509–1640* (New York and Oxford: Oxford University Press, 1990)

Todd, Janet, *The Sign of Angelica: Women, Writing and Fiction, 1660–1800* (London: Virago, 1989)

Underdown, David, *Pride's Purge: Politics in the Puritan Revolution* (Oxford: Clarendon Press, 1971)

Wall, Wendy, *The Imprint of Gender: Authorship and Publication in the English Renaissance* (Ithaca, NY and London: Cornell University Press, 1993)

Waller, Gary F., *Mary Sidney, Countess of Pembroke: A Critical Study of her Writings and Literary Milieu* (Salzburg: University of Salzburg Press, 1979)

The Sidney Family Romance, Mary Wroth, William Herbert, and the Early Modern Construction of Gender (Detroit: Wayne State University Press: 1993)

Weedon, Chris, *Feminist Practice and Post-structuralist Theory* (Oxford: Blackwell, 1993)

Wilcox, Helen, ed., *Women and Literature in Britain, 1500–1700* (Cambridge: Cambridge University Press, 1996)

Woodbridge, Linda, *Women and the English Renaissance: Literature and the Nature of Womankind* (Brighton: Harvester, 1984)

Zunder, William and Suzanne Trill, eds., *Writing and the English Renaissance* (Harlow: Longman, 1996)

Book articles

Blaydes, Sophia B., 'Nature Is a Woman: The Duchess of Newcastle and Seventeenth-Century Philosophy', in Donald C. Mell Jr., Theodore E. D. Braun and Lucia M. Palmer, eds., *Man, God, and Nature in the Enlightenment* (East Lansing, MI: Colleagues Press, 1988), pp. 51–64

Crawford, Patricia, 'The Challenges to Patriarchalism: How did the Revolution Affect Women?' in John Morrill, ed., *Revolution and Restoration: England in the 1650s* (London: Collins and Brown, 1992), pp. 112–28

Ezell, Margaret J. M., 'Re-Visioning the Restoration: or, How to Stop Obscuring Early Women Writers', in Jeffrey N. Cox and Larry J. Reynolds, eds., *New Historical Literary Study: Essays on Reproducing Texts, Representing History* (Princeton: Princeton University Press, 1993), pp. 136–50

Ferguson, Margaret W., 'A Room Not Their Own: Renaissance Women as Readers and Writers', in Clayton Koelb and Susan Noakes, eds., *The Comparative Perspective on Literature: Approaches to Theory and Practice* (Ithaca: Cornell University Press, 1988), pp. 93–116

Fitzmaurice, James and Martine Rey, 'Letters by Women in England, the French Romance, and Dorothy Osborne', in Jean R. Brink, Allison P. Coudert and Maryanne C. Horowitz, eds., *The Politics of Gender in Early Modern Europe* (Kirksville, MO: Sixteenth Cent. Jour. Pubs., 1989), pp. 149–60

Gordon, Linda, 'What's New in Women's History?' in Teresa de Lauretis, ed., *Feminist Studies/Critical Studies* (Bloomington, IN: Indiana, University Press, 1986), pp. 20–30

Hanson, Ellis, 'Sodomy and Kingcraft in *Urania* and *Antony and Cleopatra*', in Claude J. Summers, ed., *Homosexuality in Renaissance and Enlightenment England: Literary Representations in Historical Context* (New York: Harrington Park, 1992), pp. 135–51

Holm, Janis Butler, 'The Myth of a Feminist Humanism: Thomas Salter's *The Mirrhor of Modestie*', in Carole Levin and Jeanie Watson, eds., *Ambiguous Realities: Women in the Middle Ages and Renaissance* (Detroit: Wayne State University Press, 1987), pp. 197–218

Irwin, Joyce L., 'Anna Maria van Schurman: The Star of Utrecht (Dutch, 1607–1678)', in J. R. Brink, ed., *Female Scholars: A Tradition of Learned Women before 1800* (Montreal: Eden Press Women's Publications, 1980), pp. 68–85

de Lauretis, Teresa, 'Feminist Studies/Critical Studies: Issues, Terms, and Contexts', in Teresa de Laurentis, ed., *Feminist Studies/Critical Studies* (Bloomington, IN: Indiana University Press, 1986)

Mason, Mary G., 'The Other Voice: Autobiographies of Women Writers', in James Olney, ed., *Autobiography: Essays Theoretical and Critical* (Princeton: Princeton University Press, 1980), pp. 207–35

Morrill, John, 'The Church in England 1642–1649', in John Morrill, ed., *The Nature of the English Revolution: Essays by John Morrill* (London and New York: Longman, 1993), pp. 148–75

Purkiss, Diane, 'Material Girls: The Seventeenth-Century Woman Debate', in Clare Brant and Diane Purkiss, eds., *Women, Texts and Histories, 1575–1760* (London and New York: Routledge, 1992)

Quilligan, Maureen, 'Lady Mary Wroth: Female Authority and the Family Romance', in George M. Logan and Gordon Teskey, eds., *Unfolded Tales: Essays on Renaissance Romance* (Ithaca: Cornell University Press, 1989), pp. 257–80

Ransom, Janet, 'Feminism, Difference and Discourse: The Limits of Discursive Analysis for Feminism', in Caroline Ramazanoglu, ed., *Up Against Foucault: Explorations of some Tensions between Foucault and Feminism* (London and New York: Routledge, 1993), pp. 123–46

Smith, Catherine F., 'Jane Lead's Wisdom: Women and Prophecy in Seventeenth-Century England', in Jan Wojcik and Raymond-Jean Frontain, eds., *Poetic Prophecy in Western Literature* (Rutherford and London: Fairleigh Dickinson University Press and Associated University Press, 1984), pp. 55–63

Spencer, Jane, 'Not Being a Historian: Women Telling Tales in Restoration and Eighteenth-Century England', in Roy Eriksen, ed., *Contexts of Pre-Novel Narrative: The European Tradition* (Berlin: Mouton de Gruyter, 1994), pp. 319–40

Steen, Sara Jayne, 'Behind the Arras: Editing Renaissance Women's Letters', in W. Speed Hill, ed., *New Ways of Looking at Old Texts* (Binghampton, NY: Medieval and Renaissance Texts and Studies, 1993), pp. 229–38

Travitsky, Betty S., 'The New Mother of the English Renaissance: Her Writings on Motherhood', in Cathy N. Davidson and E. M. Broner, eds., *The Lost Tradition: Mothers and Daughters in Literature* (New York: Ungar, 1980), pp. 33–43

Trill, Suzanne, 'Sixteenth-Century Women's Writing: Mary Sidney's *Psalmes* and the "Femininity" of Translation', in William Zunder and Suzanne Trill, eds., *Writing and the English Renaissance* (Harlow: Longman, 1996), pp. 140–58

Wiseman, Sue, 'Unsilent Instruments and the Devil's Cushions: Authority in Seventeenth-Century Women's Prophetic Discourse', in Isobel Armstrong, ed., *New Feminist Discourses: Critical Essays on Theories and Texts* (New York and London: Routledge, 1992), pp. 176–96

Journal articles

Bayne, Diane Valeri, 'The Instruction of a Christian Woman: Richard Hyrde and the Thomas More Circle', *Moreana: Bulletin Thomas More*, 45 (1975), pp. 5–15

Beek, Pieta van, '"One Tongue is Enough for a Woman": The Correspondence in Greek between Anna Maria van Schurman (1607–1678) and Bathsua Makin (1600–167?)', *Dutch Crossing: A Journal of Low Countries Studies*, 19(1) (1995), pp. 24–48

Carrell, Jennifer Lee, 'A Pack of Lies in a Looking Glass: Lady Mary Wroth's *Urania* and the Magic Mirror of Romance', *Studies in English Literature, 1500–1900*, 34(1) (1994), pp. 79–107

Chedgzoy, Kate, 'Impudent Women: Carnival and Gender in Early Modern Culture', *Glasgow Review*, 1 (1993), pp. 9–23

Classen, Albrecht, 'Female Epistolary Literature from Antiquity to the Present: An Introduction', *Studia Neophilologica*, 60(1) (1988), pp. 3–13

Dailey, Barbara Ritter, 'The Husbands of Margaret Fell: An Essay on Religious

Metaphor and Social Change', *The Seventeenth Century*, 2(1) (1987), pp. 55–71

'The Visitation of Sarah Wight: Holy Carnival and the Revolution of the Saints in Civil War London', *Studies in Church History*, 55 (1989), pp. 438–55

Dolan, Frances E., '"Gentlemen, I have one more thing to say": Women on Scaffolds in England, 1563–1680', *Modern Philology*, 92 (1994), pp. 157–78

Dubrow, Heather, 'Navel Battles: Interpreting Renaissance Gynecological Manuals', *American Notes and Queries*, 5(2–3) (1992), pp. 67–71

Ezell, Margaret J. M., 'The Myth of Judith Shakespeare: Creating the Canon of Women's Literature', *New Literary History*, 21(3) (1990), pp. 579–92

'Elizabeth Delaval's Spiritual Heroine: Thoughts on Redefining Manuscript Texts by Early Women Writers', *English Manuscript Studies 1100–1700*, 3 (1992), pp. 216–37

Feroli, Teresa, 'The Sexual Politics of Mourning in the Prophecies of Eleanor Davies', *Criticism: A Quarterly for Literature and the Arts*, 36(3) (1994), pp. 359–82

Graves, Michael P., 'Functions of Key Metaphors in Early Quaker Sermons, 1671–1700', *The Quarterly Journal of Speech*, 69(4) (1983), pp. 364–78

Greenhut, Deborah S., 'Persuade Yourselves: Women, Speech, and Sexual Politics in Tudor Society', *Proteus*, 3(2) (1986), pp. 42–8

Guillory, John, 'Canonical and Non-Canonical: A Critique of the Current Debate', *English Literary History*, 54(3) (1987), pp. 483–527

Healey, Robert M., 'Waiting for Deborah: John Knox and Four Ruling Queens', *The Sixteenth Century Journal*, 25(2) (1994), pp. 371–86

Heertum, Cis van, 'A Hostile Annotation of Rachel Speght's *A Mouzell for Melastomus* (1617)', *English Studies*, 68(6) (1987), pp. 490–6

Howard, Jean E., 'Feminism and the Question of History: Resituating the Debate', *Women's Studies*, 19(2) (1991), pp. 149–57

Jordan, Constance, 'Woman's Rule in Sixteenth-Century British Political Thought', *Renaissance Quarterly*, 40(3) (1987), pp. 421–51

Krontiris, Tina, 'Breaking Barriers of Genre and Gender: Margaret Tyler's Translation of *The Mirrour of Knighthood*', *English Literary Renaissance*, 18(1) (1988), pp. 19–39

Lerch-Davis, Genie S., 'Rebellion against Public Prose: The Letters of Dorothy Osborne to William Temple (1652–54)', *Texas Studies in Literature and Language*, 20 (1978), pp. 386–415

Mack, Phyllis, 'Teaching about Gender and Spirituality in Early English Quakerism', *Women's Studies*, 19(2) (1991), pp. 223–37

Magnusson, A. Lynne, '"His Pen with My Hande": Jane Anger's Revisionary Rhetoric', *English Studies in Canada*, 17 (1991), pp. 269–81

Matchinske, Megan, 'Holy Hatred: Formations of the Gendered Subject in English Apocalyptic Writing, 1625–1651', *English Literary History*, 60(2) (1993), 349–77

'Legislating "Middle-Class" Morality in the Marriage Market: Ester

Sowernam's *Ester Hath Hang'd Haman'*, *English Literary Renaissance*, 24 (1994), pp. 154–83

Miller, Nancy K., 'Men's Reading, Women's Writing: Gender and the Rise of the Novel', *Yale French Studies*, 75 (1988), pp. 40–55

Neely, Carol Thomas, 'Constructing the Subject: Feminist Practice and the New Renaissance Discourses', *English Literary Renaissance*, 18 (1988), pp. 5–18

Patton, Brian, 'The Women are Revolting? Women's Activism and Popular Satire in the English Revolution', *Journal of Medieval and Renaissance Studies*, 23(1) (1993), pp. 69–87

Pearlman, E., 'Typological Autobiography in Seventeenth-Century England', *Biography: An Interdisciplinary Quarterly*, 8(2) (1985), pp. 95–118

Poole, Kristen, '"The fittest closet for all goodness": Authorial Strategies of Jacobean Mothers' Manuals', *Studies in English Literature, 1500–1900*, 35(1) (1995), pp. 69–88

Roberts, Josephine A., 'Labyrinths of Desire: Lady Mary Wroth's Reconstruction of Romance', *Women's Studies*, 19 (2) (1991), pp. 183–92

Sherman, Sandra, 'Trembling Texts: Margaret Cavendish and the Dialectic of Authorship', *English Literary Renaissance*, 24 (1994), pp. 184–210

Sizemore, Christine W., 'Attitudes toward the Education and Roles of Women: Sixteenth-Century Humanists and Seventeenth-Century Advice Books', *University of Dayton Review*, 15(1) (1981), pp. 57–67

Sullivan, D. M., 'The Female Will in Aphra Behn', *Women's Studies*, 22 (1993), pp. 335–47

Swift, Carolyn Ruth, 'Feminine Identity in Lady Mary Wroth's Romance *Urania*', *English Literary Renaissance*, 14(3) (1984), pp. 328–46

Thickstun, Margaret Olofson, '"This Was a Woman That Taught": Feminist Scriptural Exegesis in the Seventeenth Century', *Studies in Eighteenth-Century Culture*, 21 (1991), pp. 149–58

Travitsky, Betty, 'The Lady Doth Protest: Protest in the Popular Writings of Renaissance Englishwomen', *English Literary Renaissance*, 14(3) (1984), 255–83

Wade, Rosalind, 'Dorothy Osborne (Lady Temple), 1626–1695: The Missing Years', *Contemporary Review*, 248(1141) (1986), pp. 98–104

Wright, Susan, 'Private Language Made Public: The Language of Letters as Literature', *Poetics*, 18(6) (1989), pp. 549–78

Editions

Aughterson, Kate, ed., *Renaissance Woman: Constructions of Femininity in England. A Sourcebook* (New York and London: Routledge, 1996)

Blodgett, Harriet, ed., *Centuries of Female Days: Englishwomen's Private Diaries* (New Brunswick: Rutgers University Press, 1988)

Butler, Charles, intro., *Female Replies to Swetnam The Woman-Hater* (Bristol: Thoemmes Press, 1995)

Butler-Holm, Janis, ed., *A Critical Edition of Thomas Salter's The Mirrhor of Modestie* (New York and London: Garland, 1987)

Cerasano, Susan and Marion Wynne-Davies, eds., *Renaissance Drama by Women: Texts and Documents* (New York and London: Routledge, 1996)

Cope, Esther, ed., *The Works of Lady Eleanor Davies* (Oxford: Oxford University Press, 1996)

Cullen, Patrick Colborn, ed., *A Continuation of Sir Philip Sidney's 'Arcadia', Anna Weamys*, 'Women Writers in English, 1350–1850' series (New York and Oxford: Oxford University Press, 1994)

Evans, Maurice, ed., *Sir Philip Sidney, Arcadia*, (Harmondsworth: Penguin, 1977)

Graham, Elspeth, Hilary Hinds, Elaine Hobby and Helen Wilcox, eds., *Her Own Life: Autobiographical Writings by Seventeenth-Century Englishwomen* (London: Routledge, 1989)

Greene, Douglas G., ed., *The Meditations of Lady Elizabeth Delaval, Written Between 1662 and 1671*, Surtees Society, vol. CXC (Gateshead: Northumberland Press, 1978)

Greer, Germaine, Jeslyn Medoff, Melinda Sansome and Susan Hastings, *Kissing the Rod: An Anthology of 17th Century Women's Verse* (London: Virago, 1988)

Keeble, N. H., ed., *The Cultural Identity of Seventeenth-Century Woman* (New York and London: Routledge, 1996)

Lewis, Thomas Taylor, ed., *The Letters of Lady Brilliana Harley* (London: Camden Society, 1854)

Lilley, Kate, ed., *Margaret Cavendish: New Blazing World and Other Writings* (London: Pickering and Chatto, 1992)

Loftis, John, ed., *The Memoirs of Anne, Lady Halkett and Ann, Lady Fanshawe* (Oxford: Clarendon Press, 1979)

Meads, Dorothy M., ed., *Diary of Lady Margaret Hoby, 1599–1605* (London: Routledge, 1930)

Morgan, Fidelis, ed., *The Female Wits: Women Playwrights of the Restoration* (London: Virago, 1981)

Morgan, Fidelis, and Paddy Lyons, eds., *Female Playwrights of the Restoration: Five Comedies* (London: Everyman, 1991)

Nichols, John Gough, ed., *The Autobiography of Anne Lady Halket* (London: Camden Society, 1876)

Otten, Charlotte F., ed., *English Women's Voices, 1540–1700* (Miami: University Presses of Florida, 1992)

Parker, Kenneth, ed., *Dorothy Osborne: Letters to Sir William Temple* (Harmondsworth: Penguin, 1987)

Paulissen, May Nelson, ed., *The Love Sonnets of Lady Mary Wroth: A Critical Introduction* (Salzburg: University of Salzburg Press, 1982)

Pollock, Linda, ed., *With Faith and Physic: The Life of a Tudor Gentlewoman, Lady Grace Mildmay 1552–1620* (London: Collins and Brown, 1993)

Pritchard, R. E., ed., *The Sidney Psalms, Mary Sidney, Countess of Pembroke and Sir Philip Sidney* (Manchester: Carcanet, 1992)

Purkiss, Diane, ed., *Renaissance Women: The Plays of Elizabeth Cary and the Poems of Aemilia Lanyer* (London: Pickering and Chatto, 1994)

Roberts, Josephine A., ed., *The Poems of Lady Mary Wroth* (Baton Rouge and London: Louisiana State University Press, 1983)

Tanner, J. R., ed., *Tudor Constitutional Documents, 1485–1603* (Cambridge: Cambridge University Press, 1948)

Thompson, Denys, ed., *Anne Finch, Countess of Winchilsea: Selected Poems* (Manchester: Carcanet, 1987)

Todd, Janet, ed., *Aphra Behn: Oroonoko, The Rover and Other Writing* (Harmondsworth: Penguin, 1992)

The Poems of Aphra Behn, a Selection (London: Pickering, 1994)

Travitsky, Betty S., ed., *The Paradise of Women: Writings by Englishwomen of the Renaissance* (New York: Columbia University Press, 1989)

Wall, Alison, ed., *Two Elizabethan Women: The Letters of Joan Thynne and Maria Thynne* (Devizes: Wiltshire Record Office, 1983)

Wilson, Katharina M., ed., *Women Writers of the Renaissance and Reformation* (Athens, GA and London: University of Georgia Press, 1987)

Wilson, Katharina M. and Frank J. Warnke, eds., *Women Writers of the Seventeenth Century* (Athens, GA and London: University of Georgia Press, 1989)